Gendering the Europe

Gender and Politics Series

Series editors: Johanna Kantola, University of Helsinki, Finland, and **Judith Squires**, University of Bristol, UK

This timely new series publishes leading monographs and edited collections from scholars working in the disciplinary areas of politics, international relations and public policy with specific reference to questions of gender. It showcases cutting-edge research in gender and politics, publishing topical and innovative approaches to gender politics. It will include exciting work from new authors and well-known academics, and it will also publish high-impact writing by practitioners working in issues relating to gender and politics.

The series covers politics, international relations and public policy, including gendered engagement with mainstream political science issues, such as political systems and policy-making, representation and participation, citizenship and identity, equality and women's movements; gender and international relations, including feminist approaches to international institutions, political economy and global politics; and interdisciplinary and emergent areas of study, such as masculinities studies, gender and multiculturalism and intersectionality.

Potential contributors are encouraged to contact the series editors, Johanna Kantola, (johanna.kantola@helsinki.fi) and Judith Squires (judith.squires@bristol.ac.uk).

Series Advisory Board:

Louise Chappell, University of Sydney, Australia
Joni Lovenduksi, Birkbeck College, University of London, UK
Amy Mazur, Washington State University, USA
Jacqui True, University of Auckland, New Zealand
Mieke Verloo, Radboud University Nijmegen, the Netherlands
Laurel Weldon, Purdue University, USA

Titles include:

Gabriele Abels and Joyce Marie Mushaben (*editors*)
GENDERING THE EUROPEAN UNION
New Approaches to Old Democratic Deficits

Jonathan Dean
RETHINKING CONTEMPORARY FEMINIST POLITICS

Mona Lena Krook and Fiona Mackay (*editors*)
GENDER, POLITICS AND INSTITUTIONS
Towards a Feminist Institutionalism

Gender and Politics Series
Series Standing Order ISBNs 978–0–230–23917–3 (hardback) and
978–0–230–23918–0 (paperback)
(*outside North America only*)

You can receive future titles in this series as they are published by placing a standing order. Please contact your bookseller or, in case of difficulty, write to us at the address below with your name and address, the title of the series and the ISBNs quoted above.

Customer Services Department, Macmillan Distribution Ltd, Houndmills, Basingstoke, Hampshire RG21 6XS, England

Gendering the European Union

New Approaches to Old Democratic Deficits

Edited by

Gabriele Abels
Professor of Comparative Politics and European Integration, University of Tübingen, Germany

and

Joyce Marie Mushaben
Professor of Comparative Politics and Gender Studies, University of Missouri-St Louis, USA

Editorial matter, selection, introduction and conclusion © Gabriele Abels and Joyce Marie Mushaben 2012
All remaining chapters © respective authors 2012

All rights reserved. No reproduction, copy or transmission of this publication may be made without written permission.

No portion of this publication may be reproduced, copied or transmitted save with written permission or in accordance with the provisions of the Copyright, Designs and Patents Act 1988, or under the terms of any licence permitting limited copying issued by the Copyright Licensing Agency, Saffron House, 6–10 Kirby Street, London EC1N 8TS.

Any person who does any unauthorized act in relation to this publication may be liable to criminal prosecution and civil claims for damages.

The authors have asserted their rights to be identified as the authors of this work in accordance with the Copyright, Designs and Patents Act 1988.

First published 2012 by
PALGRAVE MACMILLAN

Palgrave Macmillan in the UK is an imprint of Macmillan Publishers Limited, registered in England, company number 785998, of Houndmills, Basingstoke, Hampshire RG21 6XS.

Palgrave Macmillan in the US is a division of St Martin's Press LLC, 175 Fifth Avenue, New York, NY 10010.

Palgrave Macmillan is the global academic imprint of the above companies and has companies and representatives throughout the world.

Palgrave® and Macmillan® are registered trademarks in the United States, the United Kingdom, Europe and other countries.

ISBN 978–0–230–29645–9

This book is printed on paper suitable for recycling and made from fully managed and sustained forest sources. Logging, pulping and manufacturing processes are expected to conform to the environmental regulations of the country of origin.

A catalogue record for this book is available from the British Library.

Library of Congress Cataloging-in-Publication Data
Gendering the European Union : new approaches to old democratic
  deficits / edited by Gabriele Abels and Joyce Marie Mushaben.
    p. cm.
  Includes index.
  ISBN 978–0–230–29645–9 (hardback)
  1. Gender mainstreaming—European Union countries.   2. Sex discrimination against women—European Union countries.   3. Women's rights—Government policy—European Union countries.   4. Equality—European Union countries.   5. Women and democracy—European Union countries.   I. Abels, Gabriele, 1964–   II. Mushaben, Joyce Marie, 1952–
HQ1236.5.E85G45 2011
305.42094—dc23   2011028851

10 9 8 7 6 5 4 3 2 1
21 20 19 18 17 16 15 14 13 12

Transferred to Digital Printing in 2012

To all of our children (real and virtual) and our children's children, in the hope that they will never know the horrors of World Wars, which brought about the biggest (and probably the best) peace-and-prosperity framework ever known to Europe.

Contents

List of Tables ix
List of Figures and Boxes x
Acknowledgements xi
Notes on Contributors xiii
List of Abbreviations xvii

1 Introduction: Studying the EU from a Gender Perspective 1
  Gabriele Abels and Joyce Marie Mushaben

Part I Gendering Perspectives and EU Processes

2 Gendering Theories of European Integration 23
  Annica Kronsell

3 Gendering the Institutions and Actors of the EU 41
  Anna van der Vleuten

4 Gendering the EU Policy Process and Constructing the Gender Acquis 63
  Birgit Locher

5 From Equal Treatment to Gender Mainstreaming and Diversity Management 85
  Alison E. Woodward

6 Gendering Enlargement of the EU 104
  Yvonne Galligan and Sara Clavero

Part II Meliorating Old and New EU Policy Deficits and Blind Spots

7 The Common Agricultural Policy and Gender Equality 127
  Elisabeth Prügl

8 Gendering Employment Policy: From Equal Pay to Work–Life Balance 146
  Agnès Hubert

9	Gendering the Social Policy Agenda: Anti-Discrimination, Social Inclusion and Social Protection *Maria Stratigaki*	169
10	Research by, for and about Women: Gendering Science and Research Policy *Gabriele Abels*	187
11	Women on the Move: EU Migration and Citizenship Policy *Joyce Marie Mushaben*	208
12	Conclusion: Rethinking the Double Democratic Deficit of the EU *Joyce Marie Mushaben and Gabriele Abels*	228
Bibliography		248
Index		276

Tables

1.1	Major treaties and agreements in the process of European integration	3
2.1	Major theoretical approaches in European integration theory and the feminist critique	25
3.1	Composition of the European Commission and Social Affairs Commissioners	44
3.2	Infringement proceedings: gender equality directives (1958–2008)	56
4.1	Development of the EU *gender acquis*	70
5.1	Gender mainstreaming proposals of the European Commission	99
6.1	European enlargements	106
6.2	The Copenhagen Criteria	113
6.3	Enforcing Directive 2004/113 in member states	116
6.4	Gender equality provisions in the Lisbon Treaty	120
7.1	EU actions improving the legal status of women in agriculture	132
7.2	EU actions to implement gender mainstreaming in rural development	137
8A.1	Employment provisions in treaties	165
9.1	Major turning points in EU social policy	172
10.1	Major steps in the field of 'Women and Science'	193
10.2	The 'Leaky Pipeline': Women in science (EU-27 average in 2006)	197
10.3	National policies to promote gender equality in science (2004)	204
11.1	EU initiatives on citizenship, immigration and asylum	210

Figures and Boxes

Figures

1.1	Evaluating policy through a gendered lens	8
3.1	The EU as a multilevel system	42
3.2	'Who said what and when?' The itinerary of the proposal to extend maternity leave	52
4.1	The policy cycle concept	66
4.2	Problem identification and agenda setting in the EU	67
4.3	Implementation of EU directives	79
8.1	Potential growth in GDP in the EU member states following a transition to full equality in the labour market, in percentage of GDP	162
8A.1	Gender-disaggregated employment statistics	167
10.1	Men and women in typical academic careers, EU-27, 2002 and 2006	196

Boxes

5.1	Equal treatment – what's that?	90
5.2	What is positive action?	94
5.3	What is gender mainstreaming?	98
8.1	The 2006 'Recast Directive'	156
8.2	European Employment Strategy (EES)	158
8.3	What is 'flexicurity'?	161
9.1	What is the European Social Model?	174
9.2	Definitions of gender budgeting	184
10.1	Instruments and the budget of RTD policy	190
11.1	The Hague Programme (2004)	218
11.2	Common basic principles for immigrant integration policy (2005)	221
12.1	A subversive feminist guide to achieving gender equality	243

Acknowledgements

Like so many other EU projects and 'Action Plans' dedicated to the proposition that women and men are created equal, and that they should both be endowed with inalienable rights to life, liberty, and the pursuit of happiness – along with balanced participation in decision-making – this book took a lot longer than expected to transpose and implement. We are profoundly grateful to a number of people who have supported our book since its inception several years ago on a hot summer day at a street café somewhere in Berlin; they have done so by contributing patience, time and dinner parties (thank you so much, Ryuichi). Since then, this project has taken shape by virtue of hundreds of e-mails and phone calls, and also a number of visits back and forth across the Atlantic.

Gabriele Abels expresses her thanks to the University of Missouri-St Louis, where she spent a semester as visiting professor in 2005, allowing us to co-teach a seminar entitled 'Gender and the Democratic Deficit in the European Union' and to coach student-participants in the Midwest Model EU, giving us both a lot of food for thought. Joyce Marie Mushaben is particularly grateful to our multi-national contributors who never once questioned whether an American could really grasp, much less appreciate in a deeper sense, both the complex processes of European integration and its contributions to the quality of women's lives. She also recognizes the Masters in European Studies programme at the University of Tübingen, which made it possible for us to consult in person during various stages of the 'completion, deepening and enlargement' of the text.

Our thanks likewise go to a number of researchers who supplied encouraging comments on individual chapters, as well as on different versions of our book chapters at international conferences, especially at the European Consortium for Political Research's 1st European Conference on Politics and Gender at Queen's University Belfast. We are also intellectually indebted to Johanna Kantola and Judith Squires who brought this *Gender and Politics Series* to life.

Very special thanks go to Jan Ullrich for his commitment to the project, coupled with his diligence and thoroughness in reconciling the countless stylistic differences accompanying chapters contributed by scholars based in nine different countries – qualities which make him such a great research assistant. We further extend our gratitude to Gabriele's second research assistant, Miriam Steinrücken, for her meticulousness in proofreading these chapters; to Alexander Kobusch, for his technical support in rendering many graphs and tables ready to print; as well as to Kelly Neudorfer and Dorian Woods, for their support and speedy copy-editing. We also express our appreciation to Wolfgang Schumann, for giving us permission to use and print some of the figures stemming from his Agora project. We note, with sadness, his untimely death before our book went to press. Thanks go as well to Liz Blackmore, Priya Venkat and unknown others who guided this volume speedily through the publication process.

This book is ultimately dedicated to Éliane Vogel-Polsky (a Belgian professor of labour law), Gabrielle Defrenne (plaintiff in the first cases turning Article 119 of the Rome Treaty into 'hard law'), Hanna Maij-Weggen (whose European Parliament report gave birth to a standing committee and countless recommendations to the European Commission), Simone Veil (concentration-camp survivor and the first female president of the European Parliament) and all of the other 'woman of the first hour', who were thoughtful and committed enough to set numerous paradigm-shifting changes in motion in their pursuit of a better life for the women of Europe. With this book we express our deep personal, intellectual and professional gratitude.

Notes on Contributors

Gabriele Abels is Professor of Comparative Politics and European Integration at the Institute of Political Science at the University of Tübingen, Germany. She has published on biotechnology regulation in the EU, citizens' participation and EU democracy and gender. Her current research focuses on gender and parliamentary democracy in the EU as well as on the regulatory regime of food safety. She is Editor of *Politische Vierteljahresschrift* and of *Femina Politica*. Her recent publications in English include 'Gender equality policy' in H. Heinelt and Michèle Knodt (eds) (2011), *Policies within the EU Multi-Level System*; 'Participatory technology assessment and the "institutional void". Investigating democratic theory and representative politics', in A. Bora and H. Hausendorf (eds) (2010), *Democratic Transgressions of Law: Governing Technology through Public Participation*; 'Interviewing experts in political science: a reflection on gender and policy effects based on secondary analysis' in A. Bogner, B. Littig and W. Menz (eds) (2009), *Interviewing Experts* (co-author M. Behrens) and *Die EU-Reflexionsgruppe 'Horizont 2020–2030': Herausforderungen und Reformoptionen für das Mehrebenensystem* (co-authored with Annegret Eppler und Michèle Knodt; 2010).

Sara Clavero is Senior Research Fellow at the School of Politics, International Studies and Philosophy at Queen's University Belfast. Her research focuses on gender politics and policy in the European multi-level constellation. She is currently undertaking comparative research on gender democracy in Europe as part of the RECON project (funded by the EU) and on the Europeanisation of gender equality policy in subnational governance. She is a co-author of *Gender Politics and Democracy in Postsocialist Europe* (with Y. Galligan and M. Calloni, 2007), and has recently published articles in *Gender and Society* and *Perspectives on European Politics and Society*.

Yvonne Galligan is Professor of Comparative Politics at Queen's University Belfast. She writes on women and politics in Ireland and in the EU, and theorises more broadly on gender and democracy. Professor Galligan is currently working on a new edited book, provisionally titled *Gender Justice and Democracy in the European Union*, representing the capstone output of a research project on gender and democracy as part of the EU-funded 2007–2012 project *Reconstituting Democracy in Europe*. Her books include *Gender Politics and Democracy in Post-Socialist Europe* (with S. Clavero and M. Calloni, 2007) and *Sharing Power: Women, Parliament, Democracy* (co-edited with M. Tremblay, 2005). Her recent articles have appeared in *Gender & Society* and in *Politics & Policy*.

xiv *Notes on Contributors*

Agnès Hubert is an official of the European Commission. She is a graduate in economics (Bsc and DEA) and in political science (DEA) at the University of Paris 1. She joined the Commission after having been a journalist based in Brussels. She has held responsibilities in EU Development and cooperation policy, she was head of the Unit Equal Opportunities for Women in the Directorate-General Employment of the European Commission for five years and she has since been doing policy analysis in the Forward Studies Unit, first with the team in charge of the White Paper on European Governance and currently with the Bureau of European Policy Advisers. She has also experienced the European Parliament, where she was seconded for two years to assist the President of the Women's Rights Committee. She has a specific expertise in the fields of gender, social and employment policy, and fundamental rights, and she is currently doing academic research on the mutually reinforcing dynamics of gender equality and European integration. She is the author of two books, *L'Europe et les femmes, identités en mouvement* (1998) and *Democracy and Information Society in Europe* (2000), and of many articles and academic contributions on gender equality and European integration.

Annica Kronsell is Associate Professor of Political Science at Lund University, Sweden. Her fields of expertise are gender, feminist international relations and environmental politics. Her publications include *Gender, Sex and the Post-National Defense* (2011); *Making Gender, Making War, Violence, the Military and Peacekeeping practices* (co-edited with E. Svedberg, 2011); *Environmental Politics and Deliberative Democracy. Examining the Promise of New Modes of Governance* (co-edited with K. Bäckstrand, J. Khan and E. Lövbrand, 2010); 'Gender and Governance' in R. Denemark (ed.) (2009), *The International Studies Compendium Project*; and 'Gender, Power and European Integration Theory', *European Journal of Public Policy*, 12: 6, 1022–1040 (2005).

Birgit Locher is Head of Unit 'General Affairs' in the Minister-President's Office Baden-Württemberg, Stuttgart, and Adjunct Professor of International Relations and Gender Studies at the Institute of Political Science at the University of Tübingen, Germany. Her fields of expertise are international organisations, gender issues in international relations and European governance, as well as human rights/women's rights. Her current research focuses on gender and human security. Among her recent book publications are *Transnational Activism in the UN and the EU: A Comparative Study* (co-edited with J. Joachim, 2009); and *Norms, Advocacy-Networks and Policy-Change: Trafficking in Women in the European Union* (2007). Her chapter 'Gender and European integration' (co-authored with E. Prügl) has appeared in A. Wiener and T. Diez (eds) (2009), *European Integration Theories* (2nd edition). She has published in numerous journals, including *International Studies Quarterly*, *Politische Vierteljahresschrift* and *Zeitschrift für Internationale Beziehungen*.

Joyce Marie Mushaben is Professor of Comparative Politics and Gender Studies at the University of Missouri-St Louis. She has spent many years researching in Germany by way of DAAD, Fulbright, German Marshall Fund and Alexander von Humboldt Stiftung grants. Her publications include studies of east, west and multi-cultural German identity, migration/integration policies, new social movements, gender politics, Muslim headscarf debates and women's leadership in the EU. Her most recent book is *The Changing Faces of Citizenship: Integration and Mobilization among Ethnic Minorities in Germany* (2008). Her articles have appeared in *German Politics, Democratization, Journal of Women, Politics and Policy, Citizenship Studies, Journal of Ethnicity and Migration Studies* and *Politics & Religion*, among others.

Elisabeth Prügl is Professor of Political Science at the Graduate Institute of International and Development Studies in Geneva. Her research focuses on gender politics in international organisations and global governance. Prügl's current research probes the relationship between feminist knowledge and gender expertise and the deployment of such expertise in international governance and the private sector. Among her recent publications are *Diversity and the European Union* (co-edited with M. Thiel, 2009); and *Transforming Masculine Rule: Agriculture and Rural Development in the European Union* (2011). Her articles have appeared in numerous journals, including *International Feminist Journal of Politics, Signs: Journal of Women in Culture and Society* and *International Studies Quarterly*.

Maria Stratigaki has taught gender, social policy and gender equality policies at Panteion University (Athens, Greece) since 1999. She worked at the European Commission's Gender Equality Unit from 1991 to 1999 and was Director of the Centre for Gender Studies at Panteion University from 2004 to 2009. She is currently responsible for two European research projects funded by EU FP7: GeMIC (Gender, Migration and Intercultural Interaction in South East Europe) and MIG@NET (Migration, Gender and Transnational Digital Networks). In November 2009 she was appointed Secretary-General for Gender Equality in the Greek Government. She is the author of *The Gender of Social Policy* (2007) and has edited the collective volume *Gender Equality Policies: European Guidelines and National Practice* (2008; both in Greek). She has published in *Social Politics*, the *European Journal of Women's Studies* and *Les Cahiers du genre*.

Anna van der Vleuten is Associate Professor of European Integration at the Institute for Management Research, Radboud University Nijmegen (the Netherlands). Her fields of expertise are the EU, gender and comparative regionalism/interregionalism (SADC, Mercosur, ASEAN). She is currently working on a project on the European Court of Justice and LGBT rights, on a project with the working title GRANddEUR (Gender, Regions and

Norm Diffusion: Debunking Eurocentrism) and on the diffusion of gender(ed) norms between the EU and other regional organisations. Her major publications include *The Price of Gender Equality. Member States and Governance in the European Union* (2007) and *Closing or Widening the Gap? Legitimacy and Democracy in Regional Integration Organizations* (co-edited with A. Ribeiro Hoffmann, 2007). Her articles have appeared in various journals, including *Comparative European Politics*, *Journal of Common Market Studies* and *Acta Politica*.

Alison E. Woodward is Research Professor at the Institute of European Studies and Co-Director of the Center for Gender Studies and Diversity Research at the Free University of Brussels (VUB, Belgium). Her latest books are *Teaching Intersectionality: Putting Gender at the Center* (co-edited with M. Franken, A. Cabo and B. Bagihole, 2009) and *Transforming Gendered Well-Being: The Impact of Social Movements* (co-edited with J.-M. Bonvin and M. Renom, 2011). Among recent journal articles and chapters are 'Too late for mainstreaming: The view from Brussels', *European Journal of Policy*, 18: 3 (2008) and 'International Organizations and the Organization of Gender' in D. Knights, E. Jeanes and P. Y. Martin (eds) (2011), *Handbook on Gender, Work and Organizations*.

Abbreviations

AP	Action Programmes on Equal Opportunities
Art.	Article
BMBF	Federal Ministry for Research (Germany)
BUDG	Committee on Budgets (of the EP)
BUSINESSEUROPE	Confederation of European Business
CAP	Common Agricultural Policy
CEDAW	UN Convention on the Elimination of all Forms of Discrimination against Women
CEE	Central and Eastern Europe
CEEC	Central and Eastern European Countries
CEEP	European Centre of Employers and Enterprises
COPA	Committee of Agricultural Organisations
CoR	Committee of Regions
COREPER	Committee of Permanent Representatives
Council	Council of the European Union
Court	European Court of Justice
DAPHNE	Programme of community action (2000 to 2003) on preventive measures to fight violence against children, young persons and women
DFG	Deutsche Forschungsgemeinschaft (German Research Council)
DG	Directorate-General (of the European Commission)
DG Agriculture	Directorate-General for Agriculture and Rural Development
DG EMPL	Directorate-General for Employment, Social Affairs and Inclusion
DG Research	Directorate-General for Research and Innovation
DLV	Deutscher LandFrauenverband
EAFRD	European Agricultural Fund for Rural Development
EAGGF	European Agricultural Guarantee and Guidance Fund
EC	European Communities
ECJ	European Court of Justice
ECSC	European Coal and Steel Community
ECU	European currency unit
EEC	European Economic Community
EEGE	European Expert Group on Gender and Employment
EES	European Employment Strategy

EESC	European Economic and Social Committee
EFI	European Fund for the Integration of Third-Country Nationals and the European Refugee Fund
EIT	European Institute for Innovation and Technology
EMU	European Economic and Monetary Union
ENVI	Committee on Environment, Public Health and Food Safety (of the EP)
ENWISE	Enlarge 'Women in Science' to East
EP	European Parliament
EPP	European People's Party
EPSCO	Employment, Social Policy, Health and Consumer Affairs Council
EPWS	European Platform of Women Scientists
ERA	European Research Area
ERC	European Research Council
ERF	European Refugee Fund
ESD	European Social Dialogue
ESF	European Social Fund
ETAN	European Technology Assessment Network
ETUC	European Trade Union Confederation
EU	European Union
EUREKA	European Research Coordination Agency
EURES	European Employment Services (Job Mobility Portal)
EUROJUST	Agency of the EU that deals with issues of judicial cooperation
EUROPOL	European Police Office
EWL	European Women's Lobby
FEFAF	European Federation of Women Working in the Home
FEMM	Committee on Women's Rights and Gender Equality of the EP
FP	Framework Programme for Research and Development
GAP	Gender Action Plan
GIA	Gender impact assessment
GNP	Gross national product
ILGA-Europe	International Lesbian and Gay Association (European branch)
ILO	International Labour Organization
INTI	Programme for preparatory actions for the integration of third-country nationals
LAG	Local Action Groups
LEADER	Liaison Entre Actions de Développement de l'Economie Rurale (French: EU initiative for rural development)
MEP	Member of the EP

NGO	Non-governmental organisation
NOW	New Opportunities for Women
OECD	Organisation for Economic Co-operation and Development
OMC	Open Method of Coordination
PROGRESS	The EU's employment and social solidarity program
QMV	Qualified Majority Voting
R&D	Research and development
RTD	Research, technology and development
S&D	Progressive Alliance of Socialists and Democrats
SEA	Single European Act
STOP	Sexual Trafficking of Persons (EU programme)
TCN	Third-country national
TEC	Treaty establishing the European Community
TEU	Treaty on the EU
TFEU	Treaty on the Functioning of the EU (Lisbon Treaty)
UEAPME	The European Association of Craft, Small and Medium-Sized Enterprises
UN	United Nations
URBACT	European exchange and learning programme promoting sustainable urban development
WIDE	Women in Development Europe
WIR	Women in Industrial Research
WIRDEM	Women in Research Decision Making
WTO	World Trade Organization

1
Introduction: Studying the EU from a Gender Perspective

Gabriele Abels and Joyce Marie Mushaben

> Women's point of view should be integrated from the beginning, when the structure is laid down. It is much cheaper than today, when we have to correct for women's point of view afterwards. It is like building a house and forgetting plumbing, the kitchens, bathrooms, and therefore have [*sic*] to reconstruct the entire building.
> Danish Environmental Minister Lone Dybkjaer, at the First European Summit on 'Women in Power' (Athens), November 3, 1992

Arising in the aftermath of two appalling world wars, of the horrors of the Holocaust and of the deadly effects of nationalism, European integration evolved into a fascinating process that sought to build a 'common house' for Europeans. Key architects of the European dream, the so-called founding fathers included Altiero Spinelli, Robert Schumann, Jean Monnet, Walter Hallstein and Paul-Henri Spaak. Efforts to create a new political order took place on the continent against the backdrop of the Cold War and of rapidly changing societies. Designed by all-male architects, the European dream house nonetheless featured several 'static calculation flaws' affecting the quality of life of all men and women who shared life in this structure, even determining who could occupy which rooms. The contributors to this book set out to detect these flaws and to uncover the ways in which design errors have been recognised by European Union (EU) officials, as well as to investigate the extent to which inherent flaws have (or have not) been remedied in the course of further integration.

Today the EU claims to offer the most progressive gender regime in the world. The 2009 Lisbon Treaty (TEU) formally declares gender equality a fundamental European value:

> The Union is founded on the values of respect for human dignity, freedom, democracy, equality, the rule of law and respect for human rights, including the rights of persons belonging to minorities. These values are

common to the Member States in a society in which pluralism, non-discrimination, tolerance, justice, solidarity and equality between women and men prevail. (Article 2 TEU)

Among other objectives, the EU aims to 'combat social exclusion and discrimination, and shall promote...equality between women and men' (Article 3). This objective extends to *all* EU endeavours, as the Treaty on the Functioning of the EU declares: 'In all its activities, the Union shall aim to eliminate inequalities and to promote equality, between men and women' (Article 8). Heather MacRae (2010) nonetheless speaks of a 'gender myth' that has become a part of the EU's contemporary identity, and thus warrants closer inspection: Is the EU actually as gender-sensitive and women-friendly as it claims to be? Does the EU really practise what it preaches?

In 2011, the European house turned sixty. What we now label the EU began with the European Coal and Steel Community (ECSC), created under the 1951 Treaty of Paris. It was followed by the Treaties of Rome in 1957, which established the European Economic Community (EEC) and the European Atomic Energy Community (Euratom). The establishment of a Single Market, codified in the 1986 Single European Act (SEA) subsequently converted the Community into a global economic power. The Social Protocol, simultaneously adopted by 11 member states in 1991 to avoid an impasse over the Maastricht Treaty (due to British opposition), later became part of the EU Treaties. Enacted after the fall of the Berlin Wall, the collapse of communism and the gruesome civil war in the Balkans, the 1992 Maastricht Treaty on European Union constituted a great leap forward, joining forces and pooling resources in new 'high politics' domains that include justice, home affairs and common foreign and security policy. The 1995 Schengen Agreement initially established passport-free borders among seven EU member states; today it is part of the EU Treaty.

In 1997 the Amsterdam Treaty extended individual freedoms and protections against discrimination based on gender, race, religion, nationality and sexual orientation, extending beyond the rights provided by some member states. In 2004 the Treaty establishing a European Constitution was signed in Rome but lost the ratification battle at the member state level: rejection by way of popular referenda in France and the Netherlands in 2005 triggered an institutional crisis that, in turn, led to the Lisbon Reform Treaty. Its ratification by all members was successfully completed in November 2009 – after jumping the hurdles resulting from a negative referendum in Ireland in 2008, a critical ruling by the German Federal Constitutional Court in 2009 and an obstructionist strategy pursued by the Euro-sceptic Czech President, Václav Klaus, the last to sign the document. Entering into force on 1 December 2009, the Lisbon Treaty now serves as the EU's primary legal foundation. The integration story does not end here, however: another round of far-reaching (and so far unforeseeable) sectoral reforms lies ahead

Table 1.1 Major treaties and agreements in the process of European integration

Year treaty entered into force	Treaties/Major agreement
1952	Treaty on the European Coal and Steel Community (Paris Treaty)
1958	Treaties on the European Economic Community and on the European Atomic Energy Community (Treaties of Rome)
1965	Merger Treaty (uniting the three founding communities to an EC)
1987	Single European Act (SEA)
1991	Social Protocol (appended to the 1992 Maastricht Treaty)
1993	Treaty on European Union (Maastricht Treaty)
1995	Schengen Agreement
1999	Amsterdam Treaty
2003	Nice Treaty
2004	Treaty establishing a European Constitution (ratification failed in 2005)
2009	Lisbon Treaty

in response to the 2008 global financial bust and the resulting Euro crisis, focusing on greater harmonisation of national economic and social policies.

Many perceive the EU story as a very legalistic one, consisting largely of treaties, agreements, protocols and a constant wave of treaty revisions over the last 25 years (see Table 1.1). Indeed, the body of European law – its treaties, court verdicts, regulations, directives and recommendations, known as the *acquis communautaire* – nowadays encompasses nearly 100,000 pages. But European integration also tells a story of fundamental political, economic and societal transformation in all member countries; the latter have repeatedly affected the process by 'uploading' national interests to the EU level. In turn, integration has shaped the course of national transformations, profoundly influencing national political systems ('Europeanisation' or 'downloading' EU law). Member states have engaged in constant communication processes, learning from each other's experiences; national solutions to policy problems have often travelled across country boundaries. These three processes, involving vertical as well as horizontal linkages, have also reconfigured gender policies. We claim that gender relations offer an astounding example of new interconnectedness between the social–economic and political arenas, the private and the public spheres, the domestic and the international domains growing out of European integration.

The integration process is incredibly dynamic, its subsequent directions having been entirely unpredictable at the time of its creation. Initially comprised of six Western states, the Community witnessed many rounds of *deepening and enlargement*; now encompassing 27 member states, it is home to 500 million residents, 51 per cent of whom are female. European integration clearly represents a success story; the EU today is the wealthiest region in the world. Regional integration has also functioned as a peace project on a continent where countries had engaged in conflict and warfare for centuries. The functionalist approach to integration – building peace and trust by intensifying co-operation in specific policy domains, a process gradually accompanied by strong institutions – is often projected as a developmental model for economic, political and social integration around the world.

Women were excluded from the integration project from the start; it took until the 1970s for them to begin directly sampling the fruits of regional cooperation, actively shaping Europe's expanding market and political order in accordance with their own needs and interests. Three decades later, one still finds a substantial (though shrinking) 'gender democracy deficit'. The Swedish Commissioner for Communications and Commission Vice-President Margot Wallström declared recently that the EU is still dominated by the 'reign of old men' and that 'an inner circle of male decision-makers agree behind closed doors on whom to nominate to EU top jobs' (*Sydsvenska Dagbladet*, 8 February 2008). The story of how women came to re-shape EU politics, institutions and decision-making across a variety of policy sectors is an intriguing one, which seems to follow the so-called 'law of unanticipated consequences'. Although countless experts representing diverse academic disciplines – for example political science, international relations, law, sociology and economics – have investigated the evolution of this supranational entity, accounts of women's impact and of the impact of gender perspectives on EU policy often get 'lost in translation', as mainstream academics pursue their favourite theoretical paradigms. The contributors to this volume nonetheless believe that it is imperative for students of European integration to hear 'the rest of the story'.

1. A Brief *Her*story of European integration

The general history of European integration has been written many times (see e.g. Dinan 2005). Our task is to address the significance of key events that were far from 'gender-neutral', even if they were perceived as such in the 1950s, and their effect on equalising gender relations within the Community. European integration is a very time-consuming 'political' endeavour involving multiple levels of bargaining and negotiation. Adoption of the three founding treaties and countless revisions since the mid-1980s required extensive intergovernmental conferences and years of bargaining among sovereign member states; they were first and foremost treaties of international law.

These treaties were the product of very male forms of politicking: French President Charles DeGaulle and German Chancellor Konrad Adenauer made this grand experiment a central focus of their post-war reconstruction and reconciliation efforts. Notwithstanding the presence of quite a few queens (endowed with symbolic tasks as heads of state), not a single female head of government or foreign affairs minister participated in early negotiations, although countless female secretaries and translators provided crucial services. For the first three decades women had virtually no say in setting the integration course accepted by the European Council (consisting of national leaders). Nor were women able to affect the interpretation or implementation of Treaty equality principles from within. Women were likewise few and far between among the civil servants and national lawyers charged with writing and revising the treaties.

Two of the three accords establishing the European Communities (under the 1965 Merger Treaty) concentrated on industrial sectors heavily populated by male workers: coal, steel and energy production. The third, creating the EEC, proved more interesting through a gender lens: this treaty applied integration rules to other industrial arenas, including textile production, which was dominated by female labourers. Equal pay in this sector led to highly contested intergovernmental negotiations among the six founding members (Ellina 2003; Hoskyns 1996; van der Vleuten 2007; Wobbe and Biermann 2009). Home to a strong textile industry, France already had a law mandating 'equal pay for equal work', based on an International Labour Organization Convention. The French delegation feared that its national textile industry would encounter distorted competition, should companies in other common market states not be bound by the equal pay principle. After lengthy negotiations, equal pay between women and men (for the same work, not 'work of equal value') was incorporated in as Article 119 EC Treaty, as part of the 'social policy' chapter. By the 1970s, this article would morph into the 'backbone of an ever-expanding European social-justice policy' (Cichowski 2001: 113–114). Over time, gender equality became 'one of the most legally dense domains of European Social Policy'; it is still considered 'one of the best illustrations of the EU as a "regulatory state"' (Jacquot 2010: 128).

The first opportunities for women's direct involvement in decision-making arose as a second-wave feminism swept across Germany, France and other states, being coupled with the first direct elections to the European Parliament (EP) in 1979 (Vallance and Davies 1986). Their share of seats in the EP rose from a 'high' of 5.5 per cent under the old appointment system to 16.8 per cent in 1979, then to 19.3 per cent by 1989 (Mushaben 1998: 58). Still, the EP remained the least powerful of the Community organs, even following the 2009 elections, when women's share rose to 35 per cent. As Member of European Parliament (MEP) Dame Shelagh Roberts admonished in 1981: 'I think it is the duty of governments and the Commission to practice what they preach and I have seen in the latest appointments to the Commission that somebody is not practicing what is being preached in the field of equality for women' (Vallance and Davies 1986: 14). Nearly three decades later, the EU has yet to practise what it preaches regarding the 'balanced participation' of female and male decision-makers.

Attempting to bring gender issues into the mainstream of society, the recent structural approach complements traditionally 'targeted' women's policies. *Gender mainstreaming* was adopted at the 1995 UN Women's Conference in Beijing, then by the EU in 1996. It remains a contested concept (Jacquot 2010; Schmidt 2005; Squires 2007; Walby 2005). Emilie Hafner-Burton and Mark Pollack (2009) argue that it is a lack of 'hard' incentives rather than a dearth of conceptual clarity that has undercut gender mainstreaming practices within the EU's own house. The problem, as we see it, is that there still are not enough women directly involved as architects, masons, electricians, plumbers, building inspectors and mortgage agents to ensure proper construction. What is lacking is real political will among those responsible for enforcement.

2. How the EU tackles gender

Early integration experts trained in international relations described the European Union ('European Community', EC, until 1992) as a special kind of international organisation. Later scholars trained in comparative politics found this description inaccurate, even misleading. Current conceptualisations view the EU as a political system *sui generis*, a non-state polity characterised by three outstanding features: its multi-level structure; its ever-evolving political institutions and their interactions; and very complex 'state'–society relations, multiplied by 27 (the number of members). Multi-level governance exhibits certain federal traits, but the EU is far from comprising a 'real' state. It consists of three levels – the supranational/EU level, the national/member state level, and the regional level, consisting in turn of various configurations. Each level possesses its own political institutions, cross-linked in very different ways. The *supranational level*, binding all member states, features most prominently throughout this book. The national qua *intergovernmental level* involves member states and their distinctive political systems. The third level encompasses various subunits, for example regional or local governments, which play a special role in fully fledged federal systems. Rather than envisioning this multi-level structure as a 'layer cake' where single parts can be separated from one another, we use the more apt metaphor of a 'marble cake' (Hooghe and Marks 2003: 238), in which different levels flow into each other in unpredictable ways: sometimes the dark chocolate rises to the top and the light vanilla layer extends down to the bottom, or vice versa, during processes of policy-making and implementation.

In addition to inventing new forms of multi-level or poly-centred governance, the EU has developed specialised bodies of 'law' imposing different degrees of supranational or member state obligation. The nature of EU law clearly distinguishes it from classical international law: the 1964 ruling of the European Court of Justice (ECJ) in *Costa v. ENEL* [ECR 585 (6/64a)] established the supremacy of European law over national law whenever they conflict. Member states are obliged to 'transpose' all European law, which is clearly outlined in the treaties.

As our brief *her*storical account reveals, women were economic actors from the start, but the Commission made no effort to propose equality legislation or to develop 'women-oriented' policies until the early 1970s (Hoskyns 1996; Rossilli 2000). Teresa Rees (1998) defines three equality approaches adopted by the Commission, which have guided subsequent gender policy developments: *equal treatment, positive action* and *gender mainstreaming*. The mother of all EU equality policies, Article 119 EEC Treaty, followed by Directives on equality at the (paid) workplace, is rooted in an *equal treatment* approach, embedded in a liberal concept of formal rights. This 'implies that no individual should have fewer human rights or opportunities than any other' (Rees 1998: 29).

This was enhanced by the affirmative or *positive action* approach, shifting the emphasis 'from equality of access to creating conditions more likely to result in equality of outcome' (Rees 1998: 34). A series of multi-year Action Programmes (APs) implemented since the 1980s proved to be powerful instruments for policy innovation. They introduced specific activities and requirements to improve women's starting position in the workplace, helping them to overcome age-old patriarchal barriers. The strategy includes, but is not limited to, positive discrimination in favour of women.

The third approach, adopted in 1996, is *gender mainstreaming* (Mazey 2001; Rees 1998; Schmidt 2005; Squires 2007). This approach moves beyond women-targeted policies by mandating that gender differences be systematically incorporated into *all* EU policies and activities. The Commission (1996: 2) officially defines it as

> [t]he systematic integration of the respective situations, priorities and needs of women and men in all policies and with a view to promoting equality between women and men and mobilising all general policies and measures specifically for the purpose of achieving equality by actively and openly taking into account, at the planning stage, their effects on the respective situation of women and men in implementation, monitoring and evaluation.

The innovative feature of this strategic framework is that it requires policy makers to incorporate gender perspectives deliberately and consistently into every stage of every policy process – design, implementation, monitoring and evaluation. Just as one would expect twenty-first-century architects to incorporate 'plumbing, kitchens and bathrooms' into every house design under modern building codes, mainstreaming obliges officials at all levels to

8 Introduction

anticipate and analyse the concrete impact of policy in the making on the life, position and opportunities facing women and men. It seeks to turn gender equality into a concrete reality by 'creating space for everyone within the organisations as well as in communities', thus contributing 'to the process of articulating a shared vision of sustainable human development', binding on all actors and levels.

The process for determining when, where and how gender differences ought to be recognised and accommodated (Figure 1.1) in order to share integration benefits equally among EU citizens is very complicated – but then, so are all of the other aspects of European integration, whether the issue is guaranteeing food safety from 'farm to fork', ensuring that pensions and

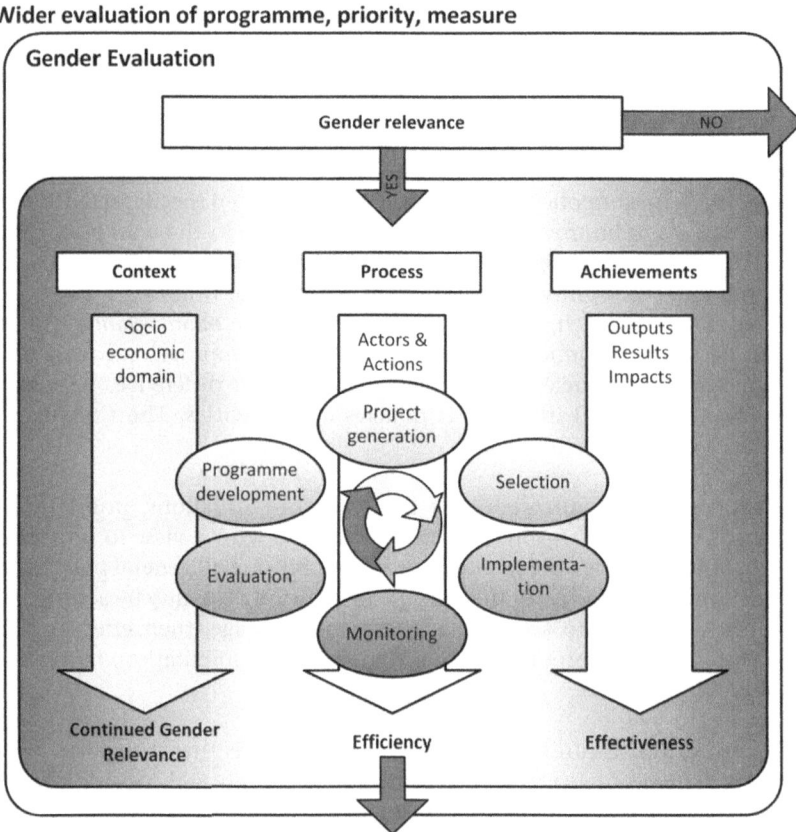

Figure 1.1 Evaluating policy through a gendered lens
Source: Polverari and Fitzgerald (2002: 5).

health benefits transfer across borders, or harmonising taxation law. Where there's a will, there's a way.

The 1997 Amsterdam Treaty codified gender mainstreaming as a primary policy tool for achieving gender equality, a policy that is now firmly embedded in the Lisbon Treaty. Unlike previous reactive and corrective approaches, gender mainstreaming comprises a pro-active, transformative approach, capable of reshaping *all* EU policy domains as well as its policy-making machinery. Starting with EU social and employment domains, gendering practices have been extended (at least rhetorically) to all policy fields, to institutional participation and to organisational practices, albeit to different degrees. Yet, in many policy fields, gender mainstreaming is still not adequately implemented, for reasons addressed in this volume.

Despite its transformative potential, some feminist critics fear that gender mainstreaming will abolish established positive action policies that remain crucial for women (Stratigaki 2005). Ideally, positive action and gender mainstreaming comprise complementary strategies. Furthermore, the adoption of more comprehensive anti-discrimination policies, including unequal treatment based on grounds other than sex, poses new challenges to the value of gender equality policy (Kantola 2010a: 168, 188; Lombardo and Verloo 2009).

3. From 'add women and stir' to a comprehensive gender approach in EU studies

Evaluating EU studies through a gender lens reveals, first, that for a long time male researchers and *male*stream analysis dominated the field, building on established – that is, gender-blind – epistemological and ontological premises. Secondly, the onset of gender analysis around 1990 has introduced new approaches, building on concepts borrowed from mainstream research as well as from gender studies. Gendered approaches make important contributions by shedding light on the otherwise invisible economic, political and social effects of integration. Today's 'feminist gender strand' began with a limited, sectoral approach, evolving into more comprehensive gender approaches. Let us now sketch out key developments and the ways in which the *male*stream and the *female*stream intersect or diverge.

For many decades, male scholars – applying different lenses – invented theories and methodologies. The 'big names' popping up include Ernst Haas, David Mitrany, Robert Keohane or Phillipe Schmitter; they have been joined by Andrew Moravscik, John McCormick, Mark Pollack, Paul Pierson, Thomas Risse, Gary Marks, Wayne Sandholz and Giandomenico Majone, to name but a few. The resulting problem is an epistemological one: the masculinity of the discipline has affected what scholars deem worthy of investigation, the questions they ask, and how they train others to 'explain' European integration. Malestream research holds profound ontological and discursive implications for 'theorising' integration. Theories, developing in several waves over the years, lead competing schools to apply very different paradigms, though most have remained oblivious or impervious to gender factors (Hoskyns 2004; Locher and Prügl 2009). The re-production of gender relations as an effect of European integration was not part of their curriculum. Despite noteworthy exceptions (Egan et al. 2010; Wiener and Diez 2009), most scholars still exclude gender analysis. The body of gender-related EU studies is growing, however, along with the 'ever expanding scope of the EU gender policy', covering issues such as violence against women, women in development, women in foreign and security policy, sex-trafficking and the like (Kantola 2010b: 321).

This expansion entails manifold challenges for researchers, some of which were first exposed by the famous episode of the blind men and the elephant – introduced in a 1972 article by Donald Puchala:

> Several blind men approached an elephant and each touched the animal in an effort to discover what the beast looked like. Each blind man, however, touched a different part of the large animal, and each concluded that the elephant had the appearance of the part he had touched. Hence, the blind man who felt the animal's trunk concluded that an elephant must be tall and slender, while the fellow who touched the beast's ear concluded that an elephant must be oblong and flat. Others of course reached different conclusions. The total result was that no man arrived at a very accurate description of the elephant. Yet, each man had gained enough evidence from his own experience to disbelieve his fellows and to maintain a lively debate of the nature of the beast. (Puchala 1972: 267)

Studying and revisiting the 'nature of the beast' is still an ambitious task for scholars. The EU is certainly not the same elephant it was in the 1950s and 1960s: this dynamic elephant moves constantly – in often unforeseen directions. This holds vast ramifications for EU research, since it is very hard to 'hit' (in other words, to describe and explain) a moving target. 'Stalking the elephant' is a complex endeavour, due to the 'diffuse nature of both the subject matter on which EU scholars focus, and the methods and approaches they use in their descriptions and analyses' (Egan et al. 2010: 3). Scholars employ concepts, theories and methodologies from international relations and comparative politics, and – in response to the debate about EU democratic deficits – also from democratic political theory. Analysing the EU simultaneously challenges established disciplinary approaches – that is, the concept of statehood.

What does all this imply for gender-sensitive EU studies? Seen through the lens of feminist epistemology, it is striking that Puchala's men display no interest in the *sex of the beast*; nor is he interested in how the beast reproduces or in how it provides for its offspring. Equally curious is how an all-male sample examines this mammal: they communicate their experiences with each other but do not jointly investigate the beast; assessments are based on individual, compartmentalised studies. Gender research around the world suggests that women would discuss what they had *collectively* experienced, perhaps (metaphorically speaking) holding hands in a circle in order to take *full measure* of the beast, including reflections on its sex, gender roles and its relations with others.

Since the 1980s, female comparative and international relations specialists have increasingly entered the male-dominated 'groves of academe'. Male EU researchers have been joined by colleagues like Helen Wallace, Alberta Sbragia, Beate Kohler-Koch, Beverly Springer, Elisabeth Meehan, Adrienne Héritier, Jo Shaw, Sonia Mazey, Vivian Schmidt, Liesbet Hooghe, Catherine Hoskyns, Ul█████████████████Antje Wiener, *inter alia*. Their innovative, some█████████████████hes to European integration have increased ex█████████████████ble political changes in the nature of the beast. Not until the Single Market project generated conflicts over the EU 'social dimension' did gender scholars question the broader implications of integration for Europe's women. Catherine Hoskyns (1996: 4) claims: 'the integration of states (and of markets) has the effect of destabilising existing patterns of social integration, including those relating to gender'. Building on an expanding body of gender studies literature, social scientists can now apply those insights, research questions, theories, concepts and methodologies to the EU. Drawing on many disciplines, the gendered endeavour of 'stalking the elephant' has followed a three-stage logic, albeit with overlapping concerns: (1) 'identifying sex discrimination'; (2) 'generating material and research'; and (3) 'challenging fundamental concepts' (Hoskyns 2004: 218–223).

The first stage, identifying discrimination, employs a *sectoral approach*. References to Article 119 EEC Treaty (equal pay for equal work) and to the *Defrenne* v *Sabena* case in 1976 initiated this phase, which lasted from the early 1970s to the mid-1980s. Concentrating on reducing workplace discrimination against women, it was sooner an activist than an academic phase.

During the 1980s, women's and gender studies began to theorise about social relations, assessing gender roles, sex-specific norms, and so on – with repercussions for feminist approaches. Elizabeth Vallance and Elizabeth Davies (1986) supplied the first such encounter with the EU, investigating the role of women in the European Parliament and their influence on equality policy development. The role of gendered actors, female experts and women's rights activists in EU institutions, and the ways in which these actors affect EU institutions and policy-making, remain predominant topics. This early research aligns with the second stage, *generation of materials and data by academics*, starting with Hoskyns' (1985) work on 'Women's Equality and the European Community'. This (ongoing) stage has added breadth and depth by focusing on diverse topics and policy sectors.[1]

Recognised as a 'classic', Hoskyns's book *Integrating Gender* (1996) marked a significant transition to the third stage, *challenging established concepts* in EU studies and developing a gender-sensitive research strand.[2] Her historical account was followed by studies utilising different theoretical concepts to review (and retell) the EU story through a gender lens (van der Vleuten 2007; Wobbe and Biermann 2009). Scholars openly criticised the gender-blindness – or the inherent male bias – of established theories, concepts and approaches, as well as that of the political integration process itself. The focus shifted from questions as to why and how the EU was adopting equality policies to 'how and why is gender difference constructed and gender inequality reproduced through EU policies' (Prügl, quoted in Kantola 2010b: 305). A new generation of integration scholars insisted that gender relations be analysed as a function of complex social developments resulting from women's specific social position as workers and mothers; in this way they render the relation between employment and 'caring' a key concern. Drawing on globalisation studies, Marxist-inspired and comparative welfare state analyses, many feminist scholars criticised the EU as a neoliberal, market-creating enterprise that disadvantaged women by neglecting the need for supranational social policy (the Single Market became key to integration as of the mid-1980s). Many found that EU equality policy focused exclusively on women's integration into the job market and the social security systems on equal terms with men. By neglecting women's social position in the family and reproductive spheres, equality policies fall short. Attempts to improve women's integration into the market on male terms were admonished for essentially endorsing the neoliberal concept (Ostner and Lewis 1995; Perrons 2005; Rubery 2005; Schunter-Kleemann 1992a; Young 2000). Such analyses highlight the significance of women's social roles. They have traced the EU's paradigmatic shift (along with gender mainstreaming) from a narrow job-market focus and employment-anchored social policy to the concept of 'employability' (Behning and Serrano Pascual 2001; Braams 2007; Guerrina 2005; Jenson 2008; Lewis 2006; O'Connor 2005a; Ostner 2000; Smith and Villa 2010). These studies take the reproductive sphere and women's caretaker roles into account in relation to their employment opportunities, drawing on comparative welfare state research. They challenge standards concepts, like those deriving from Esping-Anderson's oft-cited typology, for neglecting women's specific role in the welfare state (von Wahl 2005).

Another school of feminist EU studies investigates evolving supranational equality and gender policies and their implementation in the member states. These researchers draw on established policy-analysis concepts such as 'policy networks', framing and learning concepts, policy styles and 'regimes'. They further employ constructs borrowed from bureaucratic politics, social movement theory, norm diffusion processes, Europeanisation approaches and new institutionalism, although these concepts and theories often require elaboration in order to integrate gender factors. Birgit Locher and Elisabeth Prügl (2009: 185) argue that 'a key contribution of feminist approaches to European integration has been to theorise activism, the power of framing, and the "opportunity structures" for movement activism'. As a new governance mode (Jacquot 2010), gender mainstreaming has attracted particular attention. Gender studies reveal that political and administrative cultures underlying EU institutions and the multi-level policy-making system have not only been shaped by national heritages, bureaucratic traditions and institutional power-plays, but that these deeply gendered cultures affect government responsiveness, political will and the administrative capacities needed to implement equality policies. Mark A. Pollack and Emilie Hafner-Burton (2000), for example, pinpoint the key role of Commission Directorates-General (DG) and their respective gender cultures in formulating equality policy, explaining why mainstreaming has been more successfully implemented in some DGs than in others. Outlining specific features of the gender policy-making process, Gabriele Abels (2011a) emphasises the prominent role of what Allison Woodward (2004) has labeled 'velvet triangles'.

Implementation studies show that member states, serving as the 'policy hinterland' (Mazey 1998) for supranational equality policies, are likewise deeply gendered; different policy outcomes can be explained by the nature of national gender regimes (Liebert 2003a). Enlargement studies are particularly interesting, given that the post-communist countries re-joining the 'European family' in 2004 and 2007 were rooted in very different gender equality regimes. Economic decline in post-communist countries – triggering the elimination of public services, for example childcare facilities – had a tremendous impact on women's socio-economic position, and this was often coupled with radical rhetoric stressing traditional gender roles (Avdeyeva 2010; Galligan et al. 2007).

New integration methods are also subject to criticism, for example regarding male dominance in EU constitution-building. While the Constitutional Convention was hailed for its innovative character, more inclusive deliberation, and ambitious outcome, feminist analysts were quite ambivalent (see Lombardo 2005; Millns 2007). The open method of coordination (OMC), a 'soft' method building on intergovernmental exchange, policy diffusion and learning (introduced via the 2000 Lisbon Strategy for Growth), has also met with feminist scrutiny and scepticism. Fiona Beveridge and Samantha Velluti (2008a) show that different gender regimes influence the OMC and its success in the employment field. The 'conceptual openness' and deliberative quality of this soft strategy are seen as more advantageous than 'hard law', but OMC's lack of a comprehensive vision regarding gender equality is a core problem.

The diffusion of gender mainstreaming into new policy sectors finds scholars turning to fields outside the 'classical' women's issues (that is, social policy, employment) and setting their sights on judicial and domestic affairs, a particularly dynamic integration field over the last decade; others are assessing EU policies in relation to international norms. Kathrin Zippel (2004, 2008) and Birgit Locher (2007), for instance, illustrate norm diffusion throughout the EU, stressing the role of movement activists with regard to sexual harassment and sex-trafficking policies; others focus on enlargement's effects on sex-trafficking (Kligman and Limoncelli 2005). Amy Elman (2007) admonishes that EU policies involving violence against women have created only 'virtual equality'; Montoya (2008) delivers a more positive evaluation. Given the feminisation of migration worldwide (Askola 2007), others are zooming in on external relations (Gya 2009), on the effects of a 'fortress Europe' mentality on women as (forced) migrants and on the latter's place in development aid and trade policy (Debusscher and True 2009; Elgström 2000), as well as in security and defence fields (Eulriet 2009).

The multiplicity of EU gender studies does not allow us to supply a comprehensive overview of the field; such research has significantly broadened our conceptual and empirical approaches, however. Equally clear is the 'lack of effort among feminist scholars to engage in more coherent theorising regarding the EU as a whole' (Kronsell in this volume). Van der Vleuten's (2007) study constitutes a new effort at *theory-building*, as it seeks to gender intergovernmentalist approaches by showing that national interests vis-à-vis equality policies are shaped by economic and ideological factors.

Revisiting 'statehood', Birgit Sauer (2001) speaks of a 'European regime' combining both modern statehood and pre-modern regime structures. Her point of departure is a belief that, although European integration processes invoke an inherently new construction of statehood, relations between the sexes have not been modernised in quasi-automatic ways. Rather, existing nation–state patterns of masculinity have been 're-written' into the Community's new history. Next to state formation stands the state project, namely the creation of an economic regime rooted in male norms; this project is situated within an 'androcent   y gender-differentiated policies are used as an i   g masculinised market goals' (Sauer 2001: 12–1

In short, viewing the EU through a gender lens exposes its *double democratic deficit* – one involving women's underrepresentation across EU institutions and decision-making bodies, the other reflecting the lack of gender sensitivity in EU policy-making. Responding to both deficits by searching for new approaches and possible solutions requires more theoretical work. Only a few attempts to formulate gendered integration theories are evident thus far, but we are unlikely to see a 'comprehensive' gender integration theory emerging in the near future, and for obvious reasons. First of all, the key insight gleaned by women's and gender studies researchers to date is that there is no such thing as *one* approach to gender theory; rather, there are multiple gender perspectives, rooted in different strands of social theory (Locher and Prügl 2009: 183).[3] Secondly, feminist scholars see little point in formulating yet another 'grand theory' of European integration, most of which focus on questions, dynamics and policy fields that neglect women. Our epistemological aim is to 'enrich the understanding of European integration by making visible an under-appreciated social reality' (ibid.). At issue are empirically grounded critiques of established theories, existing decision-making structures and integration processes as they affect gender relations. While most theories are of a purely analytical nature, one feature that feminist perspectives share with other critical frameworks, for example Marxist and Gramscian paradigms, is that they are explicitly normative, investigating European integration *in order to intervene and reshape the process*. We do not claim that gender perspectives in EU studies have no blind spots of their own, only that a gender analysis of Puchala's elephant would take a definitive interest in the sex of the beast, in how it constructs and reconstructs gender realities and in how we can help it to find its way to a better habitat.

4. What we hoped to accomplish: The structure of the book

All contributors to this volume apply a gender lens in introducing students and scholars to the EU's historical evolution, theoretical parameters, institutional dynamics and policy developments across six decades. We treat gender not as a biological category, but rather as a complex series of social constructions and relations. This leads us to address gender as the by-product of deeply entrenched power relations and intricate connections between the public and the private, between political, economic and societal spheres, between the 'domestic' and the international/supranational level. Beyond reviewing broader political developments, we incorporate changes in the academic debate regarding the concepts, theories, and 'isms' applied to EU integration over the last few decades.

Part I provides a quick but comprehensive gendered overview of traditional theoretical paradigms, historical turning points, core actors, institutional dynamics, decision-making rules and community norms, supplying a 'crash course' in 60 years of European integration and preparing readers for subsequent case studies. Our authors treat different schools of integration theory, processes, strategies, tactics and concrete policies, moving from equal treatment and positive action to gender mainstreaming and diversity management. Annica Kronsell's exploration of major integration theories finds that, with the exception of liberal governmentalism, most of these theories evince some potential for raising questions of equality and could actually enrich their own paradigms by adding gender to the mix. Multi-level governance and social constructivism easily lend themselves to a deeper analysis of gender as a serious contributor to European integration processes. Anna van der Vleuten tracks the evolution of EU institutions and their gendered composition in this multi-level polity, along with the changing roles of gendered actors involved in equality policy. Birgit Locher evaluates the construction of the formal *gender acquis* that every would-be member state is now required to embrace as a condition for entry. Treating changes in EU policy and processes over time as both a cause and an effect of gendering, she highlights the significance of women's agency within the *sui generis* system of EU policy-making.

Alison Woodward then explores the conceptual qua strategic progression from equal treatment and positive action to gender mainstreaming and, more recently, to diversity management. The latter is viewed critically as an attempt to reduce the salience of gender by counting it merely as one of many protected categories, such as race/ethnicity, age, physical ability and sexual orientation. Yvonne Galligan and Sara Clavero round out the first half on the historical–institutional dynamics of EU integration, assessing gendering, or a critical lack thereof, during four waves of enlargement culminating in the incorporation of 12 Central East European states as of 2004 and 2007. Neither the transposition nor the implementation of the *acquis communautaire* have been linear processes; indeed, the pursuit of equal opportunity is the area in which national and European ambitions have repeatedly diverged.

Part II offers concrete case studies investigating gender dynamics in a number of different policy sectors. Our authors address a fixed set of questions, allowing for comparison across policy arenas:

- How has each policy evolved, and who are the core actors?
- What conceptual insights have gender studies brought to policy research in this field?
- What strategic approaches and formal instruments have EU actors employed to promote gender equality?
- To what extent has gender mainstreaming been implemented since 1996, with what observable policy outputs and outcomes?
- What major empirical and conceptual issues suggest future policy agendas for gendering EU integration?

Elisabeth Prügl demonstrates that, paradoxically, one of the oldest and biggest realms of EU responsibility, the Common Agricultural Policy, has proven quite impervious to gender equalisation strategies. The good news here is that striking changes began to kick in recently with the turn from agricultural subsidy policy to a social policy for rural areas. Agnes Hubert makes use of her 'front row seat' in Brussels to describe the gendering of employment policy, the first domain to experience pro-active intervention by the Commission. Maria Stratigaki, likewise a participant–observer in many of the processes she outlines, documents the stages by which EU social policy – for a long time the key domain of EU equality policy – moved beyond original workplace issues into more significant frameworks for 'social inclusion' and 'social protection'.

Gabriele Abels focuses on a new field of EU endeavour, research and innovation policy, which has become ever more significant since the 'relaunch' of the Lisbon Strategy (2005). She discovers that looming demographic deficits, coupled with global competition for 'best brains', render member states positively disposed towards women's inclusion in this domain, while another prospective remedy, the pro-active recruitment of foreign workers, re-invokes the image of 'Fortress Europe'. Joyce Marie Mushaben takes on one of the most fiercely defended 'last bastions' of national sovereignty, migration and citizenship policy; this domain relies heavily on shared principles and 'discursive frameworks' to compel harmonisation. Recognising the potential long-term effect of recent anti-discrimination directives, she admits that 'homeland security' still trumps human rights, undermining equality goals; but, given patterns observed across earlier decades, she remains cautiously optimistic.

One shared lesson we derive from the last 60 years of European integration is that, while most member states have transposed EU equality policies, *national implementation* leaves a lot to be desired. What our collective effort, moreover, reveals is that no matter what political leaders at multiple levels of governance may claim, virtually every EU institution and policy domain reflect some differences in their treatment of, opportunities for and impact on women and men and gender relations throughout the Union, including other fields not addressed here.

The concluding chapter, by the editors, compares the relative effectiveness of the three equality approaches to date (equal treatment, positive action, gender mainstreaming), as well as the significance of different actors and the use of various policy 'tools' in diverse policy settings. We find that certain concepts, tactics, actors or tools may lead to greater success than others *at particular points in time*. Ultimately, however, progress towards the 'balanced participation of women and men' and a more equitable distribution of individual rights in any given policy arena has depended heavily on a flexible, yet creative mix of personal commitment on the part of 'a few good women', a willingness to experiment with pilot projects and new framing concepts, the energetic pursuit of expert networks and institutional allies, and more than a little help from the Commission and the ECJ. One anticipated consequence, common to most conclusions, is our collective exhortation to others to 'do more work' regarding policy fields not covered in this text, as well as in relation to new questions that have arisen since we commenced this project five years ago, including those triggered by the enactment of the Lisbon Treaty.

In a speech delivered on 8 March 2005, Margot Wallström (2005), then Commissioner for Institutional Relations and Communication Strategy, came to a sobering conclusion:

> So here we are celebrating the International Women's Day. And as my friend's daughter asked – are all other days' [sic] men's days, then? What is there really to celebrate? [...] A balanced participation by women

and men in decision-making, both in politics and economy, is vital to developing real democracy – and it is vital, as President Barroso points out to achieve economic prosperity! And frankly, I do not think that the European institutions [...] are very good examples when it comes to a balanced participation. The statistics are not very positive: the fact remains: 29% women and 71% men in the College! Not much better in the European Parliament 30% women – 70 % men, Committee of the Regions 17% women 83 % men, Economic and Social Committee, 17% women 83% men. In the private sector there has been a rise in the number of women in the 50 publicly quoted companies in the European Union. An increase from 2% to 3 % this year! With this rate we will only achieve gender balance in the next millennium! [...]

This of course leads us to the challenge of adopting gender mainstreaming as a central strategy within Europe and within each member state by asserting that there are no gender neutral public policies or programmes [...] At the end of the day I think it is crucial that we all take gender equality into our areas of work [...] One of our goals for the years to come is to show how the Union concretely has an effect on people's lives. That is where our work on gender equality comes in. This is necessary if we want citizens, including women, to understand that Europe is not something far away and to feel involved in the European project [...] Macho doesn't prove mucho – as famous queen of glamour, Zsa Zsa Gabour once said!

All of the authors featured in this book harbour a deep appreciation for the EU's extraordinary contributions to a peaceful, prosperous Europe since 1951. Despite its slow start, the EU has become a driving force of gender equality throughout the member states – a tribute to the efforts of 'a few good women' in the 1960s, including Éliane Vogel-Polsky and Gabrielle Defrenne, who first recognised the tremendous potential embedded in Article 119 of the 1957 EEC Treaty. Yet full 'gender democracy' remains an unfulfilled promise thus far.

For many feminist and gender scholars, a focus on the ad hoc nature of EU policies and litigation throughout the 1970s resulted in a kind of intellectual scavenger hunt, teaching us a great deal about the significance of informal networking among EU officials, national 'femocrats'[4] and grassroots women's organisations. The sooner we grasped the importance of 'symbolic politics' and of 'critical mass' (a strong female-minority presence in key organs), the better positioned we were to build coalitions and to effect change at the 'interstices of procedure' (Mushaben 1998), before formal regulations were enacted. The synergy observed between empirical gender research and EU policy development has been nothing short of profound. Our attempt to analyse EU policy domains thus far presumed to be 'gender neutral' – or deliberately ignored by decision-makers pursuing 'other priorities' – pays homage to the creative scholars and courageous activists who preceded us. Together, they inscribed gender equality onto the banner of fundamental EU freedoms, for which generations of women should be most grateful. 'Stalking the elephant' with a gender lens is still an ongoing, exciting and challenging academic as well as political endeavour.

Notes

1. The 1990s were blessed by multiple EU-commissioned research projects. The more important data gatherers included the Women's Network of Legal Experts, the Group on Women in Decision-Making, and the European Women's Lobby.
2. One indicator marking the rise of a new research field is the production of textbooks such as Kantola (2010a) or Klein (2006).
3. There are essentially four main streams. The first focuses on the *fundamental equality* of women and men, calling for the same rights and benefits of societal participation; this includes liberal and socialist variations. The second, *radical feminism*, presupposes major differences between the sexes, understands gender relations as power relations, and seeks politicisation of the private sphere. *Postmodern feminism*, the third stream, recognises gender as a social construct (*sex* is a biological category); it highlights differences among women, gender comprising only one out of many types of difference. The fourth stream builds on *critical theory*, represented by Jürgen Habermas.
4. Femocrats are civil servants or bureaucrats who pursue a feminist agenda – that is, bureaucrats working in administrative bodies.

Part I

Gendering Perspectives and EU Processes

2
Gendering Theories of European Integration

Annica Kronsell

Integration theories are concerned with the processes of cooperation among EU member states, seeking to explain the trajectory of 'Europeanisation' by focusing on specific features relevant to integration generally. European cooperation was initiated in 1957, when six member states signed the Treaties of Rome, endorsing economic cooperation and trade liberalisation. The notion that former belligerent states could be tied to one another through economic dependencies is why integration is often deemed a peacemaking project, at least in Europe. Economic exchange was expected to lead to increased security via economic growth and enhanced citizen welfare.

Integration moreover refers to a process that has seen not only 'completion' but also 'deepening'. Ever more issues have become European concerns. Furthermore, 'enlargement' expanded the Union from 6 to 15 and, finally, to 27 states, and accession negotiations are in progress with Iceland, Croatia, the Former Yugoslavian Republic of Macedonia and Turkey. Although researchers who seek to explain its driving forces concentrate on various twists and turns in EU development, integration theories are not simply descriptive. They often contribute to the understanding of transnational cooperation and institution-building more generally and can help to shape expectations as to future behaviour. Following the EU's evolution over the years has therefore resulted in paradigmatic shifts in theoretical integration frameworks: theories were first concerned with explaining new forms of cooperation, then with analysing political processes and institution-building and, thirdly, with the many consequences of integration.

Despite five decades of research that have interpreted processes of Community cooperation utilising divergent approaches, attempts to grasp integration from a gender perspective remain rare. It is safe to say that both its policy-making core and many key concepts used in theorising integration have remained virtually untouched by gender analysis. Equally problematic is the lack of effort among feminist scholars to engage in more coherent theorising regarding the EU as a whole. Most studies on women and gender relations in the EU often rely on a limited, empirical case study approach.

This chapter reviews integration theories and discusses the ways in which gender analysis can contribute to 'theorising' European integration. Though we cannot consider all theories developed to date, we will revisit the major conceptual frameworks, organised here in terms of three paradigms that highlight divergent 'driving forces' of European integration. First, *liberal intergovernmentalism* and the *domestic politics approaches* see the larger process as driven by member states and their national interests. Secondly, *(neo)functionalism* and *governance approaches* define integrative forces in terms of functional or task-specific needs, arising in exchanges among multiple actors across various issue fields. The third paradigm discussed here centres on *institutional path dependency* and the *institutionalisation of norms*. I present the main arguments offered within each paradigm, using feminist theory to critique them as well as to suggest ways in which certain integration approaches might account more accurately for gender factors (see Table 2.1).

Gender analysis is based on feminist theory, which concentrates on the social construction of roles and opportunities around sex differences, especially the power asymmetries associated with gender relations. As an organising principle of social relations, gender is relevant for understanding power relations within the EU. Feminist theory and gender analysis can provide an innovative framework for assessing dominant integration dynamics as well as a foundation for challenging existing concepts and approaches, while also extending the scope of theory. Due to the epistemological basis of feminist theorising and the divergent views on EU integration introduced here, it is neither likely nor especially desirable that there be a single feminist theory of the EU. What is urgently needed are theoretically informed gender perspectives on all processes of EU integration (Abels 2011b; Locher and Prügl 2009).

1. Integration as politics between states contesting national interests

Liberal intergovernmentalism (LI) and *domestic politics approaches* are theories that explain EU integration as the result of state action based on the formation of national interests. The main focus rests on negotiations when member state interests are at stake, often occurring in conjunction with meetings and summits among national leaders. Revisions stretching from the Treaties of Rome (coming into force in 1958) to the Lisbon Treaty (2009) constitute such examples. These are formative moments for the integration process because member states have to agree upon central principles for EU politics and institutions. At such times individual members might actually choose to opt out, in other words, decide not to partake in cooperation. The United Kingdom and Sweden, for example, decided not to join the European Monetary Union (EMU); Denmark's opting out from the European Defence and Security Cooperation (EDSC) offers another case. European summits,

Table 2.1 Major theoretical approaches in European integration theory and the feminist critique

Theory	Core notions	Drives integration	Feminist critique	Suggested issues for a feminist agenda
Liberal-Intergovernmentalism	Unitary actors State's self-interest	Multilateral agreements benefit states	State defines political space Double hierarchy	Who has the authority to speak for the state? How are state interests understood when boundaries between levels are questioned and deconstructed?
Domestic politics	Various interests Compromises or most dominant = national interest	When integration conforms with the dominant domestic interests	Power asymmetries between domestic interests Women's interests viewed as special interests	How do gender gaps affect national positions in EU? Are women's interests served by dominant domestic interests? Are certain member states more women friendly?
Neo-functionalism	Transnational interactions Spill-over Transnational organisations	Need for coordination, then side-effects lead to agreement on common norms	Lacks conception of governance Some transnational groups more powerful	What is the role of transnational women's or feminist organisations? What is the relationship between different transnational groups and their influence on politics? Are women's interests served by transnational organisations?
Multilevel governance	Intertwined issues Multiple levels Fragmented authority Networks	Actors are 'sandwiched' between different levels and actors, creates 'pincer' effect (van der Vleuten)	Conceals hierarchies Democratic accountability Transparency	What is the importance of women/feminist groups in sandwiching states and creating pincer effects? Is there evidence of gender power hierarchies despite fragmented authority? Are networks democratic and inclusive?

Table 2.1 (Continued)

Theory	Core notions	Drives integration	Feminist critique	Suggested issues for a feminist agenda
Institutionalism	Norms are institutionalised. Path dependency. Institutions affect actor's behaviour and calculation of interest	Once norms agreed upon and institutionalised they create a dynamic of their own	Main focus on legal norms and formal aspects of organisations. Institutions only an intervening variable	How do supranational norms influence national norms related to women's issues and gender relations (and vice versa)? Is there any evidence of male-as-norm embedded in formal institutions?
Constructivism	Identity formation in thick/embedded institutions. Actors are enabled and constrained by institutions	Through interaction, actors, interests and institutions form and the EU is ever-changing. Different 'orders/regimes' form in issue areas	Power is external to construction	How are different gender orders contested and formed in the EU and in the interaction between member states and other actors? How is the construction of a common order in environment, agriculture, security gendered?

convened among the primary heads of state or government, are also significant insofar as they set the direction for future work, strategies and policies.

LI theory focuses on such decisive moments in the integration process, concluding that integration will proceed as long as it accommodates the various national interests articulated by member states. If intergovernmental negotiations do not effectively reconcile those interests, integration comes to a halt or slows down considerably. Basically, the particular interests of the individual member states are construed as the driving force of the integration process; this force relies on the possibility that their interests can be accommodated with the (potentially conflicting) concerns of other nation–states. LI finds its roots in international relations theory and in the intergovernmental relations of the state system.

As a grand theory of European integration, intergovernmentalism takes the state as the best level of analysis and highlights the role that governmental actors play (Moravcsik 1993, 1998). Implicit is the idea that in a world of anarchy, insecurity and fierce economic competition, the EU polity emerges as the outcome of national survival strategies. Integration advances only as long as each autonomous state finds it beneficial. Andrew Moravcsik (1993: 507) observes that integration proves acceptable as long as 'it strengthens, rather than weakens, their control over domestic affairs, permitting them to attain goals otherwise unachievable'. In other words, 'state governments call the tune in European integration' (Schimmelfennig 2004: 80).

Feminist work on international relations theory has something 'useful' to say about state-centric theories and the problems of assuming the rational aggregation of state interests. Each national government presumably forms preferences in its own best interest; it will cooperate and participate in an intergovernmental agreement as long as the latter fits those preferences. When states are deemed the most relevant actors in cooperative integration processes, the focus is limited to a specific political space, rendering national government the only arena for politics. This assumes that the state has the authority to manage practices and relations within its territorial boundaries; this political space is controlled by what happens between states in intrastate negotiations, as in the European Summits and in the Council of Ministers.

Feminists argue that this obsession with 'the state' as the only relevant political space neglects power relations within it, for example by failing to recognise its ability to exploit national resources only for select groups. The state fixation makes existing hierarchies invisible; gender relations and other power asymmetries appear irrelevant. However, what really takes place inside and outside the state in intergovernmental relations is open to question. There is a pressing need to deconstruct the boundary between state and non-state relations embedded in the LI approach, as J. Ann Tickner (1992: 27–67) does for international relations theory. The hierarchy privileging national governments has much affinity with the way gender differences are constructed. The boundaries between state and society intersect, and thus overlap with the gendered boundaries of public/man and private/woman (Elshtain 1993) to form a double hierarchy. The public sphere, thus the state and government, is associated with masculinity. Visible evidence of this double hierarchy rest with the 'family photos' often taken at EU summit meetings, the usual 'family' consisting of mostly white, middle-aged men.

LI defines the space of politics as a place where women are not. The idea that states relate to each other and interact as part of the integration process in intergovernmental negotiations ignores the fact that it is, and always has been, almost exclusively men speaking 'for' the state. Representation is certainly gendered in favour of men in all EU institutions (Kantola 2010a: 50–75; also see van der Vleuten in this volume). This is not coincidental. Citizenship, which defines the rights and duties of state subjects, is gendered to the extent that 'full' or 'real' citizens have always been male (Mushaben in this volume; Siim 2000; Voet 1998). This reinforces men's unquestionable authority to represent the state in intergovernmental affairs. Personal and gender relations are declared irrelevant by leaders whose privileged position ignores their own 'gendering'. Through the exclusion constructed by this double hierarchy, LI cares only about states as the exclusive political space. It ignores individuals and other spaces, reproducing existing gender relations.

Like LI, *domestic politics approaches* (Mauritzio 2010; Milward et al. 1992; Puchala 1975) focus on the state as the authoritative actor in intergovernmental relations. Research in this tradition has concentrated on individual states or a set of states, for example in the Scandinavian region as it relates to European integration (Archer 2005; Ingebritsen 1998; Miles 2005). Here the EU is often viewed as a negotiated order where agenda-setting, decision-making and implementation entail a two-level process of negotiation within and between states over national interest in summits and in the Council of the EU (previously called Council of Ministers). This sounds quite similar to the LI approach. However, the domestic politics approach diverges by showing that it is not always easy for a state to agree on one national position. In order to define 'the' national position, be it French or Finnish, the government often has to compromise and negotiate with multiple interests at home before a final position fit for EU negotiations can be articulated.

The domestic politics approach investigates developments within a member state, inferring that competition among national interests can impact EU integration. It opens up the 'black box' of the state, attending to the interplay between various domestic actors as they attempt to shape national preferences. It treats a broad range of interests within each state while also recognising that they may conflict. The domestic politics approach does not, by definition, automatically exclude gender interests. Christine Ingebritsen's study of the Nordic relationship to European integration affords one example (Ingebritsen 1998): in her view, Nordic national positions toward EU integration express divergent domestic preferences that have been negotiated and compromised. Integration invokes the benefits and positions of majority interests in their respective domestic settings.

Member states must be able to deliver a single national position in EU negotiations. Insofar as some groups within the same state may benefit from integration while others may not, member state governments must either compromise or allow the most influential group to dominate. Ingebritsen's study does not consider the interests of women per se as relevant for explaining the Nordic approach to European integration. Yet the gender gap in attitudes towards integration continues to be significant in those countries, as verified both in the Swedish referendum on EU membership in 1994 and on the Euro in 2003. To include women's explicit interests, we would undertake analyses comparable to Heather MacRae's (2001) study on Denmark's rejection of the Maastricht Treaty. She stresses a significant gender gap in the referendum, suggesting that Danish women feared that further integration would interfere with their possibilities for reconciling work and family life. More women thus cast a 'No' vote.

Gender differences underlie what are perceived to be 'consensual' national interests. Women's needs are ignored or construed as special interests, which cannot serve as a relevant base for national positions. This would not surprise radical feminists; they see the state as a vehicle for upholding dominant interests in society. Catherine A. MacKinnon (1989: 162) contends that the liberal state 'constitutes the social order in the interest of men as a gender'. Interests that benefit men are embodied in the state. Anna van der Vleuten's very insightful analysis of Community equality policies from 1955 to 2005 begins with a domestic politics approach, zooming in on three member states: France, Germany and the Netherlands. She proves that the interconnected interests of men and the state came to the fore in negotiating EU gender equality policies:

> In general, women are inexpensive. They are not costly citizens. They provide an enormous quantity of unpaid work, more so than men. They provide paid work at lower rates than men. But as soon as they claim the right to be treated on equal footing with male citizens, they become 'costly' [...] States panic. Despite the lip service paid to equal rights, they revise treaty articles and circumvent the law to avoid having to pay women what they are entitled to. When women become costly, states become contrary. (van der Vleuten 2007: 179)

In contrast to the radical view articulated by MacKinnon, many Nordic feminists consider the state responsive to women's concerns to the extent that it includes female decision-makers and extensive welfare policies (Hernes 1987). Women's concerns may indeed influence the national interest. Since various state types imply different gender relations (Kantola 2006: 10), we must first examine the formation of state preferences in order to assess whether those expressed by women-friendly countries during intergovernmental negotiations diverge from those with less benevolent gender orientations. The EU accession of Finland, Sweden and Austria can prove this point: the admission of these states increased female presence in decision-making bodies and brought along an active gender agenda, in stark contrast to the admission of Spain, Greece and Portugal in the 1980s. Indeed, the Nordic countries introduced gender mainstreaming (Hafner-Burton and Pollack 2002: 295; Mazey 2002a: 229).

Applying a gender lens to state-centric theories and national interest formation as a driving force of integration reveals that these approaches define 'political space' and 'national interests' quite narrowly, excluding power imbalances rooted in gender, class and ethnicity. Gender theory could, first, inform LI by accounting for the double hierarchy connecting states with the authority of men and, secondly, strengthen the domestic politics approach by questioning what relevance gender needs may have for defining national interests.

2. Integration as a function of multiple issues and actors

Functionalist-inspired theories offer a further perspective on European integration, seen as the result of bottom-up processes rooted in trade relations that gained salience in reconstructing Europe after World War II. Expanding trade increased the rate of business interactions. To facilitate this, leaders needed to coordinate rules and regulations, as well as to form transnational alliances and organisations. Economic integration began with sporadic trade and communication, but as it evolved, it supplied incentives for further cooperation in related policy areas through what the father of functionalist theory Ernst B. Haas (1958) termed 'spill-over'. As commercial interactions grew and communication intensified, problems involving 'negative' spill-over, like pollution and social costs, were consequences of trade relations and trade policies. Transnational policies in other areas were deemed necessary. Product standardisation, environmental and equal pay policy came about because of spill-over effects and ensured fair competition and a smooth running of the common market. Although Haas himself abandoned the concept in 1975 (Haas 1975), it continues to inspire integration scholars, even if its meaning has been diversified (Niemann and Schmitter 2009).

In contrast to the approaches discussed earlier, *neo-functionalism* and *multi-level governance* theories argue that everyday interactions within various issue domains create the 'European Union' phenomenon. A multiplicity of actors pursue integration across numerous policy fields. Integration results from the more or less spontaneous development of societal functions, which become increasingly sophisticated over time. Functionalism's attraction today has an ostensible empirical base. Neo-functionalist ideas fit closely with current globalisation processes, since economic relations are accorded even higher priority than during the 1970s. Decisions taken within the European Economic Community (EEC) context affected member states, making integration more political as it engaged social actors and the public to an ever-greater extent (Börzel and Risse 2008). As a more recent theoretical development, multilevel governance enjoys widespread use among contemporary scholars (Piattoni 2010). Let us take their common features, that is, the functional needs of multiple actors in transnational interaction, as our starting point.

Neo-functionalism highlights the importance of transnational organisations that mirror and represent societal concerns. They become transnational as they develop interests that transcend political and administrative boundaries, which is especially important for gender politics. Feminists like Catherine Hoskyns (2000: 58) underscore this aspect of neo-functionalism, noting that 'patriarchal structures' firmly entrenched in the EU can only be 'undermined through concerted action by a wide range of women forming alliances with other social groups'. Supranational institutions have played a crucial role in this process.

The Commission's role as treaty guardian, policy initiator and chief administrator means that it values relationships with transnational organisations that provide valuable expertise while simultaneously representing citizen interests (Tanasescu 2009). The Commission encourages 'social partners' of all kinds, even providing financial support to those with a weaker resource base; it has actually stimulated group formation in key sectors, such as the European Women's Lobby (EWL). Due to their domestic base, organised transnational interests afford alternative channels for communicating with member state governments. The European Commission can be viewed as the organiser, interest groups as the catalyst of the integration process.

The EWL has been very strong in challenging gendered politics and policies. Studies exploring the European women's mobilisation (Hoskyns 1996; Strid 2010) support the feminist view that their movements have been the main agent of change. Other investigations (Mushaben 1998) show how such mobilisation has influenced EU's political agenda. Analyses of transnational women's movements and organisations supply valuable contributions to a feminist research agenda. The EWL secures resources and influence through its particular relationship with the Commission (although the same relationship can place the organisation at its mercy). The latter's consensus-seeking character means that activist organisations presenting controversial or more conflicting positions do not stand much of a chance of having their voices heard (Edquist 2006: 515).

This is a minor issue compared to the fact that transnational groups must compete fiercely for access to the EU political arena. Organisations representing feminist politics face an uphill battle against powerful lobbies dominating policy sectors with significant gender ramifications – a factor not addressed by the neo-functional approach. Business and industrial lobbyists, the most numerous, enjoy far greater resources than groups devoted to social issues (Coen and Richardson 2009). We could learn a lot by assessing how the influence of women's organisations compares to other transnational interests present in Brussels. Neo-functionalism pays little attention to power relations, and seems ill-equipped for such analysis. This unproblematic view of power is evident in Philippe C. Schmitter's neo-functionalist work (2004: 46), emphasising the bureaucratic and technocratic role of non-state actors. The question of who is represented at the expense of what interests is not raised. Martin O'Brien and Sue Penna (2007) argue that, because it is rooted in a 'rationalist' understanding of social progress, neo-functionalist theory deals with gender inequalities as if they were simple *dysfunctions* of relations and processes (rather than *daily* occurrences), easily adjustable and external to the political system. For gender research, neo-functionalism does not seem to do the job.

One way to expose imbalanced power relations would be to examine gender composition and representation within powerful transnational actors at the EU level. Taking the European Trade Union Federation as an example, Myriam Bergamaschi (2000: 159) argues that, although women comprise '40% of the total trade union membership, they are underrepresented in decision-making bodies', with no indication that the gender ratio is improving. Women thus remain outside the collective bargaining process at both the national and the EU levels (Bergamaschi 2000: 169–172). Furthermore, transnational organised interests benefit from the increasingly corporatist structure at the EU level (Bergqvist 2004). The relationship between labour, capital and EU organs becomes institutionalised through the *social dialogue* and the increasing use of soft law (see Waddington and Hoffman 2000), with negative ramifications for women's representation.

Christina Bergqvist (2004) moreover observes that female presence in the upper echelons of nationally based corporate and labour organisations increased with the decline of the corporatist model of policy-making: when Sweden moved away from the corporatist model and government assumed more of the policy-making, women's influence in labour unions increased, making them more representative as a result. When considering the same organisations at the EU level, the trend stops or is reversed. The surge in EU interest-group politics led to a backlash against Swedish women among the leaders of other interest groups. Van der Vleuten (2007) also attests that trade union involvement has done little to put gender issues on the EU agenda. The gender composition of key social partners made them adverse to the equal pay principle. Unions were keen to represent male wage earners rather than part-time underpaid female workers. Women's small share of seats in such decision-making bodies reflects a 'male-oriented bargaining agenda' (van der Vleuten 2007: 154). Thus the gender gap among interest groups involved in EU policy-making is significant.

Many students of public administration, policy processes, organisational behaviour and governance recognise familiar features in the EU integration process and see the latter as a research domain to which they can contribute. The multilevel governance approach encompasses a wide array of insights at various levels of theorising. Beate Kohler-Koch (1999) views the EU as the outcome of numerous 'parallel' processes: of states pooling their sovereignty, influential integration discourses over time, spill-over effects and path dependency in policy-making. A new *governance theory* has also emerged out of the growing power of the market and the private sector, at the expense of state actors and the public sector. Markus Jachtenfuchs and Beate Kohler-Koch (2004) propose a multilevel governance approach with fairly clear levels of authority. Michael Zürn (2000: 185) perceives the levels as blurry, however, stressing two factors that render the EU a multilevel system of fragmented authority. First, regulations are so intertwined that they can hardly be separated out. Second, EU institutions remain autonomous from national bodies. Jürgen Neyer (2003: 689) employs the term *heterarchy*, claiming that political authority is 'neither centralized nor decentralized but shared'. Edgar Grande (1996: 325–326) argues that European policy-making can be understood as a system of multilevel bargaining; it is not a top-down process but more like the weaving of strands of issues and trends across traditional borders, administrative levels and societal actors (Piattoni 2010). Despite differences among these approaches, they share the idea that domestic politics are increasingly becoming intertwined with EU policies at all levels of governance (Bache and Flinders 2004; Hooghe and Marks 2001; Walzenbach 2006).

Contributing significantly to multilevel governance theory, van der Vleuten (2007) shows that the multilevel governance system made states accept, and later implement, gender equality directives. Member states were 'sandwiched' between domestic and supranational levels, facing combined political and judicial pressure from many levels and actors simultaneously. This created a 'pincer effect', leading to successful gender governance when pressure to reform came from both supranational and domestic sources; it was particularly relevant for implementing negotiated agreements on gender equality. Supranational pressures derived from the political prestige associated with intergovernmental negotiations as well as from Court of Justice rulings.

Domestic pressures originate in the political and party systems, in national courts and in civil society. Feminist and women's groups were shown to be most effective as actors in transnational networks, that is, as female trade union delegates and femocrats (feminist bureaucrats) who worked in tandem with women's lobbying groups. Implementation was enhanced by the pincer effect, pushing equality norms from rhetoric to practice. Women's agencies, together with civil society organisations, must create domestic pressures and sandwich the state. Confirming the crucial role of feminist movements in advancing equality, van der Vleuten enhances our understanding of multilevel governance and its impact across issue areas.

Although multilevel governance stresses the fragmented nature of authority, Mariagrazia Rossilli (2000) suggests that such interpretations still conceal hierarchies among institutional levels and actors rather than expose points of power intensity. To argue that power is fragmented – that is, distributed across levels of authority and among groups – does not rule out the fact that power is very unevenly distributed. Consider one characteristic feature of multilevel governance, namely that negotiations often take place in networks. In these networks the focus lies with relations among different actors across governance boundaries. Negotiations and policy-making typically require building trust and commonality among smaller, directly concerned sets of actors clustered around a specific issue area. One network benefit is the ability to circumscribe formal policy hierarchies, thus avoiding time-consuming bureaucratic processes. This can benefit women's issues and gender politics. Charlotte Bretherton and Liz Sperling (1996) highlight the impact of women's EU networks, and Alison Woodward (in this volume) talks about the role of 'velvet triangles' in pushing gender politics forward.

While informal interaction outside administrative boundaries makes for more efficient politics as the degree of complexity rises, we need to recognise that network formation and informal relationships render the process less transparent. Many expert-dependent policies, like environmental politics, are finalised at an early stage of policy-making, in the myriad committees within the Commission and the Council. Committees become influential policy-makers (van Schendelen 1998) in response to the regulatory needs of the 'non-unitary and non-hierarchical' EU (Joerges 2006: 779). Although networks involve individuals employed by governments and EU institutions, they are difficult to monitor and may include actors who are not democratically accountable (Bogason and Musso 2006).

Ole Elgström and Christer Jönsson (2005) argue that networks associated with informality create trust and feelings of solidarity and foster a consensus culture – esteemed features in the workings of the EU. Informal ministerial meetings, for example, deliberately aim to create a congenial atmosphere, where ministers can get acquainted. Networks afford a kind of elite collective for decision-making, implying that certain societal groups will be excluded from participation. Insofar as women experience difficulties in entering male-dominated elite circles, networks need to be assessed in terms of gender representation. Personal factors are crucial in networking, since trust and loyalty are established through familiarity. National network-building is often based on the long-term cultivation of personal relationships, fostered through professional life, education and military service, or through private associations. People tend to form ties with individuals of similar social background; thus networks are subject to pre-existing divisions based on gender, class and ethnicity (Kronsell 2009).

The historic exclusion of women from private associations, so crucial for the public scene, holds important ramifications for their inclusion in contemporary policy-making processes. The concept of *homosociality* – seeking, enjoying and/or preferring the company of the same sex (Lipman-Blumen 1976) – helps to explain this: while men might not consciously or overtly exclude women, they favour connections with other men – at work, in their research and during their leisure time. They reproduce the homosocial environment of networks in which they take part, making it hard for women to enter the scene (Alvesson and Due Billing 1997; Flood 2008). Commissioner Margot Wallström critiqued the ways in which policy-making really operates in gendered institutions and indicated the relevance of homosociality in labelling the EU 'a reign of old men'. She argued that the EU gender order is self-selecting, reproducing the existing order: 'old men choose old men, as always' (*EU Observer*, 8 February 2008).

In sum, multilevel governance approaches make it possible to generate useful studies by tracing gender effects and perspectives through the analysis of policy processes in specific sectors. However, in order to generate comprehensive feminist and gender analysis, the neo-functionalist and multilevel governance approaches must be accompanied by critical analysis sensitive to gender power dynamics.

3. Norms, institutions and EU integration

We now turn to *new institutionalism* and *constructivism*, their common feature being the centrality of institutions and established norms in the integration process. Institutionalism's central claim is that institutions matter, that rules and organisational features influence actors and have political consequences (Rosamond 2000: 113–114). Under *rational institutionalism* actors are assumed to moderate their strategies and their behaviour while taking account of institutional features (Stacey 2010). *Historical institutionalism* sees organisational structures as intervening variables but pays special attention to their effects over time: institutions lock certain EU rules and decisions in place, establishing path dependencies (Pollack 2004) while producing outcomes that are difficult for actors to foresee. Institutionalism focuses on the EU as a new political arena, establishing rules and procedures where none existed before (Olsen 2010; Stone Sweet et al. 2001: 18). The constructivist perspective deems institutions and norms important but does not perceive them simply as intervening variables. Instead, institutions are seen as integral to the construction of identities, interests and meanings in political life (Rosamond 2000: 171–172). Constructivism attributes a different logic to actors' behaviour; norms not only regulate behaviour but also create meaning and define actors (Risse 2009).

Procedures used in core EU institutions – the Commission, Parliament, the Council of Ministers and the Court of Justice (ECJ) – are key elements in rational institutionalism. National preferences, strategies and behaviour may change as a result of these institutions, while analyses of the ECJ credit it with the greatest contribution to gender advances. Institutionalism has clear affinities with legal approaches (Haltern 2004) and feminist legal approaches (Shaw 2000) to integration.

Institutionalist theories construe European organs as a response to interactions among governmental actors who have negotiated, bargained, reached compromises and established common norms, in order to tackle problems linked to intensified transaction patterns affecting trade. Obstacles posed by diverging national regulations evoke an agreement – a supranational norm – that initially takes the form of an intergovernmental solution. As Alec Stone Sweet and Wayne Sandholtz (1997: 310) argue, 'once movement toward the supranational pole begins, European rules generate a dynamic of their own'. Supranational rules evolve over time as new obstacles arise, perhaps as a result of previous rules, because their content is disputed or because circumstances change. Modified prescriptions subsequently guide future interactions, as people alter their behaviour in accordance with the new rules. Institutionalisation means that 'policy outcomes become "locked in" channelling politics down specific paths and closing previously plausible alternatives' (Stone Sweet and Sandholtz 1997: 313). Once EU agreements are in place, they become part of a dynamic largely independent of the actions of individual member states. Interesting for historic institutionalists is not simply the fact that institutions are 'sticky' or 'path-dependent', but rather that the conditions under which this occurs are as well (Ellina 2003; Pierson 1996).

One finds lots of evidence surrounding gender issues. The EU has been decisive in introducing gender equality norms in many countries, particularly where women's participation in the political and economic spheres has been lower than registered in other member states. In Ireland, more citizenship rights have come to women as a result of EU cooperation than from national institutions (Gardiner 1999). Even in Denmark, EU equal pay requirements offered an effective channel for challenging national policies (Martinsen 2007: 547). The supranational norm of *equal pay for equal work* has been a major driving force in changing member state laws and challenging national gender regimes (Liebert 2003c: 480).

The impact of EU equality norms has been striking in Germany, having resulted in several clashes between domestic and European institutions. The national gender regime was based on principles of difference rather than equality (MacRae 2006). The role of the ECJ is pivotal (see Locher and van der Vleuten in this volume): norms agreed upon at this level take 'direct effect' in the member states, becoming an integral part of the legal norm system that national judges are required to apply. The equal pay norm (Article 119, Treaty of Rome, 1957) has, through the ECJ, developed and extended

EU competence regarding gender equality (Frith 2008) well beyond what its founders imagined – just as institutionalists would argue.

Rachel Cichowski (2004: 508) demonstrates the ECJ's extraordinary impact in enforcing women's rights as well as in empowering 'social groups to bring claims against their own governments and dismantle discriminatory national practices'. Despite institutional dynamics operating in the equal rights field, one can also argue that the vision emerging from the equality principle is limiting, insofar as gender relations are now being equated with employment in the neoliberal market (Walby 2004: 5–7). Jo Shaw (2002: 220) likewise points to the constraints on ECJ rulings on women's care-work, where she notes 'the disturbing tendency to invoke outdated maternalist conceptions of women's role in the family' (Guerrina 2005).

Gender mainstreaming, embraced in 1996, entails a normative paradigm shift; it differs from the equality principle in that it is both a policy strategy and a soft law instrument. Born out of the women's movement, gender mainstreaming holds radical potential, which lies in widening the policy frame and assessing broader institutional sources of inequality (see Woodward in this volume). Incorporating gender perspectives into all policy areas, stages and levels, gender mainstreaming's strategic potential changes the way societal relations are viewed and challenges the EU's distribution of power (Stratigaki 2005: 178, 181). As a soft law instrument, however, it is not subject to ECJ review. The absence of gender and mainstreaming from the EU's 2000 White Paper on Governance reminds us of the insecure place these topics occupy among EU priorities (Shaw 2002: 225).

The focus on legal norms is both a main strength and a main weakness of the institutional approach, to the extent that research concentrates on legal norms, formalised in directives. The institutions in which those norms are embedded, as well as the political and administrative processes preceding norm adoption, are reduced to intervening variables. Gendered practices at the EU and member state levels can be traced back to well-established norms which have evolved over several decades. The historical institutional approach is inadequate, because it, too, focuses on formal aspects. The deeper problem of gender relations has to do with the dominance of the male-as-norm (woman-as-deviant) in most policy fields. For feminists, EU organs remain institutions of hegemonic masculinity, traditionally governed by men and built on norms rooted in masculinity and heterosexuality (Kronsell 2005a).

These norms are not formalised; on the contrary, their influence depends on remaining informal and invisible. The male-as-norm is essential for feminist critiques, defining the power asymmetries of social relations. Men almost exclusively hold privileged positions; the 'male' norm prevails, allowing it to shape institutional agendas and policies. For male norms to become hegemonic, cultural norms and institutional power must mutually support a particular masculinity. The EU's liberal institutional order evinces a certain hegemonic masculinity (Connell 1998).

Let us now turn to constructivism, to see what it offers from a feminist perspective. Constructivism posits EU integration as a continuous process of change, never resulting in anything fixed; the EU has a transformative impact on the state system and its constituent units – and vice versa. Agents' identities, interests and behaviour remain fluid and open to change (Christiansen et al. 1999: 529). Jeffrey Lewis (2000: 266) raises the possibility that the Council of the EU's own normative environment can construct interests and identities. Constructivism addresses institutions and norms, albeit not merely as intervening variables. Rather, institutions are 'thick' or embedded, especially at 'the nexus where structures and agency intersect' (Checkel 1999: 557); they are the 'middle ground' between micro and macro EU politics (Christiansen 1997). Individual actors reproduce institutional norms but also serve as major change agents, given institutions' simultaneously constraining and enabling effects.

Institutional practices and identity formation processes 'construct' the EU because actors engaging in organisational activities search for meaning in what they do daily. They often appeal to institutional norms in this search; by adopting and reaffirming organisational practices, they make the EU part of their professional identity (Aspinwall and Schneider 2000: 4, 9). The institution is part of a 'historically derived system of shared meanings which define agency and make action intelligible', as Stefano Guzzini (2000: 165) puts it. A reaffirmation of institutional norms takes place in every communicative act: when organisational actors speak to each other or represent the organisation vis-à-vis other associations, articulating the norms and values of the institutional setting of which they are a part, they reproduce that institution. Consider, for instance, the prevalent use of EU specific language. *Eurospeak* includes juridical terminology and obscure abbreviations; it works to connect those inside the institutions – they can recognise each other by speaking the same language; it simultaneously tends to exclude and set apart those who are outside it. Such discourses give meaning and direction to the integration process (Christiansen et al. 1999: 541) – and so do symbols, hymns and flags (Theiler 2005).

Norms also develop around non-verbal practices, such as problem-solving and work routines. Like other institutions, the EU is path-dependent: once certain choices have been made, they constrain future possibilities. Constructivism suggests that setting norms go beyond agreed-upon formal norms. Informal norms likewise make integration possible, which in turn gives meaning and identity to EU institutions and citizens (Checkel and Katzenstein 2009). Constructivism has much to say about EU gender politics insofar as feminist analysis relates directly to the social construction of sex differences. Indeed, constructivist approaches have much in common with feminist agendas because, as Birgit Locher and Elisabeth Prugl (2001: 114) argue, they share an 'ontology of becoming' – seeing the world not as having a particular form, but as an ever-changing entity.

These affinities notwithstanding, constructivism often downplays power or considers it external. Yet power is both enabling and constraining; institutions not only delimit our world but also systematically distribute privilege, thereby creating patterns of subordination – a core concern for feminist theorists (Locher 2007). Constructivism could be enhanced by adding a feminist discussion of power and highlighting the ways in which power remains integral to integration processes. The European constructivist perspective, influenced by critical feminist research, realises that organisations are deeply embedded in their environment. Embedding implies that the norms, values and procedures inherent in an institution form part of a larger spectrum of power relations, prevailing in the time and space in which it is situated. Social orders, like gender orders, have distributive effects, privilege certain groups over others, and are all connected to the practice of power, working both discursively and institutionally. Discursive power inheres in communication, symbols and texts; institutional dimensions are expressed through procedures and behaviour.

Sylvia Walby's (2004) concept of a *gender regime* (or *order*) is employed by many feminist researchers addressing EU gender relations (Liebert 2003c; MacRae 2006; von Wahl 2005). Elisabeth Prügl's research (2004; see her contribution in this volume) on the Common Agricultural Policy (CAP) reveals how the discursive dimension of a patriarchal order, in the name of the 'family farm', informed and underpinned German debates over the CAP from the start. *Gender order* is a useful concept because it embraces gender as a constructed order, exhibited in institutions and practices that come to the fore in diverse policy domains. A specific gender order offers a particular framing of gender relations as they are understood more generally, for example as either 'equal' or 'different' in certain domains. Further examples include the male breadwinner/female caretaker model of the economic domain, or the male soldier/female caretaker model prevailing in the security and defence domain.

A gender order finds expression in legislation, regulations, taxation, labour or conscription laws, as well as in subsidies and social policy. Empirical studies demonstrate that gender orders vary over time and across states and regions. When gender orders differ too much (as between Sweden and Greece), they can clash; this leads to problems for EU integration, bringing a lack of compliance and implementation. Gender orders can also converge. Angelika von Wahl (2005: 68) points to the slow formation of an EU equal employment order. Gender order research could better inform constructivist research on European integration; its findings could be used to conceptualise 'orders' in other areas (for example transportation regimes, environmental or security regimes), to explain how transport, ecological and security issues are framed, institutionalised and normalised at different levels and across EU domains. Gender regime theory could thus deepen our understanding of non-compliance, misfits and implementation deficits regarding Europeanisation.

4. Conclusions

Inherent in all EU theories reviewed here is the assumption that the *integration process* shapes politics and institutions, while influencing political actors and citizens throughout Europe. As we have seen, this process simultaneously affirms, shapes and challenges existing gender relations. However, integration theories up to now have displayed minimal interest in gender power dynamics. This chapter illustrated the (untested) potential of diverse integration theories for taking on the challenge of gender and suggests ways in which each might address gender issues through their own specific lenses. For gender to be taken seriously in integration studies, we need to engage directly with existing theories. Empirical studies concentrating on gender relations per se contribute to a deeper understanding of integration, as van der Vleuten's work on multilevel governance testifies.

Feminist scholarship on gender offers fertile ground for conceptualising other 'orders' emerging by way of integration. Conducting such research effectively, however, requires a mainstreaming of feminist critical perspectives. Otherwise EU gender studies will be restricted to equality norms, women in the labour market and, possibly, the effects of gender mainstreaming. These remain crucial research arenas, but they leave the institutionalised male-as-norm unquestioned, reproducing existing EU gender relations rather than deconstructing them. The strength of feminist analysis lies in its understanding of how power hierarchies rooted in gender are operationalised in political practices and thus 'permanently' embedded in institutions. Such critical approaches to power can contribute significantly to EU integration studies in the future.

Discussion questions
- Now that the EU consists of 27 members, and given the Lisbon Treaty which integration approach do you think offers most 'explanatory value'?
- Do you think it is useful to introduce a gender dimension to existing integration theories? Why or why not?
- Which components would you consider central to a feminist integration theory?

3
Gendering the Institutions and Actors of the EU

Anna van der Vleuten

In order to appreciate the gender outcomes of European policymaking, one needs to know how 'Europe' functions. As a multilevel political system, the European Union (EU) offers different opportunities and constraints for the promotion of gender justice than those afforded by national political systems. Unfortunately, European policymaking is often perceived as complex and obscure. In addition, the EU has witnessed several major changes in the relations among its key institutions over the last five decades. What has remained constant up to now is women's obvious underrepresentation in all EU institutions, albeit to varying degrees and with interesting patterns (Kantola 2010a: 50–75). In order to shed light on this complex and evolving polity, this chapter reviews the main actors at the supranational level, concentrating on five core institutions: the European Commission, the European Parliament (EP), the Council of the EU (in short: Council), the European Council, and the European Court of Justice (ECJ).[1]

We examine their composition, the nature and scope of female representation, their primary functions and the attention that each, in turn, gives to gender issues. We then analyse the role and impact of organised interests, including the Economic and Social Committee and the Committee of the Regions, in relation to EU gender policies, followed by an attempt to answer the question: Under what conditions can women in decision-making really make a difference? I argue that equality advocates have proved very adept at playing a multilevel game: by mobilising nationally and forging coalitions with transnational and supranational actors, women's movements have pressured their home governments from two directions, eventually allowing them to win more rights than the EU founders ever anticipated.

The EU operates as a multilevel system, analogous to David Easton's classical model of the political system, consisting of inputs, through-puts, outputs and feedback. Both the European Council and national or transnational actors (interest groups, experts, and lower level authorities) supply *inputs* in the form of demands and knowledge (see Figure 3.1). At the supranational level, inputs are converted into policies via a negotiation process involving

42 *Gendering the Institutions and Actors*

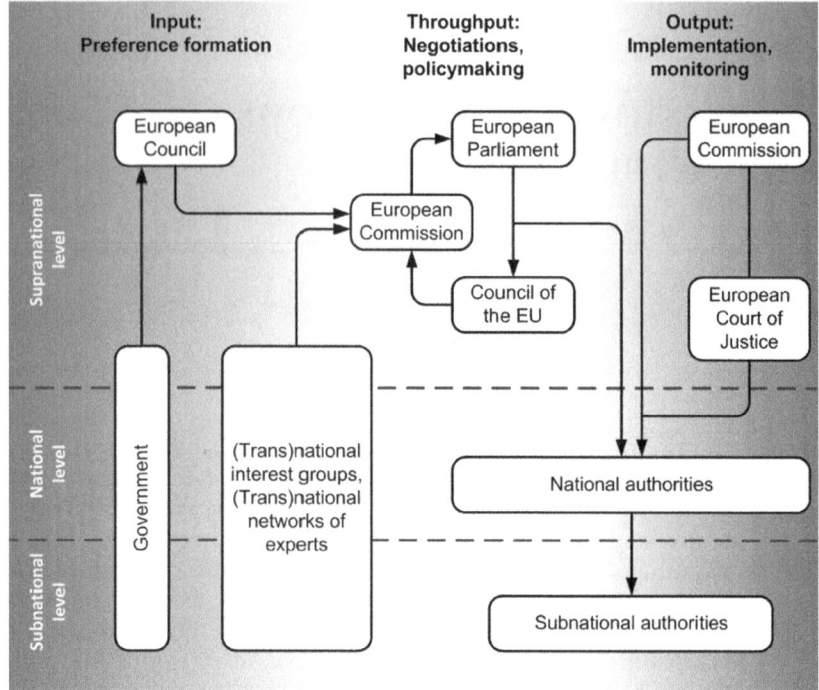

Figure 3.1   The EU as a multilevel system
Source: Charted by the author.

the Commission, the EP and the Council. The *output* feeds back into the national level, where European decisions must be 'transposed' into rules and policies by national and subnational authorities. The Commission and the ECJ monitor this implementation process.

1. The Commission

The term 'Commission' actually refers to the President and the College of Commissioners, who serve five-year terms. The President plays a role comparable to that of a prime minister. Ensuring institutional coherence, he or she is responsible for introducing major policy initiatives. The European Council (composed of the leaders of the national governments) nominates a candidate by qualified majority; the choice of the candidate has to reflect the outcome of the elections of the EP. The nominee is then elected by the EP. All Presidents to date have evinced the same profile: middle-aged men who formerly occupied high-level positions in their countries of origin. Following a Christian–Democratic victory in the June 2009 elections,

Christian–Democrat José Manuel Barroso was confirmed for a second presidential term. The President forms the College of Commissioners based on nominations submitted by the member states. After conducting a formal hearing with each potential Commissioner, the EP must approve their collective appointment by a majority vote (see section on EP).

The Commission includes one delegate per member state, totalling 27 Commissioners as of the 2007 accession of Bulgaria and Rumania. Hoping to enhance its institutional efficiency and effectiveness by curbing the expanding number of Commissioners, the Lisbon Treaty originally foresaw the introduction of a rotating system as of 2014. However, this provision was eliminated in 2009, in an effort to persuade the Irish to vote 'Yes' in their second referendum on the Lisbon Treaty.

Each Commissioner is responsible for a specific policy domain. States actively compete to secure one of the heavy 'portfolios', such as Competition, Internal Market, Agriculture, Trade and Justice. Jockeying for these positions is mainly a matter of prestige, since Commissioners are not spokespersons for their home countries: indeed, they are forbidden to take instructions from any government. The Commission ceased to be an exclusively male body in 1989; at present, nine out of 27 Commissioners (33 per cent) are female (see Table 3.1). Its composition depends on the candidates proposed by the member states, yet if each were to nominate a female and male candidate, the President could easily convene a gender-balanced College. However, there is no such rule in the European treaties.

Gender issues used to fall under the portfolio of the Commissioner for Employment and Social Affairs. A few of the 11 former Social Affairs Commissioners, like Patrick Hillery and Anna Diamantopoulou, have been strong policy entrepreneurs, fighting hard for women's interests. Others have pursued different priorities. In the 2010–2014 Commission, primary responsibility for 'gender equality in all fields of EU policy' lies with Viviane Reding, Commissioner for the new portfolio of Justice, Fundamental Rights and Citizenship, while responsibility for 'gender equality in the workplace' remains with Social Affairs Commissioner László Andor.

Beneath the College lies the Commission's own bureaucracy. It consists of 25 Directorates-General (DG) and 13 specialised services, including the Legal Service and the statistical service Eurostat. A DG is equivalent to a ministry; covering a specific policy domain, it prepares dossiers for the Commissioner in charge. Officials in DG Employment, Social Affairs and Equal Opportunities (DG EMPL) are primarily responsible for gender equality policies. They also chair the Inter-Service Group on Gender Equality, bringing together officials responsible for this quest in all other Directorates-General. The Group's main task is to develop a gender mainstreaming approach for all policies and programmes, as many services still lack specific expertise. Established in 2007 and based in Vilnius (Lituania), the European Institute for Gender Equality will further generate knowledge and provide technical assistance to the

Table 3.1 Composition of the European Commission and Social Affairs Commissioners

Term	President of the Commission, nationality between brackets	Number and percentage of male Commissioners, incl. President N	%	Number and percentage of female Commissioners N	%	Commissioner of Social Affairs, in charge of gender equality
1958–1961	Walter Hallstein (DE)	9	100	0	0	Giuseppe Petrilli (IT)
1962–1967	Walter Hallstein (DE)	9	100	0	0	Lionello Levi-Sandri (IT)
1967–1970	Jean Rey (BE)	12	100	0	0	Lionello Levi-Sandri (IT)
1970–1972	Franco Malfatti (IT)	9	100	0	0	Albert Coppé (BE)
1972	Sicco Mansholt (NL)	9	100	0	0	Albert Coppé (BE)
1973–1976	François-Xavier Ortoli (FR)	13	100	0	0	Patrick Hillery (IE)
1977–1980	Roy Jenkins (UK)	13	100	0	0	Henk Vredeling (NL)
1981–1984	Gaston Thorn (LUX)	14	100	0	0	Ivor Richard (UK)
1985–1988	Jacques Delors (FR)	17	100	0	0	Manuel Marin (ES)
1989–1992	Jacques Delors (FR)	15	88	2	12	Vasso Papandreou (EL)
1993–1994	Jacques Delors (FR)	16	94	1	6	Padraig Flynn (IE)
1995–1999	Jacques Santer (LUX)	15	75	5	25	Padraig Flynn (IE)
1999–2004	Romano Prodi (IT)	15	75	5	25	Anna Diamantopoulou (EL)
2005–2009	José Manuel Barroso (PT)	18	66	9	33	Vladimír Špidla (CZ)
2010–2014	José Manuel Barroso (PT)	18	66	9	33	Viviane Reding (LUX) László Andor (HU)

Source: Data compiled by the author.

Commission and member state authorities. As of 1996, gender mainstreaming strategies have raised awareness regarding the underrepresentation of women in middle and senior management posts. Annual targets exist for their recruitment and appointment, but in typically male policy strongholds such as External Relations change takes time. A Network of Focal Points on Equal Opportunities monitors equality in relation to Commission human resource policies.

The Commission is a supranational body, which 'shall promote the general interest of the Union' (Article 17 TEU) through its exercise of policymaking, management and control functions. Policymaking is the Commission's main task. It thus plays a crucial role in the development of European legislation by way of its monopoly on policy initiation: every EU legislative act is based on a proposal written and approved by the Commission.[2] Given its formal right of initiative, the Commission is often portrayed as the motor of European integration; but it likewise depends on the cooperation of the Council and the EP to move the process forward. During its weekly Wednesday meetings, the Commission discusses draft proposals prepared by individual Commissioners and their respective DGs. If the Commission reaches a consensus, the proposal is forwarded to the Council and the EP. In case of disagreement, it is sent back to the DG in charge. In May 2006, for instance, Commissioner of Justice Franco Frattini submitted a list of safe countries of origin to which EU member states would return asylum seekers and refugees. Commissioners Margot Wallstrom and Neelie Kroes opposed having Mali and Botswana designated as 'safe' by the EU: Mali tolerates the practice of female genital mutilation, while Botswana treats homosexuality as illegal, and also applies the death penalty. Frattini had to withdraw the list.

Given its limited knowledge-generating capacity, the Commission makes extensive use of external consultation during the preparatory process. It has established 300–400 expert committees, such as the Expert Group on Trafficking in Human Beings, comprised of specialists from the member states. Also, it has established 150 permanent advisory committees consisting of representatives for all stakeholders. The Advisory Committee on Women and Rural Areas, for instance, includes persons representing farmers, trade and consumer groups, the European Women's Lobby and trade unions. External consultation helps the Commission to develop strong proposals but also renders it dependent upon the knowledge and interests of others. It organises internet consultations, in an effort to broaden the range of stakeholders able to offer opinions on new policy ideas. The White Paper on European Communication Policy (01/02/2006), for instance, received 313 responses from different organisations. One respondent urged the Commission to adopt a gender and diversity approach to communication policy.

Moreover, the Commission manages expenditures under the Structural Funds and administers programmes in research, education, health and youth actions. Within the budgetary framework of 'Gender Equality' of the

Community Programme for Employment and Social Solidarity (PROGRESS), it offers financial support to expert networks and to projects securing the implementation of gender equality, for example, through training Greek public administration workers.

Finally, the Commission acts as the guardian of the treaties and of European law. Together with the Court of Justice, it monitors the application of EU rules. The European Network of Legal Experts in the field of Gender gathers information on the implementation of gender equality legislation. If violations come to light, the Commission may initiate infringement proceedings. First, it sends the state a formal notice indicating a possible breach of legal obligations. The member state usually replies by explaining why the rule has not (yet) been applied. If not satisfied, the Commission sends a 'reasoned opinion', summoning the member state to remedy the situation. If nothing happens, the Commission refers the case to the Court, initiating the second stage (see below). This mechanism has proven effective in many instances where national governments dragged their feet. The Dutch Equal Pay Act (1975), for instance, did not cover civil servants. After five years of pressure from the Commission, a reasoned opinion convinced the Dutch government of the necessity to amend the law (van der Vleuten 2007). The Commission also publishes scoreboards, showing the stages of transposing European regulation into national law. Governments are keen to avoid being 'named and shamed' and thus push for good rankings on these scoreboards.

Assessing the Commission from a gender perspective, we can observe that the Commission leans quite favourably towards initiatives in the field of gender equality. This derives from its strategic interest in extending its mandate as supranational policymaker, dating back to the early institutionalisation of gender equality within DG EMPL in the 1970s. The Unit Equality between Women and Men (DG EMPL G/1) plays a key role in monitoring implementation of gender equality directives and in organising and financing transnational networks – such as the Network of Experts on Employment and Gender Equality Issues and the Network of Experts in Gender Equality, Social Inclusion, Health and Long-Term Care – to warrant political support and obtain input from experts and societal groups. As chief policy initiator, the Commission is guided by ambitious hopes of advancing European integration. This is difficult in domains extensively regulated at the national level, such as social security, but easier in relatively new domains, like sex discrimination. A Commissioner needs innovative ways to convince reluctant governments 'to upgrade the common interest' and move beyond often meagre compromises reflecting minimum standards. Experts and representatives from 'pioneer states' play an active role in legitimising new constructs – like indirect discrimination, sexual harassment and gender mainstreaming. DG EMPL frames and reframes its proposals over time, to increase the chances of their adoption. Part-time work, for example, was deemed undesirable 'atypical work' in the draft directive of 1981.

It was re-introduced in 1991, as a tool for reconciling women's (paid) work and (unpaid) care. Finally, in 1995, packaged as an instrument for fighting unemployment of men and women, the directive combating discrimination of part-time workers was adopted (van der Vleuten 2007).

The Commission is limited in three ways in its promotion of gender justice. First, insofar as all of its actions require a foundation in the existing treaties, it cannot address each and every topic it deems relevant. As such, it cannot propose legislation to enable same-sex marriage or to fight sex-based violence as long as the treaty does not provide a related reference. In the latter case, the Commission has partially circumvented this obstacle by proposing a programme, named DAPHNE, on preventive measures to combat gender-based violence and to promote financial support for victims – a programme based on the treaty article concerning public health. Second, the need to secure Council approval often forces the Commission to water down its proposals, limiting the effectiveness or even undermining the goals of its action. Third, gender mainstreaming is often poorly implemented outside of DG EMPL. During accession negotiations with the Central and Eastern European countries, gender mainstreaming was not applied (Bretherton 2001). The current round of negotiations concerning new economic agreements with a host of African and Caribbean countries have thus far been conducted in a gender-blind manner, ignoring the gendered consequences of trade liberalisation. Since the 1980s the Commission has often found ways around these limitations by turning to its ever stronger ally, the EP.

2. The European Parliament

Until 1979 the EP functioned as a part-time assembly of nationally appointed parliamentarians. Ever since that date, direct elections have been held every five years in all member states, being scheduled every five years. Since the enactment of the Lisbon Treaty, the EP has consisted of 751 members. Seats are allocated in proportion to the number of inhabitants per member state; the smallest member states hold six seats and Germany, the biggest one, occupies 96. The members of the EP (MEPs) do not represent their countries but rather their political parties. The latter cooperate in overarching European party groups, consisting of national political parties with similar ideologies. As a result of the 2009 EP election there are currently seven party groups represented; the largest are the Christian–Democrat European People's Party (EPP) and the Progressive Alliance of Socialists and Democrats (S&D). Historically, most parliamentarians have been pro-integrationist, but politicians very critical of the European project have also been elected since the 1980s, thus intensifying debates within the EP itself. The issue of women's 'empowerment' has been raised in many EP resolutions and during every election campaign. After the first direct elections in 1979, the number of women in Parliament doubled from 8 to 16 per cent, further increasing over the years to 35 per cent. Women are thus represented in substantially higher numbers in the EP than in many member state parliaments.

The EP elects its own President for a (renewable) term of two and a half years. In 2009, Jerzy Buzek was elected as the first President from an Eastern European country. The Parliament meets in Strasbourg (France) every month for plenary session, during which votes are taken. All preparatory work is undertaken in parliamentary committees and party groups that meet in Brussels. This arrangement, much criticised by the European electorate and MEPs as a waste of money (costing an estimated €180 million per year), can be changed only way of unanimous agreement among all national governments. This accord is unlikely to materialise due to staunch French opposition.

Every parliamentarian belongs to one or more parliamentary committees. There are 20 committees, each with a specific policy domain. ENVI (environment, public health and food security) and BUDG (budget) are the most influential, given the EP's strong powers in these domains. The Committee on Women's Rights and Gender Equality (FEMM) prepares amendments on all proposals involving women's rights, non-discrimination and gender equality. It also organises hearings and tribunals, for example, on women and war, Muslim women and sexual and reproductive health and rights, to obtain input from NGOs and experts.

The EP has legislative, budgetary and supervisory tasks. The powers of the EP have been expanded with each treaty amendment cycle since the mid-1980s. The EP is, first and foremost, a law-making body. Each Commission proposal is assigned a *rapporteur*, a parliamentarian who prepares discussions and draws up amendments. The proposal is debated in the appropriate committee(s). Once the committee approves it, an amended proposal moves on to the plenary session for debate and approval by the full EP. It then moves on to the Council, which reaches a common position on the proposal and the amendments. Depending on the degree of agreement between the EP and the Council, this cycle of drafting by the Commission, debate in the EP, and deliberation by the Council may be repeated (second reading). If no agreement is reached, a conciliation committee enlisting EP and Council representatives is formed. The draft become law only if a majority in both institutions approves it. This procedure used to be called 'the co-decision procedure'. Since the 'Lisbon' ratification , it has become the 'ordinary procedure' and it now applies to almost all policy domains.[3]

Second, the EP possesses budgetary power. The EU revenue base consists of import levies imposed on agricultural products from third countries, import duties on industrial products, a percentage of the value added taxes (VAT) collected in member states, and the latter's contributions, which are based on the gross national income. The Commission draws up an annual draft budget for approval by the Council and the EP. The EP uses its powers to ensure and increase funding for programmes involving diversity and gender equality, among others. The EP also controls the management of the budget by the Commission. In this task it is assisted by the Court of Auditors.

Third, the EP supervises the Commission through the formal election of its President and through its confirmation of the College of Commissioners. Introduced as an act of symbolic politics, the Parliament now organises formal hearings with all candidate-Commissioners to test their knowledge and orientations regarding their prospective portfolios. The EP does not have the power to refuse individual candidates but may threaten to reject the whole Commission if certain candidates are not replaced. In August 2004, for instance, the EP successfully opposed the choice of Rocco Buttiglione (Italy) for the Justice portfolio, because his arch-conservative views on homosexuality and women did not fit with that unit's responsibility for anti-discrimination policies. The Commission is held politically accountable to the EP through the use of written and oral questions, answered during plenary sessions. Prior to the 2009 appointments, MEPs asked the Commissioners what actions they intended to undertake to ensure the mutual recognition by the member states of same-sex marriages (19 May 2009), and whether they would promote projects in Afghanistan to increase the participation of women in public life (15 April 2009). Should malfeasance or dereliction of duty come to light involving individual Commissioners, the EP can ultimately vote to censure the Commission as a whole. If the motion carries, the Commission must resign. In March 1999, accusations of fraud and nepotism on the part of Commissioner Edith Cresson led the EP to threaten a motion of censure, compelling the entire body to resign.

From its early days, the EP has been a strong supporter of gender justice. It has adopted many resolutions asking for new Commission initiatives. It has consistently voted in favour of amendments aimed at strengthening European legislation on gender equality. The high number of women MEPs has contributed to keeping women's issues on the agenda. Between 2004 and 2009, the members of the FEMM committee acted as individual *rapporteurs* on 43 occasions, voicing a gender perspective on topics ranging from the situation of handicapped women in Europe, juvenile delinquency, marketing and advertising, to the position of women in Turkey. Women MEPs have compelled Commissioners to take gender equality seriously, have prevented the European Women's Lobby from losing its financial support and have saved the FEMM Committee itself from being disbanded. The FEMM Committee is an important addressee for groups lobbying to defend the interests of women, lesbians, gays and transsexuals. Yet its room for manoeuvre is constrained by the limitations of the treaties (noted earlier) and by concomitant procedures. If the consultation procedure applies, the Council must confer with the EP, but it does not have to treat its opinion as binding. The 2004 directive to ban sex discrimination in the access to and supply of goods and services was seriously watered down in the Council, under pressure from the mass media and insurance companies; the EP was unable to do more than propose amendments. While the extension of co-decision under the Lisbon Treaty has increased potential EP influence, this procedure still requires the EP to act strategically and to forge alliances with the Commission and pioneer states in the Council in order to see its amendments adopted.

3. Council and Coreper

Formerly known as the Council of Ministers, the Council was established in 1951, as an intergovernmental counterweight to the supranational High Authority (the Commission's predecessor). Here national interests occupy centre stage. Unlike the EP or the Commission, the Council is not comprised of 'European' representatives but of ministerial level representatives from each member state. It has nine different configurations dealing with diverse policy areas, plus a General Affairs Council consisting of national leaders and foreign affairs ministers, designed to ensure consistency in the work of the different formations. Gender issues are usually handled by the Employment, Social Policy, Health and Consumer Affairs Council (EPSCO). Female representation in the Council varies according to the number of national women ministers or secretaries of state. Among the EU-27, 27 per cent of senior ministers, on average, were women in fall 2010.[4] In most Council configurations women are outnumbered by men, although EU enlargements incorporating Scandinavian and Central/Eastern European countries have increased the number of female ministers. The Secretariat-General provides administrative support for all Council activities.

The Council presidency rotates among all member states. It is held by groups of three members for a period of 18 months, each member chairing for six months. Civil servants and politicians from the presiding country chair all meetings, from the level of working groups to the Council. Serving as President means more than just directing the meetings. A presiding member state can steer the agenda, the pace and the outcome of decision-making. Member states thus attach a high value to the presidency. They can enhance their own prestige by placing appealing issues on the agenda or by bringing a complicated dossier to a happy conclusion. This implies that the attention accorded to gender issues will vary with the national salience of gender issues in the presiding member state.

The Council does not meet weekly, insofar as ministers are busy in their home countries. Daily EU business is conducted by a committee of diplomats based in Brussels. Called 'Coreper' (Committee of Permanent Representatives), it consists of member state ambassadors (Coreper II) and their deputies (Coreper I). Coreper II is in charge of institutional, financial and legal affairs as well as foreign and security policies. Coreper I prepares all other Council configurations, including EPSCO. The ambassadors and their deputies, supported by civil servants from national ministries, participate in intergovernmental working parties where they negotiate on behalf of their home country.

There are roughly 150 working groups in which all new Commission proposals are discussed and negotiated. The Working Party on Social Questions discusses many issues with a gender dimension. A Commission staff member attends the meetings to comment on the proposal. After discussion, files move up to Coreper II. If Coreper reaches an agreement, the file is transferred to the Council as an 'A item' for formal enactment. No further discussion occurs unless so requested by a member state. The system of 'A items' explains why gender equality issues occasionally appear on the agenda of Council formations other than EPSCO. If Coreper cannot reach agreement, the proposal appears on the Council agenda as a 'B item', leaving the matter to be resolved by the ministers. An estimated 75–80 per cent of Council business finds agreement at the working group level and a further 15–20 per cent at Coreper level, which leaves only 5 per cent of the time for substantive debate and approval at the ministerial level. Coreper also maintains regular contacts with the EP (see Nugent 2010).

Created in 2001, the High Level Group on Gender Mainstreaming is an informal group of senior civil servants responsible for gender mainstreaming in their respective member states. Meeting twice a year, the group considers the development of indicators and plans for following up the Beijing Platform for Action.[5] It supports the presidency in identifying relevant policy matters to address during its six-month term, while assisting the Commission in preparing the annual Report on Equality between Women and Men for the spring European Council (see below). Another informal group, similarly composed, is the High Level Group on Gender Mainstreaming in the Structural Funds, created in 2004. It provides input on gender mainstreaming to authorities managing the Structural Funds, and it exchanges 'best practices' regarding efforts to implement mainstreaming involving structural funds at the national level.

The Council's main task is decision-making, alone or jointly with the EP. Until the mid-1980s the Council had to approve all draft legislation unanimously. The veto power of individual states meant that many draft provisions remained on the shelf for years, even decades. Parental leave, for instance, was placed on the agenda in 1982 but blocked by a British veto for the next 14 years. To overcome stagnation, governments decided in 1986 to introduce qualified majority voting (QMV) for a limited number of policy domains. Since then, every treaty modification has increased the number of issues to which QMV applies – which coincided with the extension of the EP's legislative power. As regards gender equality in the labour market and at the workplace, the Council and the EP may adopt minimum norms by QMV. Legislation to combat discrimination based on sex, racial or ethnic origin, religion or belief, disability, age or sexual orientation has to be approved unanimously.

52 *Gendering the Institutions and Actors*

The rules have changed several times. As of 2014, a 'qualified majority' will consist of approval by at least 55 per cent of the member states, representing at least 65 per cent of the total EU population. A blocking minority consists of at least four member states. The shift from unanimity to QMV has changed the negotiating process among EU states: they are forced to build coalitions to create either a blocking minority or a qualified majority. In addition, it promotes cooperation between member states and 'their' MEPs.

Gendering the Council has always been critical as well as difficult. The double shift from unanimity to QMV and from non-binding EP consultation to co-decision has improved the prospects for activities promoting gender justice. In the Council, the blocking power of single states has been broken. Influencing Council politics has become still more complicated, as it requires one to address diplomats and ministers of those countries susceptible to building an alliance (a majority or a blocking minority) supporting one's point of view. How a policy proposal travels back and forth between institutions is illustrated in Figure 3.2.

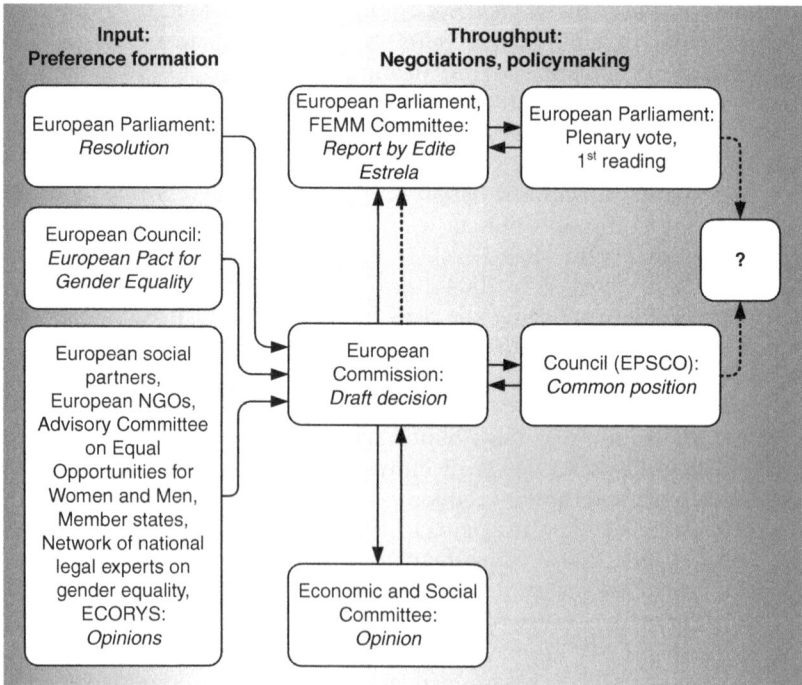

Figure 3.2 'Who said what and when?' The itinerary of the proposal to extend maternity leave
Source: Compiled by the author.

4. European Council[6]

During the early years, integration built on summits where the heads of government concluded 'grand bargains'. Beginning as an informal 'fireside chat', the European Council has become the EU powerhouse. It consists of the heads of state or government (assisted by their Foreign Affairs Ministers), the EU President, the Commission President and the High Representative for Foreign Affairs. The European Council meets twice every six months and convenes special meetings in times of crisis, for example, when violence broke out between Georgia and Russia in August 2008, or as the Euro crisis took hold in 2010. The 'family photos' taken at summit meetings clearly testify to the underrepresentation of women at government level. In March 2007 German Chancellor Angela Merkel appeared in radiant orange at the Berlin summit, surrounded by 26 dark-suited men. Presently, among the 27 presidents and prime ministers there are currently three female heads of state and three female prime ministers.

The prime minister or president of the country temporarily serving as the EU President used to head the European Council simultaneously; the Lisbon Treaty has introduced a permanent President for a renewable term of two and a half years, however. Belgian Prime Minister Herman van Rompuy was appointed by the European Council as the first 'regular' President. His task is to chair the European Council and 'drive forward its work'. Another innovation of the Lisbon Treaty involves the function of the High Representative of the Union for Foreign Affairs and Security Policy, who has the task of developing and conducting the EU's external relations. The High Representative enjoys a base in the intergovernmental Council as chair of the Foreign Affairs Council and in the supranational Commission as Vice-President. Lady Catherine Ashton (UK) is the first to occupy this post; she is assisted by the new European External Action Service.

The European Council provides political leadership, taking on the big decisions, for example, in introducing the Euro or a common asylum policy. It also tries to re-float negotiations deadlocked at lower levels. A purely intergovernmental body, it renders decisions based on unanimity. The Conclusions of the Presidency, presented after every European Council, are not binding. Rather, they function as soft law, guiding the agendas and negotiations of all other institutions. 'Eurosummits' are surrounded by secrecy. Each government presents its accomplishments at carefully orchestrated press conferences, but the processes preceding the outcome occur behind closed doors.

The European Council is very much a masculinist body. Yet, even though women are rarely present at the top, their issues do regularly show up on the agenda due to the European Employment Strategy (EES; also see Hubert in this volume). This policy strategy was devised in 1997, to counter criticisms of the EU's neoliberal orientation, public scepticism with respect to the Euro and pressure from social–democratic leaders. The European Council formulates policy guidelines regarding employability, job creation and equal opportunity policies.

These guidelines must be implemented by way of the Open Method of Coordination (OMC). This method relies on soft law mechanisms, like peer review and benchmarking, for which the European Council approves common objectives and fixes targets. Each member state subsequently draws up a National Reform Programme, outlining ways to reach the overarching objectives. The Commission assesses the outcomes, identifies pilot projects and draws up scoreboards indicating whether the targets have been met. In 2006, the European Council adopted a European Pact for Gender Equality, confirming its commitment to strengthening economic growth and competitiveness by promoting women's employment and ensuring a better work-life balance. One positive effect of the OMC is that each spring gender equality appears on the agenda of the European Council when the latter assesses whether National Reform Programme objectives have or have not been met as regards female employment rates, childcare and the gender pay gap. OMC limitations include its lack of sanctions and the focus on quantifiable aspects of gender justice and labour market issues. These features clearly hinder the effectiveness and transparency of the EES (Verloo and van der Vleuten 2009).

5. The Court of Justice

Another result of the Lisbon Treaty is that the Court of Justice of the European Union,[7] seated in Luxembourg, now consists of the Court of Justice, the General Court (formerly the Court of First Instance) and the EU Civil Service Tribunal (which deals with internal EU staffing disputes). The Court of Justice (COJ) serves as the main court. Established in 1989 to reduce the COJ's workload, the General Court rules on actions brought against European decisions concerning competition and commercial law. The Court of Justice (in short: Court) and the General Court both seat one judge from each member state. The Court is assisted by eight Advocates-General. Most cases are handled by a Chamber consisting of three to five judges. If the case is very delicate, the Full Court (minimum 15 judges) or the Grand Chamber (13 judges) deliberate. Chamber verdicts require a majority vote, but the final decision is signed by all judges; individual opinions remain the secret of the court.

The first woman, Simone Rozès from France, made her appearance at the Court in 1981 as an Advocate-General. No female judges were appointed until 1999, when Fidelma O'Kelly Macken (Ireland) and Ninon Colneric (Germany) joined the bench. As of September 2010, five women serve on the Court of Justice (19 per cent), six (22 per cent) on the General Court and two (29 per cent) on the EU Civil Service Tribunal. Even though male judges are capable of issuing gender-sensitive verdicts, an almost 'all-male bench' remains a problem for two reasons (Kennedy 2002). First, balanced participation is imperative for maintaining the legitimacy of the Court. Public confidence in European law and in the Court's rulings on gender equality, especially, is strengthened when both sexes share the bench. Second, each judge brings a specific cultural background, national traditions and experiences to bear on an interpretation. The same argument holds for women's representation, to ensure their experiences will be taken into account. However, there is no obligation for member states to jointly ensure balanced representation on the bench.

The Court plays three roles. It acts as an umpire, rules on complaints and guides the national courts. First, the Court settles conflicts among European institutions or between member states and European institutions. Furthermore, the Court upholds the implementation of European treaties and law. If a member fails to transpose an EU decision into national law or violates community rules (for instance, by supplying illicit state subsidies), the Commission or another state can initiate *infringement proceedings*, taking it to Court. European rules sometimes require more far-reaching measures than the member states anticipate. In most cases (86 per cent), 'misunderstandings' are resolved by the offending state and Commission during the first, written stage of the procedure. If this does not produce the desired result, the Commission sends a 'reasoned opinion'. If the member state still fails to take remedial action, the Commission files suit. The Court registers 400 cases annually. If the member state is found guilty of infringement, negative media coverage and a loss of prestige usually follow.

Should slights to its reputation not suffice to alter an actor's behaviour, the Commission initiates a second infringement proceeding, after which the Court can impose financial penalties. The threat of multimillion Euro fines usually persuades the member state to comply. In 2000, when France occupied the EU presidency, the Court was on the verge of imposing a daily fine of 142,425 euros when that country failed to lift the ban on night work for women. The French government succeeded in convincing its utterly divided national parliament to act immediately by stressing the consequences for its reputation (van der Vleuten 2007). The Network of Legal Experts on Equal Treatment of Men and Women monitors the implementation of equality regulations in the member states and issues annual reports that may elicit action from the Commission. Between 1957 and 2008, the Court ruled in

56 *Gendering the Institutions and Actors*

Table 3.2 Infringement proceedings: gender equality directives (1958–2008)

Case No.	Parties: Commission v.	Issue, directive	Winner?
C-58/81	Luxembourg	75/117 Equal pay	Commission
C-61/81	United Kingdom	75/117 Equal pay	Commission
C-163/82	Italy	76/207 Equal treatment	Member state
C-165/82	United Kingdom	76/207 Equal treatment; transposition	both
C-143/83	Denmark	Art. 141 & 75/117 Equal pay	Commission
C-248/83	Germany	76/207 Equal treatment	both
C-312/86	France	76/207 Equal treatment, transposition	Commission
C-318/86	France	76/207 Equal access to jobs in the civil service	both
C-229/89	Belgium	79/7 Equal treatment social security	Member state
C-173/91	Belgium	Art. 141 & 76/207 Supplementary payments	Commission
C-197/96	France	76/207 Ban on night work	Commission
C-207/96	Italy	76/207 Ban on night work	both
C-187/98	Greece	Art. 141 Equal pay, discriminatory payments	Commission
C-354/98	France	96/97/EC Social security; transposition	Commission
C-457/98	Greece	96/97/EC Social security; transposition	Commission
C-203/03	Austria	76/207 Diving for women prohibited	both
C-519/03	Luxembourg	96/34/EC Parental leave	Commission

Source: Compiled by the author, adapted from Commission 2008.

17 infringement procedures involving gender equality, which in ten cases resulted in a victory for the Commission (see Table 3.2).

The Court's third role is to provide binding interpretations of European law, in response to requests from national courts for a so-called *preliminary ruling* (explaining how the COJ itself would rule, should it hear such a case). Between 1958 and 2008 the Court supplied interpretations of EU gender equality principles in 168 cases. German, English and Dutch courts have been most active in seeking preliminary rulings. The Court often produces an interpretation of European laws that differs from member state intentions at the time of adoption. The Tanja Kreil case (285/98) offers one such example: while the German government viewed military personnel as a national security issue, the Court decided that 'equal treatment in employment' warrants women's right to serve in the Bundeswehr in all capacities, not just as musicians or nurses. Following the ECJ ruling, Germany amended its constitution, to grant women access to all Bundeswehr positions, including those involving the use of weapons.

Governments stand on the sideline in this game between national and European courts. National judiciaries usually follow 'Luxembourg'. Member states have recently blown the whistle on the Court, in declaring that new (intergovernmental) domains – foreign, security, defence policy – do not fall under its jurisdiction. The Court is also excluded from the OMC.

From a gender perspective, EU jurisprudence has always been most interesting. Analysis of rulings shows that the Court is not a feminist entity. Interpretations of European law are guided by two ideas. First, it seeks to defend its autonomy and authority vis-à-vis member governments and domestic courts, especially constitutional courts. It utilised a preliminary ruling (*Costa* v *ENEL*, Case 6/64) to affirm the *supremacy* of European law over national law. Second, it aims to act in the spirit of the treaties, thus contributing to integration by promoting peace and progress for all citizens. This has resulted in rulings protecting the rights of citizens and companies against unwilling governments, benefiting women in many cases.

The Court has more room for interpretation than holds for national courts, bound by a single constitution. European law is translated into all 23 official EU languages; due to minor (translation) differences between the texts, literal interpretations are not possible. European law is often open to multiple interpretations on purpose, for the sake of securing political acceptance in many different national contexts. The Court has used this room to maximise the implications of treaty articles and directives by 'stretching' central concepts, for example by stretching the concept of pay to include pensions as 'pay deferred' (*Barber v GRE (1990)*, Case 262/88). The Court cannot arbitrarily expand treaty articles and directives beyond the concepts embedded in them, however, lest it provoke negative reactions among national courts. Indeed, several rulings turned out to be less positive for women than anticipated, for example by limiting the entitlement to parental leave to women only (*Ulrich Hofmann v Barmer Ersatzkasse*, Case 184/83) and by accepting discrimination against lesbians (*Lisa Jacqueline Grant v South-West Trains Ltd*, Case C-249/96). The Court displays extreme caution in domains where EU competencies are limited, like social security and family law, which member states have repeatedly insisted are matters for national regulation.

6. Organised interests and social partners

A host of organised interests try to influence the European decision-making process alongside formal institutions. The expanding scope of EU policies has massively increased the array of European interest associations. An estimated 3,000 interest groups have their offices in Brussels, employing 15,000 lobbyists (Watson and Shackleton 2008). An overwhelming 62 per cent of these groups represent private economic and business interests (including law firms), 20 per cent engage on behalf of broader, non-economic aims (environmental, human rights, women's rights, public health), while 18 per cent are linked to local or regional governments, non-EU country embassies and international organisations. Within each category we find powerful players commanding many resources, such as the Committee of Agricultural Organizations (COPA), German Länder or Business Europe. Yet even the big players must build alliances with other associations, MEPs and government officials in order to influence European decision-making. Lobbyists therefore spend much time developing and nurturing national and transnational networks. Here they obtain up-to-date information on relevant initiatives and actor preferences, in an effort to coordinate their standpoints and strategies.

There are several strategies for exercising effective influence. *Inside lobbying* is when interest groups try to obtain direct access to civil servants and politicians; *outside lobbying* means they aim to mobilise public opinion and the media. European institutions are less sensitive to demonstrations and opinion polls than national governments, since they do not risk electoral punishment; it is also more difficult and expensive to organise transnational strikes and demonstrations in Brussels than at national level. Inside lobbying is generally more successful, given the open nature of the European policy arena. Organised interests offer valuable information and expertise for the Commission and the EP. The early involvement of stakeholders in EU policy development increases the probability of correct implementation at the national level. MEPs often welcome extra information to better judge the quality and feasibility of a proposal. Offering access to citizens' rights groups like the European Youth Forum and the European Citizen Action Service also helps to enhance the MEPs democratic profile.

Informal channels for inside lobbying include all direct approaches to politicians and civil servants; potential influence is greater if lobbyists are involved earlier in the process, leading them to focus their attention on the Commission. Next, lobbying is directed towards MEPs, especially the *rapporteur* and the parliamentary committee examining a specific bill. Interest groups even provide MEPs with ready-made amendments for parliamentary debate: 24 single-issue groups have been formed on a cross-party basis, for example the Gay and Lesbian Rights Intergroup and the Intergroup on Racism and Xenophobia. These encompass interested MEPs and NGO representatives. They organise hearings, pose parliamentary questions and write letters of support or inquiry. The Council is far more difficult to approach. Accordingly, groups hoping to influence Council preferences lobby national ministries and their permanent representatives in Brussels.

Foremost among formal channels are the European Economic and Social Committee (EESC), the Committee of Regions (CoR) and the European Social Dialogue (ESD). The EESC, a tripartite advisory body already established in the founding treaties, consists of a wide range of interest groups, among them trade unions, employer, environmental and consumer organisations. Women's interests are not represented by a specific group. The share of female members in the EESC is currently 23 per cent. The Commission must ask the EESC for advice on all policy proposals in domains such as environment, employment, gender equality, health, and consumers' affairs. The CoR, established in 1994 by the Maastricht Treaty, consists of local and regional authorities. Women presently constitute 19 per cent of the CoR members. The CoR's views must be solicited on all proposals of interest to local authorities. The EESC and CoR command little real influence, as they enter the decision-making process at a relatively late stage; accommodating internal conflicts of interests results in weakly compromised opinions that neither the Commission, the Council nor the EP are obliged to take into account. Since 1992 the ESD mechanism allows trade unions and employers to reach binding decisions pertaining to social affairs or employment. A recent Commission proposal allows representatives of workers' and employers' organisations to open negotiations. If they reach agreement, the Council may approve it in the form of a directive, as in the cases of parental leave and part-time work. The ESD has not proved very effective thus far, insofar as employers and workers often disagree; both prefer collective bargaining to legal regulation.

The EU is often criticised for its *democratic deficit,* which refers to the strong influence of powerful lobby groups, as well as to a broader lack of transparency in decision-making. The other side of the coin is that European decision-making remains a relatively open process, where even groups without national access, like representatives of the Roma, find an alternative arena where many can make their voices heard. In an effort to redress the over-representation of business interests, the Commission offers financial and logistic support, totalling over €1 billion annually, to several hundred NGOs; examples include the European Women's Lobby (EWL) and the European branch of the International Lesbian and Gay Association (ILGA-Europe). To increase transparency, the Commission opened a public register, requesting that all lobby groups provide information about their clients, funding and objectives. There are codes of conduct for MEPs and Commission officials regarding the receipt of gifts and relationships with outside interests. The EP website contains a register of lobbyists who can access parliamentary buildings.

The shift from national to supranational decision-making has created winners and losers. Groups who depend mainly on outside lobbying, like trade unions, have more trouble defending their interests in Brussels than women's organisations, whose expertise constitutes their primary power resource. Flexible network organisations function more effectively in a multilevel system than large, complex interest groups. Finally, the EU offers more opportunities to groups who hope to change national policies, while it is less open to groups defending the status quo. All told, the EU offers opportunities to businesses and small, well-equipped non-governmental organisations in the environmental and human rights fields, while traditional mass organisations such as trade unions have lost influence.

Gender issues typically belong to the domain in which the EU has offered new points of access to decision-making, as women have much to gain from policy change and the weakening of vested interests. Women have primarily used inside lobbying, weaving a colourful network of groups, committed parliamentarians in the EP and civil servants in DG EMPL. During the early integration years, no transnational organisations pursued gender equality in relation to social issues. Mobilisation was carried out by individual feminists such as Éliane Vogel-Polsky, a lawyer who initiated the first court cases to press for gender equality (*Gabrielle Defrenne v Belgian State, Case 80/70*). Transnational groups growing out of grassroots feminist movements first set up camp in Brussels in the 1980s. The growth in EU rule-making and equality litigation contributed to the expansion and diversification of transnational women-centred networks. Between 1957 and 2003, 57 transnational groups pursued action in the field of gender equality (Cichowski 2007). The EWL was established in 1990 as an umbrella organisation for national coordination; constituents include the Deutscher Frauenrat, the Romanian Women's Lobby, organisations such as the European Federation of Women Working in the Home (FEFAF) and the Federation of Kalé, Manouch Romany & Sinté Women. It submits position papers and amendments on policy proposals and treaty reforms. The issue of domestic violence entered the European arena through pressure from the EWL and the EP. The EWL effectively coordinated national women's groups to push for implementation of the Beijing Platform. Its legitimacy, too, has been contested, due to the dominance of 'femocrats' and 'white middle-aged women from the old member states'.

The Advisory Committee on Equal Opportunities for Women and Men offers a formal access channel. Created in 1981, it draws individuals from national ministries focusing on equal opportunities and from national committees in charge of gender equality; and representatives of employers' and workers' organisations. Two EWL members attend the meetings as observers. Meeting twice a year, this Committee assists the Commission in formulating and implementing equality policies. It suffers from the same limitations as the EESC and CoR: its members have diverging interests hard to reconcile.

The favourite lobbying strategy is to pressure MEPs from the parliamentary committee FEMM and *rapporteurs*. The Parliament's Gay and Lesbian Rights Intergroup and the Intergroup on Ageing offer privileged access to NGOs addressing gender, discrimination and equality issues. Litigation entails a different strategy. National equality agencies and feminist legal activists, such as the British Equal Opportunities Commission and the German Association of Female Lawyers, support legal claims of women who feel that their 'European' rights have been violated. These claims reach the Court as preliminary ruling requests. In many cases the rights of working women, for example regarding discrimination against pregnant workers and part-time workers, have been strengthened.

7. Gendering EU institutions: A complex system of checks and balances

It requires well-informed, well-resourced individuals to exercise influence in the EU, which would seem to reinforce unequal gender power relations. In spite of what citizens think, and despite what media or euro-sceptical politicians argue, the EU is not a super-state that only serves to concentrate huge amounts of power in the hands of Brussels' bureaucrats. Rather, the EU is rather a hybrid organisation, with intergovernmental and supranational characteristics. Its complexity stems from an effort to strike an institutional balance among three competing needs: for institutional capacity, political legitimacy and national control. Every institutional change promoting one of these objectives negatively influences at least one other aim. QMV has increased the EU's capacity for reaching decisions, but it decreases national control over outcomes. Enhancing democratic legitimacy by granting the EP co-decision powers reduces national control even further. Increasing national control through the subsidiarity principle, requiring the Commission to justify why a European instead of a national solution is needed, and the 'yellow card procedure'[8] slow down decision-making, and therewith the EU's capacity for governance. There are no easy solutions allowing the advancement of all three objectives simultaneously. One is stuck with a complex set of checks and balances. However, changes contributing to a loss of control by individual governments and national parliaments have not automatically concentrated power in the hands of Brussels' bureaucrats. The outcome has been a sharing (pooling) of power among member states, and between member states and supranational institutions.

How do women affect the European arena? Many authors credit women's growing presence in the EU arena with the success of gender equality policies (Hoskyns 1996; Kantola 2010a). But under what conditions do women become successful? In those cases where they can play a multilevel game (for a detailed account of the policy making process, see Locher in this volume), if they can mobilise nationally and build coalitions with transnational actors (European NGOs) and supranational actors (DG EMPL, MEPs), women can win, as governments are pressured from both directions and are caught in a very uncomfortable 'pincer action' (van der Vleuten 2005). This pincer action may have a legal character as well; activism vis-à-vis national courts, combined with monitoring by the Commission and the Court, may lead to the correct implementation of European legislation.

In order for the 'pincer' to work, one needs ideas and power at the national and supranational level, rendering women's presence in European institutions crucial. Committed individuals make a difference, be they feminists in DG EMPL or in the EP, judges, Advocates-General or ministers from pioneer countries. But individuals need backing at both of these levels and pressure from women's groups, female party and parliamentary activists, feminists in trade unions and in ministries – all of whom bring power to bear on their ideas. Of course, this is a mutually reinforcing mechanism. Such strong pressures legitimised the institutionalisation of gender interests in the Equal Opportunities Unit (DG EMPL) and in the Committee for Women's Rights (EP). These 'institutions', in turn, strengthened women's advocacy groups, which no longer had to lobby for access or data; they could thus concentrate scarce resources on these openings in the supranational organisation, providing expertise and 'grassroots' information. Gender mainstreaming might actually increase the number of 'privileged points of access' to this complex system.

Discussion questions

- Do you consider the EU a kind of super-state?
- Sometimes the European Court of Justice seems to act like a 'feminist court'; sometimes it seems to hinder the defence of women's rights. Elaborate on these two arguments and formulate your own position.
- To what extent and in what ways has the EU made it more or less easy for women's groups to defend and advance their interests?
- How might women's representation in the EU institutions be increased and strengthened?

Notes

1. The European Central Bank and the Court of Auditors are not treated here.
2. Major exception: regarding foreign affairs and defence, the Commission shares the right of initiative with the Council.
3. Other procedures are applied in the fields of foreign affairs and defence. There the European Parliament only plays an advisory role.
4. For data on the representation of women and men in politics in Europe, see the Database 'Women & men in decision making', online: http://ec.europa.eu/social/main.jsp?catId=764&langId=en.
5. The Platform was the outcome of the 1995 UN World Conference on Women, setting out a number of actions to be taken by governments.
6. Not to be confused with the Council of Europe, which is not part of the EU. Established in 1948; that Council currently has 46 members and it is well-known for its involvement in minority rights.
7. Not to be confused with the European Court of Human Rights in Strasbourg, which is linked to the Council of Europe (see previous note).
8. That is, if at least one-third of national parliaments is not convinced that a specific European policy is necessary. In addition, national parliaments now have a right to bring a suit to the Court of the EU.

4
Gendering the EU Policy Process and Constructing the *Gender Acquis*

Birgit Locher

Imagine a stewardess in the late 1960s being forced by her employer, the Belgian airline Sabena, to change jobs within the company at lower wages just because she had turned 40 years old. Her male colleagues of the same age were allowed to continue in the cockpit and cabin service. This stewardess, let's call her Gabrielle Defrenne, was consistently paid less than male cabin stewards and was then denied an occupational pension by her employer, Sabena Airlines. Imagine that, right about then, a feminist lawyer named Éliane Vogel-Polsky was on the look-out for a case to turn a little-known regional provision into national practice. Mandating equal pay for equal work, Article 119 of the 1957 European Economic Community (EEC) Treaty existed only on paper (*de jure*) back then; the practice in the six European Community (EC) member states looked quite different.

When Defrenne and her lawyer went to the European Court of Justice (ECJ) to challenge gender discrimination, they lost the first time around. The Court argued that Article 119 EEC Treaty did not cover equal pension claims. When Defrenne and Vogel-Polsky appealed again to the ECJ five years later, they achieved a grand victory: the Court ruled that the article was directly enforceable, granting rights to individuals in cases where remedies do not exist under national law. The ECJ, moreover, made it clear that the European Community was not only an economic union but one that should also ensure social progress, for example by requiring equal pay for equal work. The Court found Sabena's policy discriminatory, marking the start of *equal treatment*; it eventually required the airline to compensate Defrenne for her loss of income, real and deferred (Ostner and Lewis 1995: 167–168).

For a long time, Article 119 EEC Treaty and its formal ECJ interpretation constituted the 'heart' of EU gender equality policy. Today there exists a firmly established gender equality regime encompassing a wide spectrum of treaty provisions, secondary or soft law instruments, directives and court rulings (Hantrais 2000a; Hoskyns 1996; Mazey 2002b). The Community's *gender acquis*, that is, the pre-existing body of rules and policies that must be adopted by all would-be member states as a condition for admission, has been constructed in stages. In the literature (Hoskyns 2000), this incremental development is often described as a three-stage process – moving from an initial focus on *equal rights* and *equal treatment* to *positive action* and, finally, to *gender mainstreaming* (Booth and Benett 2002; Mazey 2001; Rees 1998; also see Woodward in this volume). The entire process of the development of the EU's *gender acquis* has been marked by shifting approaches and the inclusion of new issue-areas.

Starting with a narrow focus on non-discrimination in relation to equal pay in European labour markets, the regime's scope has expanded tremendously over time. It now includes measures to reconcile career and family, pregnancy and parental leave rules, directives on part-time or temporary work and warranting non-discrimination in the provision of services, as well as soft law measures addressing, for instance, sexual harassment, childcare, trafficking, violence against women, women in decision-making or in science (Hantrais 2000b; Hoskyns 2000; Ostner 2000; Walby 2004). To reconstruct the historical evolution of the EU gender regime, we need to focus not only on the key role of Community law but also on specific mechanisms – such as regulations, directives and recommendations – that have all contributed to a wide-ranging *gender acquis*. The EU *acquis* has often secured more rights for women than national governments themselves were willing to supply.

As a dense institutional environment, the EU evinces an elaborate set of norms, rules and decision-making procedures, drawing actors from many different levels and locations into deliberations among its institutions. Different stages in the policy cycle follow diverse patterns of interaction, depending on the Maastricht *pillar* (supranational, intergovernmental, and national) and the particular policy field at stake. Scholars have tried to explain the emergence and 'deepening' of the EU gender regime with the help of traditional integration theories, but feminist research rarely stops there (see Kronsell in this volume). Most mainstream approaches are missing a decisive factor, namely the central role of 'women's agency' in building the EU gender regime and equality policy. That agency becomes most visible when we explore powerful policy networks, including official actors serving in core EU institutions, as well as the many *policy entrepreneurs* based in civil society. Whereas feminist literature seeking to 'explain' such policies tends to paint the EU as a champion of gender equality, studies concentrating on the socio-economic order that EU policies produce are more critical of the EU's feminist credentials (Locher and Prügl 2009: 186–187).

This chapter provides an overview of the current EU gender equality regime. It traces key policy developments by focusing on the *sui generis* character of policy-making under a multi-level EU system that differs significantly from any and all national governance settings. It likewise reviews key turning points and specific mechanisms, such as the open method of coordination (OMC), used in policy-making to foster gender equality. Finally, the chapter offers a critical discussion of policy implementation problems in the member states – problems that are rooted in pre-existing national gender regimes; finally, it considers barriers to the implementation of gender mainstreaming.

1. Policy-making in the gender equality domain

To understand the complex mechanisms used to foster gender equality, we need to take a closer look at distinctive policy-making features shaping the EU's multi-level system (see van der Vleuten in this volume). First, the European Union has been described as 'the most densely institutionalised network of regimes and organisations in the world' (Risse-Kappen 1996: 59). As an institution *sui generis* and as a specialised polity operating at the macro-societal level, it is embedded in a dense organisational environment comprised of the EU's main institutional actors – the European Council, the Council of Ministers, the Commission, the European Parliament (EP), and the European Court of Justice (ECJ); other actors from outside, for example 'social partners', also play an important part in EU policy-making. Together and separately they build on an elaborate set of norms, rules and decision-making procedures, regulating their respective competences.

As a multi-level system, the EU is a non-hierarchical, interdependent system evincing complex linkages between different levels and actors. Policy-making involves participants from different levels and locations: Private, governmental, non-governmental, transnational and supranational actors interact with each other in complex horizontal and vertical networks, varying in terms of density as well as in depth (Welz and Engel 1993). EU policy decisions are less the result of majority votes or power politics than of communicative processes; they emerge from interactions between levels and actors showing very distinct functions, interests and resources (Kohler-Koch 1997). Due to its non-hierarchical nature and a high degree of interdependence in the EU-system, policy-making is often characterised in terms of transnational and intergovernmental coalition-building. Insofar as the EU represents a dynamic or a 'living institution' (Laffan 1999), policy tasks cannot be neatly allocated to territorially defined levels and functionally differentiated entities. Instead, the relationships among different levels and bodies tend to be flexible, depending on the policy issue or policy field at stake. Grounded in more than just a set of political and legal organs, the EU has also come to embody shared norms, commonly accepted rules and decision-making procedures. As such, the European polity is an increasingly 'rule-bound' arena for social interaction (Christiansen et al. 1999: 539). These specific features determine the institutional background for policy-making and provide the particular political opportunity structure for activism.

66 *Gendering the EU Policy Process*

Since gender mainstreaming was introduced in 1996, policies attending to equality between women and men should, in theory, be found across all EU domains, that is in all three pillars. Nevertheless, it is the first 'single-market' pillar, encompassing the fields of employment and social relations, which traditionally has been and remains the prime site for developing gender policies. A closer look at the typical EU agenda-setting and policy-formulation processes in this pillar sheds light on equality policy-making. Scholars commonly depict the policy cycle (see Figure 4.1) as progressing through the following basic stages: problem identification, agenda setting, decision making (including policy formulation, policy defending and project development), policy implementation and policy evaluation/restatement (Cini 1996).

The EU policy process entails a number of actors and peculiarities regarding problem identification and agenda setting (see Figure 4.2). Its right of initiative grants the College of Commissioners a vital role in the first pillar; it has stimulated the formation of a wide range of civil society groups who are particularly relevant at the early stages of the policy cycle. This active interest in outside expertise emerges as a result of the Commission's 'notorious shortage of resources and need for allies in its search for further European

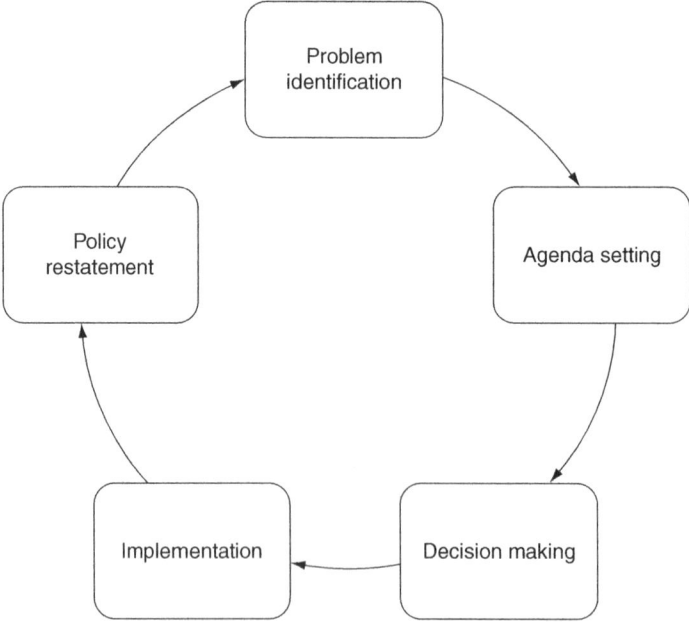

Figure 4.1 The policy cycle concept
Source: © 2011 agora-wissen (http://www.gesellschaft-agora.de), Stuttgart.

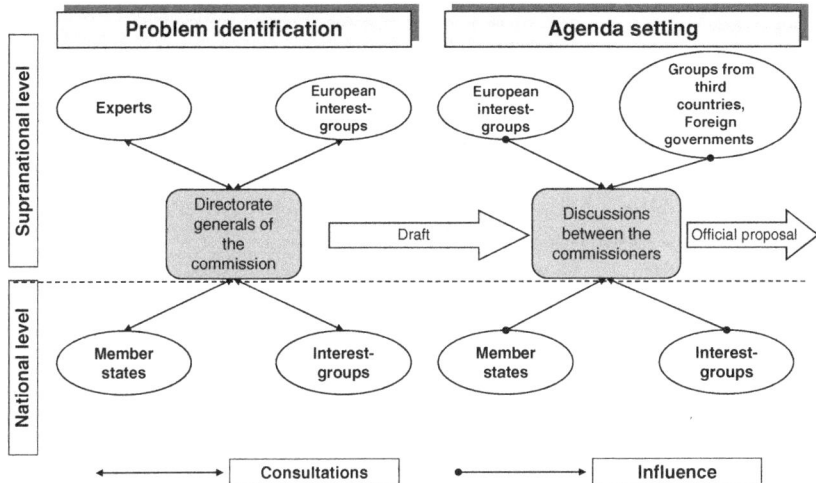

Figure 4.2 Problem identification and agenda setting in the EU
Source: © 2011 agora-wissen (http://www.gesellschaft-agora.de), Stuttgart.

integration, its continual quest for democratic legitimacy and agents capable of performing democratic functions' (Greenwood 2009: 97). Because in-house expertise in specialised fields is limited, the Commission values expert resources from outside. The Commission's Directorate-General for Employment, Social Affairs and Inclusion (DG EMPL), the unit in charge of setting the agenda for gender policies, has been rather expansionist-oriented (Greenwood 2009: 98). Typically, DG EMPL selects a topic which seems to enjoy public support, like gender equality, and launches a kick-off conference event, often coinciding with a themed European Year of Action. Very often, an umbrella lobby group emerges from this subsidised impetus, serving as a means to aggregate civil society voices across Europe, as was the case with respect to formation of the European Women's Lobby (EWL) in 1990.

Inside the Commission, the 'equal opportunities group' enjoys the most prestige and appears most powerful. This group of Commissioners serves as the main site for developing new gender equality initiatives. Directorate G 'Equality between Men and Women/Action against Discrimination' of DG EMPL deals with gender equality in different subunits. Its main tasks consist of developing new legislation, overseeing implementation processes and coordinating the new gender mainstreaming concept. This involves close interactions between the Commission and other actors, for example specific policy networks operating both inside and outside the EU institutions, at different levels and within diverse national contexts.

Once a theme has successfully been pushed onto the Commission's agenda, the policy formulation process commences. First, intensive coordination takes place among the Commission's many DGs, especially since the introduction of gender mainstreaming. The DGs with a stake in equality issues are supported by committees and working groups in which administrative personnel from the member states is also represented (Abels 2011a). The *consultative committee for gender equality between men and women*, consisting of national representatives, likewise supports the Commission in policy formulation. Both the EWL and the social partners enjoy observer status in this committee.

In most cases, the Council for Employment and Social Affairs (EPSCO) plays a central role in the policy formulation process pertaining to gender equality. Because Council members tend to uphold the norms inherent in the gender regimes of their respective countries, the Council frequently becomes a battlefield when it comes to preparing new equality policies. As long as unanimity was the rule, hardly any progressive gender equality provision found Council approval. However, the Amsterdam Treaty and introduction of the *qualified majority vote* (QMV) in 1997 allowed a new gender politics dynamic to take hold. Several sectoral coordination groups exist to support this work in the Council, for example, the working group on gender mainstreaming which prepares proposals.

Among the EU's main institutional actors, the EP has emerged as a real champion for gender equality over the decades. A high percentage of female members (MEPs), especially since 1995, means that new equality policies fall on fruitful ground or can be actively promoted by the Committee on Women's Rights and Gender Equality (FEMM). The introduction of the *co-decision procedure* under the Maastricht Treaty, expanded under the Amsterdam and the Lisbon Treaties (the latter extending co-decision to the adoption of measures concerning trafficking in women and children), has significantly strengthened the EP's role; co-decision applies in many cases affecting gender policies. Policy implementation thus follows distinct patterns, depending on the procedure used: the typical path begins with a Commission proposal, then a 'first reading' in the EP, consideration of Commission amendments, issuance of a common position by the Council, followed by a second EP 'reading', possibly a Commission 'opinion' on EP amendments and, finally, a majority decision on the part of the EP and the Council, leading to the adoption of a specific policy.

Not surprisingly, the policy formulation process absorbs a great deal of time, given the number of actors involved and the requisite step-by-step procedures. The initiative for the first DAPHNE programme to combat trafficking in women and sexual violence, for example – which eventually fell under the co-decision procedure – started in May 1998 with a Commission *communication* and a *proposal* for a Council *decision*.[1] It ended in January 2000 with a Council and Parliament *decision* to adopt the programme (Locher 2007: 271–287). In the interim, a powerful advocacy network tried to exert influence on the major institutional actors to ensure that the programme's initial intentions were not watered down.

2. The gender equality *acquis* of the EU

The core of today's EU gender regime is rooted in the wider body of Community law known as the *acquis communautaire* that must be embraced by all member states. Philippe Schmitter (1996: 162) defines the *acquis* as 'the sum total of obligations that have accumulated since the founding of the European Coal and Steel Community and are embedded in innumerable treaties and protocols'. Roger Goebel (1995: 1141–1143) captures its 'settled' quality, noting that the 'acquis communautaire essentially conveys the idea that the institutional structure, scope, policies and rules of the Community (now Union) are to be treated as "given" ("acquis"), not to be called into question or substantially modified by new states at the time they enter'. The EU gender regime, or *gender acquis,* is part of the larger *acquis communautaire*. Four types of legal provisions play a major role in advancing gender equality in the European Union: *primary, secondary* and so-called *'soft law'*, as well as settled *case law* issued by the ECJ.

The classification of legislative acts varies among what used to be called the first, second and third pillars (dissolved under the Lisbon Treaty). Since gender policies fall primarily within the first pillar (of the former European Communities), it is noteworthy that secondary legislation is classified according to whom it is directed and how it is to be implemented. *Regulations* and *directives* bind everyone, while *decisions* only affect the targeted parties (e.g. individuals, corporations, or member states). *Regulations* take direct effect: they are binding in and of themselves as part of national law; *directives* (mandating the ends but not the means) require implementation through national legislation. However, states that fail or refuse to implement *directives* as part of national law can be fined by the ECJ.

The starting point for the EU *gender acquis* was Article 119 of the Rome Treaty (EEC Treaty, revised as Article 141 Amsterdam Treaty of 1997 and today Article 157 TFEU) providing that 'men and women shall receive equal pay for equal work' (see Table 4.1). Feminists began using this bit of 'primary law' to pursue individual claims and achieve legal victories before the ECJ, as the Defrenne case illustrated. Part of the social provisions of the Treaty establishing the European Economic Community (EEC), Article 119 became the 'backbone' of the EU gender quality regime (Cichowski 2001: 113–114). Under the Amsterdam Treaty, gender equality and non-discrimination turned into 'guiding' legal principles of the Union laid out in a number of new articles extending the old 'equal pay' provision. Article 2, for example, declares: 'The Community shall have as its task [...] to promote throughout the Community a harmonious, balanced and sustainable

Table 4.1 Development of the EU *gender acquis*

Primary law*	Secondary law	'Soft law' provisions**	Case law (selection)
Treaties of Rome: Art. 119 EEC (equal pay for equal work)	1975 Equal Pay Directive 1976 Equal Treatment Directive 1979 Social Security Directive 1986 Occupational Social Security Directive and Self-Employment Directive 1992 Pregnant Workers Directive 1996 Parental Leave Directive 1996 Second Occupational Social Security Directive	1982–1986 AP1 1984 Rec. positive measures 1986–1990 AP2 1991–1995 AP3 1992 Recommendations against sexual harassment and on childcare 1996 Recommendation for women's participation and Communication on trafficking in women 1996–2000 AP4 and STOP I	1976 *Defrenne v Sabena* 1986 *Rummler v Dato-Druck*; *Bilka v Germany*

Treaties of Amsterdam (1999), Nice (2003), and Lisbon (2009; TFEU) amending the Treaty on European Union:	1997 Burden of Proof Directive	1997 DAPHNE I
Art. 2: promotion of gender equality figures as Community task	2002 Implementation of Equal Treatment Directive	2001 STOP II 2001–2006 AP5
	2004 Access to Goods and Services Directive	2004 DAPHNE II
Art. 3: gender equality as transversal objective of the EU (now Art. 8 TFEU)	2006 Recast Directive Equal Treatment in Employment and Occupation	2007 PROGRESS 2007–2013 DAPHNE III
Art. 13: entitles the Commission to take initiatives to combat discrimination based, among other grounds, on sex (now Art. 19 TFEU)		
Art. 141 (old Art. 119; now Art. 157 TFEU)		1998 *Tanja Kreil v the Germany*

* Given dates refer to the years when treaties entered into force.
** Only a few cornerstones and examples discussed above are included in this table. A complete list lies beyond the scope of this article.

development of economic activities, a high level of employment and of social protection, equality between men and women [...] '. This is reinforced by Article 3(2) requiring the Community to 'eliminate inequalities and to promote equality between men and women' in all its activities. In 1997, the EU was given a sound juridical foundation for pursuing gender issues in *any* sector, not only in relation to employment policies. Gender equality now appears as a 'guiding principle' in the Charter of Fundamental Rights as well as in the so-called Lisbon Treaty,[2] stressing non-discrimination and gender equality. The Lisbon Treaty that came into force in December 2009 reinforces the principle of equality between women and men by including it in the values and objectives of the Union and by providing for gender mainstreaming in all EU policies (Article 8 TFEU).

Primary law provisions are supplemented by way of secondary law, that is through 11 major directives on gender equality (as of this writing) that have been transposed into national law at the member state level. A directive fixes the objectives to be pursued by the EU members but assures freedom of choice as to national means for obtaining them (though it must achieve the desired goal). In practice, the Union 'addresses' directives to all member states and specifies the date by which they must have been enacted. Individual states frequently miss these deadlines; when enforcement lags too far behind, the Commission can and does initiate ECJ proceedings against the guilty countries. In 1975, the EU adopted its first equality law, reinforcing Treaty provisions banning pay discrimination (Directive 75/117/EEC). More directives followed in quick succession (see Hubert and Stratigaki in this volume), prohibiting discrimination between the sexes with regard to employment, training, and working conditions, statutory pensions and occupational social security schemes, later access to goods and services. Other directives deal with maternity and parental leave, the rights of self-employed and assisting spouses.

More recently, Directive 2002/73/EC amended the initial Directive 76/207/EEC on the implementation of *equal treatment* for men and women regarding access to employment, vocational training, promotion and working conditions. Directive 92/85/EEC introduced measures to encourage improvements in the safety and health of pregnant workers, employees who have recently given birth and/or are breastfeeding, while Directive 93/104/EC regulates certain conditions involving the organisation of working time. Directive 97/81/EC is linked to the Framework Agreement on part-time work, while Directive 2000/78/EC establishes a general framework for equal treatment in employment and occupation. Directive 79/7/EEC applies the principle of equal treatment to men and women in matters of social security; Directive 86/378/EEC extends protection to occupational social security schemes, while Directive 86/613/EEC addresses self-employment, agricultural work and the protection of self-employed women during pregnancy and motherhood.

Until the 1990s, EU gender policies focused on promoting equality through legislative measures and the strategy of *positive action*. As advanced by the Commission, the European approach was grounded in a notion of formal equality that was to be realised first and foremost at the workplace. However, the classical liberal idea of 'sameness' proved incapable of taking women's specific circumstances and specific needs into account outside the employment arena. The early 1990s brought the first signs that EU gender policies were gradually transcending the narrow realm of employment conditions in favour of a more inclusive approach, thereby rejecting faulty assumptions about 'all things being equal' outside the workplace. This broader perspective became visible by way of the expanding scope of secondary law. Directive 96/34/EC, for example, supplied a framework agreement on parental leave aiming at reconciling work and family matters. For the first time, the EU directly addressed presumably 'private matters', such as childcare. As a 'framework' agreement, this directive set out the main principles, objectives and procedures for the EU's regulatory policy; its scope was substantially expanded compared to other secondary law provisions. A year later, Directive 97/80/EC significantly redefined the 'burden of proof' in cases of discrimination based on sex, making the employer, not the woman, responsible for showing that discrimination had *not* occurred.

Intended to 'modernise' and simplify several older provisions, the Council and the Euro-Parliament approved the so-called Recast Directive (Directive 2006/54) in 2006. Bringing together four previous directives (on equal pay, equal treatment, occupational social security schemes, burden of proof), it regulates the implementation of equal opportunities and the equal treatment of men and women in employment and occupational schemes.

Over several decades, the ECJ has played a crucial role in the *de facto* implementation of gender equality legislation through its many sex discrimination verdicts. Starting with the *Defrenne* v *Sabena* verdict in 1976, the ECJ clearly turned Article 119 EEC Treaty into an 'actionable' right (Case 43/75 ECR 547, 1976). Many cases followed, gradually transforming EU legislation into national practice. In the 1980s, for example, the ECJ held in *Rummler* v *Dato-Druck* that member states had to develop job classification schemes relying on average standards for the work performance of both sexes (Case 237/85 ECR 1201, 1986). As Ostner and Lewis (1995: 170) point out, despite the fact that neither Article 119 EEC Treaty nor the Equal Pay Directive specifically mentioned different forms of discrimination, the ECJ has ruled that the former applies to indirect discrimination as well as to certain practices that produce different outcomes for men and women. In *Bilka* v *Germany* the ECJ ruled that a German department store had engaged in discriminatory practices, in that Bilka excluded part-time employees, mainly women, from its occupational pension scheme (Case 170/84 ECR 1607, 1986). The ECJ held that a company may use its wage policy to minimise part-time employment, but this is only legitimate if the enterprise proves that its measures address a real need and that the policy properly serves such a need. Bilka failed to meet these standards; this verdict marked a significant step in expanding the meanings of discrimination and pay. One of the strongest ECJ verdicts-turned-law involved Tanja Kreil in Germany; in 1998, the ECJ struck down a German constitutional ban on employing women in military units involving the use of combat weapons (*Tanja Kreil* v *Germany*, Case C-285/98).

More than 50 equal-treatment cases have reached the ECJ over the last four decades. In all such cases, its rulings have not only expanded the 'judicial review' powers of the Court itself (despite its male-dominated composition), but also clarified interpretations and extended the reach of existing EU law (for example the 1976 Equal Treatment Directive). It has, moreover, forced all national governments to comply through the mechanism of *direct effect*.

The European reach has been further expanded, and rendered ever more visible, through an increasing reliance on 'soft law', including such instruments such as recommendations, resolutions, formal opinions and Action Programmes on Equal Opportunities (APs). The APs are often used to experiment, subsidise and sort out 'best practices' among evolving EU policies. Nevertheless, it is important to note that *gender acquis* developments have always paralleled trends in 'soft' policy initiatives (Beveridge 2008: 14). Soft law can be defined as 'rules of conduct which, in principle, have no legally binding force but which nevertheless may have practical effects' (Snyder 1993: 198) and operate within a legal scope. *Recommendations* are often used by the Commission to avoid distortions of competition due to the establishment or modification of the internal norms of a member state. Recommendations differ from regulations, directives and decisions, in that they are not binding for all member states. Though lacking legal force, they do carry political weight. A recommendation is an instrument of indirect action geared toward the preparation of legislation in member states (for example, the Code of Practice on Sexual Harassment at Work), differing from a directive only by the absence of obligatory power. At other times, soft law has been used to foster progress even in the absence of a sound legal base, as happened in the case of childcare, which lay outside the Article 119 EEC remit (Beveridge 2008: 14).

Subsequent to 'completion' of the single market and ratification of the 1992 Maastricht Treaty granting the EP co-decision rights in gender matters, new soft law provisions have come into force entailing women's participation in decision-making, childcare and positive action. This period has, moreover, witnessed important discursive shifts, from the old 'discrimination-frame' to a new 'rights-frame', due not least to the increasing number of women in the EP. Building on but no longer restricted to the original 'equal pay' remit, new framing has led to recommendations and resolutions concerning domestic violence, human rights, trafficking in women and sexual violence. Since the mid-1990s, scholars have noted a third stage of EU gender equality politics marked by the introduction of *gender mainstreaming*. This process seeks to integrate a 'gender perspective' into each and every stage of the policy process – design, implementation, monitoring and evaluation – with a view to promoting equality between women and men (see Woodward in this volume).

'Soft law' measures such as APs also 'enabled the Commission to build up a constituency of interested parties, widening its policy agenda and supporting the case for greater competences to be conferred on it' (Beveridge 2008: 14). This was particularly important at times when the Council lacked the political will to further pursue equality issues, as in the 1980s. Successive APs drafted by the Commission clearly delineate the three evolutionary stages of the European gender policy-making (Hoskyns 2000). While AP1 (1982–1985) and AP2 (1986–1990) focused primarily on gender equality in the paid workplace, gender policies under the AP3 (1991–1995) 'moved into a new phase' (Hoskyns 2000: 51). Still utilising an economic perspective, this was the first Community measure to stress a need for reconciling work and family life and for integrating women in decision-making. AP3 incorporated a section on improving women's status in society as a whole. The new spirit implicit in the Action Programme materialised in different forms, resulting in a directive on pregnancy rights, a Commission recommendation on sexual harassment, and a Council recommendation addressing childcare. In contrast to regulations, directives and decisions, recommendations (as well as opinions) are non-binding.

Covering the period 1996–2000, AP4 concerned itself first and foremost with gender mainstreaming, a concentration continued under the AP5 (2001–2006) with its 'capacity building' approach – that is, an attempt to create structures and knowledge essential for the further implementation of gender mainstreaming. The Action Programmes were often accompanied by particular policy projects such as the NOW-programme (New Opportunities for Women), designed to expedite women's integration into the paid workforce, STOP (Sexual Trafficking of Persons), and DAPHNE, a joint action to combat human trafficking and the sexual exploitation of children.

Since 2007 APs have been replaced by PROGRESS, the EU's new employment and social solidarity programme. Gender equality is one of five policy programmes supporting the effective implementation of the Commission Roadmap for Equality between Women and Men 2006–2010, for instance by enhancing the reconciliation of work, private and family life through analysis, by eliminating gender stereotypes in society, by improving legislative implementation, by strengthening gender impact assessment, by promoting gender budgeting and by supporting EU-level networks in developing institutional 'capacities'. The 2006–2010 Roadmap combines the launch of new actions and the reinforcement of successful existing activities. It reaffirms the dual approach of gender equality, which calls for gender mainstreaming in all policy areas as well as for specific measures targeting women.

Since AP3, less emphasis has been placed on legislation and litigation as a means for achieving equality; instead the Commission seems to have settled for the adoption of 'soft law'. While soft law instruments possess little binding force, they still enable the Commission to advance policies going beyond employment (for example gender relations, reproduction, sexuality), slowly crossing the carefully maintained divide between public and allegedly private spheres. Just as importantly, 'soft law' over time often turns into 'hard', secondary law, as in the case of sexual harassment.

The paradigm shift to gender mainstreaming also went along with a new mode of governance developed by the EU. The OMC, first developed in the field of employment, has now also entered centre stage as a key method of governance for the entire social policy domain, both areas having been recognised as crucial for the advancement of gender equality policy (see Hubert and Stratigaki in this volume). Key features of the OMC include a reliance on political rather than legal suasion, a strong element of multilateral surveillance (by the Commission) leading to regular *benchmarking* and time-tables, the use of shared terminology, development of a common knowledge base and the systematic dissemination of knowledge (Beveridge and Velluti 2008b: 3). Thus the OMC allows actors to address policy competences through a range of non-binding measures. In a first evaluation of the OMC effects on gender policies, experts draw a mixed picture (Beveridge and Velluti 2008a): while the OMC seems promising with regard to elite learning, promoting partnership and deliberative modes of democracy, the results have been rather disappointing overall, 'particularly beyond the OMC's role as a propeller or catalyst for innovation' (Beveridge and Velluti 2008c: 197). The OMC has ostensibly been successful in maintaining momentum for policy-making in areas where there are limited interventions by the EU. Yet, as a soft mode of governance, OMC renders political commitment variable and vulnerable to exogenous events like economic recession, for example.

3. Policy-networks and 'agency'

Why have governments adopted gender equality policies at the EU level? Feminists have tried to answer this question first by drawing on the concepts and tools offered by traditional integration theories (see Kronsell in this volume). For example, scholars have used intergovernmentalist and rationalist arguments to explain the inclusion of Article 119 in the EEC Treaty as the result of French interest in levelling the economic playing field, extending national legislation to the European arena (Hoskyns 1996; van der Vleuten 2007). Intergovernmentalism also helps to explain certain innovations in European gender equality policies, for example gender mainstreaming, as a consequence of the accession of Scandinavian countries (Liebert 1999); Eastern enlargement, however, had a braking effect on EU gender equality politics (van der Vleuten 2004). Institutionalists, meanwhile, have described the emergence and development of equality policies as the by-product of path dependency. Along with Wobbe and Biermann (2009), one can argue that the short-term interests of governments in the 1950s (together with norm diffusion) led to unintended long-term consequences, namely a rather progressive EU gender regime. From a supranationalist perspective, the Commission appears to function as an autonomous actor, advancing gender equality by taking advantage of new leverage space opened by the onset of *qualified majority voting* and empirical observations of a gender gap in EU support (Abels 2001; Abels and Bongert 1998; Ellina 2003; Liebert 1999). Studies focusing on the crucial role of the ECJ often draw on 'integration through law' arguments (Cichowski 2001; Flynn 1996; Lundström 1999; Shaw 2000).

While these explanations, related to traditional theories of European integration, help to shed some light on the development of gender equality policies in the EU, a number of feminist approaches go further by focusing on the critical role of agency in the policy-making process (Locher and Prügl 2009: 185). In fact, a closer examination of EU gender policy evolution reveals that the feminist movement has been crucial in placing gender equality on the Community agenda. European gender analyses often draw on social movement theories and 'advocacy networks' (Keck and Sikkink 1998) capable of accounting for the activism of feminist lawyers, advocates and policy-makers.[3] Thus one of the key contributions of feminist approaches to European integration has been to theorise activism, the power of framing and the 'opportunity structures' for advocacy networks activism (Locher and Prügl 2009: 185).

A historical examination of the gender equality field shows that movement activism was crucial in reviving Article 119 EEC Treaty and in broadening the policy agenda (Cichowski 2007; Hoskyns 1996; van der Vleuten 2007). The EWL, an umbrella organisation representing women's associations from all member states, has played a key role in aggregating and coordinating such activism; it has worked strategically to develop a 'transnational feminist interest' (Helfferich and Kolb 2001). New frames and policy innovations have been successfully inserted into EU decision-making processes by activist networks. The introduction of gender mainstreaming provides a good example of how a strategically active network managed to change profoundly the scope and approach of European equality policy (Mazey 2002b). Obviously, such activism faces distinct 'political opportunity structures', shaped by the specific norms, rules and decision-making procedures of the EU as an institution, as well as by the dominant administrative and normative cultures that prevail in its different bodies (Kronsell 2005b). Within these opportunity structures, activists developed new policy frames that, over the years, shifted away from legislation towards 'soft law', while at the same time significantly broadening the scope of gender policies.

Another striking example illustrating feminist understandings of agency in transforming equality policies lies in the emergence of an EU policy on trafficking in women (Locher 2007). A 'velvet triangle'[4] of EU 'femocrats' (that is, feminist-inspired bureaucrats) and feminist politicians, academics and experts, as well as non-governmental organisations came together in a powerful feminist 'advocacy network' to impel trafficking onto the EU's agenda during the second half of the 1990s. Depending on their formal positions, their specific experiences and their personal backgrounds, velvet-triangle actors were endowed with special skills and unique types of knowledge (technocratic, procedural, testimonial); these were successfully combined to advance potent policy frames, using windows of opportunity to generate EU action against female trafficking. Exogenous events, such as the Dutroux scandals in Belgium, opened up a window of opportunity for action,[5] while the EU admission of Nordic states also benefited the cause. Major institutional changes, including the creation of the 'third pillar' covering justice and home affairs along with Amsterdam Treaty provisions, afforded new chances for adding trafficking to the EU agenda. The trafficking case also shows that gender equality frames are normative and changing; their resonance with other norms in the international context (such as human rights or women's rights) facilitates their adoption. International events such as the 1995 United Nation's Conference on Women in Beijing gave these norms credibility and accelerated a trickling-down not only to the national but also to the European level. This study demonstrates the explanatory power of a constructivist, agency-based approach to EU policy-making, as policy change could only occur with the help of changing constructions of gender in advocacy frames, combined with feminist activism.

4. Policy implementation in national gender regimes

While the EU has supplied opportunities for advancing equality, national gender regimes have frequently appeared as obstacles to its implementation (see Figure 4.3). As the last step in the policy cycle, implementation is decisive if gender policies are to have any real impact. EU member states are responsible for enactment; the Commission oversees implementation progress and regularly issues progress reports.

Distinctive national welfare regimes, whether liberal, conservative, or social–democratic (see Esping-Andersen 1990), coupled with their related gender regimes (von Wahl 2005), play a decisive role in explaining divergent implementation practices. Social–democratic regimes. like Sweden, tend to be pioneers in advancing gender equality, while conservative gender regimes such as Germany inadequately enforce EU equality law. National-level institutions upholding the male breadwinner model, coupled with norms espousing 'the family' as care-giver serve as 'the eye of the needle' through which European-level policy prescriptions must pass, which sometimes leads to a distortion of their intent (Ostner and Lewis 1995).

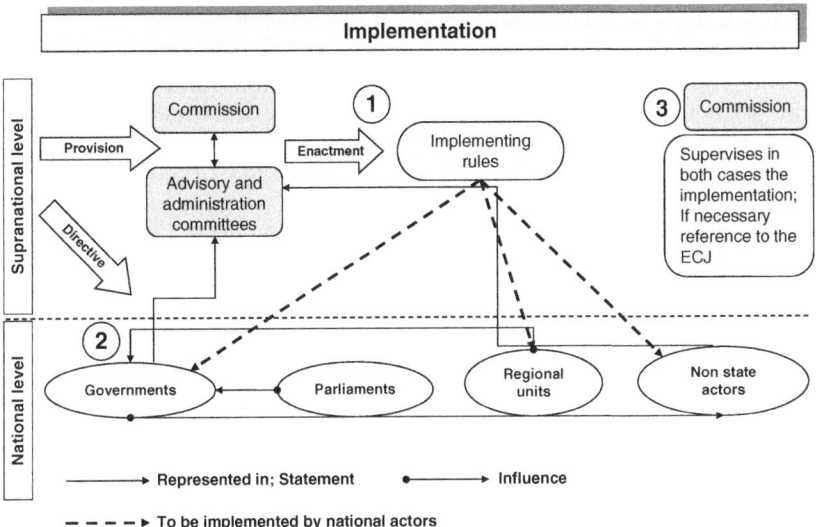

Figure 4.3 Implementation of EU directives
Source: © 2011 agora-wissen (http://www.gesellschaft-agora.de), Stuttgart.

The difficulties vary, depending on the particular member state; as Mazey (1998: 145) points out, 'national policy styles beget a dense "hinterland" of detailed programmes, policies and institutions and it takes very long time for EU institutions and policies to permeate and change this hinterland significantly'. The extent to which EU policies 'fit' or 'misfit' domestic institutions, described from a structural point of view, figures significantly in the speed and/or degree to which EU policy prescriptions are executed (Caporaso and Jupille 2001). The ECJ has played a decisive role in detecting implementation deficits (Berghahn 2002); if member states fail to implement parts of the *gender aquis* within a given period, they can eventually be forced to do so via judicial rulings.

Studies involving this last stage of the policy cycle reveal that the relationship between institutions and activism is crucial for the implementation process, particularly with respect to the use of legal mechanisms in reconstructing gender regimes (Cichowski 2007). Legal pressure from the EU, for example, was decisive in generating a public debate and elite learning in Germany (Berghahn 1998; Kodré and Müller 2003). In other instances, movement activism was the key to implementation, as in Great Britain. When the Major and (to a lesser degree) the Blair Governments opposed social policy initiatives, British feminists joined in the formulation of gender equality norms at the EU level, then mobilised around the domestic implementation of these norms (Sifft 2003). Policy entrepreneurs in advocacy networks often engage in a two-level game, using the EU to advance

80 *Gendering the EU Policy Process*

domestic agendas, in a way that Keck and Sikkink (1998) describe as a 'boomerang pattern'.

The latest EU enlargement process, incorporating 12 Eastern countries, also offers insights on policy implementation practices under national gender regimes (see Galligan and Clavero in this volume; van der Molen and Novikova 2005). The EP, especially its Women's Rights Committee, repeatedly stressed the need for greater efforts to place gender equality issues higher on the agenda during accession negotiations. This demand was supported by the EWL and a substantial number of women's organisations in Eastern and Western countries. Both the EWL and the EP shared a particular interest in promoting an understanding of gender equality extending well beyond the classical liberal approach of non-discrimination. Activists and femocrats hoped that the EU would serve as a strong ally in countering the gender backlash witnessed in most Central and Eastern European countries (CEEC) after the communist collapse (Lohmann 2005). Women's and human rights organisations placed issues such as reproductive rights, access to abortion (most notably in Poland), rights to sexual self-determination, the protection of gay rights and the battle against dramatic increases in sex trafficking high on their agendas. Moreover, activists expected the EU to advance the economic and political rights of women in the CEEC, insofar as the end of communist rule not only swept women out of parliaments and political office but also led to serious deterioration in their economic status (Funk and Müller 1993; Ruminska-Zimny 2002). Despite these efforts, gender issues did not receive much attention during the negotiation process.

During the accession negotiations with the CEECs, gender issues were only dealt with in the context of Chapter 13 (Copenhagen Criteria) and thus were limited to the equal treatment of men and women in employment. National officials preferred to understand 'gender equality' as a specific policy field rather than as a guiding principle for all policy areas. Critical issues such as violence against women and sexual and reproductive rights, as well as trafficking, could hardly be covered within this limited approach to gender equality. Even though annual progress reports for some countries (such as Poland) cited gender equality as 'critical', 'precarious' and as an 'area of concern', no visible consequences ensued.

National case studies report an impressive *de jure* harmonisation of legislation in the candidate countries, but most bemoan the dearth of enforcement and lack of *de facto* policy change. Hungary, for instance, made substantial legal progress during the first stage of accession but produced very limited consequences for political practice.[6] Only in mid-2003, close to the onset of full membership, did a more policy-oriented approach surface, linking the way gender equality issues were handled between Hungary and the EU (Krizsán and Zentai 2006). The 1997 elections In Poland triggered a policy shift towards a 'transitional backlash' against the social and political advancement of women (Titkow 1998: 29). While the Commission's

1999 progress report expressed concern over this development, the Polish government failed to make any progress in implementing women's rights legislation by 2002, a condition that did not slow down the accession process (Bretherton 2002: 9–11). Despite significant feminist mobilisation, organised opposition to EU gender equity law and its close ties to a right-conservative government delayed gender equality legislation (Anderson 2006). By comparison, the Czech Republic witnessed less feminist mobilisation but also little right-wing opposition. That country adopted a gender equity law a year earlier than Poland, but *de facto* enforcement of rights proved to be a problem there as well (see Galligan and Clavero in this volume).

Overall, an impressive degree of feminist activism did take place, but a powerful advocacy network could not be established. At the time of accession there were few 'femocrats' in high EU positions, particularly within the Commission, who could have influenced the design and process of enlargement negotiations. On the other side of the table, civil society organisations in CEEC, women's movements and feminist non-governmental organisations (NGOs) struggled hard to gain access to their national governments, with varied but often limited success (Lohmann 2005). There was a great deal of feminist activism at different levels but no functioning advocacy network that could influence the accession negotiations to advance a more progressive gender equality approach.

In summary, successful implementation of EU gender policies by individual member states depends on a number of enabling factors and mechanisms, including domestic structures, national gender regimes, litigation, elite learning, mobilisation and framing. From a feminist perspective, the interface between institutions, on the one hand, and activism, on the other, seems particularly important for the *de jure* and *de facto* implementation of the *gender acquis*.

5. Implementing gender mainstreaming

As to the implementation of gender mainstreaming, the EU is obviously not a unitary polity. The juxtaposition of EU gender equality policy against its highly gendered labour market policy suggests internal diversity. Taking into account the differential impact of policy on women and men in all domains, gender mainstreaming has made visible the degree to which gender constructions within the EU differ according to issue areas.

Gender mainstreaming has been implemented in a highly uneven fashion. Directorates-General that have 'historically been interventionist in character, and relatively open to consideration of social justice issues' (Pollack and Hafner-Burton 2000: 440) – like the structural funds and DGs charged with employment and development policy – have been very receptive to mainstreaming. By contrast, 'the most strongly neo-liberal' DGs, including those focused on competition policy, have resisted gender mainstreaming. So have

DGs in important areas such as agriculture, environment and transport, and foreign policy (Braithwaite 2000; Woodward 2003: 75). As a matter of fact, one observes significant implementation disparities that might derive from distinct institutional cultures and rivalry norms embedded in different policy fields and issue areas. Labour relations, for example, display very different gender patterns than those observed in agriculture, in manufacturing and in the service sector.

Some member states, however, had already begun to implement gender mainstreaming even before they were obliged to do so, for instance DG Research (see Abels in this volume). Studies suggest that this type of 'soft policy transfer' may be an effect of elite learning (Liebert 2002). Again, the likelihood of gender mainstreaming implementation in national settings seems to depend to a large degree on effective activism as well as on a functioning network of gender advocates that is able to play a two-level game and to translate gender mainstreaming into the domestic setting.

6. Conclusion: Two steps forward, one step backward

Today the EU *gender acquis* consists of an impressive body of legislation and soft law provisions. As this chapter reveals, the EU's gender regime has been constructed in stages, broadening its scope and shifting its focal themes as it drew in new actors. While the EU has emerged as a progressive champion of gender equality from the vantage point of most member states, we must recognise that gender policy development has been neither linear nor without backlash; nor have scholars witnessed a continuous, thorough commitment on the part of all EU institutions to follow new advancements in gender equality. The difficulties in implementing gender mainstreaming across all EU domains, as a general rule for policy-making, clearly underscores that point. Collective reluctance to push for a broader approach to gender equality in the context of Eastern enlargement, along with the failure to assess thoroughly not only *de jure* but also *de facto* implementation in the new (and in many of the old) member states, demonstrates that EU commitment to gender equality is not always as firm as the impressive *acquis* would lead us to expect.

Nonetheless, a closer look at policy-making in the European Union highlights not only the complexity of a multi-level system but also the chances and openings that can materialise, due to the existence of multiple access points in the evolving political opportunity structure. Often the EU provides a 'window of opportunity' for feminist movements that encounter reluctant governments at the national level, and Europeanisation effects have clearly challenged national gender regimes.

Feminist research on gender equality policies insists on the central role of 'agency' during all stages of the policy cycle, conceptualising 'agency' as a decisive variable in explaining both policy-making and policy change

(Locher and Prügl 2009). Very often gender activists have successfully forced new frames and policy innovations onto the EU agenda, as in the case of violence against women, trafficking or gender mainstreaming. Policy formulation often requires outside expertise that advocacy networks are anxious and able to provide. Finally, activists also play a decisive role in implementing EU policies in national contexts – whether in the old or in the new member states. Gender equality policies may be perceived as unintended outcomes from the vantage point of national governments, but not from the perspective of feminist activists.

Discussion questions

- How does policy-making typically take place in the area of gender equality?
- What are the different types of law comprising the EU's *gender equality acquis*? How and why did the strategy of the Commission change concerning the means to advance gender equality policies?
- How have scholars tried to explain the expansion of the EU's gender equality regime?
- What particular obstacles and problems impede the *de facto* implementation of the EU's *gender equality acquis* in diverse national contexts?

Notes

1. The programme name derives from Greek mythology involving Daphne, a pure, innocent young woman pursued by the god Apollo. Desperate to fend off his sexual advances, she called upon her father, the river-god Peneus, to rescue her. When Apollo touched her, she was transformed into a laurel bush (ancient Greek *daphne*).
2. The Lisbon Treaty consists of two parts, one of which is the Treaty on the Functioning of the EU (TFEU).
3. According to Keck and Sikkink, advocacy networks are particular types of networks, characterised by a shared normative goal and commitment. Advocacy networks include very different types of actors, such as international and domestic non-governmental research and advocacy organisations, local social movements, foundations, the media, and parts of the executive or parliamentary branches of governments.
4. Alison Woodward (2004), who first described the 'velvet triangle' phenomenon, refers to the women's movement as the third type of actor. Describing feminist activism in the EU context, academics prefer the phrase 'non-state actors' over 'the women's movement', mainly because the latter has become more formal and professional.
5. In June 1996 Marc Dutroux, an unemployed Belgian electrician, was found to have abducted, tortured, and killed at least seven young girls. The bodies of two young Belgian girls, kidnapped from their Liege homes in June 1995, as well as the bodies of two girls abducted from Ostend, were found on his property. Two other girls, aged 12 and 14, who were kept in a sealed cellar, could be rescued after long weeks of sexual torture. The Belgian public reacted with an unprecedented outcry. The massive 'white marches', the largest street demonstrations in the history of

Belgium, took place in October 1996 to protest government inaction and suspected police corruption. At the peak of the 'white movement', thousands of people gathered in Brussels, protesting just outside the EU buildings. Sexual violence quickly dominated the front page of European newspapers, becoming the centre of public and political attention.

6. The EU's role in the implementation of gender equality policy in Hungary was much less prominent than during the Beijing process, which brought about the development of a national strategy and the establishment of the first Hungarian gender equality agency (Krizsán and Zentai 2006).

5
From Equal Treatment to Gender Mainstreaming and Diversity Management

Alison E. Woodward

If you were a Belgian married woman in 1957, you could not have your own bank account or own property without having titles co-signed by your husband. You just recently started to vote since suffrage rights were first given to women in 1948. If you worked, not only would your salary not go into your personal account, but it would have been significantly lower than that of a man. It would be very unlikely that you had been to university: as late as 1960, women comprised less than 10 per cent of all university students. Your working life would have been shorter, since women were required to retire at 60. Even though the United Nations (UN) established a Commission on the Status of Women in 1946 and the UN Declaration of Human Rights reaffirmed the promise of equal rights for men and women in 1948, most European women remained second-class citizens.

Many of the conditions noted are now against the law. Today statistics on the position of women and men in European Union member states are kept with care, indicating each country's relative progress regarding women's social position. The EU has likewise extended protections developed for gender equality to other groups, as was celebrated during the 2007 Year of Equal Opportunities for all (Howard 2008). 'Gender equality' has become the poster-boy/girl of the European Union, one of the most frequently cited achievements of the Union. The institutions provide documentation, and write their own history in ways that have contributed to the almost mythic status of gender equality as a victory for EU social policy (MacRae 2010). Despite the positive spin, however, statistical studies also make clear that 'gender equality' still lies far ahead, even for the best students in the European class.

A story that lasts more than 50 years is a challenge to tell, and there are as many versions of this story as there are tellers. Thus far you have read about evolving EU structures dealing with gender (van der Vleuten in this volume) and about the policies adding up to a gender *acquis communautaire*

(Locher in this volume). Here the goal is to provide a pathway through a complicated conceptual landscape to help you to understand changing 'strategic approaches' to EU gender policy. Policy develops in context, and the strategies utilised in the European integration process have been shaped by increasing numbers of players, feminist theorising, grassroots organising and a growing transnational focus on gender equality issues.

As seen earlier, EU policy initially viewed women primarily as workers; early policy therefore centred on women's civil and economic rights and legislated *equal treatment*. During the second stage, policy increasingly focused on how to change conditions facing women *as women*, as well as on *positive actions* that could be used to compensate for historical disadvantages, while eliminating structural roadblocks to their progress. A third stage in policy development came to view the relationship between the sexes through a gender lens, applying feminist insights to policy formulation by using the techniques of *gender mainstreaming*. The most recent challenge for the EU is to address differences within groups of women and men, considering intersecting equality issues rooted in age, physical ability, ethnicity, race and sexual orientation. This challenge has to be met in a European Union with 27 member states in a situation of economic crisis. These policy stages, to some extent, parallel developments in feminist thinking and discourse.

1. European integration, economics and gender

There are three things to keep in mind in assessing gender equality policy within the EU context. The first is *the nature of the object of study*. European integration and the Union itself have changed dramatically across a half a century, so that we are consistently studying a moving target. The EU expanded from an arrangement intended to manage energy, coal and steel in six countries to today's unusual type of regional polity that affects a majority of legislation and policy in 27 member states. Spin-offs from EU regulations even affect global trading partners, rendering the question of where 'policy' begins and ends extremely relevant. EU policy-making has become an exercise in multi-level governance (Bache 2007; Conzelmann and Smith 2008; Hooghe and Marks 2001).

The multi-level nature of the 'transposition' (transferring policies to states and regions) is specifically illustrated in the diffusion of gender policy to member states, which some characterise as an example of the Europeanisation process (Liebert 2003a). A regulation hammered out among national actors in Brussels can have a very different impact, depending on the state and local settings evincing divergent gender regimes. Gender equality policy is subject to translation and interpretation, then it is implemented in states with varying histories of compliance with integration rules. The extent to which laws and decisions are successfully enforced depends on a myriad of national actors, lawyers, judges and particular governments.

Whether policies address fundamental structures fostering inequality, such as education, paid work, the household, citizenship and the state, sexuality and cultural institutions, also matters (Walby 1990, 1997). The EU by nature reserves social policy primarily for the member states. However, the demands of the single market have frequently brought social issues onto the EU agenda through a back door, as Leibfried and Pierson (1995; see also Leibfried 2005) suggest. Progress on gender equality issues can sometimes be understood as an example of this back and forth process.

The second analytical problem concerns *writing contemporary European Union history* insofar as the sources themselves are still in flux. Although some documents on EU decisions can be retrieved, actors generally discuss policy in closed committee rooms in Brussels and in the member states. The problem is not a lack of investigation of root causes and effects regarding equality policy, but rather that diverse stories emanate from divergent theoretical perspectives as well as from various types of evidence.[1] Policy is created in a setting that includes actors from many different levels, occupying positions both at the centre and the periphery. Thanks to enlargement, even the definition of centre and periphery has changed.

A third concern is how to identify *the role of developments in society and in feminist thinking as they affect policy-making*. Researchers attempt to link parallels in thinking about gender equality among grassroots actors, academics and policy-makers with different stages in European policy (Hoskyns 1996; Hubert 2001; Mazey 2001). This is a risky undertaking, insofar as 'European' thinking regarding equality and the dynamics of women's movements does not present a coherent picture. Debates in Germany differ significantly from those in Spain, Sweden or France. Just as there is no one 'feminism', so is there no single European women's movement, but rather many strands and interconnections that cannot be neatly restricted to a single moment in time. The heuristic division into 'stages' applied here identifies the main themes reflected in the various approaches to European gender policy, but dividing policy history in slices also does damage to reality. History writing is a question of organisation, and the story of gender policy in Europe is not one that can be neatly divided into streams. As Kronsell notes in chapter one, the different ways of understanding European integration will have an impact on approaches and research questions. This applies to gender equality policy as well.

2. EU approaches to gender equality – The role of feminism and theory

Gender policy development occurs within particular political and socio-economic contexts, involving changing networks of key actors. These can include women's movements, academic feminists, European institutions, national leaders and bureaucrats. Many authors suggest that European gender equality policy has pursued three types of approaches. These approaches follow chronologically but are also ongoing, overlapping with previous measures (Booth and Bennett 2002; Mazey 1995, 2001; Nelen and Hondeghem 2000; Rees 1998; Squires 2007). Today we are witnessing the third 'stage' gradually morphing into a new phase, as intersecting issues of diversity become more important in European law.

The first period (1950s to late 1970s) centred on demands of the liberal, equal rights feminist persuasion (Beasley 1999), seeking for women the same civil and economic rights enjoyed by men. This activism resulted in laws requiring that both sexes be *treated equally* and without discrimination. This approach can be characterised as the *sameness* approach. Feminists argued that women could achieve much more (and be on a par with men) if only the structural roadblocks treating women *differently and thus unequally* were removed. By the early 1970s an international women's movement had joined the struggle, underpinned by a diverse second wave of feminism (Ferree and Hess 2000). Pragmatic, structural analyses of sexism were accompanied by experiences with the civil rights movement in the United States, the United Kingdom and elsewhere. These experiences led to the realisation that equality before the law alone did not result in factual equality (Phillips 1995). Women seeking to achieve equal footing with men needed means to redress structural inequalities of the past in order to deal with their specific situations as women. In this approach we can see influences of radical feminism, which insisted that women evince specific qualities, rendering them 'different' from men. This is sometimes called 'difference' feminism, to underline its divergence from liberal equality feminism.

Affirmative action or positive action, as it is known in Europe, characterises this second set of measures adopted in the 1980s. The underlying logic was that governments cannot remain neutral if the goal is to achieve gender equality. Government must pro-actively combat discrimination and deliberately promote equality by recognising the differences between the sexes and by remedying historical disadvantages through positive measures, for example by fostering the active recruitment of women in places where they have been underrepresented.

The first approach underlines the need for *equal treatment* or formal equality, positing that women are 'basically' the same as men, thus policy should be 'gender neutral'. The second infers that policy has never been 'gender neutral', having always been made by men. Women sometimes require *special treatment*, if substantive equality of outcomes is to be achieved. This paradox is referred to as the *Wollstonecroft dilemma* (Lombardo 2003). These ostensibly paradoxical approaches reflect the debate between equality rights feminists and 'difference' feminists, for whom being measured by the male standards represented a tainted bargain – one that ignored women's specifically positive qualities.

Without really offering a solution to the paradox, the idea that sex is not only a biological issue but also a question of social construction became more accepted over time. Conceptualisation of a new term, *gender*, understood as a relational, socially constructed status had implications for policy. From a gender perspective, equality is not about women alone but implicates women and men together, requiring an examination of the structural factors that underwrite unequal power relationships between men and women. Conceptually speaking, 'gender' rejects a *dichotomy* in favour of a *progression*, recognising grey areas and allowing for the construction of other gendered identities (Butler 1990). Some see the third policy approach, *gender mainstreaming*, as a step towards resolving the paradox between *equal treatment* versus *special treatment* (Squires 2007; Verloo 2006) and providing a platform for dealing discursively with other kinds of inequalities. Thinking about gender as a transversal, relational concept led to the idea that the policy process itself had to be transformed to promote gender equality. Evaluating the effects of day-to-day differences on the lives of women and men at all stages – that is, during policy planning, decision-making and implementation (see below) – might help transform gendered power relations.

3. Stage one: The battle for formal equality, equal rights and equal treatment, 1957–1976

This period spans an important phase in European integration history, as the number of EU members grew from six to nine. 1973 brought in the United Kingdom, a country hesitant to legislate on social affairs; Denmark, a country with a progressive track record; as well as Ireland, a conservative Catholic country. It was also a crucial period for European women's movements, witnessing the rise of more radical forms of feminism and public activism involving a young generation. The link between economic autonomy and equality was underlined by figures such as the French philosopher Simone de Beauvoir, whose book, *The Second Sex* (1949), became a milestone in Western feminism. Creative French thinkers such as Christine Delphy likewise emphasised the economic and socially handicapped positions of women as roadblocks to emancipation. Socialist feminism, which included many British voices, stressed the link between the capitalist order and the oppression of women.

Focusing on removing barriers to economic autonomy as a key to women's liberation was a hallmark of feminist action during this era. Women's chances of achieving economic autonomy were hampered by legal frameworks rooted in social preconceptions confining women to roles as wives and mothers, thus limiting their ability to act independently on the labour market. Marriage bans, early retirement requirements, prohibitions on night work and on (unwanted) pregnancy robbed women of the right to work. Women who believed that equal civil and economic rights would lead to emancipation joined forces with groups who criticised the inherently sexist structure of society. They both aimed to remove formal legal barriers.

Formal equality means *receiving the same treatment in the same situation* (see Box 5.1). Incremental steps towards formal equality involved battles involving several venues (Hoskyns 1996, 2000), many occurring outside of public view. As Locher (in this volume) shows, litigators attempted to expand the reach of Article 119 of the European Economic Community (EEC) Treaty, which guaranteed equal pay; they presented cases before the European Court of Justice (ECJ) – such as that of Sabena stewardess Gabrielle Defrenne, who attempted to secure equal pension rights beginning in 1968. Masselot (2007: 152) argues that the ECJ was the main actor in shaping sex equality law. However, despite court action, national governments stalled and found 'practical' objections to implementing equal pay (Hubert 2001; van der Vleuten 2007).

Box 5.1   Equal treatment – what's that?

Equal treatment refers to the right of all people to receive the same treatment, and not be discriminated against on the basis of criteria such as sex, age, disability, nationality, race and religion. Since 1976 European law (in the form of directives) has guaranteed equal treatment in employment for women and men. The directives on equal treatment have been developed to prohibit both 'direct' discrimination (less favourable treatment) and 'indirect' discrimination (where an apparently neutral provision or practice puts women or men having a particular characteristic such as their sex, religion, belief, physical ability, age or sexual orientation at a disadvantage). Equal treatment is frequently coupled to the idea of equal opportunities. Equal treatment does not necessarily lead to equal outcomes, however.

Source: EuroFound (2011).

Article 119 EEC Treaty in the 1970s was ultimately turned into binding law requiring equal treatment in employment. Thanks to this narrow plank, activists were able to put pressure on other areas related to women's access to paid employment. Committed actors in EU institutions in Brussels and in civil society became more demanding as the Commission was accorded more leeway to work on social issues. The growing significance of women's socio-economic activity was a key contextual factor. Another source working to compel equal treatment in employment rested in the international context. The United Nations pushed for ratification of the Convention on the Elimination of Discrimination against Women (CEDAW) and geared up for a 1975 International Conference on Women in Mexico. This first UN conference was a watershed, bringing together not only comparative data on women's status world-wide but also policy visions and strategies for change. The subsequent UN Decade of Women included conferences in Copenhagen (1980) and Nairobi (1985). International pressure to innovate remained high, providing new venues for networking, coalition formation and the development of interpretive frames (Hawkesworth 2006; Joachim and Locher 2009; Moghadam 2005; True 2003).

The UN required its members to report on their activities, thereby promoting gender equality and forcing governments to be measured against their own rhetoric. This obligation was instrumental in pushing EU states, which resulted in binding legislation to implement Article 119 EEC by way of three equal treatment directives (see Locher, Hubert and Stratigaki in this volume). Although drafting began in 1973, it took ten years to complete the series. Some member states had already advanced beyond the minimum standards; each and every one had to adapt national laws. The UK fought bitterly against social legislation, despite the fact that its women workers were among the most disadvantaged in Europe (Gregory 1987; Walby 1997); here the equality directives became a motor for women's economic 'advancement'. The EU further served as a catalyst for the development of equal opportunities approaches, as was later the case in Italy and Ireland, and eventually in Greece, Spain and Portugal.

While equal treatment legislation helped to level the playing field for women, some criticised the idea that justice should be based on women's comparability to men. There were theoretical as well as practical objections. Using men as the standard against which women were compared was seen as increasingly problematic, as some feminists argued that women had specific and positive differences from men. Women speak, as Carol Gilligan argued, *In a Different Voice* (1982). Treating women the *same* as men under equal treatment sometimes caused women to lose ground, since framing rights in terms of formal equality did not allow for a positive valuing of *difference*. Women had often been permitted to retire earlier, for example, to join (and care for) older husbands. Now they had to wait to retire at the same age as men. Night work, known to be dangerous to health, had been prohibited for most women. This excluded them from profitable overtime but also protected them from the negative consequences of night work. A more just conclusion would have been prohibiting night work for men and women alike, except under unusual circumstances, such as emergency hospital work. Using the male norm to define equal treatment was undesirable as long as being treated 'equally' really meant being treated like a man (Prügl 2007; Rees 1998).

The critique that women were constructed only as 'workers', and thus equal to men without consideration of women's own decisions or other roles, not only prevailed among radical feminists; it was also popular with conservative thinkers such as Hakim (2000), who argued that the EU undermined women's 'choice' to be care-focused rather than career-focused. Even if Rees (1998) described this first stage of equal treatment as essentially 'tinkering' with gender relations, the revision of national sex equality regimes brought about by the directives was, in fact, fundamental. The directives of the 1970s proved to be the iron rod in the backbone of equality. Member states were forced to bring entire bodies of law (ranging from working hours to retirement age) into compliance to ensure equal treatment on the labour market.

4. Stage two: 'Difference' thinking and the growth of policy machinery, 1975–1992

The consolidation of equal treatment provisions opened the door to new approaches, spurred by the work of feminist scholars, femocrats and activists. Stressing the persistence of unequal outcomes for men and women even when conditions were 'equal', activists were increasingly supported by policy-makers inside the state. The UN Decade of Women (1975–1985) pushed countries to establish policy machinery to treat women's issues. The European Commission set up an Equal Opportunities Cell in the Directorate General for Employment, Industrial and Social Affairs in 1976. Within this agency, experts devised policy ideas and legislative proposals. New bodies consisting of female politicians and bureaucrats at the European and national levels, known as 'women's policy machinery' (Abels 2011a), drew expertise from diverse corners of Europe. In 1981, the Commission created an Advisory Committee on Equal Opportunities for Women and Men, funding research and establishing European networks of equality experts. In the same year, the European Parliament instituted its own Standing Committee on Women's Rights, an active watchdog generating data about women's circumstances in member states. Thus by 1982 both the Commission and the European Parliament, two of the EU's most powerful institutions, had women's policy machinery, even if their functions were primarily advisory.

The context became more supportive as increasing numbers of women entered into European decision-making. The Commission started applying positive action targets in relation to its own staff in 1980s (Woodward 1996). The European Parliament (EP) evinced a higher percentage of female members (MEPs) than legislatures in most member states. Civil society organisations grew and changed. Feminist researchers and academics began organising cross-nationally through groups like CREW (Center of Research on European Women), WISE (Women in Science: Europe), AIOFE (Association of Institutions for Feminist Education) and ATHENA (Advanced Thematic Network in European Women's Studies), which ultimately became AtGender in 2009. These efforts received seed money from the Commission to support research on women's issues. Gradually a forum for non-governmental women's groups organised grassroots associations, beginning with the European Network of Women (ENOW). In 1991, the European Women's Lobby (EWL) began to consolidate major national women's federations under a powerful umbrella (see Strid 2010).

Thanks to more intensive European networking and developments within international feminism (Lang 2009), the ambitions for gender equality policy grew. The contrast between the dream and the reality of policy was stark. In some ways, this appeared to be a period of stagnation at the European level in hard law terms (Leibfried 2005: 247), although national actions were proceeding apace. For example, there were clear problems with the application of equal treatment, as seen in the differential treatment of part-time workers. Most part-time workers are female, but these workers were deprived of rights to insurance, pension schemes and protection guaranteed their full-time colleagues. These discriminatory inconsistencies led to proposals for a new directive on part-time work in the early 1980s, but it did not pass until 1997. Another proposal that stagnated was a directive to regulate parental leave, first adopted in 1996.

4.1. New directives and the action programmes

Despite frustration on the legislative front, two achievements stand out during this period, both of which reflected norm changes rather than hard law, providing frames and definitions. The first achievement consisted of a refinement relative to issues of employment that, to some extent, acknowledged some of the specificities of women as workers. Two new directives targeted variations in social security schemes. As Prügl reveals (in this volume), the work of wives on farms and in small enterprises remained invisible, since they were family members, and thus not covered by social protection policies – a perfect illustration of the need to consider the specific conditions of women in equality policy. The activities of farm women had been deemed the natural role of wives rather than as 'work'; consequently, female partners possessed no workers' rights. Another directive in 1992 attended to the health of pregnant workers and young mothers. ECJ decisions during this period began to acknowledge differences between men and women as labourers, even if they avoided calculating the impact of unpaid and family work on the substantive equality of women and men.

The second achievement stemming from this era involved the reconceptualisation and intensification of activities affecting gender roles beyond the 'simple' guarantee of equal treatment. In 1984, a Council recommendation foresaw 'the promotion of positive action' (see Box 5.2) for women (Council 1984). The feminist reasoning was that structural and material issues impede women's ability to compete equally on the labour market. To achieve substantive equality, they needed targeted measures to redress previous disadvantages. This called for extra investment in building up women's job skills and training them to be more assertive at the work place, for example, while sensitising employers to women's special contributions. *Positive action* (in the United States, *affirmative action*) entailed a major shift in policy norms, acknowledging women's specificity instead of simply comparing them to men. Measures ranged from training programmes to targeted hiring practices, actively recruiting the under-represented sex. As in the United States, positive action approaches remain controversial, conflicting at first glance with the idea of equal treatment, which considers women and men basically 'the same'.

Box 5.2   What is positive action?

Positive action refers to measures targeted at a particular group to redress injustice or to offset disadvantages arising from past inequalities. Actions may include initiatives such as the introduction of preferential selection and recruitment procedures, training programmes or policies for preventing sexual harassment. 'It has the purpose of achieving full and effective equality in practice for members of groups that are socially or economically disadvantaged or otherwise face the consequences of past or present discrimination or disadvantage' (European Commission DG EMPL 2009: 6). The ECJ uses the expression *preferential treatment*, while *affirmative action* is common US usage. The term finds its roots in the US and UK civil rights legislation of the mid-1960s.

The EU explicitly allows pro-active measures to combat discrimination. Under the Treaty of Amsterdam (1997), Article 141.4 of the EC Treaty reads:

> With a view to ensuring full equality in practice between men and women in working life, the principle of equal treatment shall not prevent any Member State from maintaining or adopting measures providing for specific advantages in order to make it easier for the underrepresented sex to pursue a vocational activity or to prevent or compensate for disadvantages in professional careers.

Initiated in the mid-1980s, the Medium Term Community Action Programs for Equality between Women and Men (APs) became important instruments, allowing the Commission to sponsor actions designed to create 'equal opportunities for women and men'. Each AP, ranging from three to five years in length, contained expanding notions of what could be considered suitable terrain for governmental equality measures. The lobbying around the content and wording of these programmes succeeded in subtly stretching the frame beyond the limitations of paid employment. The APs demonstrated that outcomes in paid employment are related to many other factors defining the position of women and men. These range from educational opportunity to the organisation of personal lives and the sex composition of decision-making bodies. Action programmes both promoted improvement in the legal framework (thanks to their recommendations and resolutions) and built capacity for women's participation in international policy networks. Specific investment went to stimulating the growth of transnational expertise in women's issues and research on women in decision-making. Participation in Europe-wide consultations acted as a two-way street, bringing information into the Commission and building awareness and expertise with the European stamp of prestige in the domestic setting.

The Second AP (1986–1990) established three expert networks dealing explicitly with employment and the equality directives. Subsequent programmes went even further, creating expert networks investigating banking, business, broadcasting, childcare, education, justice, science and decision-making in a number of sectors, as well as families and work–life issues. Names figuring in the networks and in many of the reports amounted to a 'who's who' among gender equality strategists in Europe. The APs provided seed money for establishing transnational contacts among women researchers and activists. During this time, the *Women of Europe Newsletter* shared crucially comparative knowledge about the situations of women across countries, while introducing experts and researchers working on these questions to each other. Contrasting European experiences stimulated debate and opened eyes to the diversity of women's experiences as well as to the significance of policy in changing women's positions.

4.2. Moving beyond sameness and difference into gender

Rees (1998: 62) describes the first two APs as primarily focused on positive action, addressing women's differences. Drafting the third AP (1991–1995) pushed the envelope, making gender equality a broader part of all Community policies and expanding the net to include female participation not only in economic, but also in social life. Structural factors inducing gendered inequality came to the forefront, reflecting debates in the broader feminist community. Equality policy evolved rapidly through the 1980s, thanks to debates among female activists and scholars across national boundaries. Women's Studies departments were established at many universities (Bird 1996), providing a research incubator for policy ideas.

The EU brought together French, Scandinavian, German and British feminists, along with their cross-cutting and competing traditions, through international conferences and policy consultations. Their debates over the 'logic' of equality policy, for whether it was better to emphasise 'sameness' or 'difference', had an impact on goals and content. 'Difference' feminists underlined aspects of women's unique nature and demanded parity (at least

50 per cent) in decision-making and in society. English translations of French theoretical works by Luce Irigary and Helene Cixous expanded their impact on the development of the difference perspective. 'Equality' feminists looked to structural and economic contributors to women's oppression, focusing on ways to replace barriers with equal opportunities. Some reacted to positive action approaches, arguing that they pushed women into the role of 'victims' needing help, rather than underlining female positive potential.

The concept of 'gender' also gained currency during this period. The most progressive actors underlined the *construction* of inequality in inter-relational terms: the issue was not equal opportunities between men and women, but rather gender inter-relations, which implicated *both* men and women. 'Gender' equality activists sought to go beyond 'women' and beyond the labour market, to attack policy transversally for producing unequal relations between men and women. The seeds of this approach, containing elements of both difference feminism and equality feminism, were planted in the third AP. During the 1990s, the policy consequences of conceiving the equality problem in terms of gender became evident in the gender mainstreaming approach.

5. Stage three: Transformation through gender mainstreaming, 1992–2005

Institutional and contextual developments shaping the EU, including enlargement, societal changes and new academic conceptualisations of women as civil society actors, rendered this a period of dramatic policy change, as the Union increased from 9 to 25 members. New Treaties signed in Maastricht and Amsterdam introduced *EU citizenship* and a Social Protocol that supplied a broader legal basis for policy prohibiting discrimination on the basis of sex, age, belief, ethnicity and race, disability and sexual orientation. Transnational actors such as the Social Platform and the EWL were consolidated during this period (Cram 2006). Nearly half of all existing EU legislation pertaining to gender equality issues was either adopted or significantly amended after 1992. Today this legislation (re)configures the lives and opportunities of 500 million people.

The debate continued to rage over the most appropriate methods for attaining gender equality. The equality concept reflected in ECJ decisions was criticised as too androcentric, relying on male behaviour as the standard women were expected to meet. In discrimination cases the court required a comparison (to show that women were treated 'differently'). Equal opportunity and equal treatment policies had not sufficed to deliver substantive equality, as summed up in the slogan '*De jure* does not equal *de facto*'. Urging women to become 'more like men' was questioned as a model. Moreover, it became clear that formal equality could sometimes produce further inequalities in practice, for example by requiring formal certification for jobs where educational opportunity for female candidates was unavailable. The notion of *indirect discrimination* from the United States crossed the Atlantic (Gregory 1987).

The international debate increasingly underlined the diversity among women within and across countries. For Europe, discussions about new policy approaches, in anticipation of the 1995 UN Beijing Conference on Women, became intertwined with preparations for the Amsterdam Treaty. EU member state actors were also involved with activities within the broader Council of Europe based in Strasbourg.[2] This body brought together both EU countries and former socialist regimes, with special commissions working on gender equality and democracy. European feminists featured prominently in preparations for the UN Conference. The limited success of equal treatment and positive action approaches in many countries had motivated the UN Platform of Action to move beyond equality questions, to transform 'doing policy' in ways accounting for gender differences and promoting equality. Stemming from experiences in the development and disability fields, the call for the UN conference launched 'gender mainstreaming' as a cornerstone technique for fulfilling Platform for Action goals in all social arenas. It demanded that policy be assessed in terms of its impact on gender relations, by examining the position of women and men in all policy domains, in order to improve human well-being. Although the aim of making all policy contribute to gender equality through mainstreaming was clear, ways to achieve this had to be worked out by government institutions at different levels.

The EU had begun searching for a horizontal approach to equality issues in policy arenas beyond employment and family in its third AP. These international encounters united activists in the European space, including Council of Europe representatives and national actors, around a mission extending beyond equal opportunity programmes – in the hope that all policy sectors could be addressed in gender terms.

The Commission (1996) adopted gender mainstreaming as its official strategy in a 1996 communication. It first attempted to use this tool officially alongside other equality policies such as affirmative action, known as the *dual track* approach. Advocates argued that women's specific problems still needed targeted attention, although it was premature to try to transform the relations between men and women in all areas. Some feared that, as a result of focusing on gender mainstreaming, 'women's' problems would be ignored. Thanks to international obligations, coupled with declared objectives of the Amsterdam Treaty (enacted in 1999), the policy machinery devoted to monitoring gender equality in the Commission grew, as the Fourth (1996–2000) and Fifth (2001–2005/2006) APs were

98 *From Equal Treatment to Gender Mainstreaming*

approved. Gradually, a standard working definition was adopted in manuals for gender mainstreaming at the European institutions, building on input from national experts, the Commission and the Council of Europe (see Box 5.3):

Box 5.3   What is gender mainstreaming?

A Commission strategy since 1996, gender mainstreaming has been widely adopted by European governments at all levels. Gender mainstreaming systematically assesses the implications of any planned action to ensure that all policies contribute to gender equality. Starting with the policy planning stage and proceeding through the policy cycle, the aim is to evaluate policy effects in all policy areas by using a gender perspective. To implement mainstreaming, actors have developed different policy instruments, including gender equality indicators, ways to gender test policy proposals through impact assessment procedures and gender budgeting. Research grants stimulate comparative projects on how gender mainstreaming is applied. The approach was communicated to Central and Eastern European countries preparing to join the EU as part of the common *acquis*.

Thinking transversally about the equality problem in gender terms and using better legal tools provided in the Treaties was important in spreading the equality effort beyond labour market issues. While efforts to improve women's position as workers continued, new programmes addressed violence against women, trafficking, the position of women in research and gender issues in development policy. The implementation of gender mainstreaming is supposed to include four elements: (1) measurement and monitoring, which means finding out what the situation of women and men is in a specific policy area; (2) implementation, which generally implies policy analysis assessing the implications of an intended policy for gender relations and aiming to improve them; (3) creating awareness, ownership and understanding among stakeholders, to improve policy-making in the future; and (4) gender-proofing and evaluation, to determine the extent to which intended policies have had gendered effects (European Commission, DG Employment 2008: 11). Subsequent chapters in this volume offer specific examples as to how gender mainstreaming works in practice (see Table 5.1). Some critics note that the further away a policy is from a European 'social' dimension, the more difficult gender mainstreaming has been to implement (Hafner-Burton and Pollack 2009; Woodward 2008). The strategy has been accepted by governments at all levels in the European Union, however, and the experience is extremely diverse.

Table 5.1 Gender mainstreaming proposals of the European Commission

Steps	Requirements
Step 1 *Evaluation of gender relevance*	Requires analysis of *sex-disaggregated data* Q1 Does proposal concern one or more target groups? Will it affect daily life of part(s) of population?
	Q2 Are there differences between men and women in this policy field? If answer to either Q1 or Q2 is *positive*, then gender *is* relevant to the issue, and systematic gender impact assessment should be undertaken.
Step 2 *Gender impact assessment according to several criteria*	Criteria for gender impact assessment include: • participation • resources • norms and values influencing gender role • rights and access to justice
Step 3 *Implementation of results; mainstreaming respective policy*	How can the proposed policy contribute to eliminating gender inequalities and promote objectives of equality between men and women?

Source: European Commission (1997).

6. Stage four and counting? The challenges of intersections and diversity

Although the years approaching the new millennium saw many milestones, observers checking the distance between ambitions and delivery became more cautious as to the actual state of EU gender policy and equality outcomes. The late 1990s formed a kind of a peak: many constellations came together, and diversity *among* women was recognised. Transnational social actors undertook concerted action, and social ambitions became an accepted part of the European mission, enshrined in the Treaties, the work on the Constitution and the Lisbon goals. However, Union enlargement in 2004 and 2007, coupled with changing economic realities, has recently led some to fear that gender equality is under attack. Maria Stratigaki (in this volume) traces the reframing of work–family policy to focus on 'women only' rather than on gender (that is, on men's roles). Jane Jenson (2008) claims that welfare has been 'LEGO-ised', centring more on the child than on gender relations.

Besides reframing issues in ways that sideline women or put them back into 'families', one very serious challenge lies, paradoxically, in the achievements of the Amsterdam Treaty. Many hailed this Treaty as a victory for equality issues insofar as Article 13 prohibits discrimination on the grounds of sex, racial or ethnic origin, religion or belief, disability, age or sexual orientation. It explicitly outlawed different forms of discrimination and obligated member states to undertake measures to combat it; it was incorporated into the Lisbon Treaty as Article 10 TFEU.

To turn theory into practice, the Commission established a special unit to deal with anti-discrimination on grounds other than gender, thus structurally excluding gender from the new action arena. Gender equality staff succeeded in maintaining a separate set of offices to support legal and programmatic work on gender equality; this might be seen as a pyrrhic victory, frequently leading to the marginalisation of gender in discussions conceptualising and promoting policy to further equality work. The new anti-discrimination frame is similar to the equal treatment approach characterising the early years of equality work. Some argue that gender mainstreaming moves beyond mere equal treatment (Squires 2007; Woodward 2008), while the anti-discrimination framework seems like a step backward for gender. Different elements of personal identity that might intersect, compounding discrimination (Verloo 2006), have been hard to include in the new framework. Despite intensive work on new legal frameworks designed to capture the intersection of various sources of inequality—to overcome the problems of a single-strand approach only focusing on sex, or race, or age (Bagilhole 2009)—there is still no new directive.

Developments in 2011 have moved multiple equality issues, mentioned in the Treaty on the EU (TEU) and elaborated in the Lisbon Treaty or Treaty on the Functioning of the EU (TFEU), away from their old home in the Directorate-General for Employment, Social Affairs and Inclusion (DG EMPL), to the more judicially focused Directorate-General on Justice, Fundamental Rights and Citizenship (DG Justice). The Lisbon Treaty's incorporation of the Charter of Fundamental Rights should improve conditions for equality activists focusing on race and sexual orientation, but there is other mixed news: the term 'equal opportunities' is no longer included in the title of *any* offices of the European Commission. DG EMPL has dropped the title and replaced this with 'Inclusion'. It is too early to judge the extent to which the new site for equality activities will focus on 'rights' rather than 'action'.

Another indicator of the changing status of equality issues is the demise of the AP approach in favour of the Roadmap for Equality (2006–2010; see Commission 2006), which was followed by an even weaker sounding *Strategy for Equality between Women and Men* (2010–2015). These developments are seen as harbingers of declining opportunities for gender equality (Ahrens 2008; Stratigaki 2008). Without hard incentives, Hafner-Burton and Pollack (2009) argue, concrete progress towards gender-sensitive policy will become more difficult. The territorial gains achieved in comprehending the roots of inequality and in formulating public policies to redress them seem to some to have been lost. Today we frequently hear 'equality between women and men' rather than the term 'gender'. Name changes often entail changes in substance. These, as well as shifting venues – that is, moves to other Directorates General – are not merely symbolic, as Lombardo et al. (2009) argue. Such changes hold serious ramifications for future possibilities and activities.

Projections for the future are mixed. Can a supranational polity like the EU really reconfigure gender relations through policy? Policies to date have not addressed many structural roadblocks, including problems of economics and social class (Duncan 1996a). Gender watchdogs in civil society and academia still have a crucial role to play. Even on the employment front, critical observers note the decline of gender issues as a top priority (Plantenga et al. 2007). New competition from other sources of inequality, and the strange structural constellation that puts gender in one box and all other inequalities in another, reduce gender's place. Enlargement raises questions as to whether new members of the European Club will support equality initiatives, leading to further caution about the future.

7. Conclusion

Our typical Belgian married woman is no longer in the same place she occupied in 1957, thanks to European integration. She joins sisters living in 26 other countries that have also ratified EU Treaties guaranteeing equal treatment and promising to promote gender equality. Looking back, one can conclude that much has happened for the better. Parental leave was mandated in 1996; protection for part-time workers expanded (1997); and equal treatment requirements have been revised and recast (2006) under a broad directive mandating equal treatment not only in employment but also for goods and services. Gender equality was proclaimed a major EU success during the EU's 50th anniversary celebrations (2007). It led the parade as an example for other dimensions of ascriptive equality during *The 2007 Year of Equal Opportunity for All* (2007). As icing on the cake, a new piece of policy machinery, the European Institute for Gender Equality in Vilnius (Lithuania), was opened in 2007.

The social and economic distance between men and women has decreased dramatically, yet Europe's women still receive lower wages than men (on average 16 per cent less) – despite the fact that equal pay was a cornerstone of the first European treaty. Women have made substantial inroads into politics, now constituting 35 per cent of the European Parliament members; across Europe women comprise 24 per cent of the (first chamber) representatives in their national legislatures.[3] Some national governments even boast of having reached parity among governing ministers (Sweden, Spain). Still, women remain underrepresented in other arenas of socio-economic decision-making, for example business leadership (European Commission, DG Justice 2010).

Concerted efforts to re-think the problems of child-rearing when both parents are employed have led to substantial improvements in childcare access even in conservative countries, thanks to European guidelines. Yet many women 'choose' to remain childless or have fewer children than they wish (Commission 2008a). The conditions of the 1950s seem light years away. Younger women might feel that gender equality can be dropped from the agenda, not recognising that oppressive gender contracts remain comfortably intact in many countries (Prügl 2007; Stratigaki 2008): women supply the care, men enjoy their services.

Our understanding of what equality can and should mean in Europe has evolved thanks to women's activism, advances in gender theory, European enlargement, better statistics and more critical analysis. There is still much to be done: the goals of bodily integrity, of being able to profit from meaningful work, and of enjoying complete social and political equality have not yet been attained for many of Europe's women. European gender realities cover the spectrum from Malta in the South to Finland in the North, from Romania in the East to Ireland in the West. European integration provides a living laboratory for how cultures, policy and activism can redefine and alter gender relations. Thanks to this learning laboratory, European Union experiences can provide ammunition for other countries that still have a longer way to go in changing gender relations, while raising new questions about the right way to proceed in Europe itself.

Discussion questions

- Equal treatment is a fundamental right guaranteed in European Law. However, many EU policies on gender equality take a different track. What are some of the reasons why women's activists felt that equal treatment was not enough to produce real equality?
- What are some of the major challenges encountered in dealing with all grounds for discrimination and social equality issues within the same policy office?
- Which period or stage of gender equality policy development in the EU would you judge to have been the most effective? What forces do you think were important in allowing for concrete progress in gender equality issues?

Notes

1. Hoskyns (1996) provides an actor-driven description, linking policy decisions and national considerations, while van der Vleuten (2007) supplies an international relations perspective and Rees (1998) a practitioner–policy-maker approach. For the most recent in-depth treatment of gender equality policies, see Kantola (2010a).

2. Founded in 1949, the Council of Europe consists of 47 member states, stressing respect for fundamental values including human rights. It should not be confused with the European Council (of Ministers) linked to the EU.
3. For most recent data on the representation of women in EU institutions and the member states, see European Commission (2008a).

6
Gendering Enlargement of the EU
Yvonne Galligan and Sara Clavero

Originally starting in the 1950s with a membership of only six countries (Germany, France, Italy, the Netherlands, Belgium and Luxembourg), the European Union (EU) has substantially enlarged its membership in each decade since the 1970s to 27 members today – with the likelihood of more to come in the next decade. The process of enlargement began with the incorporation of Denmark, Ireland and the United Kingdom into the European Economic Community in 1973, followed by Greece (1981), Spain and Portugal (1986). In a third 'wave' of expansion, Austria, Finland and Sweden became members of the European Community (EC) in 1995. Cyprus, Malta and eight countries of Central and Eastern Europe brought the total EU membership to 25 nations in 2004; they were subsequently joined by Romania and Bulgaria, admitted in 2007. By 2010, three further countries had secured 'candidate' membership status and were actively negotiating to become members of the EU: Croatia, the Former Yugoslav Republic of Macedonia and Turkey. In addition, six other countries, the majority from the Balkan region along with Iceland, were recognised by the EU as potential candidates. Each stage of enlargement has required the countries seeking membership to adopt, transpose and implement the complete body of European law, policies, jurisprudence and practices known as the *acquis communautaire*, in force at that point in time (Iankova and Katzenstein 2003: 272).

This has not been a straightforward process, as national compliance with EU legislative and policy requirements has varied widely, while monitoring and sanctioning non-compliance belongs to the core functions of the Commission and the European Court of Justice (Börzel 2003: 197–220). We argue that the incorporation of gender directives and gender equality policies has been one point on which national and European ambitions have diverged. That European policies on equal opportunities prevail over national law has often been to the benefit of women. Over time, measures to address direct and indirect gender discrimination have informed the treaty and enlargement processes. Today candidate countries must demonstrate commitment to, and progress on, equal opportunities between women and men in the accession process as part of the requirements for EU membership.[1]

In this chapter we discuss the dynamics of gender law harmonisation during the first, second and third 'western' enlargement periods, before turning to the varied experiences of Eastern European countries in bringing national gender laws into conformity with EU requirements. We also refer to the post-Lisbon Treaty scenario for gender equality. The final section reflects on the impact of enlargement on shaping national gender relations frameworks.

1. The founding of the Union and gender equality

The harmonisation of trade relationships, the core impetus for the creation of the European Economic Community (EEC), brought nation–states into closer co-operation and instigated a particular form of supra-national governance. As other experts have noted (see van der Vleuten and Woodward in this volume), the cornerstone of the EU corpus of gender equality policies resides in Article 119 of the 1957 Treaty of Rome providing 'equal pay for equal work'. Modestly constructed as a provision to enable the harmonisation of labour costs in the interests of equalising economic competitiveness (Hoskyns 1996: 49; Warner 1984: 142–143), Article 119 would provide the anchor for the subsequent development of nearly all gender equality policies in the European Union through the 1990s.

In 1960, a progress review encompassing the first stage of economic integration (internal tariff reduction among the six member states) highlighted the lack of action on equal pay as a barrier to further progress in developing an internal market. This finding prompted the Commission to nudge member states towards implementing Article 119. The problem was rendered more urgent by France's unwillingness to proceed to the next phase of common market creation without commitments from the other countries on equal pay (Hoskyns 1996: 60–63). A non-binding resolution on the enforcement and implementation of equal pay was formally adopted by the member state governments in 1961, to facilitate the next phase of economic integration. It set the end of 1964 as the deadline for implementation. As the deadline came and went, the Commission reported that application of Article 119 remained incomplete in each country, Belgium and the Netherlands being particularly slow in advancing the implementation process (Warner 1984: 143–144). The Commission then undertook the first comparative analysis of male and female earnings across the six states, which showed that in the early 1970s the gender pay gap ranged from 25 per cent in Italy to 46 per cent in Luxembourg (European Commission 1973: 38). This finding points to the uneven implementation of equality policy, even in its most restrictive form, characterising the European integration project from its early days.

Subsequently, strike action by working women, coupled with case-law development in the European Court of Justice (ECJ), gave focus and

106 *Gendering Enlargement of the EU*

Table 6.1 European enlargements

Belgium, France, Italy, Luxembourg, Netherlands, West Germany (founding members)	25 March 1957
Denmark, Ireland and United Kingdom	1 January 1973
Greece	1 January 1981
Spain and Portugal	1 January 1986
East Germany	3 October 1990
Austria, Sweden, Finland	1 January 1995
Cyprus, Czech Republic, Estonia, Hungary, Latvia, Lithuania, Malta, Poland, Slovakia, Slovenia	1 January 2004
Bulgaria and Romania	1 January 2007

Source: http://europa.eu/abc/history/index_en.htm (accessed 6 January 2011).

substance to the equal pay provisions (Hoskyns 1996: 60–96; Kantola 2010a). The EEC's overall commitment to the realisation of gender equality during the early period lagged considerably behind that of other international bodies, such as the International Labour Organisation and the United Nations, however. It took the Community's first enlargement (see Table 6.1) from six to nine member states, a fresh Commission commitment to social policy (as a way of building public support), the activism of individual women committed to equality within the Commission, along with support from an active women's group in the newly formed European Trade Union Confederation to improve conditions for the creation of a substantial framework of supra-national laws and policies focusing on gender equality (Defeis 1999; Reinalda 1997: 208–214).

2. The first enlargement, 1973

The admission of Denmark, Ireland and the United Kingdom to the European Economic Community ended a protracted period of negotiation that had initially opened in1961.[2] Although no specific criteria existed at the time for applicant countries seeking EEC entry, the relative economic impoverishment of Denmark and Ireland prompted the Community to initiate a special assistance policy in the form of the European Regional Development Fund. This policy supplied funds to both countries in order to reduce the economic disparities between them and the better-off member states. Significantly for our purposes, this enlargement paralleled the first real effort to deepen European commitments to gender equality, framed at the time as 'equal opportunities', and focused on anti-discrimination in employment (see Woodward in this volume).

Women in Ireland mobilised to take advantage of European membership and to press their claims for equal pay in particular and for gender equality more generally (Galligan 1998: 69–79). In Denmark an agreement to introduce equal pay in the private sector was reached in 1973,[3] following campaigns initiated by women in trade unions, although it would take another three years for the law to come into effect (Siim 1993: 38). In Britain, the equal pay question was addressed prior to accession, legislation having been introduced by the Labour government in 1970 and further improvements in women's wages having already been addressed by trade unions (Chamberlayne 1993: 176). In each of the three states, the implementation of European Community rules on gender equality in employment led to the establishment of state equality bodies as part of the transposition of the equal opportunities directives.

The combined efforts of highly placed Commission officials individually committed to gender equality, pressure from women's movements pressure at the national and European levels and early Court of Justice rulings led to significant law and policy-making on gender equality from the 1970s into the 1980s (Meehan 1993b: 196). The directives on equal pay for work of equal value (75/117/EEC), equal treatment in the workplace (76/207/EEC) and equal treatment in social security (79/7/EEC) comprised the first group of equal opportunities directives. These were followed by equal treatment in private occupational pension schemes (86/378/EC) and by equal treatment of women with men in self-employment, including agriculture (86/613/EC). They were complemented by a policy supporting women's employment in the newly created European Social Fund (77/804/EEC). These legal and policy initiatives, intended to reduce inequalities in employment and social security protection between women and men, required a legislative and administrative response by national governments. This included the creation of equal opportunities agencies to monitor implementation. As Mazey (1995: 598) notes, it was unlikely that national governments, if left to their own devices, would have addressed employment-based equality issues without EU pressure.

The degree of member state compliance varied with the political, cultural and legal environment in each country, as did the lobbying effectiveness of women's movements. Due to the multiple levels of decision-making in that country's federal system, for instance, women's groups in Germany faced more obstacles in seeking to influence the political agenda than their Irish counterparts, who tried to influence national government directly, in a highly centralised state. Germany accorded low priority to the transposition of the employment directives, insofar as equality provisions in the national constitution were deemed sufficient to provide substantive protection for women (Hoskyns 1996: 118–119). Ireland, in contrast, aligned its national law on equal pay and equal treatment to the European directives as part of its preparations for accession, though even in this instance implementation of the equal pay directive was hotly contested at the national level (Galligan 1998: 69–79). Meehan (1993b: 198) notes that Denmark and Britain had to recognise the principle of equal value (defined as comparable worth) in their national equal pay laws arising from ECJ verdicts. In the UK, a parsimonious response from the Thatcher-led Conservative government regarding amendments to the Sex Discrimination Act led to considerable domestic political tension. Additional infringement proceedings against the UK were subsequently initiated by the European Commission (Duina 1999; van der Vleuten 2007).

National implementation of the social security directives also diverged. They faced a relatively unproblematic transposition in Germany, largely because the social security system was already undergoing reform in response to Constitutional Court findings. In addition, the federal ministry (Youth, the Family and Health) charged with enforcing social security legislation saw its size and remit increased under a social democratic government (Hoskyns 1996: 120, 122). In the Netherlands and Ireland, harmonisation of national law in accordance with the Community's social security directive proved especially turbulent. The crux of the problem lay with the national application of the directive to married women in ways that discriminated against them in comparison to unmarried women, as well as to married and unmarried men. In each case, conservative cultural perceptions of married women's proper role and status in society underlay the formulation of national legislation. In both instances, the European Court of Justice (ECJ) ruled in favour of upholding the equality provisions. In the Dutch case,[4] the Court ruled that national law was discriminatory in denying married women a right to claim unemployment benefits, unless the wife in question could prove that she was the 'main breadwinner'. In the Irish case,[5] the Court ruled that the 1985 social security reforms enacted by the government likewise discriminated against married women. It clarified the directive's 'fundamental principle', affirming that married women were entitled to the same level of unemployment and pay-related social security benefits as men and single women (Curtin 1988: 17–22).

Overall, this first phase of enlargement laid down the requirement for national governments to incorporate the full spirit of European provisions on gender equality. The ECJ's role as the enforcer of the directives, coupled with the power of individuals and organisations to seek national compliance, were important instruments in setting this obligation. It became clear that transposing the *gender acquis* would bring national political cultures into conflict with supra-national efforts to impose community-specific gender norms, as well as laws and practices relating to the implementation of gender equality. This clash of law and cultures continues today.

3. The second enlargement: Mediterranean states, 1981 and 1986

The admission of Greece, followed by Spain and Portugal, to the European Economic Community brought international recognition of the new democratic order in these countries. Their interest in fostering closer ties with the Community can nonetheless be traced back to 1957 in the case of Spain (De la Guardia 2004: 95–96), to 1961 in the Greek case and to 1969 with respect to Portugal (Elvert 2004: 195–196). Authoritarian leaders in Spain (Franco) and Portugal (Salazar) found it in the interest of their countries to develop links with the EEC. Greece's path to membership, interrupted by a period of military dictatorship (1967–1974), was resumed upon restoration of civilian democratic rule, culminating in its 1981 accession (Elvert 2004: 200–201). Spain and Portugal began accession negotiations in 1978, a process that resulted in their simultaneous admission in 1986. Not surprisingly, this enlargement served a political as well as an economic purpose. The candidate countries were required to uphold civil and political rights and to commit to pluralist democracy in their respective accession acts, a condition not demanded of the first enlargement states.[6] The three Mediterranean states were expected to implement the *acquis communautaire* in full, though negotiations resulted in a more flexible period of transition than had applied to the first enlargement.

Regarding the adoption of European laws on gender equality, these countries were arguably faced with bigger challenges than those prior to the first enlargement round. Indeed, the body of EC legislation pertaining to equal opportunities was already significantly larger than in the early 1970s; it included two additional directives, one on equal treatment in employment and vocational training and the other in social security.[7] Further, since these candidate countries were culturally more conservative and less secularised compared to the liberal ones comprising the first enlargement wave (with the exception of Ireland), there were doubts at the time about their capacity to comply successfully with these EU norms, laws and policies.

Thus the implementation challenges regarding the *acquis* for the new Mediterranean members were considerable. Iankova and Katzenstein (2003: 279) point to the particular difficulties encountered by Greece, despite a seven-year transition period. The Greek pattern of slow, haphazard implementation contrasts with that of Spain, where the Community *acquis* was implemented methodically and without delay (Iankova and Katzenstein 2003: 282; Valiente 2003: 191). The Spanish enthusiasm for Europe, along with the influence of the women's movement, demands for equality across the political spectrum and gender-friendly Spanish jurisprudence, made harmonisation with the *acquis* relatively straightforward (Threlfall 1997: 18–19). Greece, on the other hand, suffered from weak administrative capacity and inter-ministerial involvement, which resulted in higher transposition delays than seen in Spain and other member states (Haverland and Romeijn 2006).

The second enlargement emphasised the need to reduce inequalities between and among the Community's various regions and members; as a result, it was marked by the development of a 'social dimension' of European integration and the revival of equal opportunity policies after a period of stagnation during the early 1980s. This enlargement coincided with the signing of the Single European Act (SEA) in 1986, which provided the legal framework both for the introduction of the Social Charter in 1989 and for the subsequent implementation of Social Action Programmes.[8]

The revival of European social policy during this period, together with the consolidation of a vocal women's lobby in Europe, had a significant impact on equality policy. This policy found expression in a series of multi-annual Community Action Programmes on Equal Opportunities (1988–1990; 1991–1995 and 1996–2000)[9] that, for the first time, included *positive action* measures aimed at facilitating the effective implementation of EU equal opportunities legislation.

Gender mainstreaming was an important strategy for ensuring the implementation of equal opportunities; it was first introduced in the Third Medium Term Action Programme (1991–1995) and strengthened in successive Action Programmes. Understood as the inclusion of a gender perspective on all policies, activities and practices (European Commission 1998: 8), it required a high level of gender awareness among policy-makers. The Equal Opportunities Action Programmes contributed greatly to the development of women's networks across Europe as well as to supporting research on gender equality issues (Rees 1998: 44). Although there has been no systematic study of the impact of these programmes on national policy to date, their impact on national policy has been found to be more significant than EU directives in some second-wave countries like Spain (Valiente 2006).

4. The third enlargement: Sweden, Finland and Austria, 1995

'Mediterranean enlargement' can be seen as a product of democratisation processes, reinforced by economically strategic elite assessments (Spain and Portugal) or overriding foreign policy interests (Greece). The third wave of admissions was facilitated by the end of the Cold War. The collapse of the Soviet Union in 1991, according to Elvert (2004: 202), 'paved the way for the accession of neutral and non-aligned countries by completely transforming the European security system'. Nugent (2004b: 30–31) agrees with this assessment, adding that economic relationships among these countries (members of the European Free Trade Association) came under increasing strain as the EU's political and economic capacity to dictate trading terms grew correspondingly. The mutual benefits of an enlarged Union and the relative ease with which these prosperous developed liberal democracies with free-market economic systems could be incorporated into the existing institutional and policy structure meant that the benefits of this enlargement would clearly outweigh the costs to the Community. Sweden, Finland and Austria opened accession negotiations in 1993, becoming members in 1995, while Norway voted for a second time to remain outside the EU.

However, popular sentiment in Sweden was not as enthusiastic as that seen among other publics during previous enlargements. In the discussions preceding Swedish accession, various political parties had referred to central concepts of Swedish national identity, stressing the importance of democracy, of the workfare system and of gender equality to argue both in favour of and against EU membership (Cameron and Gonas 1999). The Swedish Left Party drew on Europe's democratic deficits, in contrast to segments of the Social Democratic Party, which argued that Sweden would make the EU a 'living democracy'. The Swedish Left, in particular, highlighted incompatibilities between the Union and Sweden's generous welfare state, gender equality rules and workers' rights. A split also opened up between Social Democrats and trade unions, which led to the creation of groups supportive of, and opposed to, membership within these organisations. There were also divisions among organised women in civil society, such as the Support Stockings network. From the onset of the Swedish referendum campaign, the 'Yes' side recognised women's importance as voters for the outcome and took to mobilising them by funding women's campaigning groups. In contrast, feminists opposed to Sweden's EU membership worked within mixed organisations that had historically represented their interests. A number of feminist intellectuals and academics contributed to the 'No' side during the campaign; one example was leading feminist academic Agneta Stark, a founder of the Support Stockings network. They also hooked up with Danish feminists who had opposed EU entry, such as Drude Dahlerup and Annette Borchorst.

However, incorporation of Scandinavian countries was welcomed by European feminists, since it brought feminist politicians from these countries into key decision-making positions in EU institutions, such as the Commission, and raised the proportion of women in the European Parliament (Roth 2008; van der Vleuten 2007). In fact, the contribution of Commissioners from these countries to the development of gender mainstreaming in the EU has been well documented (Bretherton 2002; Miles 2005; Pollack and Hafner-Burton 2000).

Austria, Sweden and Finland did not present particular implementation challenges, insofar as their legal and policy orders were already significantly aligned with European provisions (Falkner et al. 2005: 331–332). Nonetheless, transposition and implementation of certain elements of the *gender acquis* remained relatively uneven across these and other member states.

The Pregnant Workers' directive offers a case in point. In 1995, *formal notice of non-notification* (taken to indicate non-transposition) was issued to seven member states: Belgium, Denmark, France, Greece, Italy, Luxembourg and Portugal. Transposing the EU law presented few problems for Belgium, Denmark and France, as existing policies and regulations in these countries were already highly aligned with the EU measure (Falkner et al. 2005: 79–80). The failure to transpose was due to policy inertia in the case of France, where

112   *Gendering Enlargement of the EU*

officials were of the view that national legislation was sufficient, and even superior to, new EU requirements. The remaining four states had more work to do, since existing national policies only moderately reflected the EU criteria. In Portugal, timely compliance was stimulated by pressure from trade unions and the media (Falkner et al. 2005: 80–87).

The enforcement proceedings initiated by the Commission clearly prompted five states to rectify and adopt national provisions, giving effect to the directive, irrespective of prior levels of national alignment with EU requirements. Greece and Luxembourg delayed tackling the problem and were served by the Commission with a Reasoned Opinion (stage two of the formal enforcement process) in 1996. Only Luxembourg was ultimately referred to the Court of Justice in 1997 for persistent non-notification. Those proceedings ceased in 1998, when the government adopted the required rules and informed the Commission to that effect (Falkner et al. 2005: 211). In all instances, a prompt to transpose EU law was met with a compliance response from each of the offending member states.

Summarising the patterns of compliance with gender directives among the 15 member states, Falkner et al. (2005: 330–341) categorise Finland, Sweden and Denmark as having high levels of transposition, well-organised enforcement systems and fewer infringement proceedings initiated against them than other members. They describe these countries as belonging to a group where observance of EU law is accorded high priority by national governments. Germany, Austria, the Netherlands, the UK, Belgium and Spain comprise a second group of member states, where enforcement standards were deemed relatively satisfactory, although national framing of the *acquis* and the content of transposed law were often subject to domestic political contest. Finally, Falkner et al. (2005) identify a third group, whose compliance with and enforcement of the social policy *acquis* is 'characterised by neglect'. Greece, Portugal, Luxembourg, France, Ireland and Italy fall into this category. This categorisation of compliance patterns illustrates that conforming to EU membership criteria is a complex process. National political cultures, priorities and interests do not always sit easily with EU governance requirements, especially in regard to social policy in general and gender equality in particular. How far the new Eastern members have adapted to this multi-level and supra-national form of governance is the subject of the following section.

5. Expanding membership to Central and Eastern Europe

The framework for an historic eastward enlargement of the EU was laid during the European Council meeting in Copenhagen 1993, where national leaders elaborated upon the political and economic criteria for future enlargements (see Table 6.2).[10] The Council also decided that the new democracies of Central and Eastern Europe (CEE) could, if they wished,

Table 6.2 The Copenhagen Criteria

Political criteria	Democracy
	Rule of law
	Human rights
	Respect for and protection of minorities
Economic criteria	Functioning market economy
Legislative criteria	Alignment of national legislation with the *acquis communautaire*

pursue EU membership (Nugent 2004d: 35). The Copenhagen Criteria reflected the desire of the EU to foster democratic government, human rights and a liberalisation of Eastern markets in the aftermath of the Cold War. The spelling out of accession criteria in this manner raised the bar for EU membership; indeed there is no doubt that each enlargement had features particular to the countries seeking admission (Nugent 2004a: 56–58). Given their political histories, the CEE countries faced greater legal, administrative and political challenges in incorporating and transposing the *acquis* than had their nearest comparators, the Mediterranean enlargement countries (Iankova and Katzenstein 2003: 284).

Between 1994 and 1995, ten post-communist states submitted formal applications to join the EU. A European Council meeting in Luxembourg in December 1997 agreed to embark on a fourth enlargement wave designed to encompass the CEE applicants and Cyprus. The Council initially opened accession negotiations with Cyprus, the Czech Republic, Estonia, Hungary, Poland, and Slovenia. Five other new democracies – Latvia, Lithuania, Slovakia, Bulgaria and Romania – were encouraged to intensify their reform processes, with a view to joining at a later date. In March 2000, this second group, along with Malta, commenced their negotiations. By 2000, intensive, detailed discussions were underway between the EU and twelve candidate countries regarding the adoption of 31 chapters comprising the *acquis communautaire*. This process required the candidates to strengthen their national and sub-national institutions, and to raise the capacity of their managerial, administrative and judicial systems up to EU standards in a relatively short period of time (Anderson 2006: 106–107). Negotiations with eight CEE countries (excluding Bulgaria and Romania), along with Malta and Cyprus, were completed at the European Council meeting in Copenhagen, 13 December 2002.

Reflecting on the process, Iankova and Katzenstein (2003: 283–284) contend that this enlargement placed more demands on candidate countries than had previous enlargement rounds. Clearly, the move from state socialism to a democratic political order imposed considerable domestic strains on the individual states; adoption of the *acquis* by national parliaments was often a matter of procedure rather than debate. This 'voiceless' transposition, they argue, was accentuated by the blanket adoption of policies with little direct relevance to CEE states, such as Schengen and the European Economic and Monetary Union (EMU; Iankova and Katzenstein 2003: 285). Problems were further compounded by the scope and complexity of EU law and the limited number of 'derogations' from policy implementation granted to the acceding states (Iankova and Katzenstein 2003: 286).[11]

Although the Commission provided substantial financial, policy and institutional supports to facilitate the integration of CEE legal and institutional frameworks into the European order, the new democracies were afforded very little time for *acquis* transposition, administrative reform and general compliance with the Copenhagen Criteria. The twin imperatives of enlargement – consolidating fledgling democratic institutions and processes and developing a more extensive economic market across Europe – drove much of the haste accompanying this round. The complexity of the negotiations, undertaken at a time of rising unemployment and poverty in the new democracies, is summed up in an observation on the challenges of aligning social protection systems formed under state-socialism with the required EU reforms:

> The reports make some interesting general observations, namely that the grafting of external social institutions and policies by external players onto existing, culturally distinct systems with their own socio-historic identity and ethos is a complex and sometimes counter-productive process (Barbier et al. 2000: 289).

For women, the transition from state socialism to a liberal economic order brought special problems. The elimination or privatisation of childcare services, the loss of secure employment in a deregulated, open market, coupled with rising costs for goods and services, all added to the pressures on women with families (Einhorn 2006; Watson 2000). The human dimension inherent in the scale of this revolutionary transformation of the political–economic order is mirrored in the progress reports sent to the Commission by the candidate countries.

These reports reveal some of the singular challenges faced by the candidate countries, for example the problems in aligning EU regulations with labour codes rooted in socialist law. While each country followed its own timetable for transposing the equality *acquis* and creating enforcement structures, the final monitoring evaluations for each country were relatively positive. Only Romania, Bulgaria and Estonia were identified as lacking significant progress prior to accession, although this finding needs to be considered when dealing with the later admission of the first two in 2007. After a slow start, Estonia picked up the pace in transposing the *acquis*. However, the final pre-accession report called for 'immediate and decisive action' to bring Estonia's laws and structures into line with EU requirements (European Commission 2003b: Estonia, 33, 35, 54). A second group of countries, comprised of Latvia,

Slovakia and Poland, made good, if incomplete, progress in transposing and creating structures for delivering EU gender equality measures. In each case, the mechanisms and capacity of their enforcement structures were deemed less than optimal (European Commission 2003b: Poland, 40–41; Latvia, 34; Slovakia, 32).

Finally, four countries – the Czech Republic, Hungary, Lithuania and Slovenia – were identified in Commission monitoring reports as having undertaken considerable effort to transpose and create effective enforcement structures regarding the gender *acquis*. However, even the leader states shared some deficiencies with other applicants. In particular, the equalisation of pensions, the determination of pensionable age for male and female civil servants, the removal of 'protective' sex discrimination concerning night work, refinement of the burden-of-proof conditions in employment, adjustments to the parental leave directive and strengthening enforcement capacities – these were common areas identified as necessitating greater national effort across all CEE countries.

Over the monitoring period 1999–2003, the reports chart progressive compliance with the EU legal order by CEE governments. By 2001, Chapter 13 had been finalised in six states – Estonia, Hungary, Poland, the Czech Republic, Slovakia and Slovenia – indicating the Commission's satisfaction with their transposition of both the social and the equal opportunities *acquis*. The requirements of Chapter 13 were deemed to have been adequately incorporated into the national statutes of Lithuania, Latvia, Bulgaria and Romania by 2002. Only Bulgaria's compliance with transposition remained problematic at that point.

6. Enforcement since the 2004 enlargement

Much of the enlargement literature focuses on national and EU contexts in the run-up to 2004. The accession process, necessarily concentrating on matters of technical compliance, obscured the inevitable tensions between legal transposition and political expediency that came into play as the new member states integrated their national frameworks with the *acquis*. Revisiting the 2004 enlargement, Leiber (2005) provocatively asks if there is a different 'Eastern world' of compliance. Focusing on the case of Poland, she shows that, with regards to compliance with social policy directives, that country is much more similar to the old EU-15 than one might expect. She concludes that the results indicate the need to suggest a fourth world of compliance to cover Poland or other Eastern countries (Leiber 2005: 358). However, over time, it is clear that the new CEE member states have begun to conform more closely to EU transposition requirements, and also to reflect the pattern of compliance evident in older member states.

One method of assessing how far the new member states have integrated with the European gender agenda is to compare rates of transposition

116 *Gendering Enlargement of the EU*

pertaining to a single directive across all 27 members. Directive 2004/113, mandating the *equal treatment between men and women in access to and supply of goods and services*, offers a good example. It is a relatively new directive, adopted in 2004, at the time of enlargement, with an implementation deadline of December 2007. Based on Article 13 of the Amsterdam Treaty, this directive entails the first effort by the EU to outlaw sex discrimination in non-employment settings. It bans sex-based discrimination in the provision of goods and services offered to the public, such as housing, banking, insurance and transportation facilities. This directive is, moreover, the only one that applies to all member states since the 2004 enlargement, such that the CEE countries did not have to play 'catch-up' with older EU members, as was the case regarding other equality directives. An independent assessment of gender equality law in May 2007 noted that transposition had only taken place in six member states, one of which was East European – Lithuania.[12] In Austria, Bulgaria and Ireland, the directive had only been partially transposed (Network of Legal Experts 2007a). The Commission initiated the first stage of its enforcement warning, issuing letters of formal notice for non-transposition to 12 states in early 2008, five of which were CEE countries.[13]

Based on the 'types' of enforcement regimes developed by Falkner et al. (2005), one can easily identify those member states reflecting a pattern of implementation 'neglect': Ireland, Greece, France and Portugal, along with one country where 'domestic' political tensions guide implementation patterns: the UK. The remaining seven countries issued with a formal letter of notice were new community entrants (see Table 6.3). The formal notice from the Commission prompted three states to effect transposition – Portugal, France and Romania – suggesting, again, that the formal notice acted as a reminder to 'kick-start' the alignment process. By the end of 2008 the Commission had sent a second warning in the form of a 'reasoned opinion' to the nine other tardy countries; by June 2009 it had referred Poland

Table 6.3 Enforcing Directive 2004/113 in member states

Compliant by deadline	Formal notice	Reasoned opinion	ECJ referral
Belgium, Denmark, Germany, Lithuania, Netherlands, Spain, Sweden	Cyprus, Czech Rep, Estonia, France, Greece, Ireland, Latvia, Malta, Poland, Portugal Romania, UK	Cyprus, Czech Rep, Estonia, Greece, Ireland, Latvia, Malta, Poland,	Estonia*, UK**, Poland

* Estonia was deemed to be in compliance on 20 November 2009.
** In February 2010, the ECJ found that the UK failed to implement 2004/113 (Case C-186/09).

and Estonia to the European Court of Justice for non-compliance with the directive (European Commission 2009d, 2009e).

Thus an analysis of this directive's transposition does not indicate a marked difference between old and new member states. This single directive review calls into question the 'Eastern world of compliance' thesis, however, at least in relation to EU gender equality. Indeed, we need to undertake further research in the form of detailed case studies, along with extensive cross-sectoral evaluations, in order to establish full patterns of compliance among member states from former Eastern Europe and to determine whether they differ from the compliance trends in the older member states.

The fact remains, though, that accession challenges, coupled with the demands of creating democratic political structures and institutions from scratch, have rendered the Eastern enlargement process more complex than earlier enlargement rounds. The continual evolution of the *acquis* presents accession countries with the problem of forever playing 'catch-up', which is complicated by the fact that new laws and policies are still being grafted onto a socio-economic corpus of law, regulations and practices inherited from the era of state socialism. Given the dramatic increase in female unemployment in the CEE states as a result of the Iron Curtain's collapse, the structural inequalities that gender directives were designed to address in the West not only persisted but actually grew worse in the East after 1995 (Matyja 2001).

The space for a feminist challenge to the status quo is circumscribed by the weakness of civil society and by the failures of both state and market to provide the support and protection services dismantled by the state after communism (such as childcare), or to address effectively women's long-neglected health and human rights needs (Fodor 2005; Ghodsee 2006). Women's participation in social dialogue and decision-making, as representatives of legitimate civil society perspectives, has been limited at best. Consultations have been treated by government officials as a matter of formal compliance with EU expectations rather than as opportunities for substantive policy influence (Hašková 2005: 1107).

The historical legacy of the socialist past, where civil society was virtually non-existent, requires that the fabric of social dialogue be woven anew. Though varying widely in form and inclusion, the social partnerships that some older member states take for granted had to be constructed in Central and Eastern Europe under intense time pressures. At the moment of accession, an under-resourced and underfunded women's sector focused on urgent tasks of service provision (Galligan and Clavero 2007: 233–234). Since accession, some limited progress in bringing women's non-governmental organisations (NGOs) into decision-making has been achieved. In Lithuania, for example, provisions were made for formal NGO participation in the Commission on Equal Opportunities for Women and Men. Viewed as a step in the right direction, the initiative drew critical comment for not identifying the relevant NGOs and for not specifying the criteria for selection

(Network of Legal Experts 2007b: 38–39). A more positive integration of women's NGO representatives in legislative discussions is found in Slovakia. During 2007, one of its most prominent women's organisations, the Union of Mother Centres, made submissions to the government's draft revisions of the Labour Code and the Anti-Discrimination Act. The organisation maintained that the proposed legislation did not go far enough in creating conditions for the effective balancing of work and family life. The Union argued for more comprehensive treatment of these issues, to reduce the potential for discrimination against women arising from their caring duties. Although the government was unwilling to accept this argument, this is one instance where a women's civil society organisation became actively involved in a process of social dialogue (Network of Legal Experts 2007b: 51–52).

The practice of excluding or restricting women's civil society participation in policy-making contradicts the EU's efforts to foster a greater role for social partners in the legislative process at national and Community levels (Masselot 2007: 165–166). However, the EU's exhortations to engage citizens in policy and law-making are voluntary rather than binding on member states. Recent EU members are not alone in restricting public access to decision-making. Regarding equal treatment in the provision of goods and services directive, for example, few EU countries have accorded civil society a realistic opportunity to engage in the national transposition process, while the EU's own guidelines suggest that these measures are voluntary rather than obligatory by nature (Kantola 2010a).

For the Eastern EU members, enlargement nonetheless brought a more complex process of alignment than that experienced by applicants in the earlier rounds. The social security directives, consisting of 79/7 (equal treatment in statutory social security schemes), 86/378 (equal treatment in occupational social security schemes) and 2004/113 (the goods and services directive), as applied to private insurance, illustrate the conundrum (European Commission 2008c). For older member states, the application of these three directives maps closely onto three familiar models for social security provision, albeit with differing emphases in each country: statutory schemes, occupational schemes and private insurance schemes. Although the distinctions among the three models may be blurred, and although implementation of the directives has provoked correspondence between the Commission and Greece, France and the UK, infringement proceedings seem to have pushed most of the older states into addressing the legal shortcomings of national law. In the case of the recently admitted states, however, the situation is more complex. The twin processes of democratisation and accession required post-communist countries to reconfigure their social security systems substantially. This restructuring did not necessarily follow the EU-based models. In a number of instances, these countries adopted the World Bank's state schemes model, mandatory savings schemes or voluntary schemes, making the transposition of the directives more complex (Network of Legal Experts 2007c: 8–9).

Eastern enlargement studies also highlight the challenges faced by the new members in developing sufficient administrative capacity to implement, monitor and enforce the *acquis*. This requires significant resources, training for administrators and reforming judicial systems to ensure that EU laws are applied (Nugent 2004c: 16–17; Phinnemore 2004). The Commission monitoring reports on each candidate country repeatedly noted the need to enhance the capacity of national administrative systems (see for example the Commission report on Bulgaria: European Commission 1999a: 61; on the Czech Republic: European Commission 2002a: 85; on Hungary: European Commission 2001b: 60). General systemic weaknesses also featured in terms of gender mainstreaming. With the exceptions of Estonia and Slovenia, institutional mechanisms for enforcing the social *acquis* were placed at the periphery of government, in offices staffed by civil servants with limited expertise in gender issues (Galligan and Clavero 2007: 229–231). However, Daly (2005: 433–450) notes a similar 'mainstreaming' pattern in the more established EU member states. This suggests that the 'hollow' infrastructure, which looks impressive but lacks substance, reflects the ambiguous commitment of many member states, old and new, to gender equality. Liebert's (2003b: 263) observation that (older) member states wield a measure of autonomy in giving expression to EC gender requirements is readily applicable to the CEE members.

7. Gender equality and enlargement in the post-Lisbon EU

The enactment of the Lisbon Treaty on 1 December 2009 is seen by commentators as clarifying the contents of previous treaties rather than as expanding the rule and remit of the EU (Church and Phinnemore 2010: 6). For the most part, the Treaty does not hold enlargement implications. Nonetheless, along with codifying existing gender equality commitments, it places a greater emphasis on EU values and citizens' rights, gives equal status to social and economic objectives, and makes some provisions to enhance social dialogue and reduce the democratic deficit (Špidla 2009). The position of gender equality under the Lisbon provisions, as compared with previous treaties, is enhanced with its recognition as a value of the EU, more explicit commitment to upholding human rights, and a concern for women's personal integrity through combating all forms of violence against women (see Table 6.4).

This expanded gender equality agenda, given policy expression in the EU gender equality plan for the period 2010–2015, seeks to foster women's equality with men within the EU and in developing regions of the world (European Commission 2010f). Future enlargements, then, will be required to take account of this enhanced equality agenda, along with enacting new directives formulated to combat gender inequity in social relations.[14] This means that, once again, the standard of equality expected of the acceding countries has increased. This leaves Turkey in particular with a mountain to

120 *Gendering Enlargement of the EU*

Table 6.4 Gender equality provisions in the Lisbon Treaty

Area	Former Treaty Articles	As amended by Treaty of Lisbon
Equality between women and men as a value of the Union	–	Art. 2 TEU
Equality between women and men as an objective of the EU	Art. 2 TEC	Art. 3, Sect. 3 TEU
Charter of Fundamental rights	Declaration n23	Art. 6, Sect. 1 TEU
Gender mainstreaming as horizontal principle	Art. 3, Sect. 2 TEC	Art. 8 TFEU
Non-discrimination as horizontal principle	–	Art. 10 TFEU
Legal base to combat discrimination not tied to nationality	Art. 13 TEC	Art. 19 TFEU
Legal base to advance gender equality in the labour market	Art. 141 TEC	Art. 157 TFEU
Trafficking and sexual exploitation	–	Art. 79 TFEU Art. 83 TFEU
Domestic violence	–	Declaration n19
Equal treatment in public services	Art. 16 TEC Declaration n13	Art. 14 TFEU Protocol on services of general interest

Source: European Women's Lobby (n.d.).

climb in transposing gender equality laws. At the same time, as the gender equality advocacy group WIDE points out in its evaluation of the Lisbon Treaty's impact on the member states, 'much work still needs to be done to give women actual tools of equality' (Bisio and Cataldi 2008: 15). In practice, the Treaty's main effect to date has been to require governments to respond within a shorter time-frame to queries regarding the transposition and implementation of equality and other Directives.

8. Conclusion

The EU enlargement process has required applicant countries to adjust an ever-larger body of national laws, policies and procedures to simultaneously expanding European requirements across new fields of interaction. Initially, enlargement was designed to foster increased economic opportunities within Europe. This ambition has extended to developing the European region as a significant force in terms of global economics, while consolidating its position in terms of global international relations. This requires a political harmonisation with liberal democratic arrangements, in order to ensure political stability across the region. Each enlargement wave, then, has been motivated by a combination of economic and political ambitions.

Gender equality is one highly contested site in this process. This contestation takes place within the domestic political arenas of the new member states, and between each member and the Commission, adjudicated by the European Court of Justice. Previous enlargement rounds were characterised by a diversity of interactions, within member states and in a multi-layered governing context, on the subject of equal opportunities between women and men. In some instances, for example in Ireland and Portugal, the combined activities of civil society, trade union pressure and European initiatives succeeded in bringing about important legal changes that reflected social changes occurring in these countries. In other cases, as in the UK during Conservative administrations, the national government has proven stubbornly resistant to pressures of this kind; yet the latter has had a more positive record of equality *acquis* implementation than either Ireland or Portugal.

In the case of Eastern enlargement, the opportunity to join, and the motivation for doing so, came with the fall of communism. The desire to stabilise governments in a democratic direction and to rebuild economies based on free markets in a new geo-political order, as an ideological alternative to communism, led the Central/Eastern Europe states to seek membership. The fourth enlargement was a product of the convergence of two sets of ambitions: those of the EU, on the one hand, and those of the former socialist states, on the other. Indeed, in this enlargement, the twin processes of democratisation and Europeanisation are difficult to untangle. While Lendvai (2004: 330) argues that 'the debate over European enlargement seems to problematise both the institutional and political capacity of the EU', one could also argue that enlargement throws into stark relief the institutional and political challenges confronting the new member states as they integrate with the European Union.

What relationship does this bring to bear on the gendering of enlargement processes? At some level, at least, the need to accommodate EU equality norms and expectations with regard to domestic laws, policies and practices in matters of gender equality provides the public with tools to instigate, or even oppose, social change in a domestic environment. The extent to which these tools are utilised depends heavily on the particular socio-political circumstances in each individual country. Anderson (2006: 113) suggests that internal factors and actors – political parties, social movements and political institutions among them – mediate external influences and explain variations in national adoptions of EU gender equality policy. In the case of Poland and the Czech Republic, she suggests that the most significant domestic factors explaining differing rates of equality in *acquis* compliance are the extent and influence of organised opposition and the commitment of the governing party (Anderson 2006: 103). Anderson indeed mentions the role of the Catholic Church in mobilising opposition to EU equal opportunities policies in Poland, through women's organisations such as The Polish Association of Ordinary Women (2006: 114). The author contends that the Czech Republic also witnessed a significant degree of opposition to EU gender equality norms; insofar as this is a much more secularised country than Poland, opposing groups failed to mobilise the public. On the eve of accession in 2004, most CEE countries possessed a similar legacy relative to gender equality, stemming from four decades of socialism, albeit one rooted in fundamentally different 'gender regimes', requiring women's paid labour to compensate for post-war labour shortages that the West covered by recruiting migrant labourers (see Mushaben in this volume).

In the few short years since admission, this relatively monolithic pattern is rapidly coming undone, to be replaced by a wide diversity of responses to EU gender equality imperatives shaped by local conditions. For researchers, the time has now come to integrate the experiences of the new member states in their adoption of EU-instigated gender norms with those of the 'older' member states. All, new and old alike, continue to be challenged to eliminate discrimination in gender relations.

Discussion questions

- Discuss the manner in which politics and economics are inextricably bound together in successive waves of EU enlargement . How have these linkages manifested themselves in terms of gender politics?
- Can one argue for an 'Eastern world of compliance' in relation to EU gender equality policies?
- To what extent is the transposition of the *gender acquis* shaped by national attitudinal and policy contexts that inform a member state's 'gender regime'? How divergent are these national gender regimes from the EU's equal opportunities regime for gender equality?

Notes

1. The European Women's Lobby provides a brief and succinct overview of the obligations on candidate countries to adopt the equality *acquis* prior to membership. See http://www.womenlobby.org/.
2. President de Gaulle of France opposed UK membership in 1963; following his departure from political life, negotiations for admitting these three countries were re-initiated in 1967.
3. Equal pay had been in effect in the Danish public sector since 1925 (Siim 1993: 38).

4. Case 71/85, [1987] 3 C.M.L.R 767.
 5. Case 286/85, [1987] 2 C.M.L.R. 607.
 6. European Parliament, 1979, Resolution supporting the enlargement of Spain, Greece and Portugal.
 7. Directives 76/207/EEC and 79/7/EEC.
 8. The SEA constituted the first revision to the Treaty of Rome and included a number of measures to promote integration in the area of social rights.
 9. These refer to the second, third and fourth Medium Term Community Action Programmes. The first programme covered the period 1982–1985, while the fifth (and last) covered the period 2000–2005.
10. Countries aspiring to EU membership were required to achieve 'stability of institutions guaranteeing democracy, the rule of law, human rights and respect for and protection of minorities; a functioning market economy; as well as the capacity to cope with competitive pressure and market forces within the Union. Membership presupposes the candidate's ability to take on the obligations of membership, including adherence to the aims of political, economic and monetary union' (European Council 1993: 12). These conditions are often referred to as the 'Copenhagen Criteria'.
11. A derogation is permission to a member state from the EU to delay implementation of a directive for an agreed period of time beyond the legal implementation date. Derogations are commonly sought, and granted after negotiation between the member state and the Commission.
12. The other five countries with completed transposition were Belgium, Denmark, Germany, the Netherlands, Spain and Sweden.
13. The CEE countries comprised the Czech Republic, Estonia, Latvia, Poland and Romania. The other seven countries in receipt of formal notice for non-transposition were Ireland, Greece, France, Cyprus, Malta, Portugal and the UK.
14. Council Directive 2010/18/EU implementing the revised Framework Agreement on parental leave concluded by BUSINESSEUROPE, UEAPME, CEEP and ETUC, and repealing Directive 96/34/EC; Directive 2010/41/EU on the application of the principle of equal treatment between men and women engaged in an activity in a self-employed capacity and repealing Council Directive 86/613/EEC.

Part II

Meliorating Old and New EU Policy Deficits and Blind Spots

7
The Common Agricultural Policy and Gender Equality

Elisabeth Prügl

Maria Wimer grew up on a family farm in Germany and dreamt of becoming a farmer. Yet it was clear that her older brother was going to inherit the farm, as has been the practice throughout Europe. This left Maria with two options: she could marry a farmer, to gain access to land and engage in farming; or she could train to become a farmer, lease land and start her own farm. The two options by no means yield the same outcomes. If Maria chose to marry a farmer, marriage would give her both a job and a husband – she would be a *Bäuerin*. As such, her duties and rights would be fundamentally different from that of a *Bauer*. She most likely would be in charge of all the housework, childcare and much of the paperwork relating to the farm. She would engage in farming by doing jobs typically reserved for women and considered 'ancillary'. Her dual role as spouse and farmer tasked with jobs considered secondary would leave her with few rights. She would have had no occupational status, no right to the income produced from the farm. If she were to divorce, in most jurisdictions she would have no right to the assets of the farm, despite having participated in securing these through her labour. Before 1995, she would have had no independent right to a pension either.

We know from the book Maria wrote that she chose the second path: she studied to become a farmer.[1] She wanted to become a *Landwirtin* (land manager) rather than a *Bäuerin* (farmer's wife). We do not know whether she ever succeeded in this goal, but if she did, she most likely encountered considerable resistance. Margarete Schmitt (1997) has documented the struggles of women like Maria wanting to be *Landwirtinnen*. Land owners often refused to lease land to them, women training to become farmers often experienced longer probationary periods in apprenticeships, and their supervisors focused on women's physical strength when assessing their ability to farm. Maria's chances of remaining a *Landwirtin* would be greater if she did not marry. Half of the women in Schmitt's sample of female land managers were single; when men entered their lives they tended to take over farm management. Women then adopted more traditional roles; even when they remained the designated managers, men ostensibly helped out with farm work, but not with housework. Typically, women's equality strategies crumbled once they had children. *Landwirtinnen* then built their own enclaves and developed new talents: growing berries, keeping goats, marketing cheese, tending vegetable gardens and, last but not least, running the household and caring for children.

Maria Wimer and women like her run up against a deeply institutionalised gender regime in European agriculture. The family farm with its profoundly patriarchal gender order remains its core building block, long supported by public policies, including the European Union (EU)'s Common Agricultural Policy (CAP). The CAP encompasses both market-making and a structural policy, engaging in both regulatory and redistributive tasks. Because of this dual character, the EU sooner resembles an acting state in the agricultural sector than in other sectors (Majone 1996). Given the large volume of resources dedicated to the CAP, added to the fact that feminists have long thought of the state as implicated in the reproduction of masculine domination, it is particularly important to examine the relationship between the EU's gender equality policy and the CAP. This chapter argues that, by making the family farm the centre of its policies, the CAP has been complicit in reproducing masculine domination in agriculture, making feminist interventions particularly difficult and restricting them to rural development activities in a complementary services sector.

The CAP was created in the 1960s for the purpose of stabilising rural incomes and modernising farming. Its main mechanisms for accomplishing these goals included the organisation of agricultural markets and rural development policies (Roederer-Rynning 2010). Because of its focus on helping states achieve income equivalences between urban and rural areas in its early years, the CAP served as a key component of the European *agricultural welfare state* (Rieger 1995). Since the 1980s, the policy has come under attack in international trade negotiations for distorting prices in international agricultural markets. The EU has responded to this challenge by agreeing to phase out price supports gradually, providing subsidies through direct payments to farmers instead. This allows it to liberalise agricultural markets while continuing to address rural welfare goals as well as newly added *rural sustainability* goals. Liberalising the CAP has meant transforming the European agricultural welfare state into a regime of environmental liberalism (Prügl 2004). My consideration of gender in the CAP probes gender rules in the transition from the agricultural welfare state of the 1960s and 1970s to the regime of environmental liberalism emerging since the 1980s.

In analysing gender politics in the CAP, this chapter relates feminist agency to these two regimes. They encompass rules constructing agricultural markets, welfare mechanisms and development strategies. They (re)produce gender through property rights, divisions of labour, and by constituting the identities of market actors in agriculture. Feminist strategies – such as lobbying for legal change or gender mainstreaming – operate in the context of, and respond to, these regimes. The equal rights strategy of the 1970s and 1980s sought to change the rules of the agricultural welfare state, with its patriarchal understanding of the farm family and the gendered identities of 'the farmer' and 'the spouse'. Embedded in the new regime of environmental liberalism, the contemporary gender mainstreaming strategy has the potential to change rural gender divisions of labour and to constitute rural entrepreneurship in newly gendered ways.

My argument stands in the tradition of the extensive feminist literature on European gender regimes (Duncan 1996b; Kofman and Sales 1996; Lewis 1992; Sainsbury 1994; Schunter-Kleemann 1992b). In its origins, this literature focused almost exclusively on national practices. However, increasingly, it has taken into consideration the influences of the EU. Scholars have probed the EU's employment policies as a distinct type of gender regime (von Wahl 2005) and they have explored the influences of EU policies on local gender regimes (Pascall and Lewis 2004). Here I propose yet another approach by suggesting that gender regimes in systems of multi-level governance can usefully be identified along functional issue areas. Thus the gender regime in agriculture is likely to differ from the gender regime shaping other policy areas, such as science or industry. My argument also draws on constructivist approaches that have explored the EU as a rule-making enterprise – both in the sense of making laws and regulations and in regard to changing European society (Fligstein 2008; Sandholtz and Stone Sweet 1998; Shaw 2000). This approach has been particularly useful for understanding gender politics in the EU (Locher and Prügl 2009).

In what follows, I first outline the contours of the gendered agricultural welfare state under the CAP and the contemporary transition to a new regime of environmental liberalism with new gender orders. Secondly, I probe feminist agency in the context of these changing regimes. I then explore the politics around the formulation and implementation of Directive 86/613/EEC on the equal treatment of women in self-employment, including agriculture, and juxtapose them against current efforts to mainstream gender in this sector. Finally, I illustrate how these regimes circumscribe feminist agency, and how the meaning of gender equality changes in different regime contexts.

1. From the agricultural welfare state to liberal environmentalism

The CAP is frequently described as embodying a compromise between German and French interests. Whereas French agriculture was highly competitive, the German farming sector was relatively inefficient. Thus the French favoured a liberalisation of trade in agricultural products in order to create a European market for their agricultural surpluses. In contrast, the

Germans opposed agricultural liberalisation but were interested in liberalising trade in industrial products, where they were highly competitive. The compromise – a liberalisation of industry and a common market in agriculture, with relatively high fixed prices – met agrarian interests in both countries and responded to industrial interests in the construction of the common market (Moravcsik 1998). Concurrently, the CAP also institutionalised patriarchal interests represented with little contention by all states party to the negotiations.

A core element of agricultural policies at both the national and Community levels was the commitment to preserving the family farm. Documents from the 1958 Stresa conference formulating basic CAP principles convey a broad agreement among European Economic Community (EEC) member states to maintain family farming as the basic organising principle of a modernised agricultural sector.[2] Family farms combine several characteristics. First, farms and the associated land are family-owned, passed down for generations, with preference typically assigned to male heirs; second, family members provide the bulk of farm labour, with male farmers typically controlling the labour of their female spouses.[3] Third, the household and the business comprise one unit, production and reproduction are spatially and organisationally joined. In 1989, almost three-fourth of all farms in the EU were family farms; in 2005 family labour accounted for over 80 per cent of the volume of labour provided in the EU-27.[4]

A patriarchal gender order according the farmer control over his wife's labour, male control over property, and assigned household/business managerial power to men thus was a key element of the agricultural model institutionalised via the CAP; it was celebrated in rhetoric in the post-World War II era, often juxtaposed against communist policies that created large industrial-style farms. It is fair to suggest that the unpaid, unrecognised labour of women farmers made possible the post-war restructuring of European farming parallel to the preservation of family farming. Agricultural economists note that the integration of household labour and resources with the farm's labour and resources provides unique flexibility and constitutes a highly efficient regulatory system with low transaction costs. The low value attached to women's labour, including the classification of household labour as non-productive, moreover facilitated an extensive system of labour exploitation, including self-exploitation (Vogel and Wiesinger 2003).

As in the industrial sector, patriarchal rules within the family were reinforced through government policies. By accepting the definition of farmers as male, the agricultural welfare state's price mechanism distributed income primarily to men.[5] In addition, EU member states developed social insurance schemes (health insurance, accident and disability insurance, old age insurance) that complemented the Union's price mechanism to secure the welfare of farming families. Under this patriarchal gender order, states treated women quite differently within these schemes. These features of the

European agricultural welfare state became a target of attacks due to feminist activism of the 1980s, in ways outlined below.

Family farming has changed its meaning as globalisation has replaced modernisation as the rationale for agricultural policy-making (McMichael 1997). Under pressure from its trading partners at the World Trade Organization (WTO), the EU initiated steps phasing out price supports, thereby dismantling the agricultural welfare state created through the CAP. At the same time, pressures from farmer organisations and environmental groups have counteracted liberalisation. In international trade negotiations, the EU has acknowledged that price supports distort international agricultural markets while insisting that continued subsidies are justified in the agricultural sector for social, ecological and cultural reasons. In order to reduce the trade-distorting effects of the common market organisation, the EU has been gradually replacing price subsidies with direct payments to farmers.[6] It uses these new types of subsidisation to pursue a broader range of goals, like farm welfare, environmental preservation, and rural development.

These policies have become part of a new 'European model of agriculture'. The model rests on the contention that agriculture differs fundamentally from other economic sectors, in that it not only creates private goods for exchange on the market (namely food and fibre) but also provides a series of public goods, that is, externalities the market does not reward: it shapes the rural landscape, offers environmental benefits (land conservation, natural resource management, preservation of biodiversity) and contributes to the socio-economic viability of rural areas. In this way farming is becoming 'multi-functional' (Maier and Shobayashi 2001).

Multifunctionality is a crucial element in the emergence of a new regulatory regime in European agriculture, namely liberal environmentalism. It combines a commitment to free trade with state intervention to counteract trade-related detrimental environmental and welfare effects. Thus the EU's first steps towards liberalising agricultural trade during the WTO Uruguay Round of negotiations were linked to the adoption of a set of *agri-environmental* regulations (Wilson and Wilson 2001: 107–108, 194–198), which sought to channel agricultural practices into more sustainable paths. They could then be framed as providing public as well as private goods and warranting government subsidies.[7]

Along with trade liberalisation, the EU embraced an expanded policy of rural development as the second pillar of its agricultural policy. In 2005 it established a new European Agricultural Fund for Rural Development (EAFRD) to help accomplish three goals: increase the competitiveness of European agriculture; improve the rural environment; and enhance the quality of rural life while diversifying the rural economy (Council 2005). Mainstreamed throughout the text of the rural development regulation setting up the fund is the requirement to advance equality between women and men. Thus the fund's goals encompass neoliberal agendas for increasing competitiveness but also include environmental, rural welfare and gender equality objectives.

How did feminists press their agendas and how have their strategies changed in the context of the agricultural welfare state and liberal environmentalism? How do regulatory contexts circumscribe the effectiveness of feminist strategies? How have they changed the meaning of gender equality?

2. Feminists target the agricultural welfare state

By the time multiple United Nations (UN) women's conferences had galvanised the international women's movement in the 1970s and 1980s, the European agricultural welfare state was well entrenched. The EU responded to the new international discourse on women's equality with a series of equality directives guaranteeing equal pay, women's equal rights and equal treatment in the workplace and in social security (see Table 7.1; see articles by Locher, Hubert and Stratigaki in this volume). These rights were progressively implemented in the non-agricultural sector, but the issue was complicated in agriculture, so the equal rights agenda hardly impacted the sector.

This was not due to a lack of feminist effort. Starting in 1975, the Commission's Women's Information Service financed regular meetings of women farmers; the Commission's first Action Programme on Equal Opportunity (AP 1982–1985) included a priority focus on self-employment and women in agriculture. In this context, the COPA[8] Women's Committee initiated its first EU-wide inquiry into the legal status of women on family farms in the early 1980s. The survey found that member states did not discriminate between male and female farm heads, but there were very few women running farms. Instead, most were 'farmers' wives' whose work was unacknowledged: they

Table 7.1 EU actions improving the legal status of women in agriculture

1982	Grado Seminar
1986	Council passes Directive 86/613/EEC on the application of the principle of equal treatment between men and women engaged in an activity, including agriculture, in a self-employed capacity, and on the protection of self-employed women during pregnancy and motherhood
1994	Commission Report on the Implementation of the Directive
1989–2007	Five EP Reports and Resolutions
2010	EP and Council pass new Directive 2010/41/EU on the application of the principle of equal treatment between men and women engaged in an activity in a self-employed capacity and repealing Directive 86/613/EEC

typically received neither pay nor independent social security protection. If they divorced or if their husbands died, they lost not only their jobs, but also access to pension benefits accumulated by their husbands. Furthermore, farmers' wives frequently had no entitlement to compensation resulting from an inability to work due to sickness, accident or maternity – all standard provisions for women working outside agriculture. The study also found differences in training, with women rarely taking technical courses in farm work, and massive differences in women's access to farming organisations and cooperatives. Their labour was clearly not accorded the same value as that of male farmers, nor was their status equal to that of heads of households or enterprises (Sousi-Roubi and von Prondzynski 1983).[9]

The survey kicked off a series of activities that ultimately culminated in a very weak EU directive on the equal treatment of women in self-employment, including agriculture. The first was a seminar in Grado, Italy, in November 1982, organised by COPA and a Brussels-based policy think-tank with support from the Commission. The seminar discussed the results of the survey and concluded that it was necessary to write a separate directive for women in self-employment and agriculture (Commission 1988: 1–2). In the years following, rural women's organisations and 'femocrats' pursued this legal strategy to change the situation of women farmers in the context of the agricultural welfare state.

Participants in the Grado seminar suggested that the solution to improving women's status in agriculture lay in changing what it means to be a woman farmer by redefining her status and, with that, her identity. The seminar called for an EC directive addressing the occupational status of 'women farmers' with regard to property rights, tax legislation, social security, access to vocational training, farming organisations, cooperatives and relief services. The seminar received support in this demand from the European Parliament (EP). Simone Martin, a Liberal MEP from France charged by the EP's Committee of Inquiry into the Situation of Women in Europe to report on women in family businesses, attended this seminar. Her report to the EP emphasised the importance of legally recognising women's work in the household and in family enterprises, bemoaned that too many tax and social security provisions were tied to the status of the head of enterprise and recommended that all family members working in a family business be given the status of partner. Her report also took up the issues of social security, maternity leave, vocational training, access to professional organisations and cooperatives and relief services.

With support from female MEPs and input from women farmers' organisations, the Commission developed a draft proposal for a directive in 1984 that closely reflected the demands first formulated at Grado. The draft stressed the importance of granting women farmers occupational status as either partners or employees (rather than simple marital status as wives or housewives). Only occupational status would secure recognition of their contribution to family income and entitlements to social security (Commission 1984). The draft directive also included language addressing most of the other concerns discussed at the seminar.

In its reading of the proposal, the EP noted that it had previously called for a directive, voting to support the Commission proposal while seeking to strengthen certain provisions; it added language that guaranteed recognition of the spouse's work with regard to rights of succession, further requiring organisations and cooperatives to change their statutes to allow spouses to participate.[10] It also broadened the conditions that would allow for replacement of their services. In addition to adopting the Commission proposal, the EP passed a resolution expressing hope that the directive would eliminate discrimination against women in self-employment and agriculture, afford them preferential rights to inheritance, independent incomes and independent treatment for tax and social security purposes (European Parliament 1984).

Despite this groundswell of support, the Council (initially under the Dutch, then under the British presidency) radically watered down the draft directive.[11] It reformulated provisions to recognise women farmers' professional status in a way that made them meaningless: 'Member States shall undertake to examine under what conditions recognition of the work of the spouses [...] may be encouraged and, in light of such examination, consider any appropriate steps for encouraging such recognition' (Council 1986: Article 7). Gone were references to granting equal status or acknowledging the work of women farmers in the form of cash payments or allocations of profit shares. Gone was the idea of recognising their work through an entry in the register of trade organisations. Instead, governments reserved the right to take action on this issue or not. Similarly fuzzy language replaced provisions about maternity protection. The Council further weakened provisions regarding social security, substituting the reference to 'independent entitlements' with wording that called for voluntary contribution schemes for spouses, and only if they were not protected 'under the self-employed worker's social security scheme' (their husbands' insurance). In other words, derived rights were not considered a problem. Finally, the Council directive made no reference to eliminating unequal treatment in the tax code, securing female access to professional organisations or equal access to training, all of which had appeared in the Commission draft. The EP proposal to add language on inheritance rights was likewise ignored.

Not surprisingly, the directive changed little. In a 1994 review of its application, governments reported that 'it had not been necessary for them to amend or adapt their national legislation in order to implement the Directive' (Commission 1994: 6). Nothing had changed with regard to the occupational status of women farmers: 'By and large the Member States felt that there was no need for new initiatives to encourage such recognition' (Commission 1994: 6). Social security rights, for the most part, were still derived rights or rights based on costly private insurance schemes.

Only regarding maternity protection did the report find signs of movement: some states now granted allowances, but provision of genuine relief services remained the exception. The first draft of the review had included critical comments from non-governmental organisations, reiterating that the work of spouses needed to be recognised. The Commission decided to strike these comments. Furthermore, the fact that a junior sub-contracted expert, rather than a regular civil servant, was charged with writing the report may indicate the lack of importance the Commission attached to the directive.[12]

The EP and the COPA Women's Committee reacted to these unsatisfactory outcomes with continued activism, keeping alive demands for equal status and equal treatment while demanding a strengthening of the directive. In 1989 the EP passed a resolution calling to amend the directive so that spouses would be defined as 'joint partners' in a family business, enjoying 'the same rights to full social protection' as female employees. It also called for the promotion of training for farmers' wives, public information and government enforcement services (European Parliament 1988). The delayed review of the impact of the 1986 directive generated critique and new attention. The EP Committee on the Status of Women issued a report on the situation of women in agriculture in 1993, which led to a 1994 resolution calling for recognition of work done by spouses. In the context of CAP reform, the EP now demanded that vocational training measures include 'farm management courses, agri-tourism, organic farming, diversification of activities' and new technologies (European Parliament 1993). The report and the resolution were accompanied by a study from the EP's Directorate-General for Research, providing an extensive overview of the status of women farmers in Europe, of succession practices and discrimination in social welfare policies (Subhan and Angelidis 1993/1994). In 1997 the EP passed yet another resolution, calling for an amended directive to include compulsory registration of assisting spouses and reiterating the list of demands included in the original 1984 draft (European Parliament 1997: 186). It took up the issue again, in a 2003 resolution on women in rural areas in light of CAP reform (compare European Parliament 2003), as well as in a 2008 resolution that emphasised the relevance of gender mainstreaming (GM) and rural development (European Parliament 2008).

In a 1993 strategy session of experts at the Commission, participants had concluded that the chances of reviving the original proposal were very poor. Seventeen years later, following continued agitation from the EP, the EU passed a new directive, but with different emphases than those discussed at Grado. While the original directive was seen as an extension of equality legislation, the revision was framed as an instrument for job creation under the EU's Lisbon agenda. The agenda's ambitious employment goals came to include the boosting of female employment and, thus, female entrepreneurship; it puts considerable emphasis on reconciling work with family responsibilities. The new directive reflects these priorities: it considerably strengthens the original directive by adding definitions of direct and indirect discrimination and various forms of harassment. It goes beyond equal treatment, to allow for positive action enabling the member states to counteract the dearth of female self-employment. It further gives existing equality bodies competence on the issue, ensuring proactive initiatives and closer supervision of implementation. Most importantly, it strengthens provisions on maternity leave by obliging member states to set up systems that entitle self-employed and assisting spouses to maternity protection (European Parliament and Council 2010).

The directive addresses many weaknesses in the old directive, as identified by the Network of Legal Experts on the Application of Community Law on Equal Treatment between Men and Women. Yet, like the old directive, the new one stops short of legally recognising the status of assisting spouses, including women farmers. Indeed, the language recognising the economic contributions of assisting spouses dropped out of the picture. New social security entitlements may implicitly provide such recognition. However, as the experts noted, this is not enough. Formal recognition and adequate remuneration for the work of assisting spouses is desirable (Network of Legal Experts n.d.: 6). The EU's Advisory Committee on Equal Opportunities for Women and Men had gone even further, recommending the compulsory registration of assisting spouses and raising the issue of non-equality in ownership. It argued that non-recognition restricts spouses to the informal economy, considered a form of indirect gender discrimination (Advisory Committee n.d.). The closest the directive comes to recognising the work of spouses is to require that the conditions for establishing a company between spouses should be no more restrictive than the conditions between other persons.

The gendered rules that inform the agricultural welfare state are reflected in the reluctance to recognise the work of assisting spouses. Women's demand for equal partner status contradicts a farming order that construes female labour as merely complementary, distributes welfare benefits through prices paid to male heads of household and seeks to enlarge farms – as such, it dislikes the idea of splitting up farm property, for example in case of divorce or split successions. Guaranteeing women equal status would threaten this order. Given real occupational standing, women might demand regularised income or profit shares, equitable welfare benefits, equal property and succession rights. They would become equal partners in a business, rather than serving as cheap flexible labourers in someone else's business.

However, the fact that the new directive triggered no resistance among agricultural organisations (at least at the European level) also signals a shift in gender relations. This shift no doubt relates to the overall decline in family-based agriculture; as small farms die, the average farm size continues to grow, with contracted labour increasingly replacing family labour on

European farms. The shift also pertains to rural women pursuing their own equality strategies and generating their own income either through off-farm jobs or by pursing new entrepreneurial opportunities on the farm. As spouses find new income-generating options, securing their ongoing labour for the farm requires more equitable arrangements. Independent entitlements to social security and maternity protection are possible arrangements benefiting not only women farmers whose labour supports the agricultural enterprise, but also persons finding new entrepreneurial opportunities in the service sectors of a more diversified rural economy. Feminist interventions into this re-organised countryside have shifted from legal strategies to mainstreaming gender into all types of rural policies.

3. Gender mainstreaming and liberal environmentalism

When the EU adopted gender mainstreaming in the aftermath of the 1995 UN Beijing Women's Conference (see Table 7.2), the agricultural welfare state was already being replaced by a regime of liberal environmentalism. In this context, EU 'femocrats' shifted their focus from female farm labour to 'rural women' more broadly, that is, to those living in the countryside. Gender mainstreaming resonated better in rural development programmes than in regulatory discourses on welfare or market regulation. Clearly, the new regime has influenced feminist strategy. What have been the results of this strategy so far? How has the meaning of equality changed in the context of new economic politics targeting the countryside?

In the 1990s the Commission funded several studies on rural women and on women in agriculture that started with the ideal of a diversified rural

Table 7.2 EU actions to implement gender mainstreaming in rural development

1996	Commission communication on integrating a gender perspective into all EU policies and actions
1996	Council resolution on gender mainstreaming equal opportunities for men and women into the European structural funds
2002	Agricultural Council conclusion on incorporating a gender perspective into its work
2005	Rural development regulation includes mandate to promote equality and to ensure non-discrimination using the tools of gender mainstreaming
2003 and 2007	Two EP resolutions demanding gender mainstreaming in structural funds and rural development
2010	Directive 2010/41/EU requires gender mainstreaming when formulating and implementing rules pertaining to women and men in self-employment

economy, signalling a shift in its approach to gender issues. A 1994 study funded by the Commission's Directorate-General (DG) on Relays and Information Networks compiled information on rural women's work, finding substantially lower activity rates and considerably higher unemployment rates than witnessed among men, coupled with heavy concentrations in low-skilled or unskilled occupations. It recommended that governments generate more accurate, comparative statistics and that gender be mainstreamed into research and rural policy initiatives, and it suggested a range of measures to support women's economic participation. Among these were the promotion of self-employment and independent legal status, together with a revision of Directive 86/613/EC. Anticipating the theme of diversification, the report also identified opportunities for women in the tourism and leisure industries; it listed the efforts of various rural associations to create employment by producing and marketing traditional hand-crafted products, agro-tourism, rural tourism, personal and community services, or cultural activities (see Bock 2001; Braithwaite 1994: 26). Employment and self-employment in the service industries seemed to hold the promise for 'rural women', including women on farms.

A 1998 comparative study funded by DG Agriculture (Overbeek et al. 1998) focused more narrowly on female farmers and, within the new regime, explicitly concerned itself with comparing rural women's economic activity in diversified and non-diversified areas. The study found that more labour-intensive agriculture (for example organic farming) created job opportunities for women farmers without improving their working conditions in Greece, while creating paid employment in food processing industries.[13] In other regions, ongoing modernisation and intensification of farming produced contradictory outcomes for women. It led to a decline in women's agricultural employment in Northern Italy, for example, without compensating them via access to industrial jobs outside of agriculture. Such processes improved both women's levels of employment and working conditions in agriculture in a highly diversified region of the Netherlands, however. The study concluded that 'in diversified areas farm women already contribute to diminish [sic] the vulnerability for changes in agricultural policies, because they work outside [...] or work on farms with productions less dependent on EU-income policies' (Overbeek et al. 1998: 205). Indeed, women's activity rates were higher in diversified regions, while men's rates did not seem affected by diversification. The authors again recommended recognising the occupational status of women farmers, along with increased opportunities for paid services in rural areas (for example childcare), seeking balance in the demand and supply of labour qualifications, and more serious mainstreaming of gender considerations via EU regional and structural funds.

Both of these studies redefined the problem of gender equality in agriculture as one encompassing rural areas as a whole. They described women's status as affected not only by their status on the farm but also by their employment status off the farm or outside farming, as well as by the degree to which an economy was diversified. Under the new European model, women's roles no longer seemed limited to flexible farm labour. Instead, they were taking advantage of income streams created through the commodification of the rural landscape, most importantly tourism, and the professionalisation of traditionally unpaid services. By joining the rural workforce in the service industries, women assisted in cushioning the negative impacts of agricultural liberalisation.

Introduction of a new model was paralleled by a shift in feminist strategy within the EU. Calls for gender mainstreaming centred primarily on rural development policies and programmes; they tended to construct women as workers in services reserving agriculture for men. The Commission's 1996 communication on gender mainstreaming included a section on self-employed women and spouses of the self-employed. It emphasised women's fitness for service work and painted gender roles on the farm as complementary by declaring that spouses of farmers are directly implicated in the development of farm tourism and local services (Commission 1996). Thus gender mainstreaming was deemed significant in the agricultural sector.

As the Council of Ministers and the EP incorporated gender mainstreaming into their own procedures, they similarly stressed the central role of women in diversifying the rural economy, as well as the complementarity of female service work to male agriculture. In May 2002, the Agricultural Council, under the Spanish presidency, adopted a conclusion 'incorporating the gender perspective' into its work (Council of Agricultural Ministers 2002).[14] The conclusion excised all references to granting women working on farms a 'genuine farmer status', although this proposal was included in the Spanish presidency's information note to the Employment and Social Policy Council (Spanish Presidency 2002). In fact, the Agricultural Council's conclusions did not contain a single reference to women's agricultural labour, but rather constructed rural women's activity as 'diversified' labour; the Council further linked their role in the rural economy to their empowerment. The Council recognised the need to

> continue promoting the integration of women into the various sectors covered by new sources of employment as part of integrated rural development, such as new information technologies, tele-working, local services, rural tourism, leisure services, services providing childcare and care for dependants, and the promotion of environment-friendly activities (Council of Agricultural Ministers 2002: 7).

In June 2003, the EP followed with a resolution on women in rural areas that welcomed the action of the Agricultural Council, then called on the member states to implement gender mainstreaming in agricultural and rural development policy (European Parliament 2003, 2008). While the EP resolution again brought up the issue of professional status for spouses, it especially noted the role of women in strengthening the CAP's second pillar – that is, rural development – appealing for mainstreaming in the structural funds and rural development initiatives. The emphasis fell on mainstreaming rural development programmes. The idea of changing the gender order on the farm faded into the background.

Indeed, the structural funds became one of the first domains where gender mainstreaming was applied, as mandated by a 1996 Council resolution. EU rural development policies in the past had been funded through the 'guidance' section of the European Agricultural Guarantee and Guidance Fund (EAGGF); since 2007 resources have been funnelled through the EAFRD. The monies distributed through these funds must respond to national and sub-regional development plans negotiated with the Commission and have been disbursed to governments, enabling them to pursue measures set out in those plans. In addition, the EU has long run a few 'community initiatives' directly implemented by the Commission, allowing it to explore new, experimental approaches to further common goals. The LEADER programme constitutes one such initiative with regard to rural development. Run as an experimental programme since 1991,[15] it appears as a separate 'axis' in the 2005 rural development regulation that set up the EAFRD.

Despite explicit, high-level commitment, implementation of gender mainstreaming in relation to the structural funds has been uneven and often met resistance, particularly in the EAGGF:

> In spite of the clear policy commitment on the application of gender equality to *all* policy areas and programmes, certain areas of the Structural Funds have been protected from 'interference', most notably the more 'technical' areas of the EAGGF (such as [...] milk quotas, early retirement schemes) (Braithwaite 2000: 7; emphasis in original).

In other words, gender mainstreaming was hard to apply in rural development arenas associated with the agricultural welfare regime and agricultural modernisation. These domains nonetheless accounted for the bulk of rural development activities throughout the 2000–2006 budget phase. An evaluation of the later period confirms this observation: although gender mainstreaming was mandated, most programmes lacked sex-disaggregated statistics, analysis of inequalities, and gender impact assessments. Most interventions targeted 'the farm'; since women manage only one in five farms in Europe, most infusions neglect them. This was true for agricultural investments, marketing programmes, and also for agri-environmental measures in less favoured areas (Bandarra Jazra 2002). Some programmes clearly *disadvantage* women: 'Gender imbalances might even increase when, for instance, as indicated in a measure to encourage young farmers to take over or improve farms, it is explicitly foreseen that less than 6 per cent of the beneficiaries will be women' (Commission 2002: 8). Case in point: the 2003 mid-term evaluation on rural development asked two questions involving gender – as to the number of young farmers supported, and to gender ratios among people benefiting from assistance. It found that 'in most cases fewer women benefited' from aid to young farmers setting up, though in some cases aid made 'a positive contribution to the number of female entrants to farming' (Commission 2004: 46).

While the EU refused to incorporate feminist goals into its agricultural modernisation agenda under the regime of the agricultural welfare state, it did allow for such goals in its focus on rural diversification efforts early on. Mary Braithwaite (2000: 7) observed in her evaluation that, in DG Agriculture and Rural Development, 'it has not yet been possible to take equality issues beyond the most "soft" of areas (training, agro-tourism, crafts, [...])' – inferring that gender equality concerns got marginalised into areas of non-agricultural development. The Commission's 2002 communication on gender mainstreaming in the structural funds confirmed this tendency, suggesting that 'measures which might have a positive impact on gender equality mainly cover areas such as diversification, training, new employment opportunities and setting up small enterprises in rural tourism, producing and selling regional products, childcare' (Commission 2002: 8). A booklet produced by the Commission on Women Active in Rural Development affirmed this understanding: women are helped by the development of new economic sectors 'such as telecommunications, local services, tourism and leisure services, and environmental improvement' (European Commission 2000: 11). Governmental interventions should target vocational and personal training and help women to set up businesses:

> By entering into self-employment and setting up small businesses women can be at the forefront of innovation and diversification in rural areas, for example by developing agri-tourism activities, artisanal food and drinks production, craft enterprises, telecommunication and caring services. Women often have the added advantage of an awareness and knowledge of local needs, and special interpersonal and communication skills (European Commission 2000: 13).

Rural women were being reconstructed in this narrative, transformed from farming assistants into rural entrepreneurs and service providers. They were even identified as having skills that uniquely qualified them for such positions. The booklet emphasised the need to bring these women into rural decision-making structures, seeking not only their economic but also their political empowerment in this manner. While the booklet alerted the reader to the problem of women's status on farms, interventions no longer targeted this issue.

Many gaps persist regarding the implementation of gender mainstreaming in EU rural development efforts, not least because implementation remains in the hands of member states.[16] But, before it got absorbed into the

142 *The Common Agricultural Policy*

EAFRD, the Commission exercised considerable control over mainstreaming implementation in the LEADER programme, a small slice of the EU's rural development efforts. LEADER employs a participatory approach that involves creating locally based public–private partnerships ('Local Action Groups' or LAGs). These are empowered to implement innovative, area-based development strategies. The LEADER focus on diversification has provided openings for the reconfiguration of rural gender relations. The LEADER I evaluation found a high level of participation, considerable diversification, albeit mostly through the development of tourism, the creation of new enterprises, and interesting innovations in the processing and marketing of agricultural products. Though the evaluators bemoaned a dearth of record-keeping with regard to gender, women held a large number of jobs created through the programme. The high number of projects focusing on tourism apparently facilitated this: almost twice as many new jobs in tourism went to women as men (Commission 1999b: 11).

The second phase of the programme continued this record. Although tourism was somewhat less prominent (still accounting for 30 to 50 per cent of the budgets submitted by groups), women held about half the jobs created or otherwise safeguarded through the programme (European Commission, DG Agriculture 2003: 206, 209). There was considerable local variation regarding outcomes, however; 64 per cent of jobs created through LEADER II in Ireland went to women, for example, but only 21 per cent in Germany. Women's participation in the LAGs was higher in the Nordic states and in areas designated as 'Objective 1' (covering the European periphery such as Eastern Germany) than in those designated 'Objective 5b' (disadvantaged rural areas). The mid-term evaluation of the last LEADER+ phase of the programme found that women, on average, were underrepresented in the LAGs, accounting for about 30 per cent of members. Again there was considerable variation, some LAGs enlisting no women (including Fens Leap, Saarland, and Valencia), contrasting with up to 60 per cent of the LAG in Herfordshire (European Commission 2006: X, 98).

Overall, data from the first two programme phases point to some success regarding job creation, but benefits for women differed by locale, reflecting the impact of communal politics and local gender rules. Similarly, LEADER apparently makes participation possible in certain contexts but not in others: while LEADER has produced jobs for women, their employment often reproduces traditional divisions of labour. Men predominate in jobs created through small and medium-size enterprises, crafts and services, as well as in domains valorising agricultural products. Women dominate in tourism, where many jobs are part-time (European Commission, DG Agriculture 2003: 11).

In sum, an emerging regime of environmental liberalism has shifted the focus from female farmers to women residing in the countryside. Gender mainstreaming finds particular resonance in development programmes concerned with diversifying rural incomes. While women seem to benefit when gender factors are included in rural development policies, the practice cements the segregation of rural labour markets: men dominate agriculture, women prevail in the service industries. Most public support still flows into a masculinised agricultural sector (regulated by welfare state principles, albeit in a modified fashion), while governments seek to satisfy women's desire for independence by steering them into off-farm occupations or diversifying on-farm activities. In other words, gender mainstreaming has ended in defeat when it comes to women's rights and entitlements in agriculture per se. In adapting to an environmental liberalism regime, feminists have been sidelined into rural development efforts focusing on economic diversification. There is potential for female economic empowerment in this area, but the danger of reproducing hierarchical divisions of labour and affirming identities that codify masculine domination persists.

4. Conclusion

Feminist activism has long been embedded in and circumscribed by socioeconomic structures. My aim here was to show that regulatory regimes in the agricultural sector constitute one such structure. I have treated the sector not as purely economic and external to society, but as one institutionalised through market, welfare, and rural development policies. Feminist strategies fared very differently under the agricultural welfare state than they have under a regime of liberal environmentalism.

Since the 1980s, the equal rights strategy has sought to gain women farmers' equal status by legal means, with limited success. The patriarchal family, asserting male control over the means of production, family labour and income, constituting the original foundation of the European agricultural welfare state, has conflicted with equal status demands for women farmers for decades. While the equal rights strategy has shifted discourses and altered policies in some places, it has failed to undermine the larger structure of male dominance. The new directive passed in July 2010 signals some movement in this direction, acknowledging the need for equal welfare rights and seeking to make it easier for spouses to establish joint companies. Like the earlier directive, however, the new one stops short of mandating equal status for assisting spouses.

While mainstreaming was conceptualised as a tool to attack unspoken commitments and implicit gender assumptions in 'institutions' like the agricultural welfare state, it has been sidelined to date, unable to shake up the patriarchal foundations and structures that comprise the agricultural welfare regime. It has evinced some success in integrating gender considerations into rural development policies that now serve as the 'second pillar' of the CAP. In this way it has opened up avenues for women's empowerment not existing under an agriculture-oriented paradigm. Still, gender divisions of labour are reproduced in new ways within a paradigm of diversifying rural incomes: men remain farmers, while women move out of agriculture. For certain women, this has provided on-farm business opportunities; others have found highly valued jobs in the off-farm service sector. Service jobs are nonetheless notoriously low paid; thus the creation of a feminised rural services sector entails promise but also risks the creation a new feminised, low-wage workforce.

This study raises questions concerning our need for better explorations of the relationship between feminist strategy and structural context. The EU shares competence for rural development policies with national and subnational authorities; indeed, local authorities bear primary responsibility for implementing these policies. Accordingly, the question of whether and how gender mainstreaming is being implemented in the EU cannot be satisfactorily answered by probing activities only in Brussels. Future studies need to explore the dynamics of implementation in local contexts in order to capture the mechanisms in place that prevent implementation, co-opt or otherwise sidetrack feminist strategies. They also could help to identify conditions that must be in place in order to ensure that gender mainstreaming actually achieves the goal of gender equality that it set out to accomplish.

Discussion questions

– What kinds of policies did feminists primarily pursue under the agricultural welfare state?
– What kinds of policies have feminists subsequently pursued under environmental liberalism?
– If socio-economic regimes, such as the agricultural welfare state and liberal environmentalism, circumscribe feminist activism – as argued in this article – can you speculate on the mechanisms involved in such processes?

Notes

1. This anecdote is based on Wimer's public, critical reflections on her own life history, later published as Wimer (1988).
2. *Conférence Agricole des États membres de la Communauté Économique Européenne.* Recueil des Documents, Stresa, 3–12 July 1958.
3. Family farms of this type developed parallel to Fordism as industrial employment opportunities led to an accelerated exodus of agricultural labour. Through mechanisation and modernisation, farmers increasingly substituted capital for hired labour but also drew more on their wives' flexible labour. As farm women lost access to independent income from processing agricultural products and direct marketing, their labour was integrated into the specialised farm businesses of their husbands.
4. Hill's figures (1993) did not include very small part-time farms and large farms that operated with hired labour. The 2005 figure is from Agriculture in the European Union 2007.

5. The EU guaranteed the prices of the food processing industry, and farmers benefited to the extent that industry paid higher prices for commodities.
6. In addition, the EU has committed to reducing export subsidies and to 'tariffication', in other words, to the conversion of export subsidies and quotas into tariffs. This would make European subsidies more transparent and de-link them from the vagaries of the world market.
7. According to Wilson and Wilson (2001: 221), EU environmental policies have been more effective in maintaining farmers' incomes than in changing environmental practices.
8. Committee of Agricultural Organizations in the European Community – the European umbrella of national farmers' organisations.
9. In 1988, *Women of Europe* published an update including information on the new member states Spain and Portugal. Written by the COPA Women's Committee secretariat, that account included surprisingly strong language, declaring that the aim of women working on farms was 'to be fully-fledged farmers in their own right' (Commission 1988: 5). I doubt that all the member organisations of the Committee subscribed to such a radical position. Feminist discourse in Germany, for example, did not see a contradiction between gender divisions of labour and gender equality; the Deutscher Landarbeiter Verband (the German organisation represented on the Committee) tends to stress the professionalisation of home economics over making women farmers.
10. Note that the Economic and Social Committee, in its opinion on the proposal, was more circumspect about having the state mandate what the professional organisations should put in their statutes. See Economic and Social Committee (1984).
11. Proponents of the directive had waited for the Dutch presidency of the Council, hoping it would be sympathetic to the proposal (European Parliament 1988: 8).
12. Nathalie Wuiame, CESEP (who authored the report on implementation of the directive), telephone interview with the author, 22 January 2004.
13. In contrast, in Norway (not an EU member state) the more diversified economy, supporting extensive, environmentally sensitive forms of agriculture, also spawned tourist enterprises run by women farmers.
14. The Council adopting the conclusion included six female agricultural ministers: Annemie Neyts-Uyttebroeck (Belgium); Vera Dua (Flemish Minister for the Environment and Agriculture); Mariann Fischer Boel (Denmark), who became the Commissioner for Agriculture in November 2004; Renate Künast (Germany); Margareta Winberg (Sweden) as Minister of Agriculture and Equal Opportunities; and Margaret Beckett (UK).
15. LEADER I (1991 to 1994) was continued in LEADER II (1994 to 1999) and in LEADER+ (2000 to 2006).
16. For an exploration of the implementation of gender mainstreaming in Germany, see Prügl (2009).

8
Gendering Employment Policy: From Equal Pay to Work–Life Balance

Agnès Hubert

A baby and a boss, a woman can have both, says the Court: in June 1981, Elisabeth Dekker applied for employment as an instructor in a youth training centre with Stichting Vormingscentrum voor Jong Volwassenen (VJV) in Holland. She was declared the best candidate, but, being pregnant, she was denied the job on the grounds that VJV's insurance company would not cover the potential costs of her maternity leave and, unable to hire a temporary instructor, the centre would be short-staffed until she returned. The European Court of Justice (ECJ) ruled that an employer who acts in this manner violates the European Equal Treatment Directive: denying a woman employment due to sex-related factors like pregnancy is always discriminatory. Dekker did not get the job but did receive compensation equivalent to the price of a bicycle for her child's 8th birthday. At least this verdict firmly established that women could not be denied a job or fired owing to pregnancy, a very common practice back then.

Civil service pay is not as straightforward as it seems; it consists of several components allowing for sex-related discrimination practices. In Estonia, for instance, basic salaries for public servants correspond to a salary scale, differentiated according to qualification levels, working conditions, region or other characteristics of the work. Additional payment may be granted for job performance or supplementary obligations; other increments apply to length of service, academic degrees, proficiency in foreign languages and so on. A recent complaint filed by a female advisor in the defence ministry revealed that most women received supplements for university degrees or foreign languages but still collect lower salaries than their male equivalents because of lower rankings on the basic salary scale.

Also concerned about the 10 per cent pay gap in Poland, Business & Professional Women (BPW) in Warsaw organised consciousness-raising activities for Equal Pay Day on 15 April. The 79th day of the year was chosen to highlight the number of extra days a woman must work annually in order to earn the same salary as a man would receive by 31 December of the previous year. The 2011–2016 EU Strategy for Gender Equality foresees a European Equal Pay Day to encourage employers and unions to tackle the 18 per cent average pay gap still found in the 27 member states.

Cristina possesses both French and Italian citizenship. Attaining a PhD in European Law from the prestigious Sorbonne University, she was tasked by the Paris-based consulting firm employing her to open their Milan office. There she met Pierre, a French advertising executive; they married and had their first baby. Losing his job, Pierre found a good position at a major agency in Paris; her firm would not reemploy her there, so she created her own consulting firm. Her rising income moved the family into a higher tax bracket; when she became pregnant again, she had to quit work to reduce their tax burden. Over the next ten years she tended their daughters and created a small non-profit organisation to help young migrant women integrate into the job market. Pierre made ever more 'family' decisions without consulting her, and her discontent grew. When Cristina filed for divorce, Pierre waited for the court hearing before he gave her a penny in support, forcing her and the girls to rent a tiny flat in the suburbs. Separated for five years, then finally divorced, she secures consulting contracts from time to time but struggles financially. Family break-ups often plunge women into hardship. Taxation law enabling women to make independent decisions regarding labour market participation is one issue recently raised by the European Union (EU).

The predominantly economic nature of the 1957 Treaty establishing the European Economic Community (EEC) had the unintended consequence of rendering women's labour market participation a key pathway for pursuing EU policy. The process of forging a nexus between gender equality and European integration by regulating employment conditions began with Article 119 EEC Treaty mandating 'equal pay for equal work'. Pay equality and equal treatment in the labour market met second-wave feminist demands for securing women's economic independence through monetary recognition in the labour market. This did not reflect the conventional wisdom at a time when motherhood and consumption were the dominant roles assigned to women.

In this chapter we investigate how the gender question evolved into a central focus of EU employment policy. We first frame the contours of this specific policy field and then consider the conceptual issues raised by gender researchers. Next we describe specific legal, institutional and political instruments EU actors have mobilised in their pursuit of equality in employment. Thereafter we consider the major policy inputs and outcomes linked to the implementation of gender mainstreaming. Finally, viewing the upcoming challenges in the employment field, we consider the major empirical and conceptual issues raised by the 'gendering' of EU integration.

1. The creative development of employment as an EU policy field: Core actors

EU labour market regulation followed an unconventional, often rocky path, running between fluctuating market conditions and the diverse historical, legal and institutional labour regimes among member states (which multiplied with each successive enlargement). Expanding over time (see Table 8A.1), its evolution paralleled EU social policy as a peripheral and permanently contested policy field. As was true of social policy, its original Treaty foundation was quite weak, hiding deep disagreements among member states over the proper balance between national policymaking powers and the need for Community-wide regulation. In this conflicting context, measures to promote gender equality have, paradoxically, offered grounds for political compromise on various occasions. This was the case regarding Article 119 EEC, which reconciled Germany's wish to limit the development of supranational employment competences with French industrial fears of competitive disadvantage vis-à-vis countries not bound by equal pay (see van der Vleuten 2007). Parental leave and part-time work were later chosen as the least conflictual issues for social partners concluding their first collective agreements under new 'social agreement' provisions annexed to the Maastricht Treaty.

Analysing employment policy 'between efficacy and experimentation', Martin Rhodes (2005) uses the 'three pillars' metaphor to describe the creative strategies used over time by the EU employment advocacy coalition (the Commission, the ECJ, social partners, certain member states and NGOs) to overcome opposition by shifting the parameters of the regulatory system. Employment policy has offered a rich field for opening new political processes, ranging from the predominant binding instruments of the *first pillar* (directives and community method) to the binding and flexible, or rigid and non-binding, instruments of the *second pillar* (social dialogue), to the non-binding, flexible, 'voluntary approach' of the *third pillar* (European Employment Strategy, EES). While the three pillars still co-exist to a degree, each pillar marks a particular stage, supplying a useful framework for grasping the chronological trajectory of EU employment policy: the Community method originally used to produce 'hard law' gave way to a progressively 'softer' approach, involving labour market actors in the social dialogue. It eventually became a policy-coordination exercise aimed at sharing experiences and spreading best practices with the employment strategy. It has moved towards an accentuated liberalisation of the labour markets to accommodate moves towards monetary union. As an area of contested competence, employment afforded a rich policy field for actors and for creative approaches to policymaking.

During the first stage, the ECJ played a major role in supporting Commission initiatives to integrate social and employment legislation (as in the

Defrenne case). Later on, it relied on the crucial capacity of the Commission to engage in agenda-setting and coalition-building with new supporting actors like the social partners mobilising around ambitious Action Programmes (APs). In the third phase, it developed new, collaborative methods of policymaking.

Employment did not constitute a serious concern in the wake of World War II, as European economies entered the expansionary period of the golden 1960s. It only emerged as a common problem for member states following two oil shocks, as major structural changes in the economy translated into rising unemployment in the early 1990s. The main employment developments in the early years involved areas with a solid treaty basis for legislation, gender equality (commencing with two directives on equal pay and equal treatment in 1975 and 1976) and certain aspects of work-place health and safety. The original legal base was replaced by stronger Treaty provisions, especially Articles 100 and 235 EEC, for issues directly affecting, the functioning of the common market (*inter alia*). These gave rise to two employment directives during the first period: one on dismissals (1974), the other on workers' rights in the event of mergers (1975).

The Commission, along with a dynamic, enthusiastic group of young lawyers in the ECJ and a few member states who felt European regulation should be used to defend national systems from regulatory competition were the main institutional actors back then, trying to stretch weak EU competences by using directives to create a level playing field for the 'common market' (Hoskyns 1996; Hubert 1998). The legally binding approach was considerably weakened by dissension among member states during the Thatcher era, when the UK systematically opposed European initiatives in the social and employment field. Eastern enlargement (see Gallligan and Clavero in this volume) has further diversified national industrial relations regimes, keeping employment as a controversial agenda item, as illustrated by the difficult exercise of enacting a working-time directive. This is clearly an asset gender-wise, even if women face clear hurdles in defending their rights under EU legislation.

As unemployment reached record heights in most member states (11 per cent in EU-15; 16 per cent in Spain in 1992), certain jealously guarded 'national' aspects of employment won European colours when the Danes, holding the Council presidency, asked the Commission in June 1993 to generate proposals to overcome the unemployment crisis prior to the next European Council. The Commission's answer came in December 1993, articulated in a White Paper on Growth, Competitiveness and Employment (also known as the Delors White Paper): it thoroughly analysed future challenges to maintaining Europe's competitive position (European Commission 1993). Member state economies, introducing divergent policy responses at different paces, had all been shifting from models based on full-time male breadwinners in 'life-time' employment regimes in agriculture and industry towards

150 *Gendering Employment Policy*

more volatile service economies, rooted in precarious contracts and growing female employment. The Commission recommended deepening the achievements of the single market by adopting a more coordinated approach to labour market issues with substantial stakeholder involvement.

The White Paper invoked a process whereby, at least for some member states, initiatives by the Commission were expected and welcome. Structural changes triggering high levels of unemployment had ostensibly been accelerated by the 1992 completion of the single market. That same year, Maastricht Treaty referenda in Denmark and France had revealed mounting citizen resistance; the most obvious instrument in the EU toolbox for (re)gaining their confidence entailed European efforts to fight unemployment. Commensurate with the White Paper analysis, the policymaking focus shifted from employment protection to *employment promotion*. The main institutions for pursuing a more proactive policy were, first, the Social Dialogue and, second, the European Employment Strategy (EES). Both were used creatively, the former generating agreement on an action programme, the latter utilising a process leading to an employment chapter in the Amsterdam Treaty in 1997.

Focusing on employment to intensify economic growth, the White Paper, inspired by the social democratic Commission President, Jacques Delors, recognised 'the soundness of the European social model and the virtues of cooperation between the two sides of industry' as one of the "assets of European economies"' (European Commission 1993: 6). This recognition gave new life to a process introduced a few years earlier: The European Social Dialogue (ESD). Seeking the removal of barriers to the free movement of capital, goods and people among the member states, the Single European Act (1986) provided a formal legal foundation for the ESD (Article 118b). It anticipated the creation of a European industrial relations system with the potential for collective agreements and for a decentralised, structured dialogue between the partners.

After multiple meetings marked by a lack of enthusiasm on the part of employers' representatives, a Community Charter of the Fundamental Social Rights of Workers was adopted at a December 1988 summit meeting. An Action Programme containing 47 initiatives followed, including directives on atypical work, working hours, and the free movement of workers; the intense activity that ensued opened the door to an official, structured role of management and labour in the Community legislative process. Owing to UK Prime Minister John Major's refusal to accept any progress on social policy, ESD provisions were put into an 'agreement' annexed to the Maastricht Treaty. It formalised the introduction of new actors in the EU social and employment arena and extended Council use of qualified majority voting on a wider range of policies.

At the onset of the new millennium, following the Amsterdam Treaty but prior to Eastern enlargement, the new governance mode initiated in the field of employment was replicated for social inclusion, youth, health, and migration. The open method of coordination (OMC) is characterised by the setting of common objectives, peer reviews (policy coordination) and benchmarking by participating member states. National administrations were to develop detailed objectives within the framework of the Lisbon Strategy (2000–2010), 'to strengthen employment, economic reform and social cohesion as part of a knowledge-based economy' (European Council 2000a). After its 2005 mid-term assessment, the Lisbon Strategy 'refocused' its sites on two core objectives: growth and jobs, with the goal of engaging 70 per cent of the working age population (60 per cent for women) in paid employment.[1] The EU2020 Strategy for 'smart, sustainable and inclusive growth' (2010–2020)[2] raised the employment target to 75 per cent for women and men of working age (European Commission 2010c).

The coordinated policy measures framed by the EES (monitoring and measuring systems; evaluation tools and indicators to feed scoreboards; annual reports systematically scanning the efficiency of different measures in fulfilling strategy objectives) have contributed to a successful restructuring of the European labour markets. Reversing trends of the previous decade, 1996–2006 witnessed a big turnaround in employment trends across most of Europe. The proportion of working age residents in active employment rose from 60 to 66 per cent in the EU-15, growing by more than 22 million jobs, most held by women because of the high number of service sector jobs. Research on job quality establishes that along with the shift in consensus in the early 2000 – from an exclusive focus on job *creation* to a new insistence on job *quality* – most EU member states did generate *'more and better jobs'* (Hurley and Fernández-Macías 2008). This positive picture contains many different stories, however, not all so encouraging, not to mention the fact that the global economic downturn increased the number of unemployed in the EU-27 by nearly 5 million in one year from 16,771,000 in 2008 to 21,445,000 in 2009.

Two issues should be emphasised under this new approach subsequent to the Luxembourg European Council of 1997. The first entails the new association of employment (jobs) with the 'growth and competitiveness agenda' of the renewed Lisbon Strategy of 2005, creating a cleavage between social and employment policymaking, to the detriment of social policy. This is usually unfavourable to women, insofar as their labour market participation depends more heavily on welfare policies. This was corrected in 2010 by the post-crisis EU2020 strategy, which reintegrates the 'social' into the mainstream of the new growth strategy. The second refers directly to female employment: while women bore chief responsibility for employment expansion in the last decade, job creation for women has been skewed towards the bottom of the occupational ladder. The disproportionate growth in female employment involving lower paid jobs is not conducive to greater gender equality. Moreover, neither horizontal nor vertical segregation has been seriously challenged by the 'voluntary approach' over this period: most new jobs for women are found in the segregated areas of health and education. Although their share of skilled jobs has risen, women remain underrepresented in management roles: the proportion of workers with a female boss rose by 4 per cent (reaching 25 per cent) during the decade – an unremarkable change, given the greater increase in female employment over the period.

To summarise, within the complex web of interactions characterising policy development, the employment advocacy coalition has effectively used gender equality to promote employment policy objectives.

2. Gender insights regarding employment policy

Over the years, gender experts, researchers and civil society actors have brought important insights to bear on employment policy, helping to shape EU initiatives. EU actors have pushed equally for research and analysis on employment and working conditions from a gender perspective. Since the mid-1980s, expert networks financed by the Commission have produced yearly reports on women's labour market status and conditions, offering a unique source of data and analysis on gender equality in the member states. Added to policy papers issued by the European Women's Lobby (EWL), feminist economists and social scientists supply much needed analysis for anyone looking at the interface between research and policy in the employment field. Two issues have been shaped by insights from gender experts. The first concerns the organisation of the labour market and its relation to the private sphere, expressed in terms of *gender segregation* and *work–life balance*. The second, concentrating on the actors, is defined in terms of *gender democracy* in labour market institutions.

The limited EEC competences framing gender equality policy as a European labour market issue brought the core demand of feminist thinkers – women's economic autonomy – to the forefront of the political agenda in 1958, lending later support to the female liberation movement that prioritised labour market rights for women. This opening was exploited by feminist activists who, in less than two decades, secured recognition of gender equality as a fundamental right and a core EU principle. This indirectly affected employment policy insofar as gender equality could then develop as a cross-cutting issue.

The evidence accumulated by researchers can be roughly divided into four periods. The first period (1960s and 1970s) affirmed the presence of women on the paid work front and shook up old certainties relegating women to a subordinate position. The first Europe-wide survey (see Sullerot 1968) established that maternity, on average, accounted for one-seventh of women's active life-time, leaving the remaining six-sevenths free for other activities. EU institutions began to take the issue more seriously in the 1970s. The ongoing Defrenne cases (see Locher and van den Vleuten in this volume) before the ECJ, the accession of the UK, Ireland and Denmark with labour majorities, and preparations for the first UN Women's Conference in Mexico City prompted the Commission to present its first draft Equal Pay Directive to the Council in 1975.

The second period (1980s) saw the emergence of the work–life balance issue. In a major report (Meulders et al. 1993), the EU Expert Group on Gender and Employment (EEGE)[3] showed that a mass increase in women's labour market participation was accompanied by a radical change in traditional family patterns: despite variation among member states, activity curves across women's life cycles increasingly resembled those of men. The 'M curve' marking the activity patterns of those who left paid employment to care for children was being replaced by a 'bell curve', describing continuous activity from school to retirement.

Family responsibilities were recognised as a cause of workplace segregation in a limited number of occupations linked to women's traditional roles. The neoclassical school (Becker 1993) argued that segregation was the result of women choosing lower, easier positions in the labour market; they invested less in human capital because of their 'preference' for unpaid work at home, where they could maximise their welfare functions. The radical school challenged traditional economics on the 'natural' price of labour by placing the role of domestic work in determining standards of living at the centre of the economic system (Picchio 1992). Neoclassical theory was heavily criticised by feminist scholars for its crude assumptions (European Commission 1999c), based on determinism rooted in biological difference as well as on the allegedly identical interests of male and female partners (Humphries and Rubery 1995). Equally unconvincing were arguments that women choose to do unpaid work and that 'free choice' can be assumed under a gender order where 'all things are unequal' (Silvera 1998).

By the third period, starting in the 1990s, women's integration had established itself as one of the most significant labour market developments. Gender was increasingly recognised as a significant factor in explaining labour supply trends, including the development of atypical work, the growth of service sector employment and increasing 'flexibility' required by the market. The period might have been dominated by economists' straightforward supply-side approach to the labour market concentrating on waiving obstacles to women's participation – without much consideration for gender equality objectives. Gender researchers concentrated much of their work on the nature and characteristics of new segregation, linked to flexibility, service jobs and women's allocated role in the creation of the single market (Rubery et al. 1999).

The reports compiled by the EEGE presented the variable of 'time allocation' in a radically new way: distancing itself from the economist view that the gender division of labour results from decisions taken to reconcile time constraints, authors espousing equality as a priority objective calculated the length of the ideal working week for both parents, in ways that would enable them to manage their work and family responsibilities equally, providing analytical support for the 1992 EC recommendation on childcare; for the first time, an official text argued for an increased role for fathers in promoting gender equality on the labour market. This third period also saw an Organization for Economic Co-Operation and Development (OECD) study (1994) on women and structural change heralding a shift in approach: deeming the restructuring of national economies as a societal issue rendered women's employment central to socio-economic change, not a special case or 'problem'.

Recent mainstream literature has concentrated on the future of work in view of the new gender balance, societal ageing and the role of welfare in shaping labour market participation (Jouen and Caremier 2000). Emerging issues in (gender) research during this fourth period include the impact of new labour relations trends: diversification; flexibilisation of work contracts; changes in the organisation of work and production; segmentation of working life; changes in industrial relations; and strains on family and working life among disadvantaged population groups. New forms of segregation among women, skilled and under-skilled, even in the same professions (nursing, for example) attracted greater attention. Most importantly, the effect of social and labour market institutions on gender relations has been brought back into the debates (see Stratigaki in this volume).

The Council of Europe first introduced the concept of *parity democracy* in November 1989, promoting the ideal of a balanced participation of women and men in all institutions, at all levels. This strongly revived the feminist debate on women and forms of democratic representation (Cockburn 1995). In 1992, the European Commission and the EWL organised the first 'Women in Power Summit', in Athens, where parity democracy inspired a political declaration backed by high-ranking women in the member states. The call for 'equal representation of women and men in decision making bodies' (1992 Athens Declaration, http://www.eurit.it/Eurplace/diana/ateneen.html) – including the employment field – became a key demand of the 1990s. Historians exploring women's presence in the labour movement testified to the misrepresentation of their interests by men who had controlled the floor at professional labour and union conferences.[4]

When the ESD was revived with the 1992 Maastricht Treaty, the Commission sponsored the first quantitative study on women in influential posts, on committees of national trade union centres and in European sectoral industry committees (Braithwaite and Byrne 1994; Cockburn 1995). Examining women's presence at the local (intra-state) level regarding the Europe-directed activities of unions and employers' federations, Cynthia Cockburn (1995) notes that collective bargaining at EU level is even more exclusionary for women than at national level.

The reasons for women's exclusion are rooted in the classic interface between the labour market (including interest representation) and the domestic sphere, which disadvantages women as workers. Cockburn identifies unsupportive attitudes prevailing in trade unions and employers' organisations (for example rejecting positive action). She suggests strategies for intensifying women's participation in the social dialogue, including tactics for changing such attitudes at worksites and in unions; strengthening equality measures in trade unions and national confederations; taking steps to achieve sex-proportional representation, securing women's representation as a social group; mainstreaming concerns expressed by female groups within the organisations; promoting information, education and guidance for women in gaining access to Europe; and putting pressure on employers' federations to field more women in social dialogue processes. These ideas gained ground in unions and, with the advancement of individual women in employer's organisations, introduced some gender concerns to the ESD.

3. Instruments for promoting gender equality in employment

Three types of instruments have been applied: (1) *hard law or directives* enforced by the ECJ; (2) *'creative' instruments*, including financing via the structural funds, the social dialogue and action programmes managed by the Commission; and (3) formalised *soft policy instruments*, such as the EES and the OMC.

Community legislation has influenced member state sex equality laws in decisive ways. National legislation must be enacted and amended to comply with the standards set by EU directives and ECJ rulings. The hostile reaction in business circles to the updated maternity leave directive (COM (2008) 637) amends Directive 92/85/EEC on measures to encourage improvements in the workplace safety and health of pregnant workers, those who have recently given birth or are breastfeeding, providing a minimum of 20 weeks of paid leave and a paternity leave clause, illustrates the impact of EU legislation at the national level.

Article 119 EEC should have been transposed and implemented shortly after adoption in 1958 but the first 'hard law' directive requiring its actual implementation was not adopted until 1975 – just as the ECJ was rendering its judgment on the third Defrenne case. The equal pay principle was declared 'directly effective' and 'equality' acknowledged as a fundamental right under Community law on 8 April 1976. Other directives rapidly followed on equal treatment in employment and working conditions (1976), equal treatment in social security schemes (1979), the self-employed (1986), and on equal treatment in occupational schemes of social security (1986). The first directive on maternity protection (1992) as well as one reversing the burden of proof in sex discrimination cases (1997) can also be attributed to this first wave, which created a set of basic rights for equal treatment as work, albeit in a 'non-discriminatory way' for any individual wishing to claim for her or his rights before a court.

Directives adopted in the 1990s served the purpose of testing implementation of the Social Protocol provisions annexed to the Maastricht Treaty, which gave social partners a chance to agree on employment legislation prior to final decision by the Council. Two successive framework agreements, on parental leave (December 1995) and on part-time work (May 1997), were thus negotiated by Employers' (UNICE, CEEP) and trade union (ETUC) representatives approved by the Council shortly after. The former was revised in 2010, to increase the leave accorded each working parent from three to four months, at least one of which cannot be transferred to the other; any month not taken is forfeited, providing a strong incentive for fathers to use their leave entitlement.

The basic standards set by the first directives have been rendered more specific by subsequent directives, for example the 2002 ('repackaged') equal treatment directive, in response to the 1995 *Kalanke v Freie Hansestadt Bremen* (1 Case 450/93) and the 1986 *Marshall v Southampton and South West Hampshire Area* (Case 152/84) rulings on affirmative action; the 2010 revision of Directive 2001/41/EU, applying the equal treatment principle to men and women engaged and active in a self-employed capacity (Directive 2010/41/EU), thus providing a maternity allowance for self-employed workers and their spouses or life partners; the maternity directive to be approved in 2011 (see above); and the 2006 Recast Directive (see Box 8.1). Other legal instruments re-shaping gender equality in employment included 'recommendations' – that is, non-binding Council or Commission agreements, often used by the Court to interpret EU legislation – and Council resolutions or 'conclusions', representing political commitments among member states. These texts are often quite progressive, such as the Council recommendations on positive action (1984), childcare (1992), on balanced participation in decision-making processes (1996), or the Commission's recommendation on the protection of the dignity of women and men at work (1992).

Box 8.1   The 2006 'Recast Directive'

Directive 2006/54/EC of 5 July 2006 consolidated the Equal Pay Directive 75/117, Equal Treatment Directive 76/207, Occupational Social Security Directive 86/378, and the Burden of Proof Directive 97/80, taking into account both amendments and revised interpretation of those Directives issued by the European Court of Justice. It references 'work of equal value' (*comparable worth*), extends protection against discrimination arising from the gender reassignment of a person and deems sexual harassment contrary to the ideal of equal treatment, rendering it 'subject to effective, proportionate and dissuasive penalties'.

The growth of the service economy, coinciding with extended educational periods delaying labour market entry, created worker shortages in certain sectors, from the 1980s onwards. Rather than calling on migrants, as industrialists did in the 1960s, employers opted for a feminisation of the labour market. Hence, pressures from employers reinforced feminist demands, echoed in the transnational context (first UN Women's Conference in Mexico, 1975), for women's participation in the labour market. The Commission responded to this double pressure with multi-year Action Programmes (APs), as well as with key financial levers from the European Social Fund (ESF).

Moving into the *'soft law' stage*, five successive APs, stretching from 1982 to 2006, enlarged the policy scope, moving from initial equal pay concerns to a framework including affirmative action, vocational training/education, improving women's status in society, eliminating gender stereotypes, fostering equal participation in decision-making, and fighting gender based violence. The first five APs have drawn on a specific gender equality budget line (rising from €3 million to €10 million per year). Equality lawyers testified that the elimination of sex discrimination can be obstructed by specific factors: constraints on access to justice; individual litigation; difficulties in obtaining the relevant employer information; lack of court familiarity with gender equality law, inadequate sanctions and remedies; and unequal 'dominant' cultures. These could be mitigated through specialised training for lawyers and judges, recommendations, and codes of practice for procedures and remedies.

Special training for women and 'measures helping them to manage family responsibilities while remaining available for the labour market' (Verwilghen 1993) were likewise deemed necessary. The Commission promoted research and actions in these fields with the assistance of expert networks (one per member state, and a coordinator). The first networks of the early 1980s were tasked with facilitating the implementation of equality directives, monitoring the situation of women in employment and introducing positive action for women in business. In 1986, a network on childcare sought ways to make mothers more 'available' to the labour market.

By 1992, as economic and political interest in greater female labour market participation converged in a period of structural change (OECD 1994), a third AP widened the scope for action: it included legal access, training and positive action, as seen earlier, but also items designed to 'improve the status of women in society', crucial for enhancing women's employment. This amounted to a turning point: achieving EU objectives in the economic and social domains required a shift from merely concentrating on equal pay to an approach encompassing women's participation in decision-making positions, combating stereotypes and treating the social construction of gender inequalities. Altogether, nine networks assisted the Commission in this wide-ranging promotion of gender equality as women's labour market participation grew exponentially, from 32 per cent in the early 1980s to 52 per cent in the mid-1990s.

After 2006, equality promotion continued with the Roadmap for Gender Equality, two networks and supporting actions in six fields.[5] Budget rationalisation eliminated financing for former 'programmes'. Roadmap measures were to be financed by the general social budget line of PROGRESS (an employment and social solidarity programme). The new 'Strategy for gender equality 2011–2016', replacing the Roadmap, concentrates on the economy and labour market; equal pay; equality in senior positions; tackling gender violence; and promoting equality beyond the EU (European Commission 2010d). Getting more women into the labour market and helping to reach the Europe 2020 target employment rate of 75 per cent overall for women and men is likely to monopolise much of the attention.

The ESF contribution to gender equality took off in the 1990s with the development of pilot projects under the Community initiative NOW (New Opportunities for Women). This initiative, which mobilised a tiny proportion of the ESF, helped with the design and financing of specific training, positive action and childcare programmes. It opened the way for prioritising gender equality within the development of the ESF mainstream programmes for the periods 1994–1999 and 2000–2006 (European Commission 2002b); This priority disappeared in the following programming period 2007–2013 (Stratigaki 2008), abandoning multiple gender equality projects that contributed to wider labour market participation of women in member states using social policy instruments.

Another *soft-law measure*, the EES (see Box 8.2), was launched in 1997, as a follow-up to the Delors White Paper and inclusion of a new employment title (VII) in the Amsterdam Treaty. The core objective was to promote a high level of employment and social protection, using the OMC to reconcile member state employment policies on the basis of Employment Guidelines (EGL) consistent with the Broad Economic Policy Guidelines (BEPG).

Box 8.2   European Employment Strategy (EES)

The EES (Europe 2020) strives to create more and better jobs throughout the Union. It has established measures to meet three targets by 2020:

- to place 75 per cent of all people aged 20–64 in paid labour;
- to reduce school drop-out rates below 10 per cent, and to ensure that at least 40 per cent of 30–34-year-olds complete third level education; and
- to remove at least 20 million from (or 'at risk' of) poverty and social exclusion.

An explicit gender perspective was adopted establishing equal opportunities as one of the four pillars (beyond *employability, entrepreneurship* and *adaptability*). This significantly raised consciousness, positing women's behaviour as crucial to the success of the EU employment goals (see European Commission 2008d).

The high visibility of gender equality was confirmed later by the Barcelona childcare targets[6]; it will progressively disappear in subsequent growth and employment strategy exercises (Lisbon Strategy 2000-2005; renewed Lisbon Strategy 2005-2010). The EU 2020 target of 75 per cent labour market participation among women and men is quite ambitious but does not make a special case for gender equality. Recognising the important innovation brought into the first version of the EES (affording gender equality a specific status and resources under the Structural Fund guidelines), we offer two criticisms: first, the instrumentalisation of women's labour force participation for economic growth objectives left out policies related to social justice (Stratigaki 2004); second, quantitative objectives have neglected the quality of women's work, contributing to a degradation of employment status and to the emergence of a class of 'working poor' consisting of a female majority.

4. Gender mainstreaming employment policy: Outputs and outcomes

Gender equality advances in the job market, women's educational attainment, their increased participation in decision-making positions, measures against sexual harassment in the workplace, as well as enhanced provision of childcare facilities in most member states owe to EU leverage. Changes in women's aspirations for autonomy as wage earners, changes in family structures, and the EU's expanding 'gender reach' followed parallel courses in the member states, despite their diverging starting points. While Swedish and Finnish admission in 1995 foresaw little progress for Nordic women based on EU standards, the latter supplied major impulses for the French, German, Italian and Romanian labour markets, requiring them to place women on equal footing with men and enforcing the creation of a level playing-field. Beyond hard- and soft-law instruments, the ESF and benchmarking coordination foreseen by the EES, the Commission's endorsement of mainstreaming gender, coupled with developing databases to measure inequalities, has raised the profile of these issues.

Gender mainstreaming in employment policy had commenced prior to the Commission's Communication requiring the incorporation of gender equality in all appropriate domains. Women's integration into EU employment policy mechanics became a major issue in December 1991; prior to the opening of the borders in January 1992, the employment committee – the tripartite dialogue structure – dedicated one session to the risks and opportunities for women created by the single market (Conroy 1988). Vasso

Papandreou, Commissioner for employment and social policy (1988–1993), had already given instructions to mainstream equality in the Commission's annual publication, *Employment in Europe*, supplying an overview of the employment situation in the EU and analysing key labour market issues. This consciousness-raising initiative encouraged the dedicated Commission services (the Equal Opportunities Unit and its network of gender economists) to work with EUROSTAT on the production and analysis of sex-disaggregated data on the employment situation of women and men.

Over the years, this same network had produced unique comparative analyses to guide employment policy formation at the EU and national levels, contributing to 'Europeanisation'.[7] During the last decade, it has produced systematic gender impact assessments of the National Action Plans and National Reform Programmes underpinning the Lisbon Strategy through 2010; further instruments monitor gender equality progress under the new Europe 2020 Strategy. The generation of statistics and analysis has, *inter alia*, fuelled the production of annual reports on the labour market situation of women, brought to the attention of the heads of states and governments at every March European Council. Statistical tables (on female/male labour market participation, the employment impact of parenthood, the pay gap), part of the 2010 report, are published every year, allowing for a quantitative monitoring of progress (or lack thereof).

While the EU's fight against discrimination at work has seen great strides in equal treatment relative to the labour market and equal work opportunities, it has thus far failed to address the crucial impact of unpaid work on the employment patterns of women and men (Jenson 2008). The problems of combining care and employment still marginalise countless women (and some men) who 'care' in Europe. In an ageing society seeking to maximise its human resources (pushing for 75 per cent labour force participation), reconciling domestic activities and family lives with paid employment will soon become a major policy priority.

5. Emerging issues: Gendering EU employment policy

Two specific issues stand out today in projecting the future of gender equality in employment policy: the radically new context created by the Euro-crisis and the need for an EU response to put the economy back on track; and women's persistent under-representation in the employment and collective bargaining sphere. Experts with experience in combining paid/unpaid work and welfare reforms will be needed to bring about a turning point in the post-crisis world; future reforms will ultimate revolve around the three concepts of *flexicurity* (see Box 8.3), anti-discrimination and the rise of the social economy.

The *unprecedented crisis affecting global financial markets* beginning in autumn 2008 led to a recession that will be felt across the EU for years.

> **Box 8.3   What is 'flexicurity'?**
>
> *Flexicurity* is an integrated strategy to enhance flexibility and security in the labour market. Flexibility focuses on successful moves ('transitions') throughout the life-cycle: from school to work, from one job to another, between periods of unemployment (or inactivity) and work, and from work to retirement. It does not mean merely more freedom for companies to recruit or dismiss, nor does it imply that open-ended contracts are obsolete. It is about helping workers to move into better jobs, 'upward mobility' and optimal development of talent. Flexibility also refers to creating flexible work organisations, capable of quickly and effectively mastering new productive needs and skills, and facilitating the combination of work and private responsibilities. *Security* likewise entails more than just the security of keeping one's job: it is about equipping people with the skills that enable them to advance in their working lives, as well as helping them to find new employment. It also requires adequate unemployment benefits to facilitate such transitions. Finally, it encompasses training opportunities for all workers, especially for the low skilled and older workers.
>
> *Source*: European Commission (2007c).

It wiped out many gains in economic growth and unemployment reduction seen over the preceding decade due to women's increasing employment – which, in turn, created jobs in the homecare service industry. As a result of the crisis, 23 million people (almost 10 per cent of the working population) lost jobs in 2009. Disaggregating the effects on gender equality is no simple task. The initial comparison of female and male attitudes towards risk-management ('if the Lehman brothers had been Lehman sisters...') suggested a change of perspective and a potential demand for more women in decision-making in the corporate world. But attention simultaneously shifted to men losing their jobs in highly sex-segregated sectors such as car manufacturing, construction and financial services – which are more directly affected by shrinking demand and credit restrictions. Traditionally feminised sectors, such as education and health-care, evince a lower elasticity of demand.

Further consequences for equality engendered by the crisis, highlighted by a 2009 ILO report, entail an increase in housework due to declining family incomes and shrinking social services, all of which increases the burden of informal work, mainly performed by women. Feminist research (Walby 2009a, 2009b) outlined two further scenarios: either this new burden of unpaid work will take away women's time for education and paid labour, pulling them back into the home or, alternatively, it will provide a chance

162 *Gendering Employment Policy*

for enhancing productivity and value in the reproductive sphere. The EU has not radically re-directed its actions thus far, despite evidence of mounting discrimination against women: a wider share of the reproductive work has been transferred to the market for affluent families, while lone mothers and women at risk are bearing extra burdens, worsening their economic circumstances.

Against the backdrop of an ageing society and the ongoing modernisation of its social model, EU reactions to the crisis have led to a wide-ranging policy exercise. The EU 2020 strategy for new 'smart, sustainable and inclusive growth', proposed by the Commission in March 2010, sets five targets for 2020, to which member states are now committed. With the exception of the employment target, which mentions women and men of working age, gender equality is not prioritised. Still, the ambitious employment goal (moving up to 75 per cent, from the present level of 58 per cent for women, 68 per cent for men) or poverty reduction goal (20 million fewer) means that efforts to redirect growth towards a greener, more inclusive economy will have to include women and to intensify the focus on needs of the reproductive economy. Projections start with the current demographic and educational profiles in Europe (59 per cent of graduates are women), and end with growth scenarios where full gender equality will be attained in the EU (Figure 8.1).

The second question pertains to the actors shaping labour market structures and regimes. European employment policy has developed in a context open to participation and innovation; some actors have used gender equality to pursue their own objectives, but gender equality advocates have not successfully promoted their goals to the same extent, given women's under-representation in the institutions shaping labour regimes (Cockburn 1995). The demand for equal representation and participation born of the 1990s still has a long way to go: key labour market actors include public

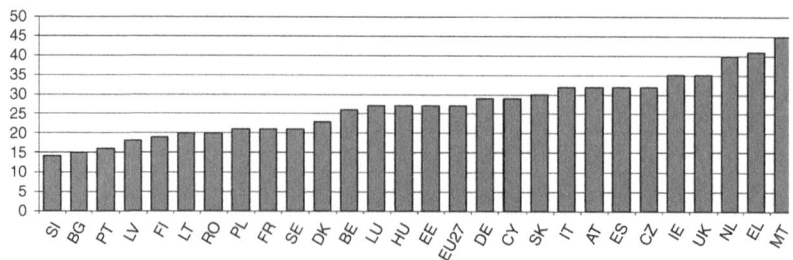

Figure 8.1 Potential growth in GDP in the EU member states following a transition to full equality in the labour market, in percentage of GDP
Source: European Commission, DG Employment 2010: 22, based on Löfström (2009).

administrations headed by labour ministers (11 out of 27 ministers at the Employment Council were female under the Belgian presidency as of July 2010); trade unions and the corporate world still account for very few women in top positions. Social partners played a greater role at the European level once they became full partners in the regulatory negotiating process under the Social Protocol (Maastricht) in 1992. Over the years, however, women trade unionists (40 per cent of the total membership) have struggled in an overwhelmingly hostile context to register small victories in policy documents, for example a resolution on the ETUC strategy to secure equal opportunities (mainstreaming and participation) and the framework agreement on parental leave (Bergamaschi 2000).

6. Conclusion

Sixty years after the Community's founding, the member states' commitment to equal pay and equal treatment at work remains an unfulfilled promise for the majority of Europe's women. Having analysed successive developments in employment, gender researchers have brought conceptual insights to bear on this policy field, as well as new institutional strategies, fostering gender equality and common standards in European labour markets. However, given the policy outputs and outcomes of gender mainstreaming (or lack thereof), we conclude that, unless structural obstacles in the social and economic realms are deconstructed, EU employment policy will continue to reproduce or reinvent segregationist and inequality patterns.

Over the years, pressures for progress regarding greater equality have come from all possible actors, such as markets (utilising women's labour power and skills) and states (more women in the labour market, to compensate for demographic deficits and encourage higher fertility). But the same logic has not penetrated the black box of the family, where gender inequalities first occur, prosper and are disseminated. Structural changes are needed to merge work performed in the private and public spheres into a set of productive solidarity mechanisms.

Flexicurity, the rise of the social economy and the fight against discrimination – policy instruments developed by the EU to modernise labour markets – hold great potential for effectively taking into account the issues of care, as well as horizontal and vertical occupational segregation hindering equal participation in the labour market: *flexicurity* would allow young parents to earn more, while working fewer hours when their children need their care; tougher *anti-discrimination policies* would effectively challenge stereotypes and labour market segregation; *social innovations* would offer new solutions to care, health and education needs. While we look forward to such policy developments, we recognise that their chances of being designed as effective triggers for overcoming structural obstacles to women's contributions to the EU economy would be greater if women – who have a vested interest in change – were significantly better represented among the decision-makers who shape these changes.

Discussion questions

- Discuss how and why the gender question evolved into a central focus of EU employment policy.
- What have been the repercussions of the European Social Dialogue for women?
- How have the different instruments employed in the employment domain affected the status of women as workers? What instruments have proven most effective thus far?
- What are some of the 'pitfalls' of the flexicurity concept from a gender perspective?

Table 8A.1 Employment provisions in treaties

Treaty	Treaty of Rome (EEC) 1958	SEA (Single European Act) 1986	TEU 1992	Treaty of Amsterdam 1997	Lisbon Treaty 2009
Content	Art. 117 (Working conditions and standards); Art. 118 (requires the Commission to promote cooperation between MS); Art. 119 (Equal pay for equal work); other articles used as a basis for employment directives: Art. 100 (completion of the Single Market) Art. 235 (matters not foreseen by the Treaty)	Social policy agreement (11 MS) and revised Art. 117–118; Art. 118a QMV Health & Safety); Art. 100a (QMV Single market)	Social Protocol (11 MS) and revised Art. 117–118; QMV for Health & safety, work conditions and equality at work	New title VIII on employment (Art.125–130 of TEC replacing Art 109 TEC in TEU); UK opt out revoked QMV extended to workers information and consultation & integration of persons excluded from the labour market; most employment policy under unanimity voting; Pay, Right of association, right to strike & lockouts are excluded from Community competence	Charter of Fundamental Rights binding for 24 MS (social and equality rights); gender equality recognised as a value of the EU (Art.1bis)a principle (Art2)+ Gender mainstreaming; (Art. 8) Equal pay (Art157); Full employment and social progress are objectives of the EU; the role of social partners is recognised and the social dialogue is reinforced

Table 8A.1 (Continued)

Treaty	Treaty of Rome (EEC) 1958	SEA (Single European Act) 1986	TEU 1992	Treaty of Amsterdam 1997	Lisbon Treaty 2009
Political context	Opposition between French and German views: Germany opposed to supranational competences in employment legislation while France wanted harmonisation to avoid competitive disadvantage Agreement ad minima on Equal Pay	Community competences bolstered for health and safety issues where regulation could prevent market distortions	Deepening of the Single Market and prospects for EMU justifies competences to avoid regulatory race to the bottom. UK disagreement (opt-out)	Preparation for enlargement to Eastern Europe. Increase in rights-based policy. Anti-discrimination clause (Art. 13) and gender mainstreaming (Art. 3 para 2) Social democratic governments: UK enters the social protocol	'We need a much stronger focus on the social dimension of Europe at all levels of government': Commission President Barroso in: Political Guidelines, Sept. 2009
Economic context	'trente glorieuses' (Thirty Glorious Years) continuous growth and full employment	Rising unemployment and declining employment rates after recession triggered by the oil shocks of the 1970s	Problems of industrial adjustment, mismatch between supply and demand of skills	Employment restructuring linked to single market; and to globalisation Investments in the service economy	Post crisis: work for a green, sustainable, inclusive economy
Women's activity rate		40%	43%	51.4%	59.1%
EU Members	6	12	12	15	27

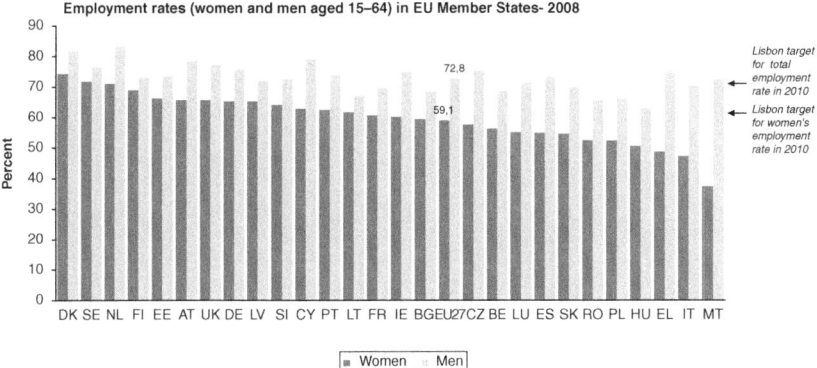

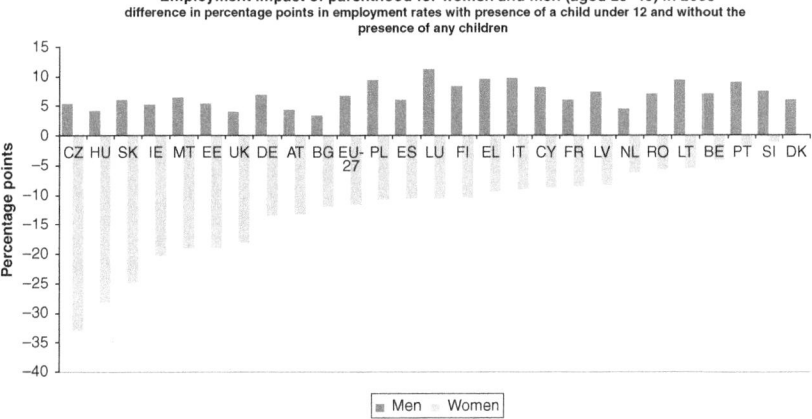

Figure 8A.1 Gender-disaggregated employment statistics

168 *Gendering Employment Policy*

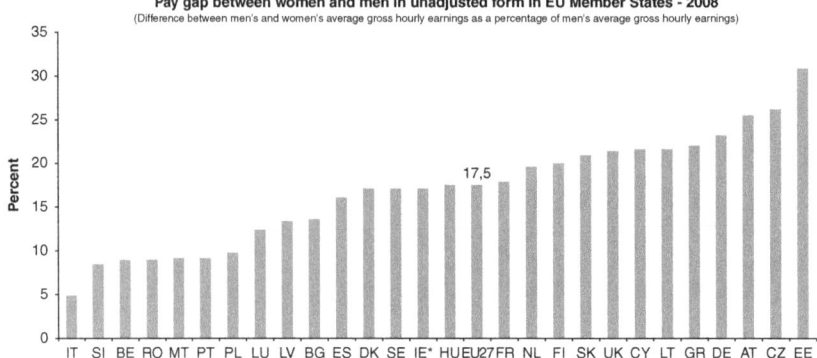

Figure 8A.1 (Continued)

Notes

1. For details, see http://ec.europa.eu/archives/growthandjobs_2009.
2. For information on the Strategy, see http://ec.europa.eu/eu2020/index_en.htm.
3. For information on EEGE, see http://www.fgb-egge.it/homepage.asp.
4. For example, the first international socialist meeting in Geneva adopted a resolution opposing night work by women in 1866, where an overwhelming majority of men vehemently proclaimed the need to protect mothers and wives, even if they were workers who needed to earn a living. A handful of female labourers voiced their concerns, not wanting to be excluded from some of the best-paid jobs, but they were too few to be heard.
5. The Roadmap specifies six priority action areas for 2006–2010: equal economic independence; reconciliation of private and professional life; equal representation in decision-making; eradication of all forms of gender-based violence; elimination of gender stereotypes; promotion of gender equality in external and development policies.
6. The goal is to provide childcare by 2010 to at least 90 per cent of children aged between 3 years and the mandatory school age and at least 33 per cent of children under 3 years of age in order to remove disincentives to female labour force participation.
7. Europeanisation is used here to mark the shift in cognition and discourse affecting EU actors at national and supranational levels in response to the development of common instruments.

9
Gendering the Social Policy Agenda: Anti-Discrimination, Social Inclusion and Social Protection

Maria Stratigaki

Eleni lives in Avra, a small town of 3,000 inhabitants, 70 kilometres away from the Greek capital city, Athens. She moved to her husband's hometown, where he worked long hours at a local Greek private bank; this meant giving up her job as an accountant at an Athens travel agency. Since Avra lacked childcare facilities, she could not look for a new job. Her mother lived in Athens, while her sick mother-in-law needed long-term care at home. Due to gender stereotypes there was no question of her husband quitting his job, although Eleni probably could have found a better one in the accounting section of a local production company. When her second child arrived, she learned that the Avra Municipality had joined a European Social Fund (ESF) programme financing the construction of a kindergarten where she could enrol her two children. The municipality, moreover, benefitted from another ESF programme, 'Help at Home', in which she placed her mother-in-law, whose daily care imposed extra burdens. Eleni was even happier to learn that, as of the following year, the public education system would extend pre-school education from one to two years, another initiative supported by the ESF. All of these programmes were funded for 'promoting women's access in the labour market' – one of the ESF's five priority objectives for the period 2000–2006. Eleni could return to the labour market because she derived support from three ESF programmes at the same time. However, these fortuitous circumstances are very rare in Greek small towns.

Efthimios Evrenopoulos argued that the principle of gender equality in social security should apply to his right to a survivor's pension following the death of his wife, a former employee of the Greek State Electricity Company (DEI). The national Court of Justice decided that he was not entitled to a survivor's pension: these were intended only for 'non-working' wives who find themselves without income after the death of a working husband. Evrenopoulos appealed to the European Court of Justice (ECJ), which ruled in 1999 that the DEI pension scheme did fall within the scope of Article 119 EEC Treaty (today 157 TFEU) stipulating equal pay between women and men. As an occupational scheme depending on the labour relation of employees, the DEI pension qualified as an occupational benefit (as 'pay deferred') that had to be allocated without discrimination on the basis of sex. With the help of ECJ Judgment C-147/95, Evrenopoulos 'forced' the DEI to revise all occupational pension schemes (Greek Law 2676/1999). However, the prerequisites for securing a survivor's pension and the benefit levels accorded were rendered stricter for female survivors than had previously been the case. As often occurs in cases involving legislative implementation, *de jure* gender equality was established in principle, but the level of protection was reduced in terms of requirements and eligibility.

Gender equality and social policy have been closely linked throughout the last 60 years of European integration, although the last two decades have seen a shift away from the predominance of the equal pay requirement, counted among the social provisions of the 1957 Treaty of Rome, to the merging of sex with other sources of inequality, that is, race, ethnicity and disability. Placed under a single EU policy roof and reclassified as anti-discrimination policy, the latter currently constitutes one of the six priority areas of the EU Social Policy Agenda (European Commission 2008e). As discussed in Part 1, gender equality has served as a driving force for increasing Community involvement in social policy matters since the 1970s.

The push for gender equality has involved several critical 'firsts', coinciding with an expansion of EU powers following the 1976 Equal Treatment Directive; equal treatment in social security was embedded in new directives (79/7/EEC and 86/378/EEC), expanding the social field beyond 'equal pay'. Next came the parental leave regulation (Directive 96/34/EC), the first to activate the Social Protocol appended to the 1992 Maastricht Treaty; the 1992 Council Recommendation on childcare marked the first time that EU policy transcended the labour market boundary to cover a 'private' domain, the family. Last but not least, Directive 2004/113/EC mandating equal access to goods and services has likewise extended the EU's gender reach beyond the labour market.

Given their respective origins in Article 119 EEC, the gender dimensions of social policy and employment policy often overlap (see Hubert in this volume). One policy objective bordering on both domains is the Community objective promoting the *reconciliation of work and family life*. Whereas 'reconciliation' has become a central component of the EU employment agenda, relevant measures like support for childcare and other forms of dependent care traditionally fall under the social agenda, and thus lie under the control of national welfare states.

In this chapter we discuss the gender dimensions of three social policy arenas falling within the purview of European Social Model concerns:[1] (a) *care for dependants* (children, elderly and the disabled), framed under the EU reconciliation objective within employment policy; (b) the *social inclusion of vulnerable people* (long-term unemployed, single mothers, migrants and so on), framed early on as an EU mechanism for combating poverty, then under strategies for combating social exclusion, and now as *active inclusion policies*; and (c) the *modernisation of social protection systems* (social security, pensions, and the like), framed under the EU prerogatives of economic convergence.

We begin with an overview of major steps contributing to EU social policy development. Next we highlight major feminist insights regarding social policy, describe major policy instruments and assess progress in the social policy field from a gender perspective. We then analyse opportunities and risks for gender equality in relation to current EU social policymaking. Finally we discuss a few empirical and conceptual elements that could be used to strengthen the gender equality perspective in future social integration processes.

1. Social policy in the EU: An overview

Research on EU social policy shows that its development was shaped by a long, difficult interaction between economic and social goals, inside and outside the meagre social policy competence inscribed in the Treaties. Continuing interaction led to the adoption of a *social integrationist* rather than a *redistributive* objective, as was the case for traditional European social welfare models.[2]

Originally the Community promoted social provisions to reduce unfair competition among member states, as in the cases of the equal pay (EEC Treaty) and Single European Act (SEA) (see van der Vleuten in this volume). Later on, social policy was enhanced to keep pace with progress in economic integration, as illustrated by the Social Protocol of the Maastricht Treaty. A limited EU approach to social benefits often served as an alibi for legitimating the restructuring (and reduction) of social protection at the national level. Empirical evidence shows that the EU has acted neither as a simple coordinator of national social policies nor as a consistent supranational policymaker. As elsewhere, social policy is developing within a multi-tiered system of decision-making; policy measures are shaped within the context of continuous conflicts between the EU and member state governments. The latter are forced to confront and accommodate changing asymmetries and contradictions between broader economic and social objectives, as well as to respond to different demands from EU citizens. While some vote for national and European parties (the Greens, Coalition of the Left), or for civil society organisations lobbying for a socially oriented Union, others (for instance conservatives) promote national sovereignty, even when the EU offers more rights to individuals. Major EU social policy landmarks since 1957 (see Table 9.1) should always be understood in light of persistent political, economic and social constraints (Hantrais 2007: 1–24).

Table 9.1 Major turning points in EU social policy

1957	Articles 118–128 EEC (Treaties of Rome)
1974	Community Social Action Programme
1979	Directive on the implementation of the principle of equal treatment for men and women in matters of social security (79/7/EEC)
1986	Directive on the implementation of the principle of equal treatment for men and women in occupational social security schemes (86/378/EEC)
1989	Community Charter of Fundamental Social Rights of Workers
1990	Judgment of the Court (Barber Case)
1992	Treaty of the EU (Maastricht) Agreement on Social Policy
1994	White Paper on Social Policy
1997	Treaty of the EU (Amsterdam) Article 13
2000	Directive on implementing the principle of equal treatment between persons irrespective of racial or ethnic origin (2000/43) (Racial Equality Directive)
2000	Directive on establishing a general framework for equal treatment in employment and occupation (2000/73) (Employment Equality Directive)
2000	European Social Agenda
2000	Open method of coordination on social inclusion
2002	Open method of coordination on pensions and retirement systems
2002	Barcelona targets for childcare facilities
2008	Open method of coordination on health and long-term care
2008	Renewed European Social Agenda
2009	Reform Treaty (Lisbon) – Charter for Fundamental Rights of the EU

The social policy section, defined by the first European Economic Community (EEC) Treaty, consisted of merely 12 articles aimed at reducing discrepancies between laws and practices among the member states. The purpose was to promote the free movement of labour, in terms of both occupational and geographical mobility. Article 119 EEC Treaty provided for equal pay between women and men, while Articles 123 to 128 permitted the creation of an ESF to facilitate geographical and occupational mobility. European Union (EU) competence in relation to other social policy areas (pensions and so on) was restricted to fostering close cooperation among member states (Article 118).

The admission of three new countries 15 years later produced the EEC's first political declaration on the need for policies tackling the social ramifications of the economic crisis experienced in the 1970s. Welfare states in the United Kingdom, Ireland and Denmark followed very different traditions from those of the founding states of France, Germany and Italy. The Community Social Action Programme, adopted in 1974, extended social concerns to include education and training, health and safety at work, worker's rights, gender equality in the labour market, and poverty. These new policy areas derived support from transnational action: comparative research conducted by expert networks advancing social policy analysis, pilot projects pursued by social actors, the exchange of good practices – all of these facilitated interaction among groups of policymakers, across member states and *beyond* the authority of national governments. A broad array of policy instruments eventually emerged, reinforcing EU authority in the employment and social policy fields.

Acceleration and intensification of the Single Market brought significant social implications to light through the political intervention of Jacques Delors, the Commission President (1985–1994), who had orchestrated the adoption of the Single European Act (SEA 1986). In 1989 Delors helped introduce the Community Charter of Fundamental Social Rights of Workers (known as the Social Charter); its subsequent action programmes (soft-law tools) were used to induce implementation in 11 member states; the UK opted out.

Delors's early concerns regarding the EU's social role were reflected in the Agreement on Social Policy appended to the Maastricht Treaty in 1992. Its provisions reinforced EU social policy, actively involving the social partners (trade-unions and employers' organisations) in the adoption of EU legislation. Delors introduced the first programmes for combating poverty and social exclusion, to counterbalance the 'side effects' of the Economic and Monetary Union (EMU) planned for the end of the decade. Social exclusion and poverty were construed as the likely consequences of unemployment among vulnerable social groups (such as the disabled), who faced special obstacles in accessing the labour market. Included in the White Paper on Social Policy (1994), these policies became operational by way of successive EU Social Action Programmes (1996–1997, 1998–2000). Under the strong influence of Sweden (admitted in 1995), social policy was no longer framed as secondary, but rather as an integral component of economic policy, intended to ameliorate the most visible externalities or social risks invoked by the EMU.

The same trend shaped the treaty revisions approved in Amsterdam in 1997. Increasing unemployment, coupled with a social–democratic majority in the Council, brought two new areas of competence to the political agenda, along with negotiations over intergovernmental versus supranational authority. The first assigned the EU the task of coordinating national employment policies through a *European strategy for employment*, aimed at generating 'a skilled trained and adaptable workforce and labour markets responsive to economic change' (Article 125 TEU; see Hubert in this volume). The second centred on EU *anti-discrimination* policy, initiated by Article 13 of the Amsterdam Treaty, providing for 'appropriate action to combat discrimination based on sex, racial or ethnic origin, religion or belief, disability, age or sexual orientation'. This extended EU anti-discrimination competence beyond the labour market, nationality and sex. Diametrically opposed in terms of their legal bases, theses post-Amsterdam policy domains serve today as social agenda cornerstones.

Both employment and anti-discrimination policy were eventually integrated into the Social Agenda (2000–2005), to 'ensure the positive and

174 *Gendering the Social Policy Agenda*

dynamic interaction of economic, employment and social policy' in modernising the European Social Model (see Box 9.1). Activities during this period focused on three central topics: creating more and better jobs; modernising social protections systems to promote social inclusion; and reinforcing fundamental rights and anti-discrimination. One innovative Agenda policy instrument was the open method of coordination (OMC) on social inclusion in 2000; it was extended to pensions and retirement systems as of 2002, and to the health and long-term care sectors by 2008. The OMC was first introduced in the employment policy in 1997 (see Hubert in this volume).

Box 9.1 What is the European Social Model?

I. Commission of the European Communities
The European Social Model is a term used to describe a number of shared values among many European states. These include democracy and individual rights free collective bargaining, the market economy, equality of opportunity for all and social welfare and solidarity. These values – which were encapsulated by the Community Charter of the Fundamental Social Rights of Workers – are held together by the conviction that economic and social progress must go hand in hand. Competitiveness and solidarity have both to be taken into account in building a successful Europe for the future. There is widespread agreement that these shared values have to be preserved, even if quite radical changes are required in the way in which they are applied in practice.' (Commission 1994)

II. European Trade Union Confederation
The European Social Model is a vision of society that combines sustainable economic growth with ever-improving living and working conditions. This implies full employment, good quality jobs, equal opportunities, social protection for all, social inclusion, and involving citizens in the decisions that affect them. In the European Trade Unions' view, social dialogue, collective bargaining and workers' protection are crucial factors in promoting innovation, productivity and competitiveness. This is what distinguishes Europe, where post-war social progress has matched economic growth, from the US model, where small numbers of individuals have benefited at the expense of the majority. Europe must continue to sustain this social model as an example for other countries around the world.' (ETUC 2009)

The Renewed Social Agenda (European Commission 2008e) reflects a new dynamic, extending EU concerns beyond social issues in the narrow sense, covering most quality-of-life concerns for all citizens – not just for paid workers! The Agenda's priorities are structured around three concepts: *opportunities*, *access* and *solidarity*. It specifically mentions seven major themes: children and youth; investing in people; mobility; longer and healthier lives; combating poverty and social exclusion; fighting discrimination; and, finally, promoting high standards protecting workers and consumers on the global scene. Counting education and health among its social priorities has led to a more holistic approach, in view of EU competences extended by the Lisbon Treaty.

The enlarged scope of EU social policy was legitimised through the incorporation of the Charter for Fundamental Rights of the EU (2000) into the Lisbon Treaty, ratified in 2009. The Charter has 'saved' the Community social *acquis* and has, moreover, provided for its expansion. Formalisation of the Charter's status rescued the Lisbon Treaty itself, paradoxically offering strong, solid arguments in favour of ratification for leftist, anti-European and feminist constituencies, who were all satisfied by the reinforcement of the status of the EU social policy. The Treaty marks a crucial step towards the formal recognition of an *EU citizen*'s social rights – not merely those of a *worker*, as prescribed in the earlier legal framework. The free movement of workers and services can easily cover care of children and the elderly, social housing and assistance, preventive healthcare and other social welfare provisions.

In sum, EU social policy development has been primarily shaped by the economic aims of the Single Market, a cornerstone objective of European integration for the last 60 years. As a driving force, this has limited it to coordination rather than to the harmonisation task, focusing on working conditions and labour market regulations rather than on redistributive interventions through social security systems. Historically weak EU competence in the social security arena was 'upheld' by member state reluctance to transfer power to the European institutions, insofar as social protection policies maximised governments' political authority over their constituencies (Hoskyns 1996).

Over the last ten years, the lack of formal EU authority over social security matters has been gradually and successfully counterbalanced by the application of regulated economic policy, which became even more restrictive during the economic crisis. National social protection systems were infected by EU pressures on member states to implement economic convergence criteria, namely through reductions in public expenditure and endorsement of regulations providing for free of circulation of services. EU social policy, as an outcome, reflects not only contradictions between economic and social constraints among policymakers but also conflicting priorities between the EU and member states over sovereignty and autonomy in policymaking.

2. Feminist insights regarding European social policy

The emergence of gender equality as a core component of EU social policy coincided with critiques of the welfare state introduced in the context of second-wave feminism in the late 1960s and early 1970s (Millet 1969; Mitchell 1971; Wilson 1977). Research on the development of EU gender equality policy has highlighted the influence of feminist politics and theories (Hoskyns 1996). Multiple studies on 'equalising' EU integration outcomes underscore the gender bias inherent in stressing economic policy and the market over social policy and the welfare state. This has a two fold impact: first, prioritising the development of the market over the welfare state regarding social protection increases gender inequalities. Feminist analysis demonstrates that women and men experience different types and degrees of economic and labour market integration; women tend to be over-represented among socially excluded population groups, which comprise a majority among heads of low-income households, at-risk pensioners and the poor. Secondly, using labour market participation as the basis for social rights likewise exacerbates gender inequalities. Feminist analysis highlights the persistence of public (workplace)/private (family) divisions, undervaluing women's unpaid family work and hiding unequal social contributions within the private sphere (Perrons 2005).

Second-wave feminist analysis reveals that economic policies have divergent, unequal impacts on women and men. Taxation, labour market and social security systems were traditionally based on male breadwinner models that privileged economic independence for working men. Female patterns of labour market participation depend upon marital status, number of children, and so on. Women comprise a majority of the poor because they also constitute a majority among three socially vulnerable groups: single parent families, low-benefit pensioners (derived rights), and low-paid part-time workers (Daly and Saraceno 2002; Lewis 1992). Women's poverty was extensively analysed by experts working for the Commission (Conroy 1994) and by non-governmental organisations (NGOs) seeking to mainstream gender into policies combating social exclusion, as did for instance the campaign against women's poverty undertaken by the European Network of Women in the 1990s.

Enhancing women's economic independence was one objective behind the individualisation of rights in social security and taxation systems at the time when it appeared in major EU social policy documents such as the White Paper on the European Social Policy (European Commission 1994). Without a doubt, the individualisation of rights promotes gender equality, reduces women's dependency on husbands and families, and further marks the end of the male breadwinner model. However, feminist economic analysis demonstrates that, given new gender inequalities in the labour market (as happens when employment patterns shift from job security/full time work to temporary/flexible part-time jobs), the individualisation of rights would cause further deterioration of living standards among countless working and non-working women.

Although EU social policy developed primarily as a tool for economic growth and labour market expansion, not as a tool of the traditional welfare state, there are some important equality opportunities inherent in market-oriented social policy, insofar as the neoliberal tradition favours opportunities for both women and men. The fact that employment policies now encompass the goal of reconciling work and family life is a positive development: the family sphere is key to employment policies, acknowledging the unequal distribution of domestic and care tasks responsible for horizontal and vertical segregation (see Hubert in this volume). The 1992 Council recommendation on childcare, placing it on the agenda as germane to equal labour market opportunities, was the first official European outcome. It recognised the importance of unpaid work in care – a recognition rooted in feminist insights of the 1970s.

Following this turn, the Commission advanced several legal provisions on working-time arrangements (parental leave and the like), childcare and elder-care infrastructure to facilitate women's full participation, a unanimously accepted EU objective (Stratigaki 2004). Although initiated as an economic goal, increasing female labour market participation has simultaneously advanced the feminist aim of fostering women's empowerment: their economic independence is a *sine qua non* prerequisite for gender equality in society, according to all schools of feminist thought. Extending the policy scope into the family arena reveals one more concern lurking in the shadow of traditional policies that must also become integral to social rights: preventing *domestic violence* (see Elman 2007; Stanko 2000). Women need to be perceived as independent *citizens*, not only as *working mothers* who should participate in paid labour or as *wives* subordinate to husbands. Both care work and bodily integrity should be construed as independent social rights for all – women and men alike.

Coordinated efforts by feminists within EU institutions and the European Women's Lobby (EWL) struggled to extend the social policy scope beyond paid work, to include domestic violence, reproductive rights and women's health (Helfferich and Kolb 2001), especially during the drafting of the 1997 Amsterdam Treaty and the directive on access to goods and services in the early 2000s. Whereas combating violence was finally incorporated into the Framework Strategy for Gender Equality (2001–2005) and a European Strategy on Combating Violence against Women was being prepared in 2010, reproductive rights (abortion) and women's health still fall outside EU policy reach.

3. Social policy instruments promoting gender equality

Almost all conventional EU policy instruments have been used in the social policy arena, being developed to 'accompany' economic growth and employment. Classic policy instruments applied here are of four types: *legislation* (directives) and law enforcement through the judicial pronouncements of the ECJ; *structural policy*, operationalised in the form of a subsequent ESF since 1989; a series of *non-binding social action programmes*, managed directly by the Commission; and use of the *OMC*. The gender relevance of these instruments is equivalent to their gender significance in other fields of Community action: *de jure* equality between women and men is promoted by legislation; *de facto* equality advances through interventions under the Structural Funds and through the Social Inclusion Action Programmes run by the Commission. Examining the social OMC in the next section, we concentrate here on select gender aspects of the first three policy instruments.

Equal treatment legislation affecting statutory social security and occupational social security schemes dates from the 1970s onwards (Directives 79/7/EEC and 86/378/EEC; Directive 2006/54/EC, recast). This legislation extended the application of the equal pay principle, recognising that social benefits based on paid employment are an integral part of one's salary. Nobody could have expected in the 1970s that such a simple principle would provoke major reconfigurations of national social security systems by the 1990s. In *Barber v Guardian Royal Exchange Assurance Group* (Case C-262/88), the ECJ ruled that pension payments indeed constituted 'pay', yet the early retirement age granted to women produced discrimination against men. The verdict's huge ramifications were technically neutralised by limiting its retroactive effect in the 1992 Maastricht Treaty. The equalisation of retirement ages for women and men still threatens political turmoil, especially in countries like Greece, where major social security schemes stress women's protection and familial perspectives. Vehement public debates surrounding this issue among women reveal major contradictions inherent in welfare state for women: measures introducing gender equality may negatively impact some groups in the short term, while contributing to a reduction of job segregation by sex and the inequalities that the latter creates in the long run.

De jure equality never suffices to promote equality regarding welfare and other social benefits. Employment-based social rights reproduce inequalities due to the unequal patterns of women's and men's economic activity. *De facto* equality would require policies ensuring equal female access to paid labour. EU structural policy has allocated specific ESF funds to promote women's labour market access through measures enhancing care infrastructures and services, for example measures to support single mothers, a priority target group among vulnerable segments of the population.

As early as 1989, the Community Initiative NOW (New Opportunities for Women) of the ESF (1989–1993) recognised that women's participation in vocational training, entrepreneurship and waged labour depends heavily on available, affordable childcare. Two consecutive ESF periods (1994–1999,

2000–2005) have allocated considerable funding for childcare, social assistance to the elderly and the disabled, along with other measures facilitating 'reconciliation' for working mothers. For countries lacking social infrastructures, like Greece, funding has included the prolongation of school hours, provision of social assistance *at home*, as well as centres for the creative leisure of children. EU funding was crucial in extending the social policy scope in Greece, where the extended family undertakes all kinds of care tasks. Still, the framing of the reconciliation objective as a measure promoting women's employment leaves the gender-biased character of care unchallenged, by excluding men not only in rhetoric but also in practice.

Social policy instruments are not limited to ESF measures, however. Formal policy documents reflect political decisions and shape the orientation of both legislation and structural policy priorities at the supranational and national level. The White Paper on European Social Policy (European Commission 1994) linked the reconciliation objective to the emergence of new forms of employment, albeit in a chapter on competition, not focused on equality. The chapter warranting equal opportunities for women and men featured the reconciliation of employment and household/family life as one out of three main topics, along with desegregating the labour market and accelerating women's participation in decision-making. Its innovative character lies in the introduction of economic arguments not only in regard to childcare provision, but also in reference to labour market desegregation. In the subsequent European Social Action Programme (1995–1997) (European Commission 1995a), the gender equality section recognised the lack of legislation and launched the debate on individualisation in social security and taxation systems.

In the 2000s the Social Agenda and the Renewed Social Agenda have incorporated gender equality in all areas of concern (mobility, healthcare, social inclusion, anti-discrimination, etc.). The 2002 European Council in Barcelona set specific childcare targets: by 2010, 22 per cent of children under 3 years of age and 90 per cent of children between 3 and the onset of compulsory education are to be cared for by nurseries and kindergartens in all member states.

4. Gender mainstreaming EU social policy

The Commission's 1996 communication on gender mainstreaming, implicitly reaffirmed in the Amsterdam Treaty (Article 3), upgraded the strategy by making it a transversal objective of EU policymaking. Still, the degree of gender equality pursued differs across policy arenas; most scholars agree that the overall result is positive but not spectacular (Pollack and Hafner-Burton 2000; Stratigaki 2005). Let us now examine two social policy components that have produced contradictory results when assessed from a gender perspective: *social inclusion/social protection* and *anti-discrimination*. In the first soft-policy field, the Community applies the OMC, a non-binding tool based on the idea of voluntary policy transfer and learning. The second rests on 'hard' competence, using the traditional tool of EU legislation. Both policies encompass risks and opportunities for gender equality: the risk inherent in social inclusion/social protection policy is linked to the 'evaporation' of gender mainstreaming in the heavy operational procedures of the OMC; the risk facing anti-discrimination policy relates to the possible 'dilution' of gender among other sources of inequality.

Gender mainstreaming strategy is supposed to be incorporated into the social OMC process that gradually came to cover *social inclusion, pensions, healthcare* and *long-term care* policies. Like its European Employment Strategy (EES) counterpart, the European Strategy for Social Protection and Social Inclusion – first launched as 'objectives to fight against poverty and social inclusion' – counts among its horizontal tasks 'the importance of mainstreaming equality between men and women in *all* actions aimed at achieving the commonly agreed objectives' (European Council 2000b: 5). Despite the political commitment to promoting gender equality across the board, the first round of results of the social OMC proved unsatisfactory, if not disappointing. National strategies evaluated in the OMC context showed that gender issues were treated sporadically; they lacked visibility in most countries, although some re-expressed their commitment to enhancing gender mainstreaming over the next two years (European Commission 2002c: 11–12). Most references to 'women' involve single parents, low-status pensioners and the victims of domestic violence (European Commission 2002c: 75).

The most recent Joint Report on Social Protection and Social Inclusion (European Commission 2010e) suggests that the salience of gender mainstreaming has weakened further: it is no longer treated as a horizontal task – and thus not evaluated in a separate joint report section. Gender equality is only mentioned as one social outcome among others, to be systematically assessed. Gender mainstreaming 'evaporates' in the Social Inclusion Strategy, reducing sexual equality to only one among many 'overarching' objectives. The OMC's gradual extension into new fields has thus undermined the implementation of gender mainstreaming, a crucial component for social policy efficacy.

The horizontal OMC principles of good governance, transparency and involvement of stakeholders in the design, implementation and monitoring of policy rarely transcend mere administrative procedure. In some cases, NGO involvement was reportedly limited to drafting opinions, with no evidence that these opinions influence national policies. In other cases even national 'machineries' reportedly failed to exercise proper gender mainstreaming in shaping their own national social inclusion and social protection policies. These cases identify serious legitimacy deficits in the way that OMC is applied in the social policy domain (Büchs 2007; Kröger 2007; Zeitlin et al. 2005).

Political and administrative obstacles to gender mainstreaming the social OMC are neither entirely the result of its 'soft' character as a non-binding policy tool nor a function of the member states' reluctance to adopt EU modes of cooperation. Even where 'strong' EU competence exists– as in the case of anti-discrimination policy – gender mainstreaming faces a significant risk of potential dilution in being merged with other sources of inequality such as ethnicity, disability, sexual orientation and age.

Rooted in Article 13 Amsterdam Treaty, the Racial Equality Directive (2000/43) and the Employment Equality Directive (2000/78) provide the legal basis for combating discrimination on the grounds of ethnic origin, religion, disability, age and sexual orientation (see Mushaben in this volume). Both directives extend the reach of the EU equal treatment principle by covering new socially disadvantaged groups. Due to its strong treaty foundation, anti-discrimination policy has become central to EU social policy and can call upon all traditional Community policy instruments: transposing legislation at the national level, monitoring implementation, following ECJ rulings, raising public awareness through campaigns and so on. Anti-discrimination policies have successfully revitalised the image of European society by promoting the advantages inherent in *equality for all*.

Within this new context, however, gender equality must 'compete' with other forms of inequality; women's organisations are being challenged by associations representing other social interests over funding, political prioritisation and visibility (Woodward 2007). One example illustrating the risks of merging these categories under the single roof of 'discrimination' is the 2007 campaign Year of Equal Opportunities for All, in which gender equality was scarcely visible among the activities highlighted.

Gender equality and equal treatment for women and men seem to be losing their special place in the EU policy; they face gradual replacement by 'mainstreaming of equality for all' in all recent social policy documents (Stratigaki 2008). Merging women with other social groups who encounter discrimination creates the impression that all women are discriminated against *in the same way*, although gender relations assume divergent forms across various societies and social arenas. Merging gender with other sources of inequality in an 'add women and stir' manner prevents policymakers from applying gender mainstreaming in anti-discrimination policy per se. It does not allow its translation into policy measures reflecting the fact that gender *cuts across all social inequalities*. This analysis has generated the concept of *multiple discrimination*, currently gaining visibility throughout the EU social policy agenda (Kantola 2010a; Verloo 2006).

5. Strengthening European social citizenship

Assessing EU social policy from a gender perspective reveals a number of considerable limitations for fostering equality (Fink 2002; Hantrais 2000a; Jenson 2008; Lewis 2006; Ostner and Lewis 1995; Ostner 2000). Securing greater gender equality and advancing women's full participation in the EU integration process could both be accelerated tremendously through the expansion and deepening of the ideal of *European social citizenship*. We now discuss two ingredients directly relevant to gender equality: the first refers to the foundation and scope of Community *social rights*, the second to the process of social decision-making or *social governance*.

Expanding and deepening European social rights requires that universal social rights be rooted in a broader concept of citizenship, entitling individuals to minimum income guarantees, health, social protection rights, dependant care provision, and protection of bodily integrity, *inter alia*; coupled with economic and social independence, this would ensure women's equality, as demonstrated by many feminist welfare-state analysts (Daly 2000; Hobson et al. 2002; Jenson 2001; Leira and Saraceno 2002; Sainsbury 1996). This necessitates changes in the existing foundation for social rights: extending the *basis* of entitlements to citizenship and residence, as well as enlarging the *scope* of social rights and social citizenship in areas remaining 'within the family', subject to interpersonal relations. Transformation of the European social citizenship concept, and its practical implications for both dimensions, could help to shift gender relations towards more substantial economic and social equality (Hansen and Hager 2009).

Social entitlements in most member states derive from employment activity or/and family relations. This discriminates against women insofar as both the labour market and the family are gendered constructions. EU social policy makes sharp distinctions between working and 'non-working' mothers when providing for childcare (though the real distinction lies between paid and unpaid work), or between married or single women in need of social protection. Individual citizenship entitlements alleviate women's dependency on families and husbands, thereby transforming 'care' from the personal responsibility of mothers into a 'universal' social and moral right for both sexes. Most feminist welfare critics agree that utilising *citizenship* as the foundation for social entitlements has reduced gender bias in Scandinavia, for example (Hobson and Lister 2002; Orloff 1993; Siim 2000).

Using *residence* as a basis for social rights would, moreover, extend coverage of social policy to migrant women who work and live in member states but do not hold any EU nationality (Morissens and Sainsbury 2005; also see Mushaben in this volume). The dearth of national care infrastructure(s) proportionate to women's steadily increasing participation in the labour market (a core objective of the EU Employment Strategy) has generated big demands for domestic and care work. This is being satisfied by countless 'third country nationals', who provide care services in the 'private' household sphere. Migrant work often falls outside of regulated labour relations, especially in southern Europe, where informal work, the usual pattern, rarely entitles one to social benefits (Anthias and Lazaridis 2000; Vaiou 2003). Recognising full social rights for female migrant care-workers would acknowledge their contribution to European societies and would facilitate their integration.

A second imperative related to the theory and practice of European social citizenship concerns its *scope*. What kinds of entitlements, benefits, allowances, pensions, services and infrastructures (education, health, housing) should be part of the social rights package? Is it better for women to access benefits or services directly? Does entitlement to early retirement or better caring facilities help them to tackle the accumulation of family and workplace tasks? What principles and features of the European Social Model should prevail, especially in the context of EU enlargement since 2004? All of these questions have gendered answers; feminist–theoretical debates infer that social citizenship must also include rights like bodily integrity and reproductive health (Vogel Polsky 1997).

Commensurate with the nature and scope of the problems discussed above, social governance – civil participation and accountability – raises the question: How do we make social decisions 'participative, visible and accountable'? This is another issue that has added significance in efforts to constitutionalise the EU. Social policy is public policy par excellence, affecting the daily lives of *all* citizens in multiple ways; good governance instruments are crucial to warranting the quality of life and the well-being of Union citizens. Social governance poses new challenges: how to balance economic pressures, monetary factors, taxation and social investment, versus how to secure the best possible welfare mix on the part of the state, the market and the household. Let us concentrate on two social governance prerequisites to applying a gender lens: ensuring the *participation of civil society groups* and *enhancing accountability* (European Commission 2001a).

The active participation of civil society in social policymaking is promoted though EU funding of associations, mechanisms and consultation processes, the aim of which is to improve institutional decision-making. Effective collective mobilisation by the EWL since 1989 has helped to coordinate action and lobbying on equality issues. Despite limited human and financial sources, the EWL actively pursued its mission, especially under Barbara Helfferich's direction as General Secretary (1992–2000). The EWL has been a key player in the civil dialogue process launched by the Commission in 1995, aiming to initiate regular consultation between EU Institutions and NGOs active in social issues, as a follow-up to the White Paper on Social Policy. The EWL later became a full member of the European Platform of Social NGOs (Social Platform), an umbrella organisation consisting of more than 40 associations, which represent countless voluntary groups and civil society interests.

The Social Platform, with EU financial backing, tries to influence the social agenda by advancing the principles of equality, solidarity, non-discrimination and respect of fundamental rights for all. The EWL's successful promotion of social concerns for female constituencies depends on several parameters, the inherent limitation of the civil dialogue per se being the most important. Contrary to the European *social dialogue* (involving trade unions and employers organisations), the *civil dialogue* was established as merely an advisory process; participating interest organisations have no decision-making power over issues in their areas of competence. EU leaders tend to use the civil dialogue to legitimise their decisions vis-à-vis member state governments rather than as a real source for voicing and hearing EU citizens' demands.

Accountability and transparency are included in the array of good governance instruments; for social policy, they are crucial in achieving a more equitable redistribution of income and other resources between women and men. Gendering accountability has primarily evolved out of the UN's institutional framing of 'state feminism', concerning balanced participation in

---

Box 9.2 Definitions of gender budgeting

'Gender budgeting is an application of gender mainstreaming in the budgetary process. It means a gender-based assessment of budgets, incorporating a gender perspective at all levels of the budgetary process and restructuring revenues and expenditures in order to promote gender equality' (Council of Europe 2005).

An example: 'In the year 2000 French Parliamentarians called on the government to present annual evidence, when the state budget was drafted, of the financial effort made to promote women's rights and gender equality. This gave rise to the *jaune budgétaire*, the yellow appendix to the budget concerning women's rights and equality. This document, which provides parliament with information and a means of monitoring the situation, and which has a legal basis, allows the government to display the results of its policy as reflected in budgetary appropriations, gauge the progress made and pinpoint shortcomings. It is up to each ministerial department to identify and take stock of the measures it has introduced to foster, or increase awareness of, gender equality. Each department is also asked to explain its approach to gender equality and submit the indicators that it considers most relevant in the area for which it is responsible' (Council of Europe 2005: 29).

'Gender budgeting aims at analysing any form of public expenditure and income from a gender perspective, i.e. it identifies the different implications that public income and spending have on girls and women, as well as different groups of women, as compared to boys and men. The final objective of gender budgeting is to shape budgets so that they actively promote gender equality' (EWL 2004).

decision-making, and spreading new principles of democratic governance (UNIFEM 2008); it thus entails both political and technical dimensions. Political factors relate to achieving explicit commitments from national leaders to include gender equality in all public policymaking. Whereas political commitments are frequently overemphasised in the EU-context, they are not always fulfilled in efficient, effective and comprehensive ways. Technical factors include the application of *gender budgeting*, a task that has been integrated into national public finances in some European countries, as well as internationally (UNIFEM 2006; Council of Europe 2005; European Women's Lobby 2004). This involves *ex ante* and *ex post facto* assessments of the gender impact of public expenditures in the social, health and education domains, affecting citizens' daily lives; it offers a way to redirect human resources and wealth (power, space, time, income and labour) between women and men. As seen above, family benefits, pensions, social services and dependent care are highly gendered fields in which public expenditures could help to decrease stereotypical inequalities (see Box 9.2). This makes gender budgeting relative to social spending even more significant than in other areas of public intervention.

Gender impact assessments (GIA) are systematically undertaken by the Commission in the case of Structural Funds, especially with respect to the ESF and EU programmes in the field of development and cooperation (European Commission 1995b, 1999b). Both realms have direct, material beneficiaries and targeted populations, which can be accurately counted and assessed.

6. Conclusion

Advocating for a stronger, more solid conceptualisation of European social citizenship through the processes described above (expanding social rights, improving social governance) creates new pressures for an increased gender equality. Placed in a wider context, enhancing European social citizenship invokes the need for a political project of *deepening the EU* rather than *enlarging* it. The close link between social citizenship and gender equality is fully compatible with the understanding of European integration and women's emancipation as two parallel but intricately connected projects (Hubert 1998). European integration and gender equality both shape identities and foster social, economic and political change in similarly cooperative, pragmatic ways. EU social policy objectives could further incorporate feminist policy analysis and adopt more specific, women-targeted measures, if there were: (a) more gender-sensitive and more deliberate implementation of the provisions of the European Charter of Fundamental Rights; (b) more systematic GIAs of ESF spending, reoriented towards gender equality objectives; and (c) more substantial participation of women's civil society organisations in economic and political decisions regarding European social integration. This would guarantee the actual practice of social rights for all European women in all aspects of everyday life.

Discussion questions

- How would a reinforcement of the role of EU in social policy affect gender equality in the member states?
- What prerequisites would have to be met for the EU to act on issues like gender based-violence and sexual and reproductive health?
- In what ways might future enlargements affect the gender equality dimension in EU social policy?
- In a period of economic crisis, do you expect gender equality measures in EU social policy to be strengthened or weakened?

Notes

1. Policies on education and public health fall outside the scope of this chapter insofar as their Europeanisation still depends primarily on Single Market priorities (that is, on the free movement of workers, to be facilitated by common criteria in diploma recognition; on the free movement of health services, etc.).
2. For details, see Fink et al. (2001); O'Connor (2005b); Leibfried (2005); Ferrera (2005); Schierup et al. (2006); Hantrais (2007); Bailey (2008) and Threlfall (2003).

10
Research by, for and about Women: Gendering Science and Research Policy

Gabriele Abels

Imagine that you have finished a PhD in philosophy in Germany.[1] You want to apply for a post-doc programme and need a recommendation from your research supervisor. You find out that you are pregnant with your second child, but you have a reliable child-care provider and an unusually supportive husband. When you inform your supervisor, he announces that he will no longer support your career, since a mother should stay home with her children rather than do research.[2]

Imagine that you have served as a biochemistry professor at a university in the Czech Republic for 20 years. Despite your heavy teaching load, you have accrued a substantial publication record; your papers and books were written mostly at night, after your 'care work' at home. When you serendipitously discover that your male colleagues earn 35 per cent more, you start to realise that they also have more lab space, more research assistants and more money for international conference travel.

Or imagine that you suffer from heavy allergies. Your doctor prescribes a new medication, which you hope will get you through your summer hayfever misery. Feeling really nauseous after a few days, you search for internet reports on the new medicine, discovering that many women with allergies have experienced the same negative side-effects. Digging deeper, you learn that clinical tests for this drug used all male test-subjects who encountered no serious side-effects. Experts link the side-effects to women's biologically 'different' metabolisms.

Science and society are highly interdependent, each constantly affecting the other. Scientific research and technological innovation are not gender-neutral activities. According to gender-sensitive science and technology studies, the gender dimension is deeply embedded in the way we do science and develop new technologies, influencing the entire process of scientific and technological innovation from the lab to the market. European Union (EU) research policy – known in 'Eurospeak' as research, technology and development (RTD) – dates back to the 1950s. Over time these three domains have undergone incredible conceptual, institutional and instrumental transformation, yet one aspect has remained unchanged: 'science' is still based on an allegedly gender-neutral, 'purely technical' approach. The mid-1990s bore witness to significant changes, thanks to the EU focus on women and science in connection with its new commitment to gender mainstreaming. This major shift has come about largely because gender equality has gained significance as one of the Community's core values, and because globalisation has reconfigured the active parameters of European RTD policy.

Community activities in RTD have been an essential part of the integration project since the 1950s.[3] Due to strong linkages between scientific and technological innovation and economic competitiveness, policy-making in this area has been quite controversial among EU member states and EU actors. Securing the economic competitiveness of European industry has been, and remains, the driving force of such policy-making. Many conflicts have affected RTD policy, being fuelled by different visions of industrial policy; they are deeply rooted in different forms of 'techno-nationalism' (Peterson and Sharp 1998: 4) found in member states. Material conflicts, especially, have always been the Achilles' heel of Community RTD policy. At the same time, research policy heavily relies on a 'politics of expertise' (Peterson 1995).

Against the backdrop of growing economic competition, the failure to integrate women into science and research systems has been reframed as an unacceptable 'waste of human resources'. The following chapter analyses the development of European RTD policy. I discuss the gender dimension of RTD policy and then consider the implications of gender mainstreaming for the entire field. From a gender perspective, the development of RTD policy can be divided into two stages, the first extending from the early 1950s to the mid-1990s, and the second beginning in the mid-1990s.

1. European RTD activities through the mid-1990s

Both the 1952 Treaty on the European Coal and Steel Community (ECSC) and the 1958 Euratom Treaty affirmed a role for Community-funded RTD, but only in these sectors. Its role was to coordinate national programmes and to develop collectively funded programmes through the Joint Research Centre, mainly creating 'jobs for the boys' (Rose 1999: 34). Curiously, the 1958 European Economic Community (EEC) Treaty did not mention RTD policy. Peterson and Sharp (1998: 41) claim that the lack of success to create a technology community goes back to '[a]rguments between governments, differences in national policies and priorities, and difficulties in establishing effective management formulae'.

The 1970s oil crisis, added to a perceived 'technological gap', unleashed an intense debate on the role of Community-funded research. Europeans feared being sandwiched between their old competitor, the USA, and a new one, Japan. Compared to those economic powerhouses, the European Community (EC) countries clearly lagged behind regarding the classical indicators of technological performance – that is, the share of gross national product (GNP) devoted to RTD, the number of researchers, patents filed and the like. Increasing Community-funded research was expected to remedy under-financing and to balance the gap to some extent, by creating synergies. Information and communication technologies, added to biotechnology, were among the first research sectors attracting Community attention.

Community RTD policy did not witness a great leap forward until the mid-1980s, when it was closely linked to the Single Market project, as well as to the promotion and strengthening of competitiveness among European industries. The Single Market would be accompanied by the creation of a 'technological community' connecting RTD policy to industrial policy; the environmental and consumer effects of technological development were neglected, however. The broader economic vision required new instruments, fundamental institutional changes, as well as decisions on technological priorities.

The 1986 Single European Act (SEA), the foundation for accelerated market integration, ascribed a new role to Community RTD policy. First, Article 130 SEA introduced a firm legal basis for RTD policy,[4] linking it to key objectives promoting European industrial competitiveness. While the Commission had funded single research projects in multiple fields since the early 1980s, it lacked a coherent strategy. The pivotal instrument, introduced in 1984, was the first Framework Programme for Research and Development (henceforth FP; see Box 10.1). The focus rested with pre-competitive (basic) research rather than with applied research, which is 'closer to the market' and thus involves economic stakes. Secondly, the SEA granted a stronger role to the European Parliament (EP). The new cooperation procedure became effective for all *specific* research programmes (Article 130q, section 2 SEA) and included limited veto rights. For FPs, however, only EP consent was necessary.

One of the major problems of the policy, which was criticised as ineffective, was the lack of participating industrialists, due to the fact that Community research was under-funded and that corporations preferred in-house research to joint projects with potential economic competitors. Scientists, meanwhile, disapproved of the 'political' selection criteria. Finally, the Commission played no direct role in coordinating national RTD policies or in addressing science policy in a broader sense, in ways including higher educational issues and human resource management.

> **Box 10.1 Instruments and the budget of RTD policy**
>
> Framework Programmes (FPs) are multi-annual programmes that outline common research objectives, identify priority areas for funding and allocate the research budget to these priorities. Priority areas are operationalised via thematic programme lines. Researchers can apply for grants for collaborative projects based on 'calls for proposals' for thematic programmes. The budget is used to co-finance research, technological development and demonstration projects; the Commission administers the budget and the highly competitive peer review process for selecting worthy proposals. FP1 commenced in 1984, running until 1987 (total budget 3.75 billion ECU); FP7 (2007–2013) draws on a budget of 53.2 billion Euro to cover its seven-year lifespan – the largest allocation ever.

The 1990s brought an incredible acceleration to European integration affecting also RTD policy. Economic pressures grew stronger with globalisation. Information and communication technology became key, as technological innovations assumed paramount importance in a globalised economy; all three were crucial to economic competitiveness. Unlike the 'technology gap' debate of the 1970s, the new debate was framed in terms of a wide-ranging transformation moving Europe towards a 'knowledge-based society'. This required novel mechanisms and venues for knowledge production and understanding its relation to technological progress. *Innovation policy* became the new catchword which encompasses a broader concept, building, *inter alia*, on the integration of 'user perspectives' and diverse social actors (stakeholders) in the production of new technological and scientific knowledge, and on the integration of RTD-related policy domains. The need for integration re-conceptualised the relationship between science and society.

The 1992 Maastricht Treaty introduced the *co-decision procedure* between the EP and the Council, which extended to FPs. Indeed, the adoption of FP4 (1994–1998) was the first co-decision ever taken. However, specific programmes no longer required parliamentary *co-operation* but only *consultation*. The EP began using its enhanced legislative power to boost the role of Community RTD policy and its budget. FP4 was also the first to introduce EU funding for 'Targeted Socio-Economic Research'. Under previous FPs, the social sciences had been relegated, at best, to serving as 'handmaiden disciplines', that is, to studying the impact of technological innovation on society and helping the latter to adjust to technology-induced social change (Rose 1999: 36–37).

The efficiency of RTD policy was subject to concurrent debate. The Amsterdam Treaty, coming into force in 1999, introduced the promotion of research and technological development as a community task (Article 3). In 1997 a group of experts led by former Commissioner of Research (and Vice President) Etienne Davignon had published a critical evaluation report, lambasting the FPs as too fragmented and decompartmentalised, in thematic and administrative terms. It criticised decisions on thematic priorities, as well as the project-selection process, as non-transparent. Overall, the report called for greater coherence and synergies. The following FP5 (1998–2002; budget 15 Billion ECU) responded directly to this critique by focussing on four thematic and three horizontal programmes.

The giant conceptual qua instrumental leap forward in RTD policy occurred by way of the Commission's January 2000 communication on the development of a European Research Area (ERA). The ERA concept (Commission 2000) foresees the transformation into a knowledge-based society and brings the idea of a 'true' technology community back in. The Commission proposed the ERA to render the EU 'the most competitive and dynamic knowledge-based economy in the world' by 2010. ERA was considered a central pillar of the 2000 Lisbon Strategy for Economic Growth and Jobs – linked to the creation of the Single Market and a European Higher Education Area. The Commission diagnosis read:

> Decompartmentalisation and better integration of Europe's scientific and technological area is an indispensable condition for invigorating research in Europe. We need to go beyond the current static structure of '15+1' towards a more dynamic configuration [...] based on a more coherent approach involving measures taken at different levels: by the Member states at national level, by the European Union with the framework programme and other possible instruments, and by intergovernmental cooperation organisations. A configuration of this kind would make for the essential 'critical mass' in the major areas of progress in knowledge, in particular to achieve economies of scale, to allocate resources better overall, and to reduce negative externalities due to insufficient mobility of factors and poor information for operators. (Commission 2000: 7)

ERA called for the mobilisation of *all* resources involved in knowledge production; human resources in RTD became a key issue (Hansen 2009). ERA also foresaw a new role for the Commission in coordinating national RTD policies. Public investment in RTD was to increase from a European average of 1.9 per cent to 3.0 per cent of the member state gross domestic products (GDPs) by 2010 (the USA spent about 2.7 per cent on RTD, Japan about 3.0 per cent). The increase necessitated a rise in the number of qualified researchers. First assessments of the ERA strategy by scholars and

EU policy-makers themselves have been quite critical. Scholars diagnosed a number of barriers to deepening integration in this policy area; due to RTD's key economic role, a lack of political will too often result in fragmentation (Delanghe et al. 2009; Edler et al. 2003). The European Commission (2007b) introduced the ERA Green Paper, which was aimed at remedying these shortcomings.

Seen through a gender lens, ERA is of paramount importance for two reasons: firstly, it highlighted the *human resource dimension*, rendering the underrepresentation of women scientists a serious problem. Secondly, ERA was built on a *comprehensive picture of science/society relations*, re-conceptualised in response to recent public concerns – for example, over the food safety crisis – and controversies over biotechnology (Abels 2003). The Commission realised that technological innovations require receptive social environments, sorely lacking in Europe, in order to become economically successful; EU-funded research had to be made 'more socially relevant and sensitive to the "needs of society"' (Peterson and Sharp 1998: 20). This idea was further developed in multiple Commission policy papers, such as the 2001 *Science and Society Action Plan* (Commission 2001a).

Finally, ERA assigned a new strategic role to FPs and the Commission. FPs needed to support the creation of ERA, a concept first operationalised via FP6 (2002–2006). New instruments included Networks of Excellence.[5] FP6 further earmarked funding (225 million Euros) to study 'citizens and governance in a knowledge-based society'. FP7 (2007–2013) identifies four key programmes entitled cooperation, ideas, people and capacities.

Assessment of the 2000 Lisbon Strategy made clear that the ERA's ambitious goals had not been met. However, there is evidence that a vast number of member states have actually prioritised public research and development (R&D), as government budgets increased between 2000 and 2007. The overall share of GDP spent on R&D in the EU rose marginally from 1.82 per cent in 2000 to 1.9 per cent in 2008. Critical evaluations led to a 're-launch' of the Lisbon Strategy in 2010 (Europe 2020), supposedly a 'strategy for smart, sustainable and inclusive growth'; accordingly, economic success, social inclusion and ecological responsibility should be reconciled. Deeming science and research to be crucial factors, developing an 'Innovation Union' was described as one of the seven flagship initiatives of the European Commission (2010a: 3).

The Lisbon Treaty, which took effect in December 2009, further supports the key role of research and innovation; Article 179 of the Treaty on the Functioning of the EU (TFEU) rendered research and innovation policy an objective in its own right; it included matters of health, climate and outer space, thus enabling the EU to adopt legislative measures to secure such objectives.[6]

2. Gendering research policy since the mid-1990s

Against the backdrop of research policy, we observe a maturing discourse over women *and* science and women *in* science as of the mid-1990s (Genetti 2010: 186–203; Zimmermann and Metz-Göckel 2007). As in many policy fields, these innovations owe their prominence to a change in Commission policy. The Council and the EP have likewise legislated in this field, when we look at gendering processes (see Table 10.1).

Among the initial steps undertaken, the Commission organised a small conference on women in science in 1993, 'which put forward recommendations designed to improve the collection of statistics on the participation of women scientists in EU research programmes, and to encourage women scientists to apply for EU funding' (Pollack and Hafner-Burton 2000: 448) – with no lasting effect. Not many women served in leading positions in the Commission's Directorate-General for Research (hereafter DG Research) at the time; the advisory committees were just as male-dominated.

French Research Commissioner Edith Cresson (1995–1999) highlighted women and science in 1995, subsequently supported by the Commissioner's Group. The issue was also important for her Belgian successor, Philip Busquin (1999–2004). The opportunity structure changed for three reasons: gender mainstreaming was about to be formally adopted as a guiding principle for EU policies; Cresson took the 'science and society' issue seriously, presupposing they were interrelated;[7] placing women in science became a human resource issue linked to economic competitiveness. Over the next ten years, DG Research became a pioneer in implementing mainstreaming, even though the Commission's 1996 landmark communication did not even mention science and technology. The 'women and science' emphasis was first specifically mentioned in FP5 in relation to the horizontal programme of improving human research potential and the socio-economic knowledge base.

Table 10.1 Major steps in the field of 'Women and Science'

1999	Commission Communication *Women and Science* published
1999	Council Resolution *Women and Science* adopted
1999	*Helsinki Group on Women and Science* established
2000	EP resolution on the Communication *Women and Science*
2000	ETAN report *Promoting excellence through mainstreaming gender equality*
2002	FP 6 establishes link between science policy and gender mainstreaming
2002	Report on *National Policies on Women and Science in Europe* Helsinki Group
2003	WIR report on *Women in Industrial Research*
2004	ENWISE report *Waste of talents: turning private struggles into a public issue*
2006	EPWS established
2008	WIRDEM report *Mapping the Maze*
2008	Commission report *Benchmarking Policy Measures for Gender Equality in Science*

194 *Gendering Science and Research Policy*

A working group on women and science was created within DG Research's Directorate Science and Society in late 1997, later becoming the Women and Science Unit (hereafter Unit). As of this writing, this Unit remains the key actor, holding together top-down and bottom-up networking. Its mandate is to promote research 'for, by, and about women' by 'collecting statistics, developing indicators, publishing research, documenting policies and exchanging good practices on women and science' (Rees 2007: 18, note 3). This applies in the EU member states and in other countries participating in the FPs.

One of the Unit's first activities was to form a special group of gender and science experts as part of the European Technology Assessment Network (ETAN), a tool available in FP4. The ETAN group convened a conference on women and science in April 1998, jointly organised with the EP. The results of this workshop fed into the Commission's (1999a) Communication *Women and Science: Mobilizing Women to Enrich European Research* and in the resulting Action Plan. Given the limited mandate, it aimed to simulate discussion and to exchange experiences among the member states, as well as to increase the number of female scientists involved in research funded by the Union – signifying the growing importance of the field. The report's main argument is the human resource one.

With the Council and the EP backing the communication, the Research Council adopted its first resolution on 20 May 1999, inviting the member states to

> (a) make available existing information on the gender balance of R&D personnel; and establish methods and procedures to collect and produce appropriate data and indicators [...]; (b) actively engage in the dialogue [...] by exchanging views on policies pursued at the national level so as to be able to analyse the situation and make a joint assessment of ongoing policies, taking into account benchmarking and best practice in Member states; (c) pursue the objective of gender equality in science by appropriate means, including through other national policies. (Council of the EU 1999: 4)

A second Research Council Resolution (2001) requested the Commission to report on the progress made after several years.

Traditionally an advocate of gender equality, the European Parliament supported the Commission; its own resolution in February 2000 rested on a report by the EP's Committee on Women's Rights and Equal Opportunities (FEMM), stressing the need for gender mainstreaming in research, especially where human subjects were concerned:

The old jibe of 'toys for the boys' is probably unfair but, in fields such as the life sciences, environmental and energy research, it is not clear that the health implications for women of certain research is well understood or taken into account. The question of differential access to information technology could also result in unequitable [sic] expenditure of research funding. Since EU research is undertaken on behalf of all the citizens of Europe, including women, efforts must be made to ensure that their wishes and priorities are met. (EP 1999: 9)

The Commission's Action Plan proposed a Gender Watch System for the evaluation and monitoring of the situation and a Policy Forum to foster discussion and exchanges of experiences among the member states. Both affected FP6, the first to implement the ERA strategy, which dedicated around 20 million Euros to 'women in science' activities.

The Gender Watch System is a quantitative instrument for monitoring and evaluating women's roles in science, focusing directly on 'research by women' – data were scarce in the late 1990s. It also tracks 'research on and about women', that is, the ways in which gender issues are addressed in European research activities. The first mechanism has proven more fruitful thus far. To support the system, the Commission established an inter-service working group in 2000.

Providing quantitative oversight, the Unit commissioned several reports on the situation of women in science conducted by scientific 'gender experts' networks. The first such group was ETAN (ETAN Expert Working Group 2000), supplying a statistical overview of women not only in higher education but also at research institutes and in scientific policy-making bodies at the EU and member state levels. The report strongly criticised sexism (reflected in the gender pay gap) and nepotism in science (via the peer-review system, often flawed, to women's detriment). It highlighted the lack of high quality, comparative statistics and indicators – for example on female researchers in the industrial sector. It strongly affirmed the blatant under-representation of women in science and the 'leaky pipeline' problem, which is as follows: although women constitute a majority of undergraduates in many subjects, they drop out of the academic system at every stage of the career hierarchy. Rather than registering numerical increases among higher academic ranks (lecturers, professors), women seem to be disappearing (see Figure 10.1).

Sparking serious public debate, the ETAN report led the Commission to organise a conference, 'Women and Science: Making Change Happen' in April 2000, to expand the report's conclusions. Overall, it revealed that 'gender appears still to be a significant organizing principle in academic life' (Rees 2007: 8).

196 *Gendering Science and Research Policy*

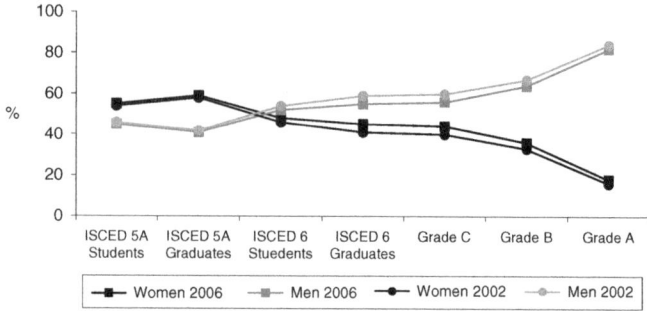

Figure 10.1 Men and women in typical academic careers, EU-27, 2002 and 2006
Source: European Commission (2009a: 73).

Definition of grades:

A: The single highest grade/post at which research is normally conducted.

B: Researchers working in positions not as senior as top position (A) but more senior than newly qualified PhD holders.

C: The first grade/post into which a newly qualified PhD graduate would normally be recruited.

ISCED 5A: Tertiary programmes to provide sufficient qualifications to enter into advanced research programmes & professions with high skills requirements.

ISCED 6: Tertiary programmes which lead to an advanced research qualification (PhD).

Created in late 1999, the Helsinki Group on Women and Science held its first meeting during the Finnish Council presidency; meeting twice a year, it consists of civil servants from the national ministries, including gender experts and representatives from countries participating in the FPs. The modus operandi is the open method of coordination (OMC). National delegates exchange information and ideas on how to gender science policy, coordinate national statistics and develop indicators for gender equality. The group combines a top-down with a bottom-up approach to data collection. It uses new public management techniques, for instance exchanging 'best practices' for promoting women scientists; it also utilises benchmarking exercises covering the number of women as well as issues like productivity, patenting, bibliometric data and so on. Its report on *National Policies on Women and Science in Europe* (Rees 2002) depicted conditions in various countries and actions taken to tackle the leaky pipeline syndrome. The study *Benchmarking Policy Measures for Gender Equality in Science* supplied an update (European Commission 2008b), analysing the situation in the 33 participating countries, including Western Balkans states.

Commission services have begun to develop a database with primary, sex-disaggregated data since 2003 (European Commission, DG Research 2006): the co-called 'She Figures' clearly attest to the leaky pipeline phenomenon. The 2006 data still show strong vertical segregation (European Commission 2009a), but also differences among countries as well as between sectors (see Table 10.2).

For example, the proportion of female researchers ranged from 49 per cent in Lithuania to 18 per cent in the Netherlands (EU-27 average: 30 per cent). The increase in female researchers, 2002 to 2006, varied from 13.7 per cent in Malta to 0.9 per cent in Poland (EU-27 average: 6.3 per cent). The number of female PhD graduates ranked below the EU average in France (41 per cent), the UK (43 per cent) and in Germany (41 per cent), compared to 66 per cent in Cyprus (EU-27 average: 45 per cent). In the state sector, where most female researchers are employed, growth rates ranged from 21.3 per cent in Sweden to –0.8 per cent in Poland (EU-27 average: 5.4 per cent); female participation was even lower in the business sector (EU-27 average: 19 per cent), topping 41 per cent in Romania but only 10 per cent in the Netherlands.

A breakdown by academic disciplines reveals that female researchers are much more prevalent in the humanities and social sciences, and better represented in the medical sciences than in natural sciences and engineering. Again, there is quite a range in the natural sciences, from 35 per cent in Cyprus to 4 per cent in Malta. In the humanities, women account for 35 per cent in Hungary, but only 1 per cent of Romanian scholars. Assessing female academic staff according to rank, one finds that women comprise 19 per cent of the grade A academic positions (the highest grade, usually

Table 10.2 The 'Leaky Pipeline': Women in science (EU-27 average in 2006)

	Women in %
Graduates	59
PhD graduates	45
Grade C academic staff	44
Grade B academic staff	36
A level researchers	19*
Total number of researchers	30
Overall growth rate 2002-2006	6.3
Business and enterprise sector	19
Government sector	39
Growth rate in government sector	5.4**

* Reference year: 2007.
** Compound annual growth rate (2002–2006).
Source: European Commission (2009a).

equivalent to full professors), with a low of 2 per cent in Malta to 32 per cent in Romania. Women remain a minority among scientific board members, ranging from 4 per cent in Luxembourg to 49 per cent in Sweden (EU 27 average: 22 per cent).

Finally, science evinces its own gender pay gap (European Commission, DG Research 2007). The average (weighted) gross annual salary in 2006 reveals that the gap between male and female research salaries is greatest in Estonia (47 per cent), lowest in Denmark (11 per cent). A breakdown by countries complicates the usual picture about 'pacemakers' and 'laggards' in equal opportunities policy.

The Commission's response in 2005 was to concentrate on boosting women's numbers in leading positions, aiming for 25 per cent of all leading positions in science by 2010. Included in the final declaration of the Council for Competitiveness in April 2005, this goal has still not been realised.[8]

The Commission further addressed two specific groups identified as requiring further support, by introducing the initiative Women in Industrial Research (WIR) in late 2001 – insofar women's numbers in the business and enterprise sector were even smaller than in the public sector. The WIR group was designated an action item (No. 26) in the Commission's Science and Society Action Plan. Again, the first step established a High Level STRATA-ETAN Expert Group,[9] charged with analysing the position of female researchers in the private sector and exploring strategies to promote gender equality. Commencing work in January 2002, the group presented its report a year later (High Level Expert Group on WIR 2003). The key barrier affecting women's careers in industrial research was 'old-fashioned ideas and practices'. The report devised recommendations aimed at companies and governments and called for closer monitoring and supplying 'best practices' to companies.

A third expert group established was ENWISE, investigating women's status in the Eastern candidate countries; it deliberated from October 2002 until December 2003, delivering its report in January 2004. Regional results are striking insofar as one legacy of communist gender policy has been a 'considerable proportion of highly-qualified women active in all public spheres and notably in science' (ENWISE Expert Working Group 2004: 6). The new member states evince a higher share of female graduates, and women scientists are much more visible in the natural science and engineering fields. Still, several of these countries display a substantial gender pay gap, over 35 per cent in Estonia or in the Czech Republic, for instance.

To counter the dearth of women in leading positions, the EU created an independent expert group on Women in Research Decision-Making (WIRDEM), with a mandate 'to identify and review positive actions and gender equality measures at institutional and national level to promote women into senior positions in public research' (European Commission,

DG Research 2008: 1). The WIRDEM report 'describes in detail nomination procedures, obstacles, facts and funding limitations that women need to overcome in their academic careers. It reviews the procedures for evaluating and promoting research personnel to senior positions and identifies examples of good practice at national and institutional levels' (European Commission, DG Research 2008: 1).

In addition to its national level analyses, the Unit attended to the EU level, where there is obviously a shortage of women participating in research policy-making within the Commission. DG Research subsequently set a minimum target of 40 per cent women for its Advisory Groups, Proposal Evaluation Panels and Monitoring Panels. Although some improvement ensued, the targets have not been met, partly because the member states do not propose more female delegates (Commission 2005: 8–9). The Unit commissioned a gender impact assessment (GIA) of some projects funded under FP5. The question was how to deal with the inclusion of women scientists and to ensure gender-relevant awareness in research content. The assessment made clear that gender mainstreaming is missing at the level of individual research projects (European Commission, DG Research 2001), leading the Unit to engage actively in the development of ERA and FP6. DG Research encourages women scientists to submit proposals, but no 'preferential treatment' (positive action) is used.

ERA concentrates on higher educational institutions, explicitly linking science policy and equality issues to strengthen women's position in science and research. FP6 outlined three specific objectives: to increase women's scientific presence at universities, in research institutions and in industrial research; to include gender issues in EU-funded projects; and to sponsor studies on indirect forms of discrimination facing women scientists. All proposals for so-called 'integrated projects' must consider the gender balance among research partners and design a Gender Action Plan (GAP) outlining how gender dimensions feature in the actual research content. According to the Commission (2005: 9), a 'good GAP' contains three steps: '(i) a diagnosis of the current situation regarding women's participation and gender aspects in the research field; (ii) proposed actions based on this diagnosis; and (iii) concrete information about how the gender dimension will be integrated in the research content'. GAPs can include the use of gender awareness groups to encourage networking or mentoring activities; the organisation of outreach activities, such as girls' days; fellowships and training activities for women scientists; or the statistical monitoring of women scientists' participation in programmes and activities. Too often, however, the quality of GAPs has not been decisive for actual funding.

GIA was continued for FP6. At least in some thematic fields, like 'science and society', 'a significant contribution was made in terms of progress towards gender equality' (Mergaert 2008: 5). There was nonetheless a great need for continuing efforts to realise the objectives declared at the start of

FP6. The GAP instrument contributed significantly to progress: the '40% target for women's participation in committees and panels of FP6 has been met or nearly met' (Mergaert 2008: 5). Continuing weaknesses include 'uncertainty and a lack of understanding among the evaluators of the significance of the gender dimension'; a lack of action in relation to gender mainstreaming by National Contact Points; fairly low participation rates of women as coordinators and participants; a failure to identify gender relevant issues in research proposals; and flaws in the Commission's central data management (Mergaert 2008: 5–6). An expert committee evaluating FP6 addressed the need for 'much more pro-active approaches such as (re)introducing specific gender equality actions after quality criteria as a condition of funding in large instruments' (Rietschel 2009: viii) to increase female research participation in FP projects substantially.

Nevertheless, in FP7 (2007–2013) GAPs became voluntary. Weaker instruments (i.e. 'gender toolkits') were developed to cover research fields ranging from health, energy, environment to nanotechnology. Toolkits make potential grant applicants aware of gender factors in diverse research fields, since 'investing in a gender-sensitive approach to the research content makes for higher quality and validity', thereby makings 'research results more relevant for society' (European Commission 2009b: 1). GIA remain in place for FP7. Allocating a stronger role to women in scientific research and in scientific decision-making bodies, strengthening the gender dimensions of research, and gender mainstreaming EU research policy and programmes are still significant objectives. While gender equality has advanced in some thematic areas, it remains very limited in others. Recent evaluations note 'that without robust policies at the Member State level to promote female researchers, the FP alone cannot succeed' (European Commission 2010b: 44).

The second instrument embedded in the 1999 Commission communication centred on a *political platform* for debate at the member states and EU levels (also seen in the Helsinki Group). The Commission fostered several networks for Europe's women scientists. The challenge was how to link them in ways that both aggregated their interests and lobbied for them. A Unit-organised conference, 'Networking the Networks'(1999), sought 'to mobilise existing networks with a view to increasing the participation of women scientists in the Fifth Framework Programme, while also examining the extent to which a European-level network of networks could bring added value, and if so, what form such a structure could take' (Commission 2001b: 10).

FP6 money funded specific support actions under the programme line 'women and science', pinpointing opportunities and recommendations for network creation (Bradley Dunbar Associates 2003). Officially launched in March 2006, the European Platform of Women Scientists (EPWS) saw earmarked funding from FP6. Its core task entailed 'the representation of the interests, needs, concerns and aspirations of women scientists in the research policy debate on the European level [...] EPWS seeks to influence the decision-making process regarding European research policy through negotiation of interests among decision-makers and other stakeholders' (EPWS 2006: 2). A lack of funding, inter alia, shut down its Brussels-based Secretariat in 2009; it now exists only as a platform.

The Commission continues to perceive gender inequality in science and research, above all, as a human resource issue. The Council adopted a resolution on family-friendly scientific careers in May 2008; the ERA revision (European Commission 2007b) links gender issues to human resources. Several policy tools focus on building up data-bases, creating indicators, supporting benchmarking and so on, to improve the empirical statistical basis for policy recommendations in member states. The Helsinki Group likewise fosters collaboration and exchanges among the member states. In 2005 a progress report requested by the Research Council found that, while women have made some progress in EU research and in the member states, conditions are 'far from satisfactory' (Commission 2005: 3). The former recommended narrowing the focus to certain disciplines (e.g., engineering); attending to definitions and measurements of excellence; and revisiting 'the role of men in ensuring or hampering progress towards gender equality in science [...] with a view to better understanding the mechanisms involved' and envisioning measures that encourage men to promote actively gender equality in science (Commission 2005: 13). The Slovenian Research Commissioner Janez Potočnik (2004–2009) renamed the Unit 'Scientific Culture and Gender Issues' (as part of the Directorate L – Science, Economy and Society). The current Commissioner for Research, Innovation and Science is the Irish Máire Geoghegan-Quinn.

These developments indicate some change in perceptions of the problem: scientific cultures are gendered and thus reproduce discriminating gender relations. However, the shift from a primarily economic perspective on statistics and indicators does imply fundamental change in FP7 (2007–2013), which builds on four pillars, seeking to strengthen the autonomy of the scientific community. It formed a European Research Council (ERC) to fund basic, investigator-driven pioneering research in Europe. A second element, from September 2008 on, is the European Institute for Innovation and Technology (EIT), inspired by the Massachusetts Institute of Technology (MIT), and designed to promote 'world-class knowledge and innovation communities'. The EIT Governing Board consists of 'innovators, academic, scientific or business leaders with widespread reputation and outstanding leadership abilities' (European Commission 2008b).

Not one of these new influential bodies meets the EU's own 40 per cent gender-balance quota: only 3 (16 per cent) of the ERC Scientific Council's 19 members are currently women, along with only 5 of 18 (28 per cent) on the EIT Governing Board. Both organisations, and the research priorities outlined in the FP7 budget, remain dominated by natural sciences and engineering, disciplines that traditionally engage fewer female researchers and present less gender awareness.

The Lisbon Treaty places great emphasis on R&D, while stressing equality between men and women and the gender mainstreaming principle as key EU goals. Directives require active implementation, however. Limitations on gendering research policy became obvious in the 2009 Lund Declaration, which emphasised that 'European research must focus on the Grand Challenges of our time'; it highlighted the need for stakeholder involvement but lacked a systematic gender perspective. The Lund Declaration calls for the involvement of women and men on equal terms, yet the challenges are presented as gender-neutral. FP8 (2014–2020) will comprise a litmus test for the gendering of EU science policy.

3. The gender dimension of research policy

Science, technology and innovation are not gender-neutral social activities. Feminist scholars and science philosophers present a strong critique of modern science and its gendered epistemology and methodology; they also offer alternative interpretations (Rose 1999: 33; Wajcman 2000). Policy-oriented research sponsored by the Commission and conducted by independent experts exposes the over-representation of men at all levels of the research system and the manifold mechanisms working to the detriment of women scientists.

The quantitative, human resource approach has triggered the greatest response at both the EU and member state levels. Although the debate over science, technology and economic competitiveness began in the 1970s, no connection was made back then between the science question and the women's question. For many decades, DG Research remained fixated on technical criteria; including political initiatives and assessment criteria in EU-funded research has always been a touchy issue, widely criticised by the scientific community. DG Research was initially quite gender-blind (Pollack and Hafner-Burton 2000: 447–448). Gender did not feature as a science-policy focus until the mid-1990s, due to increasing pressures on European competitiveness through globalisation, debates about self-transformation into a knowledge society (with implications for the science/society relationship), and the evolving gender mainstreaming debate. Various expert groups involved in framing women's marginalisation in science and research as problems of efficiency (human resource mismanagement) were vested in neoliberal thinking (Genetti 2010: 203–208). This becomes obvious in multiple Commission documents regarding the ERA:

> Indeed, the underrepresentation of women in science prevents its full realisation. First, because this represents an unacceptable and unaffordable *waste of human resources*. And second, because the underrepresentation of women in science compared with their representation in society induces a *distortion between science and society* at a moment where it is

of utmost importance to increase confidence in science. (Commission 2001b: 3; emphasis in original)

The human resource argument generated significant momentum; gendering this policy field has been backed by the EP, and, more importantly, by the Council, which influences the conduct of science and higher educational policies in member states. To a limited extent, the Commission (2001b: 12) does reference the feminist epistemological argument:

The studies found that the perception of technology and science is gender blind. Science, as such, through its search for objectivity, tends to dismiss the gender dimension [...] Integrating the gender dimension in research requires a deep transformation of research design and also of paradigms and concepts underlying this research design. It touches upon the very nature of science.

Expert reports have raised crucial questions as to the gendered nature of key science and research institutions, for example the peer-review system, the concept of excellence, empirical indicators, and assessment criteria.

A review of European research policy makes two things clear. First, gendering research policy has thus far relied on a *soft policy* mode; there is no hard legislation at the EU level and no ECJ rulings re-shaping the field. Policy coordination is based on the OMC, which is in turn backed by Council resolutions. Policy changes therefore depend on the good-will of member state governments and industrial stakeholders. Still, policy changes are occurring as some member states set up special programmes for women scientists (see Table 10.3).

Secondly, the primary reliance on a quantitative approach means that EU policy-making in this field meets the prerequisites for a gender mainstreaming approach. Gender statistics and indicators, GIA, gender awareness and GAP are leading to some success, as FP evaluations show. Still, the field has seen no gender budgeting, although this could have major (re)distributive effects: research funding comprises the third largest segment of the EU budget, after agriculture and structural policy. Women and science activities are funded under the science/society programme, by far the smallest component amount in the research budget. Most money goes to male-dominated science and engineering programmes, where it proves difficult to gender research plans and to design research targeting women. Most policy recommendations follow an equal treatment or positive action approach, focusing on women, not on gender; they focus on increasing the share of women scientists in public and (private) industrial research. Still missing is a comprehensive approach gendering the epistemological foundations of EU research policy and the underlying scientific cultures.

Table 10.3 National policies to promote gender equality in science (2004)

Equality Measures in Science	BE	CY	CZ	DK	DE	EE	EL	ES	FR	IE	IT	LV	LT	LU	HU	MT	NL	AT	PL	PT	SI	SK	FI	SE	UK
Equal treatment legislation (general)	x		x	x	x	x	x	x	x	x	x	x	x	x	x	x	x	x	x	x	x	x	x	x	x
Commitment to gender mainstreaming	x	x	x	x	x	x	x	x	x	x	x	x	x	x			x	x	x	x	x	x	x	x	x
National Committee on Women & Science	x	x	x	xx	x	x	xx	x	x	x	x	x	x		x	x		x	x	x	x	x	x	x	
Women & Science Unit in Research Ministry							x5	x	x	x								x							x
Publication of Sex-disaggregated Statistics	x	x	x	x	x	x	x	x	x	x		x	x	xx	x	x	x	x	x	x	x	x	x	x	x3
Development of Gender equality indicators	x4		x	x	x		x		x	x	x	x	x		x	x	x	x		x			x	x	x
Gender balance targets: public committees	x2			x			x		x	x													x	x	x
Gender balance targets: on university committees		x		x					x								x4	x					x	x	x4
Gender equality Plans in Univ. & Research I.	x4		x	x	x				x	x	x			xx			x4	x					x	x	
Gender[1] Studies & Research at Universities	x	x	x	x	x	x	x	x	x	x	x	x	x	xx	x	x	x	x	x	x	x	x	x	x	x
Programmes on W&S, special funding available					x		x			xx	x	xx	xx			x	x	x			x				x
Nationwide Centres on Women & Science			x		x																				x

EU-Member States (25)

*Source: Information provided by the members of the Helsinki group & EOWIN, Summer 2004, DG RTD, UNIT C4; xx = preparation; [1]) or women studies/research X1 = only BE French-speaking; X2 = only BE Dutch-speaking; x3 = not for industrial R&D; x = yes x4 = set by certain universities; x5 = person only responsible for W&S; Commission (2005: 11).

4. Gender mainstreaming in science and research policy – A critical assessment

Given the initially unfavourable conditions, it is amazing that DG Research became a pioneer in implementing a top-down gender mainstreaming strategy. Yet DG Research is not a homogenous actor; internal divisions as well as a very specific interpretation of gender mainstreaming by the DG's Gender Unit help to explain its piecemeal approach and the persistent gap between EU rhetoric and practice (see Cavaghan 2010). Gender is a significant science focus today, and gender mainstreaming offers 'transformative potential' (Schäfer 2005) for European research policy.

Working in Brussels, Agnès Hubert (2010) claims that evolving women and science policies constitute an important institutional innovation for promoting gender equality. As for major policy outputs and outcomes, there is now a solid institutional structure, the Unit inside DG Research, and also the inter-service working group. The Gender Watch System has brought new procedures and rules that apply to community funded research (for example GIA, GAP); toolkits are available to improve implementation; a quota system moreover applies to committees and panels. Furthermore, dramatic improvements in the statistical base make it easier to examine gender-oriented science policy. Multiple expert studies and continuing Commission efforts allow for statistical analysis of conditions at the EU and member state levels, affording an empirical foundation for policy recommendations. However, there is still no 'hard' EU legislation. The *gender acquis* and countless work regulations do apply to the research system as an employment sector; however, no law covers the peculiarities of scientific careers and the research system. A (weakened) political platform, the EPWS, can sustain a broader debate and lobby for the interests of women scientists at the EU level.[10] Finally, even though the EU's mandate affecting women's status in science is very limited, European initiatives have impelled changes in national policies primarily via the Helsinki Group and its instruments – information sharing, benchmarking and best practices. Rees (2007: 12) concludes that the group has 'enabled countries to learn from each other and to push the agendas forward more easily than they might otherwise have done'. Consequently, women and science appear as regular items on the national research agendas; member states, in turn, are introducing equality measures in science (see Table 10.3).

In Germany, for example, the Federal Ministry for Research (BMBF) houses a unit informing women scientists about EU research programmes and offering training on how to apply. The BMBF has introduced gender-specific grants and mobility programmes, like its 2008 initiative creating 200 new positions for female professors within five years. It has, moreover, introduced an annual Total E-Quality award for universities most actively promoting work/life balance. Finally, all major research organisations in Germany now have policies, and often special programmes, promoting women in science. Main policy actors like the German Research Council (DFG) and the Science Council (*Wissenschaftsrat*) have adopted their own recommendations for advancing women.

5. Conclusions

In May 2009 the Czech presidency celebrated these developments with a conference in Prague, titled '10 years of EU Activities in "Women and Science", and Beyond'. Gender and science comprise a vibrant issue-area; gender mainstreaming – interpreted here as science conducted *by* women – has become an effective means for shaping the EU agenda and influencing policy discourse in the member states. Today's emphasis falls on mobilising women scientists, perceived as a precious human resource in the new economy. Ironically, this offers major political justification for action, while genuine equality concerns have taken a back seat. Progress relative to the numbers and positions of women in the EU and in national science is too slow, and the pipeline remains 'leaky'. The national level still displays a lack of strong commitment and real action, affecting the participation of women in EU projects and, hence, the success of the FPs.

Progress has been quite halting when it comes to science *for* and *about* women. Gender mainstreaming has yet to display its transformative potential, since many mechanisms have rested on an equal treatment or positive action approach. Bear in mind that much collaborative research is conducted outside the Community framework (for instance, through transatlantic or other international ties), although EUREKA is linked to the ERA. When we examine research budget allocations, most money still goes into the natural sciences and engineering, fields still dominated by men, which remain more 'resistant' to gender concerns than the humanities. Thus gender mainstreaming in research policy has been sectorally limited to the science/society issues; mainstreaming across the entire research domain is inadequate. The social sciences and humanities, heavily populated by women, are still underrepresented in EU policy. Future research must focus not only on quantitative indicators but also on qualitative changes in the gendered culture and economy of science.

The European Commission (2009c) concluded: 'no true modernisation of universities and research institutions can take place if the social relationships governing them remain based on and ruled by stereotypes'. The challenge today is to gender the institutional structures in which science and research is embedded. Major innovations have been introduced over the last ten years, but many challenges still lie ahead.

Discussion questions
– Why has gender mainstreaming been more successful in the field of technology and research policy?

– What instruments have been effective, at the national and EU level, in increasing women's participation in science? What instruments could be effective in the future?
 – What does 'doing science about and for women' mean in science, engineering and the humanities? How does this relate to gendering science?

Notes

1. I am grateful to Ann-Catherine Roth and Jan Ullrich for background research and technical assistance. All remaining errors are mine.
2. For an amusing, real-world version, see von Flowtow (1997).
3. Much of European RTD is conducted outside the Community framework, as part of the intergovernmental EUREKA (European Research Coordination Agency) founded in 1985 by the EC and further European countries. EUREKA fosters cooperation among universities, research institutes and private facilities. Funding comes from national RTD budgets and private sources; the European Commission is a partner to EUREKA.
4. Until then Community RTD activities had to be based on Article 235 EC Treaty authorising community actions, if it had been considered appropriate for achieving the general goal of economic integration.
5. Networks of Excellence grant much more autonomy to the research consortium partner in setting research priorities and in administering the research budget than the previous mode of project funding controlled by the Commission.
6. 'The Union shall have the objective of strengthening its scientific and technological bases by achieving a European research area in which researchers, scientific knowledge and technology circulate freely, and encouraging it to become more competitive, including in its industry, while promoting all the research activities deemed necessary by virtue of other Chapters of the Treaties' (Article 179 TFEU).
7. 'The gender dimension is at the core of the science/society issue, which is itself at the core of the European Research Area' (Commission 2001b: 16).
8. This aim is also included in the Roadmap for Gender Equality.
9. The acronyms stand for Strategic Analysis of Policy Issues (STRATA) and European Technology Assessment Network (ETAN). This group consists of 17 members, most of whom are chief executive officers, vice-presidents or directors of international companies from different branches of industries with significant research departments, along with some political actors (see http://ec.europa.eu/research/science-society/women/wir/general_en.html#strataetan).
10. Research policy affords another example of the Commission's role as a network creator and its strategy of intensifying close relations with its policy clients by helping to set up groups representing 'weak' or 'diffuse' public interests. The European Women's Lobby and the European Environmental Forum are further examples.

11
Women on the Move: EU Migration and Citizenship Policy

Joyce Marie Mushaben

Imagine that you were forced to flee your homeland due to a sudden wave of 'ethnic cleansing' in 1995. You were an accomplished university professor who frequently attended international conferences and held dinner parties for your multi-cultural colleagues in Sarajevo. Married to a Muslim taken away by masked soldiers, you have seen your comfortable life destroyed by ultra-nationalists engaging in mass rape to terrify people like you into abandoning their neighbourhoods. You arrive in Germany with your two children after three weeks of trekking across mountains, grateful to have found refuge, although you cannot speak the language. For the next three years you will be required to live in an asylum hostel outside of town, sharing a room with six people. You are forbidden to work legally until your case is 'decided'. Luckily you find a cleaning job at a local hospital, working the night shift so that you can care for your children, attending half-day German schools. They now speak better German than Bosnian, but because your country was not an EU member, you might be deported if authorities decide it is safe for you to go back.

Or imagine that your spouse has been offered a five-year temporary work visa, given Europe's growing need for IT specialists. You run your own software business in Mumbai but this is a great opportunity for your husband. Since Germany lacks child-care facilities and will not allow a 'dependent spouse' to pursue paid labour, you become a reluctant homebody. The marriage suffers and your husband divorces you after 18 months. Your return to India as a divorcee will bring shame upon your family, but you could be deported (without your children), since your residency status depends on the 'family breadwinner'.

Or perhaps your parents migrated to work in Europe a decade ago. You arrived as a child, but due to language requirements and emotional attachments to the homeland, your parents have kept their Turkish passports. Members of the extended family persuade them to send you 'home' at age 16 to marry a cousin you have never met, although you want to study medicine. As soon as they put you on the plane, they cancel your residency permit, making it impossible for you to return legally. Will the EU come to the rescue?

By 2008, 30.8 million foreigners accounted for 6.2 per cent of all Community residents, 11.3 million (37 per cent) of whom hold citizenship in another member state; the EU-27 population of 497 million encompassed 19.5 million (4 per cent) third-country nationals (TCNs), a figure reaching 25 million if we add undocumented estimates to the mix (Vasileva 2009: 1–2). The number of TCNs has risen by 9.2 million since 2001; net immigration lies between 1.5 and 2 million new arrivals annually. Subject to intergovernmental regulation until the late 1990s under the Justice and Home Affairs pillar, migration, asylum and refugee policies are now among the EU's most politically charged issues.

Recognising the obstacles inherent in national policies, the Commission is searching for collective remedies to looming demographic deficits, labour shortages and globalised competition for 'the best brains'. The 9/11 terrorist attacks, coupled with Eastern enlargement, have brought new problems, not easily reconciled with the free movement of people enshrined in the 1957 Treaty of Rome. Admission of 12 new members since 2004 has turned 'external migration' into 'internal mobility' (Traser et al. 2005). The proliferation of illegal labour pools, human trafficking, organised crime, refugee surges and home-grown terrorism has resulted in shifting migrant typologies, as well as surprising re-alignments among sending and receiving countries.

Routinely classified as spouses of newly arriving male workers, regardless of their occupational histories, migrant women become provisional residents, excluded from employment for waiting periods of up to five years. The EU has yet to adopt binding regulations concerning gender-specific persecution or dependency on 'head of household' asylum status. Nor has it adequately addressed problematic family unification practices, for example the admission of multiple wives, forced marriages among underage women or the exploitation of countless females working as domestics, au-pairs and prostitutes behind closed doors in European cities.

This chapter examines core EU initiatives and barriers to gender-sensitive migration policies, including new occupational and security linkages shaping this policy domain. Starting with key agreements establishing a common approach to immigration and asylum, it then describes the broader gender context underlying member state regulations. Next we consider an evolving set of basic principles and policy parameters seeking to redirect migrant flows. Finally, we analyse specific gender dilemmas inherent in the mechanisms thus far adopted for EU 'migration management'.

210 *EU Migration and Citizenship Policy*

1. Developing EU migration and asylum policies: The rise of 'Fortress Europe'

Especially since the 1990s, we have seen a number of EU initiatives on citizenship, immigration and asylum (see Table 11.1). Anticipating completion of the Single Market, five member states agreed in June 1985 to eliminate passport controls to facilitate free movement within Community boundaries. France, Germany, Belgium, Luxembourg and the Netherlands signed the Schengen Agreement prior to the fall of the Berlin Wall (1989), never imagining that it would soon be overtaken by a new world order. The Southern Mediterranean and North African flank comprised the most porous border regions at the time. Mounting complaints regarding the Community's 'democratic deficits' led national leaders to highlight EU citizenship, embedded in the Maastricht Treaty (1991); they also called for a harmonisation of asylum procedures by 1993. Before the Commission could act, Western states were overwhelmed by the first of three waves of Yugoslav refugees. What began as an effort to eliminate controls within EU boundaries has evolved into an ever more impenetrable fortress to keep undocumented migrants and asylum-seekers out.

Table 11.1 EU initiatives on citizenship, immigration and asylum

1992	Maastricht Treaty (Art. 8), defining EU citizenship
1997	Amsterdam Treaty (Art. 13) prohibits discrimination based on sex, religion and national origin, *inter alia*; it also shifted responsibility for migration and asylum issues from 'third' intergovernmental to 'first' supranational pillar
1999	European Council meeting in Tampere (Finland) in October
2000	Directive 2000/43/EC, implementing the principle of equal treatment between persons irrespective of racial or ethnic origin Directive 2000/78/EC, Equal Treatment in Employment, prohibiting discrimination based on religion or belief, disability, age or sexual orientation
2002	Council Regulation (EC) No 1030/2002, laying down a uniform format for residence permits for third-country nationals Creation of National Contact Points on integration
2003	Directive 2003/109/EC, concerning the status of third-country nationals who are long-term residents
2004	The Hague Programme First Annual Report on Migration and Integration First edition of the Handbook on Integration for Policy-Makers and Practitioners Regulation (EC) No 491/2004 of the European Parliament and of the Council of 10 March 2004 establishing a programme for financial and technical assistance to third countries in the areas of migration and asylum (AENEAS)
2005	Common Basic Principles for immigrant integration policy Policy Plan on Legal Migration
2007	Framework Programme on Solidarity and Management of Migration Flows (2007–2013)
2010	Appointment of a Commissioner for Justice, Fundamental Rights and Citizenship

The supplemental Dublin Accord (1995) was a knee-jerk response to fears that collapsing Central Eastern European economies would trigger a tidal wave of job-seekers and refugees. The signatories consented to common asylum processes, adopting a 'one chance rule' and a 'safe list' of countries used to disqualify throngs of potential applicants. Despite documented gender violence and human rights violations, in India, Pakistan, Bulgaria, Cyprus, Poland and Romania, all were declared 'safe'. The blanket exclusion of minorities facing persecution – like the Roma, Kurds or women under the Taliban – was quasi-institutionalised, based on male-normed definitions of 'political' activity. The United Nations estimates that 85 to 90 percent of the world's refugees are 'women and children', yet 90 percent of asylum applicants are male. Schengen amendments foresaw identical procedures for external border controls, standardisation of visas and asylum rules, greater police and judicial cooperation to tackle organised crime and centralised data-banks.

Thirteen more member states were incorporated into *Schengenland* in 1997. The Amsterdam Treaty (enacted in 1999) nonetheless transferred immigration policy from the third 'intergovernmental' pillar to the first 'supranational' pillar, although the European Council insisted on national control in some areas. Further measures included separate processing of non-Schengen residents at the main points of entry such as airports, established common surveillance and training requirements for border personnel – and re-defined carrier responsibility for illegal immigration. Participating states restricted asylum applications to 'the first country of arrival'; they extended cross-border authorisation for police forces in hot pursuit of criminals, accelerated extradition processes and allowed cross-national dissemination of criminal-conviction information. Although Denmark, Ireland and the UK exempt themselves from certain provisions, an Amsterdam Treaty protocol rendered Schengen decisions part of the EU *acquis* in 1999.

The parameters for future immigration policies were defined at the European Council meeting in Tampere (Finland) in October 1999. Attending to the plight of long-term alien residents and the need for *social cohesion*, the Council called for vigorous integration efforts; it introduced 'an arsenal of instruments' to promote family reunification rights and secure status for permanent third-country residents. Supporting common conditions of entry and residence for the purpose of paid- or self-employment, the Council agreed to grant third-country nationals *equal protection* regarding social security, to develop shared rules for admitting students and volunteers, set minimum standards for receiving asylum seekers and recognising the qualifications of non-EU nationals or persons meriting international protection. It simultaneously proposed rigorous measures against discrimination (Directives 2000/43/EC and 2000/78/EC). Relying on open methods of coordination (OMC), it adopted the European Employment Strategy (EES), requiring national action plans to combat poverty and social exclusion while reinforcing best-practice exchanges. The latter are crucial for promoting integration among long-term 'foreigners', especially for youth of migrant descent.

Finally, the Tampere Council installed National Contact Points on integration, commensurate with the Justice and Home Affairs Council conclusions of 2002. This network fosters information exchanges to ensure policy coordination and coherence between national and EU initiatives; it seeks implementation of best practices grounded in shared principles, specific targets and benchmarks. The Thessaloniki Council (2003) 'invited' the Commission to present an Annual Report on Migration and Integration, mapping EU-wide migration and tracking integration practices. Its first report (European Commission 2004) reinforced an earlier Commission communication on integration and employment; both projected a need for future labour imports to counter demographic trends and skilled worker shortages. The second and third reports called for systematic integration policies to ensure migrants' labour market incorporation as well as their participation in cultural and civic life.

Like the High Level Group on Gender Mainstreaming, the recently formed Commissioners' Group on Migration Issues seeks to incorporate integration objectives into all relevant EU initiatives. In 2005 it launched a five-year Action Plan pertaining to terrorism, migration management, visa and asylum policies, measures addressing privacy, security, organised crime and criminal justice. It was labelled 'a major policy initiative and a cornerstone of the Commission's Strategic Objectives for 2010 – built around prosperity, solidarity and security' (European Movement – Malta 2005). A European Integration Forum links stakeholders and umbrella organisations; participants range from public officials, civil society groups and migrant associations to private enterprises and social partners. The Commission began promoting transnational cooperation at the municipal level after the 2006 Rotterdam Conference under the rubric 'integrating cities'. It supports best-practice studies in major cities like London, Berlin and Rome as part of its Europe Land of Asylum project (European Refugee Fund 2004). The Ministerial Conference of Groningen (2004) brought a new round of *intergovernmental* debates, followed by an informal meeting of EU Ministers responsible for integration in Potsdam in May 2007. Under the German Presidency, the Council resolved to strengthen integration by 'promoting unity in diversity' in June 2007.

Immigration and integration have come to occupy a prominent place on the Commission's agenda due to decades of national neglect as well as to globalisation. The integration theories embraced by the EU, coupled with a plethora of strategic objectives, principles and action plans, hold lots of promise for millions of long-term foreign residents, especially for migrant women. Yet even actively supported best practices will do little to bring about Community integration in a dual sense, as long as equality is forced to take a back seat to 'security' by member state governments.

2. Migration and citizenship through a gendered lens

Despite an obvious globalisation of 'women's work' stretching from the *maquiladoras* of Mexico to the sneaker-stichers of South Korea (Enloe 2004), the *feminisation of migration* was largely ignored even by EU equality advocates prior to 1990. Reflecting a complex constellation of social relations, gender often determines 'who stays, who moves, where, why, how often' (Pessar and Mahler 2001) – and what they do once they get there (Mushaben 2008). Before we examine specific directives and principles shaping EU migration policies, let us review migratory 'gender gaps' highlighted by feminist scholars. Among the nearly 11 million third-country nationals who entered EU territory in 1990, at least five million were female (Kofman and Sales 2000: 196). As noted by Moravcsik (1984), Donato (1992) and others (Gabaccia et al. 2006; Kofman 1999), however, 'female birds of passage' have long constituted an invisible stream of migrants, subsumed under the label of 'family migration.'

Not all member states guaranteed family unification early on; national regulations were rooted in a double standard, allowing male breadwinners but not female workers to bring in their dependants. Some countries issued an entry permit for a migrant's spouse only after 'he' had qualified for permanent residency; waiting periods ranged from one to eight years (although 12 months of separation is proof of marital breakdown in Germany). Wives and children still do not enjoy independent residency rights in all member states, compelling them to stay in abusive households or face possible deportation. Ostensibly neutral in form, national immigration laws are highly gendered in content.

Article 119 EEC Treaty accorded 'equal pay for equal work' to both sexes but extended no protection with regard to race or ethnicity. Differences in legal status result in disparate economic opportunity structures, depending on one's country of origin; they also affect the ways in which migration reconfigures gender relations within a specific community (Raghuram 2004; Zulauf 2001). 'Dependent' wives are often denied employment, regardless of their previous work records; host states refuse to recognise skill certification acquired elsewhere, leading to their disproportionate *de-qualification* (Mushaben 2009). National accreditation requirements hit women hardest in fields historically dominated by men, such as medicine and engineering. Job-training in the country of settlement is extended to men as breadwinners; women are excluded 'since they are unlikely to find work anyway' (Westphal 1999: 139). Unemployment forces women into traditional caretaking roles, paradoxically isolating them just when they need to help other family members to integrate socially. When they do become economically active, women purportedly support family enterprises (at no/low pay) or become domestic labourers 'operating in the shadows of affluence' (Hondagneu-Sotelo 2001).

Migrant women often lack human capital due to limited educations in their countries of origin. One consequence is a twofold 'women's gap' (Heron 2005): foreign-born females lag significantly behind native-born women *and* foreign-born men in labour market participation in Australia, Canada, Germany, the Netherlands, Sweden and the UK. Although these gaps depend partly on 'mismatches' between migrant skills and host-country needs, labour market access and prior experience, the most significant factor remains a dearth of affordable child-care; Belgium, Denmark and Sweden constitute the exceptions. Bearing children at earlier ages than native women (especially academics) gives them less workplace experience from the start. A lack of child-care provides fewer opportunities for acquiring a new language and thus better wages later on. The longer women remain outside the labour force, the greater an employer's reluctance to recognise their homeland qualifications, beyond the usual 're-entry' problems incurred by mothers. Employment has a beneficial effect on language proficiency (Heron 2005), suggesting that waiting periods imposed on 'dependent' spouses actually hinder family integration.

Direct and indirect discrimination remains 'an enduring fact in the labour market' (Iredale 2005: 10), despite the EU's mandate to advance occupational opportunity, pay equity and equal treatment. Iredale pinpoints market criteria that reinforce inequality, starting with *'supply side' biases on behalf of the sending countries*, reluctant to allow their women to work abroad. Secondly, the *occupations in high demand*, though new (information technologies), are already male-dominated. Thirdly, only the *profile of the principal breadwinner* is used to test eligibility for admission, forcing female professionals to enter as dependants. Fourth, women put off having their *qualifications recognised* until a spouse has completed the process. This means postponing language acquisition in order to stay home 'for the family'; accreditation comes at higher cost the longer it is postponed.

Ostensibly gender-neutral *mutual recognition agreements* differ for occupations (psychotherapy, actuarial science) as well as for certain regions. The EU Directive on the Recognition of Professional Qualifications (1985) accords mutual recognition to degrees/diplomas held for at least three years; such job-seekers cannot be excluded from regulated professions if they meet the criteria of their own member state. Yet occupational recognition can be hindered by secondary criteria (like headscarf bans), or if 'experience' is defined in terms of continuous working years. Competency tests may limit gender bias, but on-the-job assessments and interviews reflect ethno-gender biases among evaluators, for example in engineering. Poor evaluations may reflect a lack of language courses for 'non-principal' breadwinners: even strictly standardised *knowledge-based examinations* can place persons not exposed to colloquial terms or acronyms at a disadvantage. Testing fees may also be prohibitive. Doctorates, diplomas or licences do not guarantee 'substantial equivalence', insofar as rising standards (for example publications) work against women who leave the workforce for a few years. Unfamiliar with host-country laws, women find discrimination difficult to prove; employers, reluctant to deal with pregnancy and family leave, can resort to smokescreen arguments, for example citing a lack of segregated toilets in rejecting female construction workers.

Still, there is lots of money to be made exploiting undocumented female labour, given the dramatic increase in sex trafficking since the rending of the Iron Curtain. Controlling borders has become one more way to regulate women's sexual behaviour, but not that of male consumers of prostitution or pornography. Moved by the 1993 UN Convention on the Elimination of all Forms of Discrimination against Women (CEDAW) and the Vienna World Conference on Human Rights (1994), a 1997 meeting in The Hague led to the EU Ministerial Declaration on European guidelines for effective measures to prevent and combat trafficking in women for sexual exploitation. Although women are the primary victims, national leaders adhere to a male-normed definition of 'the problem': trafficking is construed, above all, as illegal migration, then as a form of unregulated or slave labour; as a threat to 'public order', undermining family and community stability; as a 'moral problem' (for women); and, finally, as a vehicle for organised crime (Wijers 2000). Decision-makers fail to grasp it as the inevitable by-product of unequal power relations, a dearth of economic opportunity and a market problem rooted in a heinous type of gendered 'supply and demand'.

The EU's early conceptualisation of citizenship is partly to blame: 'Every person holding the nationality of a Member State shall be a citizen of the Union. Citizenship of the Union shall complement and not replace national citizenship' (Article 8 TEU). Member states reserved for themselves 'sole authority' over decisions shaping the criteria for the acquisition or loss of citizenship status. The privileges conferred upon EU nationals include the right to move and reside freely within Union borders (Article 18 TEU), subject to gender limitations noted above. After six months, EU citizens acquire the right to vote and to run as candidates in municipal and European Parliament elections where they reside (Article 19 TEU); TCNs who have lived there for decades do not. The former possess the right to diplomatic/consular protection by another member state when outside the EU (Article 20 TEU), along with the right to petition the EP and to register administrative complaints with the European Ombudsman (Article 21 TEU). Further 'fundamental rights and obligations' derive from the EU Treaties, ECJ case law and member state constitutions. The Amsterdam Treaty expanded 'citizen rights' by enabling EU organs to take active measures against discrimination rooted in sex, racial or ethnic origin, religion or belief, disability, age or sexual orientation.

Like most fields of EU endeavour, this one constitutes a 'moving target'. Under the combined influences of the four freedoms, the Single Market and EU enlargement, the immigration policies of one member state inevitably produce spill-over effects for others. Looming demographic deficits likewise leave the Union no choice but to plan for future immigration in efficient, effective and humane ways. Integration must become a two-way process based on mutual rights and corresponding obligations, engaging legal non-nationals and their host societies at multiple levels; it should, moreover, instil a shared respect for fundamental, democratic norms, preservation of valued cultural identities and the active participation of all EU residents on equal footing.

The last three years have brought a shift from symbolic politics to transversal soft-law instruments, heralding an ever more holistic response to immigration and integration concerns. The Commission is leading member states to abandon their traditionally rigid, legalistic interpretation of 'belonging' in favour of more fluid notions of active qua social citizenship. As the next section reveals, mechanisms that previously proved effective in advancing the equality agenda are reflected in recent efforts to enhance EU-citizenship: namely *equal treatment, positive action, mainstreaming, anti-discrimination* and *social inclusion* policies. If member state governments would only practise the principles underlying these mechanisms half as much as the EU preaches them, the result would be a great leap forward for women in general and ethnic minorities in particular.

3. Plans, programmes and priorities: Waiting for gender balance

As a knowledge-generating enterprise *sui generis*, the EU has adopted an impressive array of migration frameworks, programmes, action plans and directives, grounded in annual member state reports, research projects and 'best practice' exchanges, only a few of which can be described here. In November 2000, the Commission called for a 'fresh look' at Community immigration policy (European Commission 2000), stressing the need for the 'fair treatment' of TCNs based on integration policies granting them rights and obligations comparable to those of EU citizens. Labelled *civic citizenship*, the idea here is to 'phase in' core rights and duties over time, to ensure equal treatment across many domains even without naturalisation. 'Active citizenship' among TCNs is to be grounded in 'volition' (willingness to take part) and 'competence' (the capacity to take part) at the local, national and European level. The Treaty of Nice (enacted 2001) rendered legislation pertaining to free movement and residence subject to qualified majority voting in the Council, explicitly declaring the principle of non-discrimination 'a cornerstone of the whole construction'.

Presented jointly by Commissioners Diamantopoulou (Employment and Social Affairs) and Vitorino (Justice and Home Affairs), the Communication on Immigration, Integration and Employment (European Commission

2003a), advocates a 'structure of rights' allowing for 'fair participation' in economic, social, cultural and civil life, coupled with mutual responsibilities for migrants and their host societies. It calls for the coordination of national approaches by way of holistic integration policies that nonetheless reflect the special needs of specific groups. The Commission hinted that according civic citizenship would constitute a first step in migrant acquisition of host-state nationality. It highlights gender differences, noting that nearly half of all new arrivals are females, coming to work as 'caring professionals', for example nurses, nannies and domestic servants. Many face double, even triple discrimination (gender + ethnic origin + religion), necessitating special measures to secure equal access to education, language skills, occupational training and lifelong learning. The Commission acknowledges the family's central role in integration; hardships in securing work often push women into the unregulated informal sector. The Directive on Family Reunification (2003/86/EC) not only promotes women's access to the labour market but also grants them independent residence status – if they face a 'particularly difficult situation'.

Endorsed by the European Council in 2004, the Hague Programme (see Box 11.1) identifies ten 'top priorities' for community action, accompanied by a five-year timetable for adoption and implementation. Beginning with fundamental rights and citizenship, the EU strives to protect personal data, eliminate discrimination, eradicate violence and secure rights for women and children; it has converted its Vienna-based European Monitoring Centre for Racism and Xenophobia into a Fundamental Rights Agency (www.fra.europa.eu). The fight against terrorism concentrates on prevention, preparedness and enhancing national capabilities. In 2006 it added a pilot project creating reception centres to supply aid and psychological counselling for terrorist victims. Migration management looks towards strategies that transcend (or by-pass) national laws, with a common definition of third-country national rights, readmission and return procedures, in response to fluctuating market needs.

Internal borders, external borders and visas anticipate the full integration of CEE members into the Schengen *acquis*, adding biometric identifiers to travel/identification documents and a Visa Information System. A fifth priority entails building a common asylum area utilising shared procedures, status determinations and 'regional protection programs' commensurate with international humanitarian obligations. Drawing attention to the positive impact of migration and integration on society and the economy follows next. In 2007, the EU issued its second handbook of best practices, incentives and support measures to strengthen integration efforts. The Union must simultaneously strive to balance privacy and security in sharing information among law enforcement agencies, border personnel and court authorities.

> **Box 11.1 The Hague Programme (2004)**
>
> 1. *Fundamental rights and citizenship:* Ensure the full development of policies enhancing citizenship, monitoring and promoting respect for fundamental rights.
> 2. *The fight against terrorism:* Focus on different aspects of prevention, preparedness and response in order to further enhance, and where necessary complement, member states capabilities to fight terrorism.
> 3. *Migration management:* Define a balanced approach by developing common policy at the Union level, while strengthening the fight against illegal migration and trafficking, especially women and children.
> 4. *Internal borders, external borders and visas:* Further develop an integrated management of external borders and a common visa policy, while ensuring the free movement of persons.
> 5. *A common asylum area:* A common asylum area must take into account the humanitarian tradition and international obligations of the Union, and the effectiveness of a harmonized procedure.
> 6. *Integration: the positive impact of migration on our society and economy:* Adopt, support and incentivize measures to help member states deliver better policies on integration so as to maximize the positive impact of migration on our society and economy.
> 7. *Privacy and security in sharing information:* Strike the right balance between privacy and security in sharing available information among authorities, respecting fundamental rights of privacy and data protection.
> 8. *The fight against organized crime:* Implement a strategic concept for tackling organized crime at EU level, including law enforcement, judicial cooperation, while involving third countries, international organizations, EUROPOL and EUROJUST.
> 9. *Civil and criminal justice: an effective European area of justice for all:* Guarantee an effective European area of justice by ensuring an effective access to justice for all and the enforcement of judgements.
> 10. *Freedom, Security and Justice: sharing responsibility and solidarity:* Promote shared responsibility and solidarity between member states, utilizing policy and financial instruments that can meet these objectives in the most efficient way.
>
> *Source*: European Commission (2005a).

Ranked seventh is the fight against organised crime, requiring greater cooperation among judges, national law enforcement agencies, third-country actors and international organisations; European Police Office (EUROPOL) and EUROJUST are included in efforts to detect cross-border patterns for human trafficking and criminal financial transactions. Developing an effective European area of civil and criminal justice for all will ensure fair access to judicial processes and enforcement of standing judgements. The frequency of international marriages is covered in a Green Paper on jurisdiction regarding divorce and child custody, since 'marital breakdown' criteria range from 6 to 12 months of separation across the EU-27. Finally, the EU accords priority to freedom, security, justice, shared responsibility and solidarity – for example equitable member state contributions to these efforts.

Noteworthy among the Hague 'priorities' is, first, the heavy emphasis on security and, secondly, the essentially negative understanding of migration management: the EU budget share devoted to these aims brought a six-fold increase in security allocations, 2006–2013. Women appear primarily as victims, or as persons whose 'privacy' must be protected in operationalising other priorities. There is no positive obligation to promote equal opportunities for women or minorities, for example, in law enforcement or border control agencies.

The Policy Plan on Legal Migration (European Commission 2005c) relies on gender-neutral terminology, although migrant employment rights depend on sex qua marital status in most member states. Framework Directive 2003/109/EC warrants employment rights for all legally admitted workers, even without long-term residence status. It covers recognition of qualifications and ordains a single application for a joint work/residence permit. Four more directives *in spe* address salaried workers, highly skilled workers, seasonal workers, intra-corporate transferees (ICTs) and remunerated trainees whose admission is contingent on time-limited work contracts and an 'economic needs test'.

A second element centres on knowledge-building and information. The Commission has established a European Job Mobility Portal (EURES) and links to national integration websites. It promoted information campaigns and research projects for the European Year of Workers' Mobility (2006), the Year of Equal Opportunities for All (2007) and the Year of Intercultural Dialogue (2008). The EU has also become pro-active regarding migrant integration, urging member states to supply information packets, language courses, civic orientation classes, job training and cultural initiatives for new (legal) arrivals.

The Policy Plan stresses greater cooperation with countries of origin, to identify sectors in developing states hit by brain-drain. Funding training programmes through local authorities and/or of non-governmental organisations (NGOs) in the sending states would foster technical skills helping migrants to adapt to EU job market conditions. 'Circular migration' would create long-term multi-entry visas, according priority to former migrants while simplifying eligibility rules for renewed employment; this would generate a database of (potentially acculturated) TCNs who left the EU when their temporary permits expired. Unfortunately, the Plan's gender-neutral language does little to mitigate inequalities already inherent in labour migration, namely the extent to which skilled females are disproportionately subject to de-qualified, part-time or insecure service work upon arrival.

The Commission has pushed the member states to adopt Common Basic Principles for Immigrant Integration Policy (see Box 11.2), along with a Common Agenda for Integration (European Commission 2005b), linking EU integration goals to broader treaty values and social inclusion objectives. The lack of explicit references to gender equality could imply that an emerging emphasis on diversity management will water down female-targeted programmes; but gender mainstreaming might also give rise to *ethnic mainstreaming* (Szczepaniková et al. 2006). If the history of EU gender policies has taught us anything, it is that symbolic politics – implicit in the declaration of common principles – gradually evolves into supranational mandates that supply the leverage grassroots activists need to 'sandwich' or squeeze national governments into effective policy overhauls (van der Vleuten 2007), even if some members take longer than others to see the light.

The Commission has thus formed a Network of National Contact Points, obliging member states to actively identify integration priorities and to render them mutually reinforcing at all levels; this includes regional policy mechanisms (URBAN, URBACTII 2007–2013). Recalcitrant governments insisting on the 'need for further study' can easily be referred to 'best practices' elaborated in the *Handbook on Integration for Policy-Makers and Practitioners* (three editions, 2004, 2007, 2009) including useful monitoring indicators, tips on building integration infrastructure and assessing implementation across policy domains, for example, regarding urban housing. For those blaming a failure to act on scarce resources, the INTI Programme for preparatory actions for the integration of third-country nationals allocated € 5,000,000 in 2005 for promoting dialogue, developing models, evaluating best practices and fostering cross-national networks. Member states can also draw on the European Fund for the Integration of Third-Country Nationals and the European Refugee Fund (EFI) allocating € 825 million for 2007–2013; the ERF supports the beneficiaries of subsidiary protection whose stay in the EU 'is of a lasting and stable nature'.

The Commission's Framework Programme on Solidarity and Management of Migration Flows (2007–2013) explores nationally diverse concepts of participation and citizenship affecting integration; the 'added value' of common European modules (such as orientation courses) promoting local migrant engagement; media influences on public awareness; processes

Box 11.2 Common basic principles for immigrant integration policy (2005)

1. 'Integration is a dynamic, two-way process of mutual accommodation by all immigrants and residents of Member states.'
2. 'Integration implies respect for the basic values of the European Union.'
3. 'Employment is a key part of the integration process and is central to the participation of immigrants, to the contributions immigrants make to the host society, and to making such contributions visible.'
4. 'Basic knowledge of the host society's language, history, and institutions is indispensable to integration; enabling immigrants to acquire this basic knowledge is essential to successful integration.'
5. 'Efforts in education are critical to preparing immigrants, and particularly their descendants, to be more successful and more active participants in society.'
6. 'Access for immigrants to institutions, as well as to public and private goods and services, on a basis equal to national citizens and in a non-discriminatory way is a critical foundation for better integration.'
7. 'Frequent interaction between immigrants and Member State citizens is a fundamental mechanism for integration. Shared forums, intercultural dialogue, education about immigrants and immigrant cultures, and stimulating living conditions in urban environments enhance the interactions between immigrants and Member State citizens.'
8. 'The practice of diverse cultures and religions is guaranteed under the Charter of Fundamental Rights and must be safeguarded, unless practices conflict with other inviolable European rights or with national law.'
9. 'The participation of immigrants in the democratic process and in the formulation of integration policies and measures, especially at the local level, supports their integration.'
10. 'Mainstreaming integration policies and measures in all relevant policy portfolios and levels of government and public services is an important consideration in public policy formation and implementation.'
11. 'Developing clear goals, indicators and evaluation mechanisms are necessary to adjust policy, evaluate progress on integration and to make the exchange of information more effective.'

Source: Council of the EU (2004: 17–18).

preventing social alienation and discrimination, for example among youth; common indicators and indices for comparative analysis; and ways to redesign the Annual Migration Report to render it a comprehensive monitoring tool. The Commission has adopted an Action Plan for the collection and analysis of migration statistics, commensurate with the launch of its European Migration Network.

The European Council further endorsed a European Pact on Migration and Integration (2008) focusing on tighter border controls and organising the 'selective repatriation' of illegal immigrants, commensurate with a (proposed) Return Directive. The Commission, meanwhile, has joined metropolitan authorities in defining integration as 'a dynamic, two-way process of mutual accommodation'; its ongoing Territorial Dialogue links national authorities and urban areas (URBACT, CLIP, Euro-Cities); local and regional officials evince more competence in implementing integration policies in all member states, though who finances their measures/programmes varies significantly.

Despite persistent security and illegality concerns, the last decade has engendered a positive shift by recognising a need for integration activity on the part of all EU citizens, not only among migrants and their offspring. The trend is towards less confrontational language regarding values and adoption of nuanced, targeted programmes mirroring the special needs of divergent ethnic groups. Finally, immigration has been brought into the holistic framework, acknowledging that social exclusion, poor neighbourhoods, and educational segregation are detrimental for all European residents.

4. Civic citizenship and the Lisbon Treaty

Moves towards hard law, pre-ordained by Article 13 of the Amsterdam Treaty, include the Racial Equality Directive (2000/43/EC) and the Employment Equality Directive (2000/78/EC), extending EU competence in combating discrimination rooted in ethnic origin, religion, disability, age and sexual orientation. The former bans discrimination based on race or ethnic origin in employment, vocational training and non-employment areas like social protection, health care, access to goods/services and public housing. Recognising that women often fall victim to 'multiple discriminations' (Szczepaniková et al. 2006), it construes employment as quintessential to equal opportunity and thus full participation in economic, cultural and social life. Both directives prohibit direct and indirect discrimination and harassment – a primary legal instrument for combating structural inequality.[1] Pledging to 'take into account the different ways in which men and women experience discrimination on grounds of religion', it seeks a 'workable unity in the European approach to the regulation of religion' (Doe

2010: 152). Still, Directive 2000/78/EC permits national laws deemed necessary for guaranteeing security, public order, public health, crime prevention and the freedoms of others. Both directives were to be transposed into national law by 2003, with the exception of age and disability provisions, granted an extra three years.

A further (proposed) directive would extend equal treatment regardless of religion, belief, age or sexual orientation to social protection, health, education, housing, transportation, access/supply of goods and services, 'to complete the EU anti-discrimination legal framework'. Legal consolidation creates linkages to the European Employment Strategy (see Hubert in this volume), economic and social cohesion and cooperation in education (Bologna). Migrants now enjoy specific references under the EU Social Inclusion Strategies and the OMC on Social Protections and Social Inclusions; the Renewed Social Agenda earmarks € 1.2 billion for their labour market participation.

Even more significantly, the Commission is using *civic citizenship* to address the controversial issue of real enfranchisement (Meehan 1993a). Here we observe an evolving synergy between the immigration, employment and social policy domains. Expanding and deepening European social rights means extending the basis of entitlements. Using residence rather than formal citizenship as a prerequisite for social rights would enlarge the scope of social policy coverage for working women and men who lack EU-national status. Commensurate with its social governance, civil participation and accountability objectives (see Stratigaki in this volume), the Commission's desire to make social policy decisions 'participative, visible and accountable' suggests the need to accord non-citizen residents (for example guestworker descendants who speak the language, attended neighbourhood schools and pay taxes) at least the same local voting rights granted to EU nationals (such as subcontracted 'Polish plumbers') after only six months.

Welcoming recent liberalisation of naturalisation criteria among certain member states, the Commission supports more direct forms of political participation among long-term TCNs, many of whom are active in parties, community organisations and interest associations. The Commission Communication on immigration, integration and employment notes:

> On the premise that it is desirable that immigrants become citizens, it is reasonable to relate access to citizenship to the length of time they have been living in the country concerned, and to apply different principles for 1st and 2nd/3rd generation immigrants. For the latter, nationality laws should provide automatic or semi-automatic access whereas it is reasonable to require the first generation to make a formal application for citizenship. Naturalisation should be rapid, secure and non-discretionary. States may require a period of residence, knowledge of the language

and take into account any criminal record. In any case, criteria for naturalisation should be clear, precise and objective. Administrative discretion should be delimited and subject to judicial control. (European Commission 2003a: section 3.3.6)

Moreover, 'it is obvious that local franchise should derive from permanent residence, rather than from nationality'. Half of the member states accord some participatory rights to non-EU nationals; following (legal) residency periods ranging from six months to five years, migrants can vote or pursue candidacies in local/municipal elections in Denmark, Ireland, Netherlands, Sweden and Finland. Others permit elected foreigners' councils whose functions are largely advisory.

The dilemma for migrant women continues to lie with national laws rendering their status dependent on male 'heads of household' whose status is also derived, limited and insecure, especially among asylum applicants. Replacing the rejected Constitution, the 2009 Lisbon Treaty extends the hard-law foundation for EU immigration and citizenship policies; the Treaty allowed the UK to opt out of the (appended) Charter of Fundamental Rights but accorded it 'the same legal value as the Treaties' for the Community as a whole. With the exception of Chapter 5 (citizens' rights), the Treaty's 54 articles and seven chapters apply to all individuals within EU boundaries. Lisbon thus extends EU competence to develop common immigration policy, establish shared conditions of entry and residence, common long-term visa standards and residence (crucial for family unification), conditions governing freedom of movement/residency and incentives for integration in other member states – all by way of qualified majority vote.

Some rights embodied in the civic citizenship construct are universal in nature (human rights); others derive from those conferred earlier on EU nationals: the right to access Commission, Council and Euro-Parliament documents, equal opportunity vis-à-vis the Community civil service, freedom of movement, residency, the right to access and provide services, protection against discrimination on the basis of nationality, et cetera. The Commission can add to existing citizenship rights, subject to unanimous Council adoption, in consultation with the European Parliament (Article 22 TEC). In 2010, Viviane Reding became the first Commissioner for Justice, Fundamental Rights and Citizenship.

5. Conclusion: Gender and migration synergy

The EU has become a mover-and-shaker with regard to citizenship, migration and asylum policies, especially since 9/11. There is little evidence that immigration increases unemployment for native citizens, although many of the dirty, difficult and dangerous jobs for which migrants were recruited have disappeared. National leaders are scrambling to respond to demographic deficits, conflicts over religious diversity, residential segregation and concentrated pools of jobless youth. A common EU framework makes it easier for them to do what should have been done to integrate migrants and their offspring decades ago: supply real educational and employment opportunities for all. Still, defining who can/not enter their territory or acquire citizenship remains one of the last bastions of national sovereignty, explaining many barriers to implementation. The gradual shift from intergovernmental to supranational competencies in this domain suggests that EU equal treatment and anti-discrimination precepts will eventually prevail. Like earlier gender-policy success stories, however, this one will take another decade to reach a happy ending.

This raises the question: How much positive action and gender mainstreaming has been directly incorporated into EU migration policies to date? The short answer, based on the wording of key agreements, is 'not much'. But deeper analysis points to a crucial synergy between gender and ethnic mainstreaming, as highlighted by the Commission:

> Promotion of fundamental rights, non-discrimination and equal opportunities plays a crucial role in the context of integration [...] Efforts to tackle structural barriers faced by immigrants are being reinforced in the context of the '2007 European Year of Equal Opportunities for All' launching a major debate on benefits of diversity. As women are a majority of the immigrant population in the EU-27, addressing their specific needs is increasingly reflected in gender mainstreaming mechanisms such as the Roadmap for Equality between Women and Men 2006–2010. (European Commission 2007a: 6)

Prior to the global financial crisis of 2008/2009, the EU set itself the ambitious goal of reducing by 50 per cent the unemployment gap between citizens and non-nationals. Unable to realise that goal by 2010, national leaders cannot escape the reality of aging populations and looming skilled labour vacancies, giving them a vested interest in securing future workers from outside the EU. They must convince employers of the benefits of workplace diversity (language skills, intercultural competence, transnational networks), albeit without depriving the 'sending' states of the human capital needed to develop their own economies, and without permanently gendering or 'racializing' European labour markets. The EURES Network involves enterprises in non-discriminatory practices, fostering corporate social responsibility. The re-launched Lisbon Strategy (2005) sets concrete benchmarks for educational attainment among youth of migrant descent, as do many of the National Action Plans.

The Commission has repeatedly stressed the need for a holistic approach, obliging member states to tackle not only the economic dimensions of integration but also socio-cultural and religious diversity, local participation, citizenship and political rights. The main actors include government authorities, social partners, the research community, public service providers, NGOs and civil society groups, including ethnic organisations. The EQUAL[2] programme, the Amsterdam Treaty, the Charter on Fundamental Rights and recent Directives (see Box 11.1) are providing new parameters for integration at multiple levels. Drawing attention to poor quality housing in ethnically mixed districts, this holistic approach is leading cities like London, Rome, Berlin and Amsterdam to review unsustainable refugee policies as well as failing educational systems, ethnically insensitive health- and elderly care systems, neighbourhood security policies, public transportation links, urban and regional planning strategies. *Sustainable integration* of third-country nationals does not mean ignoring real problems of undocumented labour, unregulated informal economies or human smuggling. It does, however, require a new emphasis on the enormous *brain gain* potential implicit in communities of migrant descent, especially among women. Restrictions on the employment of 'migrant spouses' contradict other EU strategic objectives, like raising female labour market participation to 75 per cent under the Europe 2020 campaign. As to the broader question of gendering integration, the Commission itself notes:

> [T]he EU should consider how its experience of combating sex discrimination and promoting gender equality may be transferable to other grounds of discrimination. In line with the principle of gender mainstreaming, it should take into account the different ways in which women and men experience discrimination on grounds of racial or ethnic origin, religion or belief, disability, age and sexual orientation [...] it may be appropriate to consider the development of an integrated approach to the promotion of non-discrimination and gender equality (addressing the reality that) people may experience multiple discrimination on several grounds. (European Commission 2005b: 2–3)

EU migration, asylum and citizenship policies to date make it clear that one can only promote supranational integration by maximising access to the national rights necessary for full participation in society. Social cohesion *across* the member states cannot be achieved without the genuine social inclusion of all groups *within* each nation–state. No matter how carefully we craft our social scientific distinctions with respect to various types of citizenship in democratic society, in the real world only one thing matters: either you enjoy all of the rights that citizenship brings, or you don't. Though regularly stymied by dominant economic interests and stubborn national egos, the EU remains a trail-blazer in matters of mainstreaming and social inclusion, even regarding migration and asylum policies. The problem, as always, is turning its more enlightened theories into everyday practice.

Discussion questions

- Given the Community's original emphasis on 'freedom of movement', why have member states been so reluctant to create common immigration policies? What new pressures have led to accelerated developments in this policy field?
- In what ways do the migration experiences of women and men differ? What structural, legal and socio-cultural factors contribute to these differences?
- What 'framing' principles, legal instruments and strategic approaches seem to hold the greatest promise for advancing gender equality in this policy domain? What are the biggest barriers to effective implementation at the member state level?
- What effect(s) will a new emphasis on 'diversity management' have on immigration and integration policies?
- How has the EU helped to redefine the concept of 'citizenship'?

Notes

1. The directive paradoxically leaves it to 'Member States alone to take decisions on questions such as whether to allow selective admission to schools, or prohibit or allow the wearing or display of religious symbols in schools, whether to recognise same-sex marriages, and the nature of any relationship between organised religion and the state' (Commission 2008c: 6) – clearly ensuring unequal treatment of headscarf-wearers in France and Germany.
2. EQUAL stands for the Community Initiative concerning transnational cooperation to promote new means of combating all forms of discrimination and inequalities in connection with the labour market.

12
Conclusion: Rethinking the Double Democratic Deficit of the EU

Joyce Marie Mushaben and Gabriele Abels

Since the late 1970s, widening circles of feminist experts and activists have produced a multitude of studies focusing on extensive gender policy developments within the EU. Despite the Community's reputation as a 'rich men's industrial club', the first wave of European equality activism brought us together, our national, political, class and age differences notwithstanding. Attempts to render European Economic Community (EEC) Treaty provisions both binding and directly effective in the 1970s and 1980s made us realise that we needed 'data', lots of them, to overcome entrenched male assertions that 'there is no problem here, and the problem that there is not is best solved by voluntary agreement' (Dipak Nandy, cited in Vallance and Davies 1986: 112). Conference papers blossomed into 'expert reports' commissioned by the EU itself; at first these were little more than blurred, type-writer manuscripts stapled between flimsy lavender covers that we hauled back in heavy suitcases after research trips to Brussels. Revised reports gave birth to intrepid journal articles and a few books (Vallance and Davies 1986; Springer 1992; Hoskyns 1996). Today there are whole journals and presses specialising in these concerns, voluminous examples of which can be accessed on-line.

The collective of feminist EU researchers constructed, refined and expanded its own investigative paradigms. The second wave of expert reports displayed increasing methodological sophistication; random comparisons were replaced by more systematic treatments of 'women targeted' policies (Duina 1999; Elman 1996; Rossilli 2000). The third wave introduced 'theorising' about gender in the Community context, viewed as completely separate from mainstream qua malestream theorising about integration. As more women found places in the academy, gender terms became so established that they became 'strangely depoliticising', offering only one among many options for theorising EU integration (in fact, gender concerns should not be ghettoised but rather used to contribute continuously to all policy debates). Feminist scholars took less direct aim at mainstream integration theory than did their international relations counterparts: feminist critiques in that field 'were regarded as so disruptive that a defence had to be mounted by Robert

Keohane, among others [...] This involved a paternalist attempt to tell feminists what kind of theorizing was and was not acceptable' (Hoskyns 2004: 234).

Our theorising took on qualitative and quantitative dimensions relative to EU equality pursuits, most clearly reflected in Commission-sponsored projects and final reports. It would take another few years, however, before scholars followed up with independent implementation studies (on gender mainstreaming, for example); enlargement is one area that has seen noteworthy exceptions (Watson 2000; Bretherton 2001; Galligan et al. 2007; Avdeyeva 2010). We hope that this book has taken us one step further, starting with Annica Kronsell's efforts to assess the validity and reach of *all* major EU integration theories through a gender lens.

Returning to Donald Puchala's (1972) metaphor of the EU as an elephant (see Introduction), the problem is that no one researcher can simultaneously cover all parts and track all movements of 27 national 'beasts' stemming from very different habitats, while monitoring the behaviour of the mother-elephant back in Brussels. Nowadays studies with EU gender themes are appearing in rapid succession in many places, in many languages. Contemporary scholars are expanding their investigative reach with collaborative cross-national research teams, engaging in longer-term investigations (Mazur 2009).

In the following pages, we review what we have learned individually and collectively and then offer free but hopefully good advice to students and scholars reading this text. We ultimately conclude with an exhortation to EU gender scholars, present and future, 'to do more work' in areas this text was unable to cover.

1. Writing *her*story: Collective lessons

First of all, we tried to cast a wide net, drawing on experts in nine different countries evincing diverse areas of expertise, hoping they would help us to compile the Big Picture – or at least a bigger one than we could mange on our own. The challenge to our contributors was to make consistent use of a *gender lens* in introducing you to the historical evolution, theoretical parameters, institutional dynamics and concrete EU policy developments across a span of 60 years. Regarding Part II, each author moreover pursued five fixed questions allowing for easy orientation as well as for comparisons between policy fields: (1) How has each policy evolved, and who are the core actors? (2) What conceptual insights have gender studies brought to policy research in this field? (3) What strategic approaches and formal instruments have EU actors employed to promote gender equality? (4) To what extent has gender mainstreaming been implemented since 1996, with what observable policy outputs and outcomes? (5) What major empirical and conceptual issues suggest future policy agendas for gendering EU integration?

While this is a lot to digest for students and academics new to the field, especially when we had no choice but to use 'Euro-speak', all authors have provided you with a sense of the legal foundations, evolutional dynamics, core actors, institutional entanglements, conceptual frameworks, policy instruments, policy outputs and even 'unanticipated consequences' of gendering European policies dating back to the serendipitous adoption of Article 119 EEC Treaty on equal pay in 1957.

Our effort to trace the history of gendering in concrete policy domains illustrates, first, the extent to which gender per se has become *a dominant factor* in some policy domains, and at least a consistent variable in others. Secondly, our policy studies demonstrate the extent to which *different instruments* have proven sometimes more, sometimes less effective across various stages of EU development. Third, contextual factors *have sometimes helped or sometimes hindered* the application of *equal treatment, positive action* and *gender mainstreaming* at different points in time; multi-level governance can serve both purposes. Fourth, we tried to determine the *degree of progress attained thus far*, zooming in on persistent stumbling blocks in each policy arena.

The short answers as to what we have learned fall into five categories (explored further below). (1) The incorporation of gender factors into formal EU policy documents and policy frameworks has become breath-taking in its normality. 'Gender equality' is (almost) everywhere in rhetoric, though the practice often lags behind. (2) Next, we observed that the general trend is to move from *symbolic politics* to *soft law* to *hard law* instruments over periods ranging from one to two decades. (3) We established that specific mechanisms are better received by some member states than by others, but that *new framing* can be used to win over laggards; the trick is to turn gender equality into a win–win proposition for would-be naysayers, for example by adopting the language of 'economic efficiency'. (4) It emerges that certain instruments work better in *particular policy arenas*, and that administrators in select settings make better use of available tool-kits and 'best practices'. (5) The EU is not really practising what it preaches within its own institutions; procedural changes that would automatically incorporate gender experts as social partners to same extent as the 'usual suspects' (employers, labour unions and traditional interest groups) could propel us farther, faster. Still, the biggest barriers to effective implementation have been and remain the dearth of female decision-makers, member state resistance, a lack of political will and the absence of effective supranational sanctions.

The societal changes evoked by the 'supranationalization' of gender equality policies have been observable and dramatic; our ability to witness *herstory* in the making – moving from the 'empty glass' days in 1957, to a glass that is half full in some policy fields, if still only wetting the surface in others – has been a life-transforming experience; this is true not only for us as researchers but also for 'average citizens'. The incorporation of EU equality principles into successive treaties, along with the recognition of gender equality as a legally enforceable, directly effective 'fundamental right', renders us cautiously optimistic that greater changes lie ahead. The push towards a reconciliation of family and career that directly engages men and challenges prevailing norms in the work sphere, for example, augurs the kind of 'completion, deepening and enlargement' of the equality principle we long ago espoused via the mantra, *the personal is the political.*

2. The big picture: Rethinking his- and herstorical institutionalism

As an institutional complex 'starting from scratch' in the 1960s and 1970s, the EEC offered unique mobilisational opportunities for women that fortuitously coincided with a postwar Baby Boom, the dramatic expansion of educational opportunity in most European countries, and a revolution in communications technology. While mainstream democratic theorists abjured fuzzy competences, a lack of transparency, questionable legitimacy and the general *under-institutionalisation* of EU decision-making practices prior to the 1992 Maastricht Treaty, we argue that it was exactly the absence of entrenched incumbents, codified procedures, institutional hierarchies and official data bases that opened the door to women's multi-level mobilisation and participation in EU problem-definition and policy-formulation concerning gender issues. This gives rise to a first institutional paradox: *the democratic deficit as conventionally defined in terms of a lack of 'representative elites' (men + parties + elections) allowed new players onto the field*, giving women their first chance to remedy a 'problem that had no name' (with all due respect to Betty Friedan) prior to the launch of second-wave feminism. A second, more deeply rooted *democratic deficit* soon became known as 'the gender gap' or the 'gender democratic deficit'.

The Commission's desire to overcome the *Euro-malaise* or *Euro-scepticism* of 1970s, coupled with the Court of Justice's (ECJ) expansion of its own powers of judicial review, coincided with consciousness-raising among better-educated female Baby Boomers. Add to this the relative youth of the European Parliament (EP) and its lack of 'real' powers, facilitating women's great leap forward in 1979. Hardly visible under the 1957 system of appointment by the national legislatures, women's presence in the EP rose significantly after the first direct elections, largely because male party leaders could reward female party activists without sacrificing legislative seats equipped with substantially greater powers at home. Even the EP's architecture was new and modern. Familiar with the centuries-old, exclusive men's club atmosphere of the British House of Commons, UK-MEP Joyce Quin noted that it has '[N]o holy of holies where women aren't supposed to go [...] and there's no place to hang your sword!' (quoted in: Vallance and Davies 1986: 10).

The exponential increase in female MEPs, from 5.5 per cent (1978) to 11 per cent (1979) to 35 per cent today (2011), enabled women to engage in *critical acts* – symbolic politics intended to raise consciousness that unexpectedly triggered 'an irreversible take-off into a new situation or process' – before they attained *critical mass* (Dahlerup 1988: 276; Mushaben 1998).[1] By rallying investigative expertise and networking supporters across the member states, women forged informal alliances with the Commission and *femocrats*[2] within its Directorates-General; they operated and lobbied 'at the interstices of procedure', that is, in areas where formal competencies and decision-making rules did not yet exist (Mushaben 1998: 53). This led to the creation of 'velvet triangles' (Woodward 2004).

Observable changes emerging from new, cross-cutting forms of cooperation (and cooptation) included: (1) shifts from negative or diffident reactions to women's presence in decision-making organs to signs that decision-makers welcomed their input; (2) improvements in the performance and efficiency of individual politicians, thanks to 'old girl' networks that short-cut learning processes for new recruits; (3) modifications in the political culture of the institution, accepting women's and gender issues as a routine part of the agenda; (4) a gradual transformation of prevailing political discourses; (5) legislative changes affecting policy substance and approaches to decision-making (QMV); (6) changes in the underlying norms (internal and external); and (7) observable increases in the power of women working collectively, reinforced by professionalised networks. By 2000, women had also reached critical mass in many member state parliaments, lending ever more pressure in the sense of van der Vleuten's (2007) 'pincer effect'.

Besides compelling all member states to eliminate national laws tolerating various forms of sex discrimination, women activists raised public awareness regarding the EP's institutional potential for democratising the EU overall. Despite the frustratingly small number of women occupying top positions in the Commission, the Council and even the ECJ, the Community has come to embody a *feminist concept of power-sharing*, building on a pooling of capacities and resources in ways suggesting a second paradox inherent in the double democratic deficit. Since the 1980s, a *distinctive mode of what feminists label 'power with'* (Deutchman 1993) *has come to replace the more conventional mode of decision-making, 'power over'*, throughout the EU itself; the latter was defined by Max Weber, and later Robert Dahl, as 'A's ability to make B do what B would not necessarily do'.[3] The supranationality practised by the member states entails neither an abdication of national authority nor the outright imposition of decisions from above, but rather a transformation of governance that involves a 'pooling' of sovereignty (Kohler-Koch 1999); it precludes an exercise of power understood as a winner-take-all proposition, having learned that the most efficacious use of power in an age of global interdependence is one employing a *win–win* strategy.

This nonetheless points us towards a third paradox regarding new institutionalisation measures embodied in the 2009 Lisbon Treaty. As 'a representational system still in the making' (Abels 1998: 23), the Community structures and procedures of the 1960s and 1970s reflected the prevailing gender biases of the founding fathers. It became more difficult to justify female underrepresentation in European organs as the result of a simple 'time lag' throughout the 1980s, however, as more women completed university degrees and commenced their 'long march' through the institutions. By the next decade, the European Women's Lobby (EWL)'s push to secure more female appointments to the Delors (1990) and Santer (1995) Commissions, data compiled by the expert network on 'Women and Decision-Making' in 1994, as well as the Council Recommendation (Council of the EU 1996) embracing 'the balanced participation of women and men' should have triggered more 'positive action' inside the European house. By the time national leaders opted to create a Constitution for Europe, gender mainstreaming had become part of the *acquis*, and the Commission had promised to accord women 40 per cent of the committee and expert-group seats. Thus there was *no* excuse for the overwhelmingly male composition of the European Convention charged in 2002 with 'writing' a document whose main purpose was to codify the EU's standing *as a democratic value community* committed to fundamental freedoms, *including gender equality*. The Constitutional Convention was chaired by a president and two vice-presidents, all men; women accounted for only 18 of 105 delegates in 2003, including only 3 (of 15) heads of state/government, and only 3 of 30 national parliamentarians. They comprised 31 per cent (5 of 16) of the MEP convention delegates but only 16 per cent (2 of 12) of the Presidium members (Leon et al. 2003; Millns 2007).

The Lisbon Treaty that supplanted the Constitution, following its rejection by French and Dutch voters in 2005, was the outcome of intense intergovernmental bargaining. The aim of both was to remedy the highly fragmented nature of EU decision-making, to supply it with effective leadership, to reconnect the EU to national parliaments, to increase transparency and democratic accountability. According to Ingeborg Toemmel (2009: 10), 'Efficiency plays the most prominent role; democratic accountability is of minor importance and transparency is not achieved at all'; the result, she holds, is that the new Treaty 'clearly privileges the position of the Councils' – and therefore the member states. As this volume attests, one major stumbling block to gender quality has been foot-dragging and outright resistance on the part of member states! If the Lisbon Treaty shifts 'the power balance between member states, those that actively promote European integration and those that prefer to slow it down or to give it another direction' (Toemmel 2009: 17), then how can we expect the Union to bring about the balanced participation of women and men in decision-making – perhaps the biggest barrier to deliberative implementation of the *gender acquis*?

Still, the protocol appended to the Treaty strengthens the role of the EP and intensifies relations with national parliaments by enhancing their power to control EU policy-making; it also adds new mechanisms for greater citizen input (European Citizens' Initiative, adopted in 2010). This gives rise to a fourth paradox revealed by our investigations: multi-level governance is a messy process, to be sure, *but formalisation and 'streamlining' of EU-internal institutional relations and competencies offers a superficial remedy to the first 'democratic deficit' – at a high cost to the second, gender-democratic deficit.* The greater the degree of *institutionalisation*, that is, the more the EU starts to look like a 'real government', embracing routine procedures, hierarchical information flows, 'organised' interest groups, the 'usual' office-holding requirements, set management/control functions and formal feedback channels, the less likely it becomes that new groups will be able to effect the kind of 'unanticipated' social–cultural revolution witnessed over the last 30 years. The White Paper on European Governance (European Commission 2001a) stresses the need to integrate more stakeholders, yet the lack of transparency potentially accompanying this type of informalisation triggers other problems for the feminist agenda: being 'heard' is not the same as being guaranteed amending or veto powers. Equally problematic, informalisation nowadays could marginalise the role of democratic institutions, just as more women are entering the institutionalised political sphere; in short, the relationship between formalisation, transparency, accountability and 'unanticipated' opportunity structures is fraught with ambivalence. Thus the next generation of equality advocates will face ever more complex negotiations with ever more recognised stakeholders, every step of the way, as seen under the rubric of diversity management (Woodward in this volume). This clearly raises questions for future research.

3. Lessons from the field: Cautious optimism in hard times

Annica Kronsell reveals the extent to which dominant theoretical paradigms have neglected gender power dynamics. Among the mainstream integration theories, all but *liberal intergovernmentalism* display some potential for incorporating equality issues; all could enrich their own paradigms as a result. Feminist scholarship offers fertile ground for conceptualising other emerging 'orders' (for example ethnic or religious minorities) in the integration process, but this requires feminists to engage directly with existing theories and necessitates that 'others' question *their* invisibly gendered assumptions concerning EU norms, processes and institutions. To overcome gender marginalisation, we need theoretical treatments directly challenging the 'institutionalization' of male norms (as in the Lisbon Treaty) that reproduce power asymmetries across the Union rather than deconstructing them. Big Theories to date leave us with a very incomplete picture of how integration really came about, why implementation often falls short, and how consequences for women, men and gender relations differ across member states.

Anna van der Vleuten assesses the functions of key EU institutions and actors, as well as the attention each accords to gender issues; exploring the impact of organised interests on gender policies reveals that 'women in decision-making' really do make a difference. Committed individuals ranging from feminists in DG EMPL's Equal Opportunity Unit, or in the EP, to ECJ judges or Advocates-General, as well as ministers from countries with a strong commitment to equality proved quite adept at playing a multi-level game: mobilising nationally and forging transnational coalitions with supranational actors helps women to generate a crucial 'pincer effect', squeezing their home governments into policy compliance and norms from above and below. Women have consequently secured more equality rights than EU founders ever anticipated.

Describing the EU 'as a progressive champion of gender equality' relative to most national regulatory frameworks, *Birgit Locher* reminds us that this development has neither been linear nor backlash-free. EU norm-development usually outpaces national practice, as affirmed by the collective failure to push for more equality under Eastern enlargement; implementation is much more lax than the impressive *gender acquis* leads us to expect. Still, the complexity of a multi-level system creates new openings for equality agency: multiple access points have, up to now, allowed for new types of policy framing, for the infusion of crucial external expertise and for (unintended) opportunities to push for national implementation.

While many contributors find the glass 'half full', positing that gender mainstreaming should increase women's 'privileged points of access' within the complex European system, *Alison Woodward* sees a troubling tendency among national decision-makers to water down gendered successes, present and future, given a new emphasis on diversity management. Changes in conceptual framing, from *equal treatment* to *positive action* to *gender mainstreaming*, reflect deeper changes in the feminist logic underlying gender advances across the decade. Equality advocates initially believed that the main barrier to women's participation in paid labour rested with formal requirements and bans (for example excluding married, pregnant or 'older' women – like Defrenne – from certain professions, denying them occupational training, barring them from night work, et cetera). As gender-friendly as the ECJ has been, its proclivity to use the male standard in judging what was 'equal' was one factor pushing feminists towards new paradigms. Reflective texts by early feminist intellectuals, crucial exchanges at international meetings and campaigns run by grassroots movements were just as significant in framing – and re-framing – core concepts and strategies. Gender equality activists, one could argue, learned how to 'upload' and 'download' policy ideas long before these terms were associated with the Internet.

Intended to foster democratic development in Europe as well as to increase economic opportunities across Europe, *Yvonne Galligan* and *Sara Clavero* show that enlargement has indeed consolidated Europe's position within the global economy. Gender equality has nonetheless remained a highly contested site throughout successive enlargement waves. While Greece, Spain and Portugal were eager to consolidate newly democratised systems to foster their own economic development, the larger, synchronised incorporation of Central/East European states challenged the institutional and political capacities of the EU itself; in short, it is easier to admit three poor countries than ten all at once! Less than a decade later, a 'relatively monolithic pattern' of transposing the *acquis* 'is rapidly coming undone'. The Polish and Czech cases, especially, see early instrumental harmonisation efforts being replaced by widely divergent responses to gender equality imperatives, largely shaped by local conditions (Sedelmeier 2009). The marginalisation of gender issues during the accession process underscores the idea that the more 'formal powers' are at stake in negotiations, the less open decision-makers are to alternative problem definitions and policy frames.

Taking on one of the oldest, best subsidised EU policy domains, *Elisabeth Prügl* attests to the limits and potential for gendering inherent in (neo)functionalism; Common Agricultural Policy (CAP) proved fiercely resistant to gender equality strategies through the 1990s; the good news is that recent directives are slowly but surely gendering even this male occupational bastion. She demonstrates the ways in which the meaning of 'gender equality' changed, as women took on the agricultural welfare state (defining 'farm work'), rural development and environmental policy regimes. Feminist strategies fared very differently under the agricultural welfare state than under a liberal environmentalism regime. While mainstreaming was invoked as a tool to attack implicit gender assumptions in the CAP's 'institutional' framework, it has been sidelined to date, unable to shake up the patriarchal foundations and structures that comprise the agricultural welfare regime. New social security entitlements, for example, have filled some holes, but not others, regarding the unrecognised status of 'assisting spouses'. Women are nonetheless being actively recruited for self-employment ventures involving agro-tourism, artisanal food production, craft enterprises, telecommunication and caring services, given their 'special sensitivity' to local conditions and needs. Inclusion of rural development policies in the CAP's second pillar has opened up new female empowerment opportunities while reproducing old gendered divisions of labour in novel (low-paid) ways. This treatment thus raises new questions concerning fluctuations in the relationship between 'feminist strategy' and 'structural context'.

Agnès Hubert makes use of her 'front row seat' in Brussels to describe the gendering of employment policy, the first domain to experience proactive intervention by the Commission; her case study offers empirical confirmation of Locher's arguments regarding the all important shift from 'soft' to 'hard law' – and, in part, back again to 'softer' mechanisms involving 'dialogue' and 'best practices' in the midst of a global financial crisis. Female participation in paid labour began as an instrumental concern but soon evolved into a central focus of EU employment policy, albeit as a strategy favouring economic growth. The EU has chipped away at formidable barriers to women's economic autonomy rooted in occupational segregation, neglect of work–life balance issues, and the dearth of women in labour-market management structures, including trade unions. The 1997 European Employment Strategy (EES), reinforcing a new employment title (VII) in the Amsterdam Treaty, stresses quantitative goals, neglecting the qualitative aspects of women's work. The post-2008 financial crisis has seen the transfer of reproductive work back into the private sphere for many, despite the EU 2020 promise to pursue 'smart, sustainable and inclusive growth'.

Likewise a participant–observer in the processes she describes, *Maria Stratigaki* examines the stages by which EU social policy moved beyond original workplace issues into more significant frameworks for 'social inclusion' and 'social protection'. Initially well beyond the reach of Article 119 EEC Treaty, social policy gained firm legal footing in the Amsterdam Treaty. Deemed essential for economic growth and labour market participation, issues usually falling under the remit of national welfare-state provisions, such as dependent care, incorporation of vulnerable groups (single mothers, the disabled) and the modernisation of social protection systems required ever more 'coordination', if not harmonisation. Despite a shift to the open method of coordination (OMC) as a non-binding policy tool (unlike the 'money talks' impact of structural funds and the European Social Fund), equality advocates need to recognise the potential inherent in expanding notions of *social citizenship* and *social governance* and to push for gender-sensitive implementation of the Charter of Fundamental Rights.

Soft law, a treasure trove of ECJ verdicts, the OMC, new anti-discrimination directives and, above all, a new push to create a 'Europe of Knowledge' have no doubt made life a lot easier for equality advocates demanding women's inclusion in the expanding science and technology arenas. *Gabriele Abels* discovers that women are making 'quantum leaps' in these policy domains based on new instruments such as Gender Actions Plan (GAP). This is one case where Central and East European enlargement has strengthened women's mobilisation, given their heavier presence in the natural and engineering sciences prior to the collapse of socialism. Early indicators suggest that gender mainstreaming in these areas may affect the texture of 'science' itself as a male-normed human endeavor.

Looming demographic deficits, coupled with global competition for 'the best brains', render the member states positively disposed towards women's inclusion in science and technology, while another prospective remedy, the pro-active recruitment of foreign workers, re-invokes the image of 'Fortress Europe'. The picture regarding migration and citizenship policy is still hazy, rendering EU commitment to gender equality in this domain more rhetorical (read: 'principled') than real, as *Joyce Marie Mushaben* illustrates. This case shows that 'homeland security' still trumps human rights in the post 9/11 era, undermining equality goals; this author remains hopeful, however, invoking the potential long-term effect of recent anti-discrimination directives, in light of patterns observed across earlier decades. Commensurate with the shift of migration policy from the second (intergovernmental) to the first (supranational) pillar, the Framework Directive (2000/43/EC), applying the equal treatment principle to all Union residents irrespective of racial or ethnic origin, parallels the first Equal Treatment Directive of 1976. Given the standing accorded the Charter of Fundamental Rights under the Lisbon Treaty, efforts to render it 'actionable' by way of the ECJ may take five to ten years, but 'the handwriting is on the wall', projecting the eventual outcome.

Certain lessons stand out when one compares the policy chapters. First, the 'oldest' area of Community responsibility is not the one witnessing the greatest progress in matters of equality, as our treatments of CAP and more recent science/technology policies demonstrate. Secondly, the move from symbolic/creative instruments to soft-law, and finally to hard-law instruments does not amount to a linear progression. Employment is one policy domain that owes its start to a formal treaty provision and a few well-timed, 'directly effective' ECJ verdicts; it nonetheless took countless pilot projects, multi-year Action Programmes, lobbying by expert networks and other activities falling 'outside the legal box' to compel the implementation of directives regarding equal treatment in employment and rudimentary social policy issues. Thirdly, in some areas concrete policy changes across the member states (Sweden, Denmark, Finland) far outpaced changes in the discursive framing and EU norm-development, while others rely heavily on the invocation of supranational value-constructs (*EU citizenship, social governance, fundamental rights* in social policy and migration fields) to set the parameters for legislating change.

With respect to 'core actors' shaping the gendering of EU policies, there is no clear, one-size-fits-all template. Efforts to turn Article 119 EEC Treaty into binding law began with women mobilising outside the EEC's institutional walls, for example those employed in the Belgian Herstal defence industry, Defrenne and her lawyer Vogel-Polsky. The ECJ unintentionally became a driving force in employment policy, given palpable resistance on the part of member states. The Commission then took up the charge, actively searching out allies, subsidising the creation and consolidation of women's networks, including the EWL. The door opened further, to include social partners (still male-dominated unions, employers' associations). The recent shift to OMC re-inserts the member states as core actors, albeit tethered by way of annual reporting requirements, quantitative indicators and concrete benchmarks. Riding piggy-back on employment developments, social policy could draw on the ever stronger alliance between the Commission, the EWL, women's transnational and expert networks, with occasional boosts from the Court of Justice and targeted use of the ESF.

The predominance of national ministers with strong ties to their respective farmers' organisations did not allow the Commission as much room for manoeuvre in the CAP; despite the engagement of the Committee of Agricultural Organisations (COPA) Woman's Committee and the European Parliament (prior to co-decision), national leaders failed to recognise, much less calculate the economic contributions of 'the farmer's wife' at the most basic levels. The equal treatment strategy made little headway, and mainstreaming has already been sidelined. The ECJ only adjudicated 'social dimensions' at the margins, being called upon for the most part to resolve 'single-market' questions in this domain. Decades later, the search for alternative forms of 'sustainable' economic activity (to supplement farm income) enlarges the space for women, without allocating a key role to women's own interest representatives and networks.

As a relatively new domain, research and technology could again rely heavily on the Commission, equality-oriented DGs and transnationalised, professional women's networks. The statistical databases generated by networks of professionals (established by the Commission) have proven to be powerful tools, in view of the call for a 'European innovation community' and the 2000 Lisbon Agenda on European competitiveness. Yet the role of the Commission is restricted. Now it is basically up to the member states to implement the necessary measures, which are all on the table, to improve the situation of 'women in science'. Here the OMC is potentially a powerful tool for change.

Because the final domain, migration and asylum policy, strikes at the very heart of national sovereignty concerns – security, citizenship and occupation of national territory – the European Council, along with national interior, justice and home affairs ministers quickly moved to centre stage but allowed the Commission to advance significant value premises as a foundation for what remains 'intergovernmental' action. This area has seen little direct involvement on the part of unions and employers' associations (despite imminent skilled labour shortages), and no active participation with regard to women's networks.

The effectiveness of specific instruments has also varied, not only from one domain to another but also across divergent points in time. The field of employment clearly served as an incubator for a panoply of symbolic, creative and soft-law mechanisms subsequently extended to other arenas. Given the centrality of employment in the Single Market, it is not surprising that the cumulative impact of Action Programmes, Roadmaps, directives, recommendations, ECJ verdicts and extensive subsidies would be a broadening and deepening of 'hard law' in the form of major Treaty revisions, occurring in very quick succession since 1991. Each policy domain has nonetheless contributed new framing concepts (multi-functionality, balanced participation of women and men, social inclusion, work-life reconciliation, leaky pipelines, civic citizenship, social governance, common principles) along the way. New constructs, in turn, have led to the embrace of new mechanisms, ranging from a panoply of women-targeted programmes (DAPHNE, European Platform of Women Scientists, Gender Watch System) to the Lisbon Strategy, the Social Dialogue, the Bologna Process and the OMC – many of which are now being extended to not-yet-gendered policy fields.

If we had to choose favourites, we would cite the directives and ECJ verdicts as the most effective tools to date. Time and again, directives – binding as to the goals but open with regard to the means – have unleashed creative, programmatic energies, while also supplying critical leverage for willing lawmakers in the member states to overcome resistance at home. Council directives, for example, gave Germany's Social Affairs Minister Ursula von der Leyen the leverage she needed to force her conservative compatriots to extend paid parental leave to men and to guarantee sufficient care facilities for 90 per cent of 3- to 6-year-olds and 33 per cent of toddlers under 3 (von Wahl 2011). The ECJ even required that country to change its constitution (Article 12a of the *Grundgesetz*), having ruled that barring women from *Bundeswehr* military units utilising weapons amounted to employment discrimination, plain and simple. By contrast, directives in the agricultural domain have been few and far between; the European Agricultural Fund for Rural Development, the LEADER programme and Local Action Groups are beginning to make inroads, but the results are not evenly distributed across the member states.

Not that we underestimate the paradigm-shifting potential of gender impact assessments (GIA) required for all mainstreaming processes. The problem is that very little gender mainstreaming has been taking place, despite the proliferation of training programmes, 'toolkits' and handbooks replete with best practices intended to spread this process throughout the system of multi-level governance. While actors in the employment and social domains are supposed to apply the mainstreaming of equality as a 'horizontal' task extending to all policy actions geared toward common objectives, the results relative to the EES and the Social OMC have been quite disappointing – even declining (Behning and Serrano Pascual 2001; Corsi and Lodovici 2009; Villa and Smith 2010). Mainstreaming practices have barely penetrated the agricultural and migration spheres to date. The one area offering evidence of some progress is the research, science and technology field. Yet in this field the GAPs – a potentially powerful tool – are no longer mandatory, only voluntary for EU 'soft money' applicants.

Several of the major conceptual challenges highlighted by our authors clearly transcend policy boundaries; the need *to modernise social protection regimes* in response to shifting demographics will require ever more coordination among the educational, employment, migration, social policy, and science/technology domains. Reconceptualising the proper relationship between residency rights, social citizenship and political enfranchisement will pit member states against the Commission, the EP, the ECJ and municipal authorities (Euro-Cities) in heretofore unexplored ways. Last but certainly not least, finding effective ways to 'measure' the gendered nature and value of *time* holds significant implications for the future of employment (care-work), social policy (active aging), migration (civic citizenship) and the balanced participation of the sexes in political and economic decision-making.

The vignettes opening each policy chapter attest to the very real ways in which EU equality policies have, sooner or later, improved the everyday lives of women – and men – in virtually every member state. The democratic accountability problem here is that the EU often gets very little credit for such achievements. The fact that policies are ultimately implemented at the member state level leads average citizens who benefit most to see them as progressive changes undertaken by their own governments, rather than as the result of hard work on the part of countless transnational actors and multi-level pincer effects. This helps to explain women's diffidence and even scepticism (Liebert 1999) regarding the EU in a broader sense. Having served in Brussels for several years, two of our contributors have a special understanding of the wheeling and dealing that has often delayed, watered down or completely pulled the brakes on holistic policies. However, even the worst laggard states (Zeff and Pirro 2006) have been impelled over time to generate databases, file national reports, bow to court referrals and, ultimately, to cross that gender-equality bridge to the twenty-first century.

4. Where do we go from here?

Long viewed as the 'locomotive' for equal treatment, EU employment policies may be heading for new setbacks (Smith and Villa 2010), underlining the significance of the 'dual strategy' specified by gender mainstreaming requirements. Dating back to 1996, officials at all levels have spent years trying to figure out what gender mainstreaming means; it is no coincidence that the English term is used in several EU states, unable (or unwilling) as they are to find their own linguistic equivalent. National leaders are all too quick to ignore the dual-strategy obligation, hoping to use 'diversity management' to do away with women-targeted programmes. Noticing a significant increase in women's presence in lots of important political institutions, some attempt to argue (without reviewing the hard data) that 'we are all equal now'. The dramatic increase in rights for women is sometimes interpreted as a loss or as 'too much competition' for men, especially in times of mass unemployment. Each major step forward inevitably produces a measure of backlash on the part of governments, employers and persons most privileged by the status quo. Hence the logic of two steps forward, one step back: it pays to remind ourselves that women are still significantly better off today as the direct result of EU gender policies than they were in 1957, or even in 1979.

Divisions among feminist scholars, politicians and activists as to whether the glass is half-full or half-empty owe to at least three factors: (1) disparate units and levels of analysis employed by researchers; (2) the 'Puchala effect'; and (3) generational differences among the scholars involved. The first problem is one shared across the entire field of comparative politics. The second owes to the size, complexity and dynamic 'nature of the beast'. Since no scholar is able to study the entire EU at one time, our focus on individual policy domains leads us to different optimistic, pessimistic or 'missing in action' conclusions. Gender pessimism regarding 50+ years of CAP was certainly justifiable until new economic pressures unrelated to equality campaigns unexpectedly opened new doors for women under the rubric of rural development. Investigating women's ability to break through another glass ceiling, both as researchers and as the long overdue 'subjects' of scientific investigation, sooner leads to optimism. The main difference between these two cases is that the latter found a critical mass of women already 'on the ground and ready for battle' – armed with networks, data and personal academic experiences – at a time when the EU decided to launch a dramatic campaign in the science and technology fields. It is still too early to tell whether the Lisbon Treaty will help or hinder progress towards gender equality, due to the institutionalisation paradox already noted. At first glance, it represents another 'great leap forward' insofar as its new equality references will become actionable before the ECJ as 'hard law'.

As to the third factor, younger women today enjoy a better starting position and, moreover, expect instant gratification; the combination of these two elements will undoubtedly give policy implementation a boost as they move into positions of influence. But we caution our younger readers not to reject earlier speed limits and strategies as old-fashioned; we urge them to revisit the personal and political synergies that gave rise to extremely effective networks and coalitions to create the policy foundations they now take for granted (for a quick overview, see Box 12.1). To succeed within the framework of multi-level governance, one needs to cultivate allies at all levels, as well as to find the kind of 'framing' that will draw in what, at first glance, looks like 'the opposition'. Rather than fighting over whether the elephant consists of tails or ears, we call for a willingness to move a few steps to the 'right' or 'left' – or even to hold hands with potential adversaries on occasion, to get the full measure of a policy problem.

There are undoubtedly many feminist scholars who do not share our optimism. They worry that the glass, only half-full, is perhaps in danger of being emptied, either because the EU is not moving fast enough (Elman 2007), or because 'diversity management' sidelines gender in favour of other equality gaps – like ethnicity, ageism, sexual orientation or 'disabilities' (Kantola 2010a). We believe that the fundamental overhaul of historically male-normed, market-driven governmental institutions and policies triggered by

Box 12.1   A subversive feminist guide to achieving gender equality

Stage One: Consciousness-raising

- Form an *ad hoc* committee with 'a few good women' or committed persons at lower levels of decision-making, even if they appear relatively powerless. Begin collecting preliminary data regarding a fairly self-explanatory variable like equal pay, no matter how hard it may be to find them. When the data show that things are worse than you thought, urge your home government to begin disaggregating its own official statistics according to sex. Do not expect it to jump at your request.
- Publicise the gaps through an official agency or public organisation. Emphasise the need for 'more data'. Look for contradictions in the institution's own goals. Read its statutory documents very carefully and ask if they apply to you. Take immediate or spontaneous advantage of 'unanticipated consequences' or changes in the political opportunity structure. Do not consider any prospect for change 'too small'. Do not be afraid to cultivate allies in strange places, even if others' motives do not always overlap with your own.

Stage Two: Building a policy community

- Stimulate a 'public outcry' to discriminatory findings among groups tied directly to the issue or data at hand. Use this (small but loud) response to pressure an appropriate agency into funding an 'initiative' or 'pilot project'. Find a few Big (preferably corporate) Players willing to experiment at someone else's expense. Praise them publicly.
- Form a division or office within an existing agency to 'monitor' and, later, to implement the initiatives; put them in charge of 'analysing' the results. Arrange for a regular flow of subsidies, no matter how limited, to institute longer term pilot projects or 'action plans'. Bring in stakeholders by stressing words like 'efficiency' and 'productivity'. Gather more data, and initiate annual reporting requirements for participants. Emphasise the positive in publicising results.
- Utilise your expanding database to hire 'experts'. Insist on using your own terminology where possible, but use Euro-speak with modifiers whenever necessary to keep disinterested (or potentially adversarial) parties engaged in a 'dialogue'. Cultivate some degree of *gender expertise* in every agency connected to your issue. Routinise

Box 12.1 (Continued)

contacts and information-exchanges among experts, allowing them to develop a supportive 'culture within a culture'. Encourage experts to form their coalitions, building networks with external organs of their own choosing.

Stage Three: Professionalisation and internationalisation

- Develop recognisable spokespersons and cultivate select media relationships. Expand external networks through links with professional associations (and cite each other regularly as experts!). Urge networks to establish cross-sectional and inter-institutional ties. Commission studies that promote regional and international comparisons; use these studies to establish more cross-national and grassroots networks. Never assume one is more important than the other.
- Hold international conferences and 'summit meetings' as functions officially subsidised by the home institution. Require member states to send official delegations and country reports; if they don't have a gender expert, they will have to appoint one to write a report.
- Have your 'language' gradually recognised as official parlance. Develop new indicators for use in presumably 'gender-neutral' domains; make sure they have some connection to longer term goals of the established powers. Help isolated 'gender experts' to use the 'official parlance' to introduce new strategic frameworks within their own agencies. Come together as a unified group (despite your differences) to lobby higher authorities: the more organisational units promote your cause, the better, even if it does lead to problems of coordination and control.

Stage Four: Institutionalisation, 'norming' and mainstreaming

- Persuade external contacts and networks to utilise *your* experts, offices and data as the point of 'first contact' with the main institution. Foster increasing specialisation among recognised gender scholars; apply for grants, produce 'counter-expertise' and invent ways to incorporate it into all 'official findings', as a 'critical response'.
- Draw up legislative proposals based on cross-cutting rationales, and have your experts appointed to organs overseeing 'equality policies'. Overwhelm recalcitrant officials with longitudinal data, especially when they argue 'there is no problem here'. Present your own positions as 'the majority view'.

- Seize the right to participate during the 'problem definition' and 'policy-formulation' stages. Conduct symbolic hearings on policies (or against officials) detrimental to your cause. Lobby to have your self-assumed powers incorporated into core legal documents (first as protocols, then as Treaty provisions).
- Push to have subsequent treaties expand your influence, not only in procedural–operational terms, but also by inserting new 'values' and 'objectives' into constitutional documents as a launching pad for future pilot projects, legal actions, compliance monitoring and the like. Add a requirement for yearly national progress reports.
- Develop a corps of cross-national legal experts and lawyers. Introduce courses on your expanding body of jurisprudence at all member state universities, presenting it as a 'growth industry'. Keep your eyes open for precedent-setting cases at lower levels.
- Think about ways to 'consolidate' the array of experts you now have spread throughout the institution, before someone unfriendly to your cause does it in the name of budget cuts. Engage in 'self-study' and propose reforms, using a 'pincer' effect. Get it in writing that new programmes will not be eliminated at the expense of tried and true ones.
- Act as if your once 'radical agenda' has become 'the routine'. Have officials sign on to your innocuous-sounding language, like *gender mainstreaming*, even if most have not yet figured out what that means. Initiate more 'Stage One' activities at the highest level of decision-making, even if it temporarily alienates ostensible 'allies' intent on using your networks to achieve their own institutional goals. Do not forget to use 'symbolic politics', to prove to your grassroots constituencies that you have not been co-opted by 'the system'.
- Appoint more experts, develop more indicators, publish your data in multiple languages, and recruit hordes of sympathetic academics to write scholarly articles on your progress. Convince them that 'institutions matter', and that institutions sometimes transform themselves in ways they never anticipated, opening the door to societal transformation. Encourage them to 'mainstream' their own research in 'non-feminist' journals.
- Repeat often that 'it is a new millennium', and wait for *generational change* to kick in.

feminist mobilisation, massive data-collection and theoretically grounded GIAs is about as radical as you can get! New emphasis on the reconciliation of family and career, for example, means 'going back to the roots' of discrimination, namely challenging the unequal division of household labour, the separation of the personal and the political, and the centuries of homage to 'natural law' qua essentialism.

The next ten years will hopefully witness a dramatic improvement in the one thing that has most thwarted women's progress since the Community's founding: namely the Commission's and the Council's failure to practise what they preach regarding the balanced participation of women and men in their own decision-making circles. Better educated than ever before, and likely to benefit from a future need for skilled labourers, women are moving 'through the pipeline' at an impressive pace. Although they still face a 'longer march through the institutions' in some policy arenas, their increased presence should ameliorate the foot-dragging failure of their respective member states to implement gender mainstreaming across every field of EU endeavour. It is more than a question of 'getting the incentives right' (Hafner-Burton and Pollack 2009). The problem, first and foremost, is one of political will; but the latter will soon emerge out of looming demographic deficits on the European horizon. Demographic change has indeed become a driving force for the changes we are witnessing with regard to women's and gender policies in a number of fields.[4]

Returning to our primordial concern – the connection between gender equality and meaningful democratic participation – we conclude that remedies proposed in response to a *democratic deficit* defined in narrow, institutional terms will not only fall short of redressing the current gender gap but might even shrink the political and economic opportunity structure for other inadequately represented EU-citizen groups (for example ethnic minorities, the elderly) in the future.

The second lesson that needs to permeate the EU institutions is that ensuring equal *gender power*, that is, the balanced participation of the sexes, cannot be understood merely as the ability to vote up or down in proportionate numbers on a given issue. Substantive equality infers the ability to *define the policy problem* from one's own experiential perspective, the *chance to establish relevant, experiential criteria* for monitoring member state activities, as well as the *power to choose the actual indicators* measuring implementation and outcomes. Finally, equality entails the recognition that women have taken on and successfully mastered the need for fundamental changes in their own role identities, qualifications, support structures and policy logics, and that it is high time for *men* to undertake equally fundamental changes along these axes.

We foresee a three fold task for scholars, feminists and others we would exhort to 'do more work' over the next decade. First, we need to see more deliberate integration of gender theorisation on the part of so-called 'mainstream' integration theorists (neo-functional, multi-level governance, new institutionalism, neo-Marxist theory and so on), as well as more feminist engagement with gender-theory sceptics. Second, we welcome a wider assortment of empirical studies comparing the evolution of gender policies in heretofore neglected EU policy domains, including (but not limited to) transportation, energy, environmental sustainability, development assistance, regionalisation, foreign/security policy and EU finance/taxation policies. Finally, we urge more cross-national, collaborative teams of scholars to undertake long-term implementation studies across multiple member states in a given policy domain.

As a process now extending over 50 years, gendering the EU has consistently confirmed the wisdom of trail-blazing anthropologist Margaret Mead: 'Never doubt the ability of a small group of committed, thoughtful people to change the world. Indeed, it's the only thing that ever has.' This book is a testimony to women like Simone Veil, Éliane Vogel-Polsky, Gabriella Defrenne, Hanna Maij-Weggen and all the rest who were thoughtful and committed enough to set a number of key paradigm-shifting changes in motion in their pursuit of a better life for the women of Europe. We likewise concur with former Commission President Jacques Santer, who noted on the occasion of International Women's Day, 8 March 1995:

> We like to remind everyone of the essential role as a driving force that the Commission has played with regard to equality, and the considerable legislative work which has laid the legal groundwork for important changes in attitudes, in the practices on the labour market and in the development of women's individual rights. But if it can be said that Europe has done much for women, it can also be said that women have done much for Europe.

Notes

1. Borrowed from nuclear physics, *critical mass* involves the smallest number of atoms one needs to 'split' by way of external force to generate sufficient energy to induce a self-sustaining chain-reaction (a small explosion, to detonate a much larger atomic bomb). Unlike non-rational atomic particles, committed, thoughtful women can strategise, undertake symbolic actions and seek out powerful coalition partners to trigger fundamental changes in their surroundings long before they accrue seats numerically proportionate to their share of the population.
2. Femocrats are civil servants or bureaucrats who pursue a feminist agenda by working in administrative bodies.
3. Consider, for example, the elimination of a member state's veto-right (initially imposed by French president De Gaulle under the 1966 Luxembourg Compromise), followed by the introduction of QMV; and the more recent OMC.
4. See, for example, the report of the EU Reflection Group (2010), whose mandate was to think about the future of the EU 10 to 20 years from now. The 'women's question' regularly appears in the final report relative to changing demographics and their effects on social systems and employment.

Bibliography

Abels, G. (1998), 'Engendering the Representational Democratic Deficit in the European Union', WZB Discussion Paper FS 98–106, Berlin.

Abels, G. (2001), 'Das "Geschlechterdemokratiedefizit" der EU. Politische Repräsentation und Geschlecht im europäischen Mehrebenensystem', in E. Kreisky, S. Lang and B. Sauer (eds), *EU. Geschlecht. Staat*, Wien: WUV Universitätsverlag, pp. 185–202.

Abels, G. (2003), 'The European Research Area and the Social Contextualisation of Technological Innovations: The Case of Biotechnology', in J. Edler, S. Kuhlmann and M. Behrens (eds), *Changing Governance of Research and Technology Policy: The European Research Area*, Cheltenham, Northhampton: Edward Elgar, pp. 311–332.

Abels, G. (2011a), 'Gender Equality Policy', in H. Heinelt and M. Knodt (eds), *Policies within the EU Multi-Level System. Instruments and Strategies of European Governance*, Baden-Baden: Nomos, pp. 325–348.

Abels, G. (2011b), 'Feministische Perspektiven', in H.-J. Bieling and M. Lerch (eds), *Theorien der europäischen Integration*, 3rd edition, Wiesbaden: VS Verlag für Sozialwissenschaften.

Abels, G. and E. Bongert (1998), 'Quo vadis, Europa? Einleitung, Stand und Perspektiven feministischer Europaforschung', *Femina Politica*, 7: 2, 9–19.

Advisory Committee on Equal Opportunities for Women and Men (n.d.), 'Proposal from the Working Group on the Revision of Directive 86/613/EEC on the Application of the Principle of Equal Treatment between Men and Women Engaged in an Activity, Including Agriculture, in a Self-employed Capacity, and on the Protection of Self-employed Women during Pregnancy and Motherhood', Online: http://www.zdruzenje-manager.si/storage/3373/Bruselj,%20direktiva..doc (accessed 23 January 2009).

Agriculture in the European Union – Statistical and Economic Information (2007), Europa website, Online: http://ec.europa.eu/agriculture/agrista/2007/table_en/35151.pdf (accessed 3 June 2008).

Ahrens, P. (2008), 'More Actors Butter No Parsnips: Gaining Insights into Gender Equality Programs of the European Union', Paper presented at the ECPR Pan European Conference on EU Politics, Riga, Latvia, 25–27 September.

Alvesson, M. and Y. Due Billing (1997), *Understanding Gender and Organization*, London: Sage.

Anderson, L. S. (2006), 'European Union Gender Regulations in the East: The Czech and Polish Accession Process', *East European Politics and Societies*, 20: 1, 101–125.

Anthias, F. and G. Lazaridis (eds) (2000), *Gender and Migration in Southern Europe*, Oxford: Berg.

Archer, C. (2005), *Norway outside the European Union: Norway and European Integration from 1994 to 2004*, London: Routledge.

Askola, H. (2007), 'Violence against Women, Trafficking, and Migration in the European Union', *European Law Journal*, 13: 2, 204–217.

Aspinwall, M. and G. Schneider (2000), 'Same Menu, Separate Tables: The Institutionalist Turn in Political Science and the Study of European Integration', *European Journal of Political Research*, 38: 1, 1–36.

Avdeyeva, O. (2010), 'States' Compliance with International Requirements: Gender Equality in EU Enlargement Countries', *Political Research Quarterly*, 63: 1, 203–217.
Bache, I. (2007), *Europeanization and Multilevel Governance: Cohesion Policy in the European Union and Britain*, London: Rowman & Littlefield Publishers.
Bache, I. and M. Flinders (eds) (2004), *Multi-Level Governance*, Oxford: Oxford University Press.
Bagilhole, B. (2009), *Understanding Equal Opportunities and Diversity: The Social Differentiations and Intersections of Inequality*, Bristol: Policy Press.
Bailey, D. (2008), 'Explaining the Underdevelopment of "Social Europe": A Critical Realisation', *Journal of European Social Policy*, 18: 3, 232–245.
Bandarra Jazra, N. (2002), 'Intégration de l'égalité des chances dans les Programmes de Développement Rural (2000–06)', *Revue du Marché commun et de l'Union europeenne*, 462, 615.
Barbier, C., C. de la Porte, C. D. Ghailani and P. Pochet (2000), 'European Briefing', *Journal of European Social Policy*, 10: 3, 173–188.
Beasley, C. (1999), *What is Feminism? An Introduction to Feminist Theory*, London: Sage.
Becker, G. (1993), *A Treatise on the Family*, Enlarged edition, Cambridge, MA: Harvard University Press.
Behning, U. and A. Serrano Pascual (eds) (2001), *Gender Mainstreaming in the European Employment Strategy*, Brussels: ETUI.
Bergamaschi, M. (2000), 'The Gender Perspective in the Policies of European Trade Unions', in M. Rossili (ed.), *Gender Policies in the European Union*, New York: Peter Lang Publishers, pp. 159–174.
Berghahn, S. (1998), 'Zwischen marktvermittelter Geschlechtergleichheit im europäischen "Herrenclub" und den patriarchalischen Traditionalismen von Mitgliedstaaten: Gibt es einen "Mehrwert" der europäischen Gleichheitsentwicklung für Frauen?', *Femina Politica*, 7: 2, 46–55.
Berghahn, S. (2002), 'Supranationaler Reformimpuls versus mitgliedstaatliche Beharrlichkeit. Europäische Rechtsentwicklung und Gleichstellung', *Aus Politik und Zeitgeschichte*, B 33–34/2002, 29–37.
Bergqvist, C. (2004), 'Gender (In)Equality, European Integration and the Transition of Swedish Corporatism', *Economic and Industrial Democracy*, 25: 1, 125–146.
Beveridge, F. (2008), 'Implementing Gender Equality and Mainstreaming in an Enlarged European Union: Prospects and Challenges', in F. Beveridge and S. Velluti (eds), *Gender and the Open Method of Coordination. Perspectives on Law, Governance and Equality in the EU*, Aldershot: Ashgate, pp. 11–34.
Beveridge, F. and S. Velluti (eds) (2008a), *Gender and the Open Method of Coordination. Perspectives on Law, Governance and Equality in the EU*, Aldershot: Ashgate.
Beveridge, F. and S. Velluti (2008b), 'Introduction – Gender and the OMC', in F. Beveridge and S. Velluti (eds), *Gender and the Open Method of Coordination. Perspectives on Law, Governance and Equality in the EU*, Aldershot: Ashgate, pp. 1–10.
Beveridge, F. and S. Velluti (2008c), 'Gender and the OMC: Conclusions and Prospects', in F. Beveridge and S. Velluti (eds), *Gender and the Open Method of Coordination. Perspectives on Law, Governance and Equality in the EU*, Aldershot: Ashgate, pp. 191–208.
Bird, E. (1996), 'Women's Studies in European Higher Education: Sigma and Coimbra', *European Journal of Women's Studies*, 3: 2, 151–166.
Bisio, L. and A. Cataldi (2008), *The Treaty of Lisbon from a Gender Perspective: Changes and Challenges*, Brussels: WIDE.

Bock, B. (2001), 'The Problems, Prospects and Promises of Female Employment in Rural Areas', Paper presented at the conference 'The New Challenge of Women's Role in Rural Europe', Nikosia, Cyprus, 4–6 October.

Bogason, P. and J. Musso (2006), 'The Democratic Prospects of Network Governance', *American Review of Public Administration*, 36: 1, 3–18.

Booth, C. and C. Bennett (2002), 'Gender Mainstreaming in the European Union. Towards a New Conception and Practice of Equal Opportunities', *The European Journal of Women's Studies*, 9: 4, 430–446.

Börzel, T. A. (2003), 'Guarding the Treaty: The Compliance Strategies of the European Commission', in T. A. Börzel and R. A. Cichowski (eds), *The State of the European Union, Volume 6: Law, Politics and Society*, Oxford: Oxford University Press, pp. 197–220.

Börzel, T. A. and T. Risse (2008), 'Revisiting the Nature of the Beast – Politicization, European Identity, and Postfunctionalism: A Comment on Hooghe and Marks', *British Journal of Political Science*, 39, 217–220.

Braams, B. (2007), 'Equal Opportunities between Men and Women and Gender Mainstreaming under the European Employment Strategy (EES) and the Open Method of Coordination (OMC) – A New Policy Approach to Combat Gender Discrimination?', *European Integration Online Papers*, 11: 6, Online: http://eiop.or.at/eiop/texte/2007-006a.htm (accessed 21 March 2011).

Bradley Dunbar Associates Ltd (2003), 'Study on Networks of Women Scientists. Recommendations Report', Online: http://ec.europa.eu/research/science-society/pdf/reco_report_250703.pdf (accessed 3 January 2009).

Braithwaite, M. (1994), 'The Economic Role and Situation of Women in Rural Areas', *Green Europe 1/94*, Luxembourg: Office for Official Publications of the European Communities.

Braithwaite, M. (2000), 'Mainstreaming Gender in the European Structural Funds', Paper presented at the Mainstreaming Gender in European Public Policy Workshop, University of Wisconsin-Madison, 14–15 October.

Braithwaite, M. and C. Byrne (1994), *Women in Decision Making in Trade Unions*, Brussels: European Trade Union Confederation.

Bretherton, C. (2001), 'Gender Mainstreaming and EU Enlargement: Swimming against the Tide?', *Journal of European Public Policy*, 8: 1, 60–81.

Bretherton, C. (2002), 'Gender Mainstreaming and Enlargement: The EU as Negligent Actor?', National Europe Centre Paper No. 24, Online: http://dspace.anu.edu.au/bitstream/1885/41760/2/bretherton.pdf (accessed 18 March 2011).

Bretherton, C. and L. Sperling (1996), 'Women's Network and the European Union: Towards an Inclusive Approach?', *Journal of Common Market Studies*, 34: 4, 487–508.

Büchs, M. (2007), *New Governance in European Social Policy. The Open Method of Coordination*, Basingstoke: Palgrave Macmillan.

Butler, J. (1990), *Gender Trouble*, New York: Routledge.

Cameron, B. and L. Gonas (1999), 'Women's Response to Economic and Political Integration in Canada and Sweden', in L. Briskin and M. Eliason (eds), *Women's Organizing and Public Policy in Canada and Sweden*, Montreal; Kingston: McGill-Queen's University Press, pp. 51–86.

Caporaso, J. and J. Jupille (2001), 'The Europeanization of Gender Equality Policy and Domestic Structural Change', in M. Green Cowles, J. Caporaso and T. Risse (eds), *Transforming Europe: Europeanization and Domestic Change*, Ithaca: Cornell University Press, pp. 21–43.

Cavaghan, R. (2010), 'Gender Mainstreaming as Translation. The Case of EU Science and Research Policy', Paper presented at the 5th Interpretive Policy Analysis Conference in Grenoble, 23–25 June.
Chamberlayne, P. (1993), 'Women and the State: Changes in Roles and Rights in France, West Germany, Italy and Britain, 1970–1990', in J. Lewis (ed.), *Women and Social Policy in Europe: Work, Family and the State*, Cheltenham: Edward Elgar, pp. 170–193.
Checkel, J. T. (1999), 'Social Construction and Integration', *Journal of European Public Policy*, 6: 4, 545–560.
Checkel, J. T. and J. P. Katzenstein (eds) (2009), *European Identity*, Cambridge: Cambridge University Press.
Christiansen, T. (1997), 'Tensions of European Governance: Politicized Bureaucracy and Multiple Accountability in the European Commission', *Journal of European Public Policy*, 4: 1, 73–90.
Christiansen, T., K. E. Jørgensen and A. Wiener (1999), 'The Social Construction of Europe', *Journal of European Public Policy*, 6: 4, 528–544.
Church, C. H. and D. Phinnemore (2010), 'Understanding the Treaty of Lisbon', *Romanian Journal of European Affairs*, 10: 2, Online: http://papers.ssrn.com/sol3/papers.cfm?abstract_id=1629143 (accessed 18 March 2011).
Cichowski, R. A. (2001), 'Judicial Rulemaking and the Institutionalization of European Union Sex Equality Policy', in A. Stone Sweet, W. Sandholtz and N. Fligstein (eds), *The Institutionalization of Europe*, Oxford: Oxford University Press, pp. 113–136.
Cichowski, R. A. (2004), 'Women's Rights, the European Court, and Supranational Constitutionalism', *Law & Society Review*, 38: 3, 489–512.
Cichowski, R. A. (2007), *The European Court and Civil Society. Litigation, Mobilization and Governance*, Cambridge, UK: Cambridge University Press.
Cini, M. (1996), *The European Commission: Leadership, Organisation and Culture in the EU*, Manchester: Manchester University Press.
Cockburn, C. (1995), 'Women and the European Social Dialogue, Strategies for Gender Democracy', *EC Social Europe*, Supplement 4/95, 65.
Coen, D. and J. J. Richardson (eds) (2009), *Lobbying the European Union: Institutions, Actors and Issues*, Oxford: Oxford University Press.
Commission of the European Communities (1984), 'Documents: Proposal for a Council Directive on the Principle of Equal Treatment for Men and Women in Self-employed Occupations, Including Agriculture, and on Protection during Pregnancy and Maternity (Submitted to the Council by the Commission)', COM (84) 57 final, Luxembourg: Office for Official Publications of the European Communities.
Commission of the European Communities (1988), 'Women in Agriculture', Supplement No. 29 to Women of Europe, Brussels: Commission of the EC, Directorate-General Information, Communication, Culture, October.
Commission of the European Communities (1994), 'Report from the Commission on the Implementation of Council Directive of 11 December 1986 on the Application of the Principle of Equal Treatment between Men and Women Engaged in an Activity, Including Agriculture, in Self-Employed Capacity, and on the Protection of Self-Employed Women during Pregnancy and Motherhood (86/613/EEC)', COM (94) 163 final, Brussels.
Commission of the European Communities (1996), 'Communication from the Commission: Incorporating Equal Opportunities for Women and Men into All Community Policies and Activities', COM (96) 67 final, Brussels.

252 Bibliography

Commission of the European Communities (1997), 'A Guide to Gender Impact Assessment', Doc. EQQP 42-97en, DG V/D/5, Online: ec.europa.eu/social/BlobServlet?docId=4376&langId=en (accessed 28 March 2011).

Commission of the European Communities (1999a), 'Women and Science: Mobilising Women to Enrich European Research', Communication of the Commission, COM (99) 76 final, Luxembourg.

Commission of the European Communities (1999b), 'Ex-Post Evaluation of the LEADER I Community Initiative 1989–1993: Executive Summary (1999)', Online: http://ec.europa.eu/comm/agriculture/rur/leader1/index_en.htm (accessed 12 May 2006).

Commission of the European Communities (2000), 'Communication from the Commission to the Council, the European Parliament, the Economic and Social Committee and the Committee of the Regions. Towards a European Research Area', COM (2000) 6, Brussels.

Commission of the European Communities (2001a), 'Science and Society. Action Plan', 4 December 2001, COM (2001) 714 final, Brussels.

Commission of the European Communities (2001b), 'Women and Science: The Gender Dimension as a Leverage for Reforming Science', Commission Staff Working Paper SEC (2001) 771, Online: ftp://ftp.cordis.europa.eu/pub/improving/docs/g_wo_sec771_en_200101.pdf (accessed 1 March 2008).

Commission of the European Communities (2002), 'Communication from the Commission to the Council, the European Parliament, the European Economic and Social Committee and the Committee of the Regions – Implementation of Gender Mainstreaming the Structural Funds Programming Documents 2000–2006', COM/2002/0748 final, Brussels.

Commission of the European Communities (2004), 'Impact Assessment of Rural Development Programmes in View of Post 2006 Rural Development Policy. Final Report', Brussels: DG Agriculture.

Commission of the European Communities (2005), 'Women and Science: Excellence and Innovation – Gender Equality in Science', Commission Staff Working Paper SEC (2005) 370, Online: http://ec.europa.eu/research/science-society/women/wir/pdf/sec_2005_370_en.pdf (accessed 1 March 2008).

Commission of the European Communities (2008a), 'Commission Staff Working Document Demography Report 2008: Meeting Social Needs in an Aging Society, Full Report and Annexes', SEC (2008) 2911, Brussels.

Commission of the European Communities (2008b), 'Proposal for a Directive of the European Parliament and of the Council on the Application of the Principle of Equal Treatment between Men and Women Engaged in an Activity in a Self-employed Capacity and Repealing Directive 86/613/EEC', Online: http://ec.europa.eu/social/BlobServlet?docId=608&langId=en (accessed 26 January 2009).

Commission of the European Communties (2008c), 'Proposal for a Council Directive on Implementing the Principle of Equal Treatment between Persons Irrespective of Religion or Belief, Disability, Age or Sexual Orientation', COM (2008) 426 final, Brussels.

Connell, R. W. (1998), 'Masculinities and Globalization', *Men and Masculinities*, 1: 1, 3–23.

Conroy, P. (1988), *The Impact of the Completion of the Single Market on Women in the European Community*, Brussels: Commission of the European Communities.

Conroy, P. (1994), 'Women and Poverty in the European Community. Issues in the Current Debate', European Commission DG V/A/3 (V/42/94-EN), Brussels.

Conzelmann, T. and R. Smith (eds) (2008), *Multi-Level Governance in the European Union: Taking Stock and Looking Ahead*, Baden Baden: Nomos.

Corsi, M. and M. Samek Lodovici, in collaboration with A. Cipollone, C. D'Ippoliti and S. Sansonetti (2009), *Gender Mainstreaming Active Inclusion Policies* (DG V, November).

Council (1984), 'Council Recommendation of 13 December 1984 on the Promotion of Positive Action for Women (84/635/EEC)', *Official Journal L 331*, 19 December, 34–35.

Council of Agricultural Ministers (2002), 'Conclusion: Incorporating the Gender Perspective into the Agricultural Council', 2428th Meeting, 27 May, Brussels, 8959/02 (Presse 184).

Council of Europe (2005), 'Gender Budgeting. Final Report of the Group of Specialists on Gender Budgeting (EG-S-GB)', Strasburg, Online: http://www.coe.int/t/dghl/standardsetting/equality/03themes/gender-mainstreaming/EG-S-GB%282004%29R APFIN_en.pdf (accessed 17 February 2011).

Council of the EU (1996), 'Council Recommendation 96/694/EC of 2 December 1996 on the Balanced Participation of Women and Men in the Decision-Making Process', Brussels.

Council of the EU (2004): 2618th Council Meeting: Justice and Home Affairs, Press Release, 19 November 2004, Brussels, Internet: http://www.consilium.europa.eu/uedocs/cms_data/docs/pressdata/en/jha/82745.pdf (accessed 30 March 2011).

Council of the European Communities (1986), 'Council Directive 86/613/EEC of December 1986 on the Application of the Principle of Equal Treatment between Men and Women Engaged in an Activity, Including Agriculture, in a Self-employed Capacity, and on the Protection of Self-employed Women during Pregnancy and Motherhood', *Official Journal L 359*, 19 December, 56–58.

Council of the European Union (1999), 'Council Resolution on "Women and Science"', Brussels, Online: ftp://ftp.cordis.europa.eu/pub/improving/docs/g_wo_res_en.pdf (accessed 1 March 2008).

Council of the European Union (2001), 'Council Resolution on Science and Society and on Women in Science', Brussels, Online: http://register.consilium.eu.int/pdf/en/01/st10/10357en1.pdf (accessed 1 March 2008).

Council of the European Union (2005), 'Council Regulation (EC) No 1698/1005 of 20 September 2005 on Support for Rural Development by the European Agricultural Fund for Rural Development (EAFRD)', *Official Journal L 277*, 21 October, 1.

Cram, L. (2006), 'Inventing People: Civil Society Participation and the Enhabitation of the EU', in S. Smismans (ed.), *Civil Society and Legitimate European Governance*, Cheltenham: Edward Elgar, pp. 241–259.

Curtin, D. (1988), 'Equal Treatment and Social Welfare: The European Court's Emerging Case-Law on Directive 79/7/EEC', in G. Whyte (ed.), *Sex Equality, Community Rights and Irish Social Welfare Law: The Impact of the Third Equality Directive*, Dublin: Irish Centre for European Law, Trinity College, pp. 39–59.

Dahlerup, D. (1988), 'From a Small to a Large Minority: Women in Scandinavian Politics', *Scandinavian Political Studies*, 11: 4, 275–297.

Dahlerup, D. (2010), 'The Development of Gender and Politics as a New Research Field within the Framework of the ECPR', *European Political Science*, 9, 85–97.

Daly, M. (2000), *The Gender Division of Welfare*, Cambridge: Cambridge University Press.

Daly, M. (2005), 'Gender Mainstreaming in Theory and Practice', *Social Politics*, 12: 3, 433–450.

Daly, M. and C. Saraceno (2002), 'Social Exclusion and Gender Relations', in B. Hobson, J. Lewis and B. Siim (eds), *Contested Concepts in Gender and Social Politics*, Cheltenham: Edward Elgar, pp. 84–104.

de Beauvoir, S. (1953), *The Second Sex*, New York: Vintage (French: Le Deuxième Sexe, 1949).

Debusscher, P. and J. True (2009), 'Lobbying the EU for Gender-Equal Development', in J. Orbie and L. Tortell (eds), *The EU and the Social Dimension of Globalization*, Abingdon: Routledge, pp. 186–206.

Defeis, E. F. (1999), 'The Treaty of Amsterdam: the Next Step towards Gender Equality?', Online: http://www.bc.edu/bc_org/avp/law/lwsch/journals/bciclr/23_1/01_TXT.htm (accessed 24 July 2008).

De la Guardia, R. M. (2004), 'In Search of Lost Europe: Spain', in W. Kaiser and J. Elvert (eds), *European Union Enlargement: A Comparative History*, London; New York: Routledge, pp. 93–111.

Delanghe, H., U. Muldur and L. Soete (eds) (2009), *European Science and Technology Policy: Towards Integration or Fragmentation?*, Cheltenham: Edward Elgar.

Deutchman, I. E. (1993), 'Feminist Theory and the Politics of Empowerment', in L. Lovelace Duke (ed.), *Women in Politics. Outsiders or Insiders?*, Englewood Cliffs, NJ: Prentice Hall, pp. 3–15.

Diez, T. and A. Wiener (2004), 'Introducing the Mosaic of Integration Theory', in A. Wiener and T. Diez (eds), *European Integration Theory*, Oxford: Oxford University Press, pp. 1–21.

Dinan, D. (2005), *Europe Recast: A History of European Union*, Basingstoke: Palgrave Macmillan.

Doe, N. (2010), 'Towards a "Common Law" on Religion in the European Union', in L. N. Leustean and J. T. S. Madeley (eds), *Religion, Politics and Law in the European Union*, London/New York: Routledge, pp. 141–160.

Donato, K. M. (1992), 'Understanding US Immigration: Why Some Countries Send Women and Others Send Men', in D. Gabaccia (ed.), *Seeking Common Ground. Multidisciplinary Studies of Immigrant Women in the United States*, Westport: Greenwood Press, pp. 159–184.

Duina, F. G. (1999), *Harmonizing Europe. Nation–States within the Common Market*, New York: SUNY Press.

Duncan, S. (1996a), 'Obstacles to a Successful Equal Opportunities Policy in the European Union', *The European Journal of Women's Studies*, 3: 4, 399–422.

Duncan, S. (1996b), 'The Diverse Worlds of European Patriarchy', in M. D. García-Ramon and J. Monk (eds), *Women of the European Union: The Politics of Work and Daily Life*, London: Routledge, pp. 74–110.

Economic and Social Committee (1984), 'Opinion of the Economic and Social Committee on the Proposal for a Council Directive on the Application of the Principle of Equal Treatment as between Men and Women Engaged in an Activity, Including Agriculture, in a Self-Employed Capacity, and on the Protection of Self-Employed Women during Pregnancy and Motherhood', *Official Journal C 343*, 24 December, 1.

Edler, J., S. Kuhlmann and M. Behrens (eds) (2003), *Changing Governance of Research and Technology Policy: The European Research Area*, Cheltenham: Edward Elgar.

Edquist, K. (2006), 'EU Social-Policy Governance: Advocating Activism or Servicing States?', *Journal of European Public Policy*, 13: 4, 500–518.

Egan, M., N. Nugent and W. E. Paterson (eds) (2010), *Research Agenda in EU Studies: Stalking the Elephant*, Houndsmill: Palgrave Macmillan.

Einhorn, B. (2006), *Citizenship in an Enlarging Europe: From Dream to Awakening*, Basingstoke: Palgrave Macmillan.
Elgström, O. (2000), 'Norm Negotiations. The Construction of New Norms regarding Gender and Development in EU Foreign Aid Policy', *Journal of European Public Policy*, 7: 3, 457–476.
Elgström, O. and C. Jönsson (2005), 'Introduction', in O. Elgström and C. Jönsson (eds), *European Union Negotiations. Processes, Networks and Institutions*, Abingdon: Routledge, pp. 1–9.
Ellina, C. A. (2003), *Promoting Women's Rights. The Politics of Gender in the European Union*, New York, London: Routledge.
Elman, R. A. (1996), *Sexual Politics in the European Union. The New Feminist Challenge*, Providence, Oxford: Berghahn Books.
Elman, R. A. (2007), *Sexual Equality in an Integrated Europe. Virtual Equality*, London: Palgrave Macmillan.
Elshtain, J. B. (1993), *Public Man, Private Woman*, 2nd edition, Princeton: Princeton University Press.
Elvert, J. (2004), 'A Fool's Game or a Comedy of Errors? EU Enlargements in Comparative Perspective', in W. Kaiser and J. Elvert (eds), *European Union Enlargement: A Comparative History*, London and New York: Routledge, pp. 189–208.
Enloe, C. (2004) *The Curious Feminist: Searching for Women in the New Age of Empire*, London: University of California Press.
ENWISE Expert Working Group (2004), 'Waste of Talents: Turning Private Struggles into a Public Issue. Women and Science in the Enwise Countries. A Report to the European Commission from the Enwise Expert Group on Women Scientists in the Central and Eastern European Countries and in the Baltic States', Luxembourg, Online: http://ec.europa.eu/research/science-society/women/enwise/enwise_report_en.html (accessed 1 March 2008).
Esping-Andersen, G. (1990), *The Three Worlds of Welfare Capitalism*, Princeton: Princeton University Press.
ETAN Expert Working Group (2000), 'Science Policies in the European Union: Promoting Excellence through Mainstreaming Gender Equality. A Report from the ETAN Network on Women and Science', Luxembourg, Online: http://ec.europa.eu/research/science-society/pdf/g_wo_etan_en_200101.pdf (accessed 1 March 2008).
EU Observer (2008), 'Margot Wallstrom Fed up with EU "Reign of Old Men"', Published 8 February 2008, Online: http://euobserver.com/9/25631 (accessed 18 March 2011).
Eulriet, I. (2009), 'Towards More Coherence? Policy and Legal Aspects of Gender Equality in the Armed Forces of Europe', *Journal of European Integration*, 31: 6, 741–756.
EuroFound (2011), 'Tripartite EU Agency on Living and Working Conditions', Online: http://www.eurofound.europa.eu/areas/industrialrelations/dictionary/definitions/equaltreatment.htm (accessed 28 February 2011).
European Commission (1973), 'Report to the Council on the Application of the Principle of Equal Pay between Men and Women: Situation on 31 December 1972', SEC (73) 3000 Final, 18 July, Online: http://aei.pitt.edu/9269/ (accessed 21 January 2011).
European Commission (1993), 'White Paper on Growth, Competitiveness and Employment', Brussels: European Commission.
European Commission (1994), 'European Social Policy. A Way Forward for the Union. A White Paper', COM (94) 333, Brussels.

256 Bibliography

European Commission (1995a), 'Medium-Term Social Action Programme 1995–1997', COM (1995) 134, Brussels.
European Commission (1995b), 'Communication on Integrating Gender Issues in Development Co-Operation', COM (1995) 423, Brussels.
European Commission (1998), 'Interim Report of the Commission to the European Parliament, the Council, the Economic and Social Committee and the Committee of the Regions on the Implementation of the Medium-Term Community Action Programme on Equal Opportunities for Men and Women (1996–2000)', 17 December, COM (98) 770 final, Brussels.
European Commission (1999a), '1999 Regular Report from the Commission on Bulgaria's Progress towards Accession', Online: http://ec.europa.eu/enlargement/archives/key_documents/reports_2003_en.htm (accessed 27 March 2008).
European Commission (1999b), 'Guidelines for Systems of Monitoring and Evaluation of ESF Assistance in the Period 2000–2006', Directorate-General for Employment, Industrial Relations and Social Affairs. Monitoring and Evaluation Unit, Online: http://ec.europa.eu/employment_social/esf/docs/guidelines/evaluation/en.pdf (accessed 2 March 2011).
European Commission (1999c), 'Women and Work. Report on Existing Research in the European Union', Brussels: European Commission.
European Commission (2000), 'Communication from the Commission to the Council and the European Parliament on a Community Immigration Policy', COM (2000) 757, Brussels.
European Commission (2001a), 'European Governance. A White Paper', COM (2001) 428 final, Brussels.
European Commission (2001b), '2001 Regular Report from the Commission on Hungary's Progress towards Accession', Online: http://ec.europa.eu/enlargement/archives/key_documents/reports_2003_en.htm (accessed 27 March 2008).
European Commission (2002a), '2002 Regular Report from the Commission on the Czech Republic's Progress toward Accession', Online: http://ec.europa.eu/enlargement/archives/key_documents/reports_2003_en.htm (accessed 27 March 2008).
European Commission (2002b), 'Implementation of Gender Mainstreaming in the Structural Funds Programming Documents 2000–2006', COM (2002) 748 final, Brussels.
European Commission (2002c), 'Joint Report on Social Inclusion 2002', Brussels.
European Commission (2003a), 'Communication on Immigration, Integration and Employment', COM (2003) 336 final, Brussels.
European Commission (2003b), 'Comprehensive Monitoring Reports', Online: http://ec.europa.eu/enlargement/archives/key_documents/reports_2003_en.htm (accessed 30 March 2008).
European Commission (2004), 'First Annual Report on Migration and Integration', COM (2004) 508 final, Brussels.
European Commission (2005a), 'The Hague Programme: Ten Priorities for the Next Five Years. The Partnership for European Renewal in the Field of Freedom, Security and Justice', COM (2005) 184 final, Online: http://eur-lex.europa.eu/LexUriServ/LexUriServ.do?uri=CELEX:52005PC0184:EN:HTML (accessed 30 March 2011).
European Commission (2005b), 'A Common Agenda for Integration: Framework for the Integration of Third-Country Nationals in the European Union', COM (2005) 389 final, Brussels.

European Commission (2005c), 'Policy Plan on Legal Migration', COM (2005) 669 final, Brussels.
European Commission (2006), 'Communication from the Commission to the Council, the European Parliament, the European Economic and Social Committee and the Committee of the Regions – A Roadmap for Equality between Women and Men 2006–2010', SEC (2006) 275, COM (2006) 92 final, 1 March, Brussels.
European Commission (2007a), 'Strategy Paper for the Thematic Programme of Cooperation with Third Countries in the Areas of Migration and Asylum 2007–2010. Third Annual Report on Migration and Integration', COM (2007) 512 final, Brussels.
European Commission (2007b), 'The European Research Area: New Perspectives', Green Paper, COM (2007) 161 final, Brussels.
European Commission (2007c), 'Towards Common Principles of Flexicurity: More and Better Jobs through Flexibility and Security', Luxembourg: Office for Official Publications of the European Communities.
European Commission (2008a), 'Women and Men in Decision-Making 2007: Analysis of the Situation and Trends', Luxembourg: Office for Official Publications of the European Communities.
European Commission (2008b), 'Benchmarking Policy Measures for Gender Equality in Science', EUR 23314, Brussels.
European Commission (2008c), 'Commission Acts on Gender Equality Legislation', Press release 25 July, IP/08/1014, Online: http://ec.europa.eu/employment_social/gender_equality/legislation/index_en.html (accessed 25 July 2008).
European Commission (2008d), 'Manual for Gender Mainstreaming: Employment, Social Inclusion and Social Protection Policies', Luxembourg: Office for Official Publications of the European Communities.
European Commission (2008e), 'Renewed Social Agenda: Opportunities, Access and Solidarity in 21st Century Europe', COM (2008) 412, Brussels.
European Commission (2009a), 'She Figures 2009. Statistics and Indicators on Gender Equality in Science', Brussels, Online: http://ec.europa.eu/research/science-society/document_library/pdf_06/she_figures_2009_en.pdf (accessed 20 December 2009).
European Commission (2009b), 'Toolkit: Gender in EU-Funded Research', EUR 23857 EN, Brussels.
European Commission (2009c) 'Changing Research Landscapes to Make the Most of Human Potential', Online: http://ec.europa.eu/research/science-society/index.cfm?fuseaction=public.topic&id=1701 (accessed 28 March 2011).
European Commission (2009d), 'Commission Refers Estonia to European Court of Justice on Gender Equality Legislation', Press release 25 June, IP/09/1036, Brussels, Online: http://europa.eu/rapid/pressReleasesAction.do?reference=IP/09/1036&type=HTML&aged=0&language=EN&guiLanguage=en (accessed 21 January 2011).
European Commission (2009e), 'Commission Refers Poland to the European Court of Justice on Gender Equality Legislation', Press release 14 May, IP/09/785, Brussels, Online: http://europa.eu/rapid/pressReleasesAction.do?reference= IP/09/785&type=HTML (accessed 21 January 2011).
European Commission (2010a), 'Europe 2020: A European Strategy for Smart, Sustainable and Inclusive Growth', Brussels, Online: http://ec.europa.eu/eu2020/pdf/COMPLET%20EN%20BARROSO%20%20%20007%20-%20Europe%202020%20- %20EN%20version.pdf (accessed 5 August 2010).
European Commission (2010b), 'Interim Evaluation of the Seventh Framework Programme. Report of the Expert Group', Brussels.

258 Bibliography

European Commission (2010c), 'Europe 2020: A Strategy for Smart, Sustainable and Inclusive Growth', COM (2010) 2020 final, Brussels.

European Commission (2010d), 'Strategy for Equality between Women and Men 2010–2015', COM (2010) 491 final, Brussels.

European Commission (2010e), 'Joint Report on Social Protection and Social Inclusion 2010', Brussels.

European Commission (2010f), 'Strategy for Equality between Women and Men 2010–2015', COM (2010) 491 final, Brussels.

European Commission, DG Agriculture (2000), 'Women Active in Rural Development: Assuring the Future of Rural Europe', Luxembourg: Office for Official Publications of the European Communities.

European Commission, DG Agriculture (2003), 'Ex-Post Evaluation of the Community Initiative LEADER II: Final Report (2003) Volume 1: Main Report', Online: http://ec.europa.eu/comm/agriculture/eval/reports/leader2/index_en.htm (accessed 5 June 2008).

European Commission, DG Agriculture (2006), 'Synthesis of Mid-Term Evaluations of LEADER+ Programmes. Final Report', November, Online: http://ec.europa.eu/agriculture/eval/reports/leaderplus/ (accessed 31 December 2008).

European Commission, DG Employment, Social Affairs and Equal Opportunities Unit G1 (2008), 'Manual for Gender Mainstreaming: Employment, Social Inclusion and Social Protection Policies', Luxembourg: Office for Official Publications of the European Communities.

European Commission, DG Employment, Social Affairs and Equal Opportunities Unit G4 (2009), 'International Perspectives on Positive Action Measures: A Comparative Analysis in the European Union, Canada, The United States and South Africa', Luxembourg: Office for Official Publications of the European Community.

European Commission, DG Employment, Social Affairs and Equal Opportunities Unit G1 (2010), 'Report on Equality between Women and Men 2010', Luxembourg: Office for Official Publications of the European Communities.

European Commission, DG Justice (2010), 'Report on Progress on Equality between Women and Men in 2010: The Gender Balance in Business Leadership', Luxembourg: Publications Office of the European Union.

European Commission, DG Research (2001), 'Gender in Research: Gender Impact Assessment of the Specific Programmes of the Fifth Framework Programme. An Overview', Brussels.

European Commission, DG Research (2006), 'She Figures 2006. Women and Science: Statistics and Indicators', Brussels, Online: http://ec.europa.eu/research/science-society/pdf/she_figures_2006_en.pdf (accessed 1 March 2008).

European Commission, DG Research (2007), 'Remuneration of Researchers in the Public and Private Sectors. Final Report', Brussels.

European Commission, DG Research (2008), 'Mapping the Maze. Getting More Women to the Top in Research', Brussels, Online: http://ec.europa.eu/research/science-society/document_library/pdf_06/mapping-the-maze-getting-more-women-to-the-top-in-research_en.pdf (accessed 3 March 2008).

European Council (1993), 'Presidency Conclusions, Copenhagen European Council 21–22 June', Online: http://www.europarl.europa.eu/enlargement/ec/pdf/cop_en.pdf (accessed 21 March 2011).

European Council (2000a), 'Presidency Conclusions', Lisbon European Council 23 and 24 March, Online: http://www.consilium.europa.eu/uedocs/cms_data/docs/pressdata/en/ec/00100-r1.en0.htm (accessed 29 March 2011).

European Council (2000b), 'Council Conclusions Annex: Objectives in the Fight against Poverty and Social Inclusion', 30 November, Online: http://ec.europa.eu/employment_social/social_inclusion/docs/approb_en.pdf (accessed 2 March 2011).

European Movement – Malta (2005), 'Our Europe, Our Europe', 22 May 2005, Online: http://www.euro-movement.org.mt/page.asp?p=739&l=1&i=594 (accessed 30 March 2011).

European Parliament (1984), 'Resolution Closing the Procedure for Consultation of the European Parliament on Proposals from the Commission of the European Communities to the Council for a Directive on the Principle of Equal Treatment for Men and Women in Self-Employed Occupations, Including Agriculture, and on Protection during Pregnancy and Maternity', *Official Journal C 172*, 2 July (EN).

European Parliament (1993), 'Report on the Situation of Women in Agriculture in the Member States of the Community', Rapporteur: Mrs. Térésa Domingo-Segarra, 3 December, PE DOC A3-0409/93.

European Parliament (1997), 'Resolution on the Situation of the Assisting Spouses of the Self-Employed', *Official Journal C 085*, 17 March, 186.

European Parliament (2000), 'European Parliament Resolution on the Communication from the Commission Entitled: "Women and Science" – Mobilising Women to Enrich European Research', COM(1999) 76., EP document A5-0082/1999, Online: ftp://ftp.cordis.europa.eu/pub/improving/docs/g_wo_parl_resol_en.pdf (accessed 1 March 2008).

European Parliament (2003), 'Resolution on Women in Rural Areas of the European Union in the Light of the Mid-Term Review of the Common Agricultural Policy', Adopted 3 July, A5-0230/2003.

European Parliament (2008), 'Resolution on the Situation of Women in Rural Areas of the EU', Adopted 12 March, A6-0031/2008.

European Parliament and Council of the European Union (2010), 'Directive 2010/41/EU of 7 July 2010 on the Application of the Principle of Equal Treatment between Men and Women Engaged in an Activity in a Self-Employed Capacity and Repealing Council Directive 86/613/EEC', *Official Journal L 180*, 15 July, 1–6.

European Parliament, Committee on Women's Rights (1988), 'Report on Spouses in Agriculture and Family Businesses. Part B: Justification', Rapporteur: Mr. Andrew Pearce, PE DOC A 2-0416/88/Part B.

European Parliament, Committee on Women's Rights and Equal Opportunities (1999), 'Report on the Communication from the Commission Entitled: "Women and Science" – Mobilising Women to Enrich European Research', A5-0082/1999, PE 231.841/DEF.

European Platform of Women Scientists (2006), 'Representing the Interests of Women Scientists EU Level', *EPWS Newsletter*, 4, 2–3.

European Refugee Fund (2004), 'Europe Land of Asylum. Reception and Social Inclusion of Asylum Seekers and Refugees in Three European Capital Cities', Online: http://europelandofasylum.net (accessed 20 July 2004).

European Trade Union Confederation (2009), Online: http://www.etuc.org/a/111 (accessed 11 September 2009).

European Union (2010), 'Consolidated Versions of the Treaty on European Union and the Treaty on the Functioning of the EU, Charter of Fundamental Rights of the European Union', *Official Journal of the European Union*, C 83/2010, 1–408.

European Women's Lobby (2004), 'Gender Budgeting. An Overview', Online: http://www.womenlobby.org/SiteResources/data/MediaArchive/policies/gender%20equality/Gender_en.pdf (accessed 29 September 2010).
Falkner, G., O. Treib, M. Hartlapp and S. Leiber (2005), *Complying with Europe: EU Harmonization and Soft Law in the Member States*, Cambridge: Cambridge University Press.
Ferree, M. M. and B. B. Hess (2000), *Controversy and Coalition: The New Feminist Movement across Three Decades of Change*, London, New York: Routledge.
Ferrera, M. (2005), *The Boundaries of Welfare: European Integration and the New Spatial Politics of Social Protection*, Oxford: Oxford University Press.
Fink, J. (2002), 'Silence, Absence and Elision in Analyses of "The Family" in European Social Policy', in J. Fink, G. Lewis and J. Clarke (eds) (2001), *Rethinking European Welfare. Transformation of Europe and Social Policy*, London: Sage, pp. 163–179.
Fink, J., G. Lewis and J. Clarke (eds) (2001), *Rethinking European Welfare. Transformation of Europe and Social Policy*, London: Sage.
Fligstein, N. (2008), *Euro-Clash: The EU, European Identity, and the Future of Europe*, Oxford: Oxford University Press.
Flood, M. (2008), 'Men, Sex, and Homosociality', *Men and Masculinities*, 10: 3, 339–359.
Flowtow, L. von (1997), 'Dr. Mama: Ein Bericht aus der Universität', *Streit*, 2, 61–64.
Flynn, L. (1996), 'The Body Politic(s) of EU Law', in T. K. Hervey and D. O'Keeffe (eds), *Sex Equality Law in the European Community*, Chichester: Wiley, pp. 279–297.
Fodor, E. (2005), 'Women at Work: The Status of Women in the Labour Markets of the Czech Republic, Hungary and Poland', Occasional paper, Geneva: UNRISD.
Frith, R. (2008), 'Cosmopolitan Democracy and the EU: The Case of Gender', *Political Studies*, 58: 1, 215–236.
Funk, N. and M. Müller (1993), *Gender Politics and Post-Communism: Reflections from Eastern Europe and the Former Soviet Union*, New York: Routledge.
Gabaccia, D., K. M. Donato, J. Holdaway, M. Manalansan and P. R. Pessar (eds) (2006), 'Special Issue on Gender and Migration Revisited', *International Migration Review*, 40: 2.
Galligan, Y. (1998), *Women and Politics in Contemporary Ireland: From the Margins to the Mainstream*, London; Washington: Pinter.
Galligan, Y. and S. Clavero (2007), 'Gender Equality and Multi-Level Governance in East Central Europe', in J. de Bardeleben and A. Hurrelmann (eds), *Democratic Dilemmas of Multilevel Governance*, Basingstoke: Palgrave Macmillan, pp. 216–239.
Galligan, Y., S. Clavero and M. Calloni (2007), *Gender Politics and Democracy in Post-Socialist Europe*, Opladen: Barbara Budrich.
Gardiner, F. (1999), 'The Impact of EU Equality Legislation on Irish Women', in Y. Galligan, E. Wardand and R. Wilford (eds), *Contesting Politics: Women in Ireland, North and South*, Boulder: Westview, pp. 38–54.
Genetti, E. (2010), *Europäische Staaten im Wettbewerb: Zur Transformation von Geschlechterordnungen im Kontext der EU*, Münster: Westfälisches Dampfboot.
Ghodsee, K. (2006), 'Nongovernmental Ogres? How Feminist NGOs Undermine Women in Postsocialist Eastern Europe', *The International Journal of Not-for-Profit Law*, 8: 3, 43–58.
Gilligan, C. (1982), *In a Different Voice*, Cambridge: Harvard University Press.
Goebel, R. J. (1995), 'The European Union Grows: The Constitutional Impact of the Accession of Austria, Finland and Sweden', *Fordham International Law Journal*, 18, 1141–1143.

Grande, E. (1996), 'The State and Interest Groups in a Framework of Multi-Level Decision-Making: The Case of the European Union', *Journal of European Public Policy*, 3: 3, 318–338.

Greenwood, J. (2009), 'Institutions and Civil Society Organizations in the EU's Multi-level System', in J. Joachim and B. Locher (eds), *Transnational Activism in the UN and the EU. A Comparative Study*, London, New York: Routledge, pp. 93–104.

Gregory, J. (1987), *Sex, Race and the Law*, London: Sage.

Guerrina, R. (2005), *Mothering the Union. Gender Politics in the EU*, Manchester: Manchester University Press.

Guzzini, S. (2000), 'A Reconstruction of Constructivism in International Relations', *European Journal of International Relations*, 6: 2, 147–182.

Gya, G. (2009), 'Gender Mainstreaming and Empowerment of Women in the EU's External Relations Instruments. Study for the European Parliament', PE407.002, Online: http://www.isis-europe.org/pdf/2009_artrel_306_09-04-epstudy-gender-extrel-gya.pdf (accessed 4 April 2011).

Haas, E. B. (1958), *The Uniting of Europe: Political, Social, and Economic Forces 1950–57*, Stanford: Stanford University Press.

Haas, E. B. (1975), *The Obsolescence of Regional Integration Theory*, Berkeley: University of California, Institute of International Studies, Research Series, No. 25.

Hafner-Burton, E. and M. A. Pollack (2002), 'Gender Mainstreaming and Global Governance', *Feminist Legal Studies*, 10, 285–298.

Hafner-Burton, E. M. and M. A. Pollack (2009), 'Mainstreaming Gender in the European Union: Getting the Incentives Right', *Comparative European Politics*, 7: 1, 114–138.

Hakim, C. (2000), *Work-Lifestyle Choices in the Twenty-First Century: Preference Theory*, Oxford: Oxford University Press.

Haltern, U. (2004), 'Integration through Law', in A. Wiener and T. Diez (eds), *European Integration Theory*, Oxford: Oxford University Press, pp. 177–196.

Hansen, P. and S. Hager (2009), *The Politics of European Citizenship: Social Rights, Migration and Political Economy*, Oxford: Berghahn Books.

Hansen, W. (2009), 'The European Research Area and Human Resources in Science and Technology', in H. Delanghe, U. Muldur, and L. Soete (eds), *European Science and Technology Policy: Towards Integration or Fragmentation?*, Cheltenham: Edward Elgar, pp. 237–255.

Hantrais, L. (ed.) (2000a), *Gendered Policies in Europe. Reconciling Employment and Family Life*, London: Macmillan.

Hantrais, L. (2000b), 'From Equal Pay to Reconciliation of Employment and Family Life', in L. Hantrais (ed.), *Gendered Policies in Europe. Reconciling Employment and Family Life*, London: Macmillan, pp. 1–26.

Hantrais, L. (2007), *Social Policy in the European Union*, London: Macmillan.

Hašková, H. (2005), 'Czech Women's Civic Organizing under the State Socialist Regime, Socio-Economic Transformation and the EU Accession Period', *Czech Sociological Review*, 41: 6, 1077–1110.

Haverland, M. and M. H. Romeijn (2006), 'Do Member States Make European Policies Work? Analysing the EU Transposition Deficit', Paper presented at the CES Conference in Chicago, 29 March – 2 April.

Hawkesworth, M. (2006), *Globalization and Feminist Activism*, Lanham, MD: Rowman and Littlefield.

Helfferich, B. and F. Kolb (2001), 'Multilevel Action Coordination in European Contentious Politics: The Case of the European Women's Lobby', in D. Imig and

S. Tarrow (eds), *Contentious Europeans. Protest and Politics in an Emerging Polity*, Lanham, MD: Rowman & Littlefield, pp. 143–161.
Hernes, H. (1987), *Welfare State and Women Power*, Oslo: Norwegian University Press.
Heron, A. (2005), 'Migrant Women into Work – What is Working?', OECD and European Commission Seminar: 'Migrant Women and the Labour Market: Diversity and Challenges', Brussels.
High Level Expert Group on WIR (2003), 'Women in Industrial Research: A Wake Up Call for European Industry. A Report to the European Commission from the High Level Expert Group on Women in Industrial Research for Strategic Analysis of Specific Science and Technology Policy Issues (STRATA)', Luxembourg, Online: http://ec.europa.eu/research/science-society/women/wir/report_en.html (accessed 1 March 2008).
Hill, B. (1993), 'The "Myth" of the Family Farm: Defining the Family Farm and Assessing Its Importance in the European Community', *Journal of Rural Studies*, 9: 4, 359–370.
Hobson, B., J. Lewis and B. Siim (eds) (2002), *Contested Concepts in Gender and Social Politics*, Cheltenham: Edward Elgar.
Hobson, B. and R. Lister (2002), 'Citizenship', in B. Hobson, J. Lewis and B. Siim (eds), *Contested Concepts in Gender and Social Politics*, Cheltenham: Edward Elgar, pp. 23–55.
Hondagneu-Sotelo, P. (2001), *Doméstica. Immigrant Workers Cleaning and Caring in the Shadows of Affluence*, Berkeley: University of California Press.
Hooghe, L. and G. Marks (2001), *Multi-Level Governance and European Integration*, Oxford; Lanham, MD: Rowman & Littlefield.
Hooghe, L. and G. Marks (2003), 'Unraveling the Central State, But How? Types of Multi-Level Governance', *American Political Science Review*, 97: 2, 233–243.
Hoskyns, C. (1985), 'Women's Equality and the European Community', *Feminist Review*, 20, 71–88.
Hoskyns, C. (1996), *Integrating Gender: Women, Law and Politics in the European Union*, London: Verso.
Hoskyns, C. (2000), 'A Study of Four Action Programmes on Equal Opportunities', in M. Rossilli (ed.), *Gender Policies in the European Union*, New York: Peter Lang, pp. 43–58.
Hoskyns, C. (2004), 'Gender Perspectives', in A. Wiener and T. Diez (eds), *European Integration Theory*, Oxford: Oxford University Press, pp. 217–236.
Howard, E. (2008), 'The European Year of Equal Opportunities for All – 2007: Is the EU Moving Away from a Formal Idea of Equality?', *European Law Journal*, 14: 2, 168–185.
Hubert, A. (1998), *L'Europe et les femmes. Identités en mouvement*, Rennes: Éditions Apogée.
Hubert, A. (2001), 'From Equal Pay to Parity Democracy: The Rocky Ride of Women's Policy in the European Union', in J. Klausen and C. S. Maier (eds), *Has Liberalism Failed Women? Assuring Equal Representation in Europe and the United States*, New York: Palgrave Macmillan, pp. 143–164.
Hubert, A. (2010), 'Dynamiques transnationales dans le développement de la politique européenne Femmes et Sciences', in B. Marques-Pereira, P. Meier and D. Paternotte (eds), *Au dela et en deça de l'Etat, le genre entre dynamiques transnationales et multiniveaux*, Brussels: Academia BRUYLANT, pp. 153–167.
Humphries, J. and J. Rubery (eds) (1995), *The Economics of Equal Opportunities*, Manchester: Equal Opportunities Commission.

Hurley, J. and E. Fernández-Macías (2008), 'More and Better Jobs: Patterns of Employment Expansion in Europe', ERM Report 2008, Luxembourg: Office for Official Publications of the European Communities, Online: http://www.eurofound.europa.eu/publications/htmlfiles/ef0850.htm (accessed 21 January 2011).

Iankova, E. A. and P. J. Katzenstein (2003), 'European Enlargement and Institutional Hypocrisy', in T. A. Börzel and R. A. Cichowski (eds), *The State of the European Union*, Volume 6: Law, Politics and Society, Oxford: Oxford University Press, pp. 269–290.

Ingebritsen, C. (1998), *The Nordic States and European Unity*, Ithaca: Cornell University Press.

Iredale, R. (2005), 'Gender, Immigration Policies and Accreditation: Valuing the Skills of Professional Women Migrants', *Science Direct GEOFORUM*, 36: 2, 155–166.

Jachtenfuchs, M. and B. Kohler-Koch (2004), 'Governance and Institutional Development', in A. Wiener and T. Diez (eds), *European Integration Theory*, Oxford: Oxford University Press, pp. 97–115.

Jacquot, S. (2010), 'The Paradox of Gender Mainstreaming: Unanticipated Effects of New Modes of Governance in the Gender Equality Domain', *West European Politics*, 33: 1, 118–135.

Jenson, J. (2001), *Who Cares? Women's Work, Childcare and Welfare State Design*, Toronto: University of Toronto Press.

Jenson, J. (2008), 'Writing Women Out, Folding Gender In: The European Union "Modernises" Social Policy', *Social Politics*, 15: 2, 131–153.

Joachim, J. and B. Locher (eds) (2009), *Transnational Activism in the UN and the EU. A Comparative Study*, London: Routledge.

Joerges, C. (2006), 'Deliberative Political Processes Revisited: What Have We Learnt about the Legitimacy of Supranational Decision-Making', *Journal of Common Market Studies*, 44: 4, 779–802.

Jouen M. and B. Caremier (2000), 'The Future of Work', Forward Studies Unit, Luxembourg: Office for Official Publications of the European Communities.

Kantola, J. (2006), *Feminists Theorize the State*, Basingstoke: Palgrave Macmillan.

Kantola, J. (2010a), *Gender and the European Union*, Basingstoke: Palgrave Macmillan.

Kantola, J. (2010b), 'Feminist Approaches', in M. Egan, N. Nugent and W. E. Paterson (eds), *Research Agenda in EU Studies: Stalking the Elephant*, Houndsmill: Palgrave Macmillan, pp. 305–328.

Keck, M. E. and K. Sikkink (1998), *Activists beyond Borders: Advocacy Networks in International Politics*, Ithaca: Cornell University Press.

Kennedy, S. J. (2002), 'Breaking the Silence: Gender Mainstreaming and the Composition of the Court of Justice', *Feminist Legal Studies*, 10: 3, 257–270.

Klein, U. (2006), *Geschlechterverhältnisse und Gleichstellungspolitik in der Europäischen Union: Akteure – Themen – Ergebnisse*, Wiesbaden: VS Verlag.

Kligman, G. and S. Limoncelli (2005), 'Trafficking Women after Socialism: To, Through, and From Eastern Europe', *Social Politics*, 12: 1, 118–140.

Kodré, P. and H. Müller (2003), 'Shifting Policy Frames: EU Equal Treatment Norms and Domestic Discourses in Germany', in U. Liebert (ed.), *Gendering Europeanisation*, Brussels: Peter Lang, pp. 83–116.

Kofman, E. (1999), 'Female "Birds of Passage" a Decade Later: Gender and Immigration in the European Union', *International Migration Review*, 33: 2, 269–299.

Kofman, E. and R. Sales (1996), 'The Geography of Gender and Welfare in Europe', in M. D. García-Ramon and J. Monk (eds), *Women of the European Union: The Politics of Work and Daily Life*, London, New York: Routledge, pp. 31–60.

Kofman, E. and R. Sales (2000), 'The Implications of European Union Policies for Non-EU Migrant Women', in M. Rossilli (ed.), *Gender Policies in the European Union*, New York: Peter Lang, pp. 193–208.

Kohler-Koch, B. (1997), 'Organized Interests in European Integration: The Evolution of a New Type of Governance', in H. Wallace, H. Young and R. Alasdair (eds), *Participation and Policy Making in the European Union*, Oxford: Clarendon Press, pp. 42–68.

Kohler-Koch, B. (1999), 'The Evolution and Transformation of European Governance', in B. Kohler-Koch and R. Eising (eds), *The Transformation of Governance in the European Union*, London: Routledge, pp. 14–35.

Krizsán, A. and V. Zentai (2006), 'Gender Equality Policy or Gender Mainstreaming? The Case of Hungary on the Road to an Enlarged Europe', *Policy Studies*, 27: 2, 135–151.

Kröger, S. (2007), 'The End of Democracy as We Know It? The Legitimacy Deficits of Bureaucratic Social Policy Governance', *European Integration*, 29: 5, 565–582.

Kronsell, A. (2005a), 'Gendered Practices in Institutions of Hegemonic Masculinity: Reflections from Feminist Standpoint Theory', *International Feminist Journal of Politics*, 7: 2, 280–298.

Kronsell, A. (2005b), 'Gender, Power and European Integration Theory', *Journal of European Public Policy*, 12: 6, 1022–1040.

Kronsell, A. (2009), 'Negotiations in Networks. The Importance of Personal Relations and Homosociality', in K. Aggestam and M. Jerneck (eds), *Diplomacy in Theory and Practice*, Malmö: Liber, pp. 241–256.

Laffan, B. (1999), 'Becoming a "Living Institution": The Evolution of the European Court of Auditors', *Journal of Common Market Studies*, 37: 2, 251–268.

Lang, S. (2009), 'Assessing Advocacy: Transnational Women's Networks and Gender Mainstreaming in the European Union', *Social Politics*, 16: 3, 327–367.

Leiber, S. (2005), 'Implementation of EU Social Policy in Poland: Is there a Different "Eastern World of Compliance"?', Paper presented at the Ninth Biennial International Conference of the European Union Studies Association (EUSA) in Austin TX, 31 March – 2 April.

Leibfried, S. (2005), 'Social Policy', in H. Wallace, W. Wallace and M. A. Pollack (eds), *Policy-Making in the European Union*, Oxford: Oxford University Press, pp. 243–278.

Leibfried, S. and P. Pierson (1995), 'Semisovereign Welfare States: Social Policy in a Multi-Tiered Europe', in S. Leibfried and P. Pierson (eds), *European Social Policy. Between Fragmentation and Integration*, Washington, D.C.: The Brookings Institute, pp. 43–78.

Leira, A. and C. Saraceno (2002), 'Care: Actors, Relationships and Contexts', in B. Hobson, J. Lewis and B. Siim (eds), *Contested Concepts in Gender and Social Politics*, Cheltenham: Edward Elgar, pp. 55–83.

Lendvai, N. (2004), 'The Weakest Link? EU Accession and Enlargement: Dialoguing EU and Post-Communist Social Policy', *Journal of European Social Policy*, 14: 3, 319–333.

Leon, M., M. Mateo Diaz and S. Millns (2003), '(En)Gendering the Convention: Women and the Future of the European Union', Paper presented at the ECPR Conference in Marburg, Germany, 18–21 September.

Lewis, J. (1992), 'Gender and the Development of Welfare Regimes', *Journal of European Social Policy*, 2: 3, 159–173.

Lewis, J. (2000), 'The Methods of Community in EU Decision Making and Administrative Rivalry in the Council's Infrastructure', *European Journal of Public Policy*, 7: 2, 261–289.

Lewis, J. (2006), 'Work/Family Reconciliation, Equal Opportunities and Social Policies: The Interpretation of Policy Trajectories at the EU Level and the Meaning of Gender Equality', *Journal of European Public Policy*, 13: 3, 420–437.

Liebert, U. (1999), 'Gender Politics in the European Union: The Return of the Public', *European Societies*, 1: 2, 197–239.

Liebert, U. (2002), 'Europeanising Gender Mainstreaming: Constraints and Opportunities in the Multilevel Euro-Polity', *Feminist Legal Studies*, 10, 241–256.

Liebert, U. (ed.) (2003a), *Gendering Europeanisation*, Brussels: Peter Lang.

Liebert, U. (2003b), 'Gendering Europeanisation: Patterns and Dynamics', in U. Liebert (ed.), *Gendering Europeanisation*, Brussels: Peter Lang, pp. 255–285.

Liebert, U. (2003c), 'Europeanization and the "Needle's Eye": The Transformation of Employment Policy in Germany', *Review of Policy Research*, 20: 3, 479–492.

Lipman-Blumen, J. (1976), 'Toward a Homosocial Theory of Sex Roles: An Explanation of the Sex Segregation of Social Institutions', *Signs*, 1: 3, 15–31.

Locher, B. (2007), *Trafficking in Women in the European Union. Norms, Advocacy Networks and Policy Change*, Wiesbaden: VS Verlag.

Locher, B. and E. Prugl (2001), 'Feminism and Constructivism: Worlds Apart or Sharing the Middle Ground?', *International Studies Quarterly*, 45: 1, 111–129.

Locher, B. and E. Prügl (2009), 'Gender and European Integration', in A. Wiener and T. Diez (eds), *European Integration Theory*, 2nd edition, Oxford: Oxford University Press, pp. 181–197.

Löfström, A. (2009), 'Gender Equality, Economic Growth and Employment', Report presented at the conference 'What does Gender Equality Mean for Growth and Employment?' in Stockholm, 15–16 October, Online: http://ec.europa.eu/social/BlobServlet?docId=3988&langId=en (accessed 18 April 2011).

Lohmann, K. (2005), 'The Impact of EU Enlargement on the Civic Participation of Women in Central and Eastern Europe – The Perspective of the Karat Coalition', *Sociologický ústav AV ČR*, 1111–1117.

Lombardo, E. (2003), 'EU Gender Policy: Trapped in the Wollstonecroft Dilemma', *The European Journal of Women's Studies*, 10: 2, 159–180.

Lombardo, E. (2005), 'Integrating or Setting the Agenda? Gender Mainstreaming in the European Constitution-Making Process', *Social Politics*, 12: 3, 412–432.

Lombardo, E. and M. Verloo (2009), 'Institutionalizing Intersectionality in the European Union? Policy Developments and Contestations', *International Feminist Journal of Politics*, 11: 4, 478–495.

Lombardo, E., M. Verloo and P. Meier (2009), *The Discursive Politics of Gender Equality, Stretching, Bending and Policy-Making*, London: Routledge/Taylor & Francis.

Lundström, K. (1999), *Jämlikhet mellan Kvinnor och män i EG-rätten. En feministik Analys*, Göteborg: Iustus.

MacKinnon, C. A. (1989), *Toward a Feminist Theory of the State*, Cambridge: Harvard University Press.

MacRae, H. (2001), 'Engendering Europe: The What, Why and How of a Feminist Perspective on European Integration', Paper presented at the ISA convention in Chicago, IL, 20–24 February.

MacRae, H. (2006), 'Rescaling Gender Relations: The Influence of European Directives on the German Gender Regime', *Social Politics*, 13: 4, 522–550.

MacRae, H. (2010), 'The EU as a Gender Equal Polity: Myths and Realities', *Journal of Common Market Studies*, 48: 1, 155–174.

Maier, L. and M. Shobayashi (2001), *Multifunctionality: Towards an Analytical Framework*, Paris: OECD.

Majone, G. (1996), *Regulating Europe*, London: Routledge.
Martinsen, D. S. (2007), 'The Europeanization of Gender Equality, Who Controls the Scope of Non-Discrimination?', *Journal of European Public Policy*, 14: 4, 544–562.
Masselot, A. (2007), 'The State of Gender Equality Law in the European Union', *European Law Journal*, 13: 2, 152–168.
Matyja, M. (2001), 'Subsidiarity: A Tool for Gender Equality in an Enlarged EU', Online: http://www.eumap.org/journal/features/2001/dec/toolforgender (accessed 22 July 2008).
Mauritzio, C. (ed.) (2010), *National Politics and European Integration. From the Constitution to the Lisbon Treaty*, Cheltenham: Edward Elgar.
Mazey, S. (1995), 'The Development of EU Equality Policies: Bureaucratic Expansion on Behalf of Women?', *Public Administration*, 73, 591–609.
Mazey, S. (1998), 'The European Union and Women's Rights. From the Europeanisation of National Agendas to the Nationalisation of a European Agenda?', *Journal of European Public Policy*, 5: 1, 131–152.
Mazey, S. (2001), *Gender Mainstreaming in the EU: Principle and Practice*, London: Kogan.
Mazey, S. (2002a), 'Gender Mainstreaming Strategies in the EU: Delivering on an Agenda?', *Feminist Legal Studies*, 10, 227–240.
Mazey, S. (2002b), 'The Development of EU Gender Policies: Toward the Recognition of Difference', *EUSA Review*, 15: 3, 1–2.
Mazur, A. (2009), 'Comparative Gender and Policy Projects in Europe: Current Trends in Theory, Method and Research', *Comparative European Politics*, 9: 1, 12–36.
McMichael, P. (1997), 'Rethinking Globalization: The Agrarian Question Revisited', *Review of International Political Economy*, 4: 4, 630–662.
Meehan, E. M. (1993a), *Citizenship and the European Community*, London: Sage.
Meehan, E. M. (1993b), 'Women's Rights in the European Community', in J. Lewis (ed.), *Women and Social Policies in Europe*, Aldershot: Edward Elgar, pp. 194–205.
Mergaert, L. (2008), 'Monitoring Progress towards Gender Equality in the Sixth Framework Programme: Science and Society, Citizens and Governance in a Knowledge-Based Society', Brussels: European Commission, Online: http://ec.europa.eu/research/science-society/document_library/pdf_06/monitoring-progress-towards-gender-equality-in-fp6_en.pdf (accessed 23 February 2009).
Meulders, D., O. Plasman and V. Vander Stricht (1993), *Position of Women on the Labour Market in the European Community*, Aldershot: Dartmouth.
Miles, L. (2005), *Fusing with Europe? Sweden in the European Union*, London, Aldershot: Ashgate.
Millet, K. (1969), *Sexual Politics*, New York: Granada Publishing.
Millns, S. (2007), 'Gender Equality, Citizenship, and the EU's Constitutional Future', *European Law Journal*, 13: 2, 218–237.
Milward, A. S., G. Brennan and F. Romero (1992), *The European Rescue of the Nation-State*, London: Routledge.
Mitchell, J. (1971), *Women's Estate*, London: Penguin.
Moghadam, V. M. (2005), *Globalizing Women: Transnational Feminist Networks*, Baltimore, MD: Johns Hopkins University Press.
Montoya, C. (2008), 'The European Union, Capacity Building, and Transnational Networks: Combating Violence against Women through the Daphne Program', *International Organization*, 62, 359–372.
Moravcsik, A. (1993), 'Preferences and Power in the European Community: A Liberal Intergovernmentalist Approach', *Journal of Common Market Studies*, 31: 4, 472–524.

Moravcsik, A. (1998), *The Choice for Europe: Social Purpose and State Power from Messina to Maastricht*, Ithaca: Cornell University Press.

Morissens, A. and D. Sainsbury (2005), 'Migrants' Social Rights, Ethnicity and Welfare Regimes', *Journal of Social Policy*, 34: 4, 637–660.

Morokvasic, M. (1984), 'Birds of Passage Are Also Women', *International Migration Review*, 18: 4, 886–907.

Mushaben, J. M. (1998), 'The Politics of Critical Acts: Women and Leadership in the European Union', *European Studies Journal*, 15: 2, 51–91.

Mushaben, J. M. (2008), *The Changing Faces of Citizenship. Integration and Mobilization among Ethnic Minorities in Germany*, New York and Oxford: Berghahn Books.

Mushaben, J. M. (2009), 'Up the Down Staircase: Reconfiguring Gender Identities through Ethnic Employment in Germany', *Journal of Ethnicity and Migration Studies*, 35: 8, 1249–1274.

Nelen, S. and A. Hondeghem (eds) (2000), *Equality Oriented Personnel Policy in the Public Sector*, Amsterdam: International Institute of Administrative Sciences, IOS Press.

Network of Legal Experts in the fields of employment, social affairs and equality between women and men (2007a), 'Access to Goods and Services: Implementation of Directive 2004/113/EC', Online: http://ec.europa.eu/social/main.jsp?catId=641&langId=en&moreDocuments=yes (accessed 30 July 2008).

Network of Legal Experts in the fields of employment, social affairs and equality between women and men (2007b), 'Bulletin Legal Issues in Gender Equality', No. 2/2007, Online: http://ec.europa.eu/employment_social/gender_equality/legislation/bulletin_en.html (accessed 30 July 2008).

Network of Legal Experts in the fields of employment, social affairs and equality between women and men (2007c), 'General Report on Developments in EU Gender Equality Law June 2006–May 2007', Online: http://ec.europa.eu/employment_social/gender_equality/legislation/bulletin_en.html (accessed 25 July 2008).

Network of Legal Experts on the application of Community Law on equal treatment between men and women (n.d.), 'Report on Directive 86/613/EEC', Online: http://ec.europa.eu/employment_social/gender_equality/legislation/report_draft2.pdf (accessed 26 January 2009).

Neyer, J. (2003), 'Discourse and Order in the EU: A Deliberative Approach to Multi-Level Governance', *Journal of Common Market Studies*, 41: 4, 687–706.

Niemann, A. and P. C. Schmitter (2009), 'Neofunctionalism', in A. Wiener and T. Diez (eds), *European Integration Theory*, 2nd edition, Oxford: Oxford University Press, pp. 45–66.

Nugent, N. (2004a), 'Distinctive and Recurring Features of Enlargement Rounds', in N. Nugent (ed.), *European Union Enlargement*, Basingstoke: Palgrave Macmillan, pp. 56–69.

Nugent, N. (2004b), 'Previous Enlargement Rounds', in N. Nugent (ed.), *European Union Enlargement*, Basingstoke: Palgrave Macmillan, pp. 22–33.

Nugent, N. (2004c), 'The EU and the 10+2 Enlargement Round: Opportunities and Challenges', in N. Nugent (ed.), *European Union Enlargement*, Basingstoke: Palgrave Macmillan, pp. 1–21.

Nugent, N. (2004d), 'The Unfolding of the 10+2 Enlargement Round', in N. Nugent (ed.), *European Union Enlargement*, Basingstoke: Palgrave Macmillan, pp. 34–55.

Nugent, N. (2010), *The Government and Politics of the European Union*, 7th edition, Houndmills: Palgrave Macmillan.

O'Brien, M. and S. Penna (2007), 'Social Exclusion in Europe: Some Conceptual Issues', *International Journal of Social Welfare*, 17, 84–92.

O'Connor, J. S. (2005a), 'Employment-Anchored Social Policy, Gender Equality and the Open Method of Policy Coordination in the European Union', *European Societies*, 7: 1, 27–52.

O'Connor, J. S. (2005b), 'Policy Coordination, Social Indicators and the Social-Policy Agenda in the European Union', *Journal of European Social Policy*, 15: 4, 345–361.

OECD (1994), *Women and Structural Change*, Paris: OECD.

Olsen, J. P. (2010), *Governing through Institution Building. Institutional Theory and Recent European Experiments in Democratic Organization*, Oxford: Oxford University Press.

Orloff, A. S. (1993), 'Gender and the Social Rights of Citizenship: The Comparative Analysis of Gender Relations and Welfare States', *American Sociological Review*, 58: 3, 303–328.

Ostner, I. (2000), 'From Equal Pay to Equal Employability: Four Decades of European Gender Policies', in M. Rossili (ed.), *Gender Policies in the European Union*, New York: Peter Lang, pp. 25–42.

Ostner, I. and J. Lewis (1995), 'Gender and the Evolution of European Social Policy', in S. Leibfried and P. Pierson (eds), *European Social Policy. Between Fragmentation and Integration*, Washington D.C.: The Brookings Institution, pp. 159–193.

Overbeek, G., S. Efstratoglou, M. S. Haugen and E. Saraceno (1998), *Labour Situation and Strategies of Farm Women in Diversified Rural Areas of Europe*, Luxembourg: Office for Official Publications of the European Communities.

Pascall, G. and J. Lewis (2004), 'Emerging Gender Regimes and Policies for Gender Equality in a Wider Europe', *Journal of Social Policy*, 33: 3, 373–394.

Perrons, D. (2005), 'Gender Mainstreaming and Gender Equality in the New (Market) Economy: An Analysis of Contradictions', *Social Politics*, 12: 3, 389–411

Pessar, P. R. and S. J. Mahler (2001), 'Gender and Transnational Migration', Conference on Transnational Migration: Comparative Perspectives, Princeton University, 30 June.

Peterson, J. (1995), 'EU Research Policy: The Politics of Expertise', in C. Rhodes and S. Mazey (eds), *The State of the European Union*, Volume 3, Harlow: Lynne Rienner, pp. 391–412.

Peterson, J. and M. Sharp (1998), *Technology Policy in the European Union*, Houndmills, London, New York: Macmillan and St. Martin's Press.

Phillips, A. (1995), *The Politics of Presence: The Political Representation of Gender, Ethnicity and Race*, Oxford: Oxford University Press.

Phinnemore, D. (2004), 'Institutions and Governance', in N. Nugent (ed.), *European Union Enlargement*, Basingstoke: Palgrave Macmillan, pp. 118–131.

Piattoni, S. (2010), *The Theory of Multi-Level Governance. Conceptual, Empirical and Normative Challenges*, Oxford: Oxford University Press.

Picchio, A. (1992), *Social Reproduction: The Political Economy of the Labour Market*, Cambridge: Cambridge University Press.

Pierson, P. (1996), 'The Path to European Integration: A Historical Institutionalist Analysis', *Comparative Political Studies*, 29: 2, 123–163.

Plantenga, J., C. Remery and J. Rubery (2007), *Gender Mainstreaming of Employment Policies – A Comparative Review of Thirty European Countries*, Luxembourg: Office for Official Publications of the European Communities.

Pollack, M. (2004), 'The New Institutionalism and European Integration', in A. Wiener and T. Diez (eds), *European Integration Theory*, Oxford: Oxford University Press, pp. 137–156.

Pollack, M. A. and E. Hafner-Burton (2000), 'Mainstreaming Gender in the European Union', *Journal of European Public Policy*, 7: 1, 432–456.

Polverari, L. and R. Fitzgerald (2002), 'Integrating Gender Equality in the Evaluation of the Irish 2000–06 National Development Plan', Volume 2: 'Tool Kit for Gender Evaluation', University of Strathclyde/NDP Gender Equality Unit.

Prügl, E. (2004), 'Gender Orders in German Agriculture: From the Patriarchal Welfare State to Liberal Environmentalism', *Sociologia Ruralis*, 44: 4, 349–372.

Prügl, E. (2007), 'Gender and European Union Politics', in K. E. Jorgensen, M. A. Pollack and B. Rosamond (eds), *Handbook of European Union Politics*, London: Sage, pp. 433–448.

Prügl, E. (2009), 'Does Gender Mainstreaming Work? Feminist Engagements with the German Agricultural State', *International Feminist Journal of Politics*, 11: 2, 174–195.

Puchala, D. J. (1972), 'Of Blind Men, Elephants and European Integration', *Journal of Common Market Studies*, 10: 2, 267–284.

Puchala, D. J. (1975), 'Domestic Politics and Regional Harmonization in the European Communities', *World Politics*, 27: 4, 496–520.

Raghuram, P. (2004), 'The Difference That Skills Make: Gender, Family Migration Strategies and Regulated Labour Markets', *Journal of Ethnic and Migration Research*, 30: 2, 303–321.

Rees, T. (1998), *Mainstreaming Equality in the European Union. Education, Training and Labor Market Policies*, London: Routledge.

Rees, T. (2002), 'The Helsinki Group on Women and Science: National Policies on Women and Science in Europe. Final Report', Luxembourg, Online: http://www.cordis.lu/improving/women/policies.htm (accessed 1 March 2008).

Rees, T. (2007), 'Pushing the Gender Equality Agenda Forward in the European Union', in M. A. Danowith Sagaria (ed.), *Women, Universities, and Change: Gender Equality in the European Union and the United States*, Houndmills: Palgrave Macmillan, pp. 7–21.

Reflection Group (2010), 'Project Europe 2030: Challenges and Opportunities. A Report to the European Council by the Reflection Group on the Future of the EU 2030. May 2010', Brussels.

Reinalda, B. (1997), 'Dea ex Machina or the Interplay between National and International Policymaking: A Critical Analysis of Women in the European Union', in F. Gardiner (ed.), *Sex Equality Policy in Western Europe*, London: Routledge, pp. 197–215.

Rhodes, M. (2005), 'Employment Policy: Between Efficacy and Experimentation', in H. Wallace, W. Wallace and M. A. Pollack (eds), *Policy-Making in the European Union*, 5th edition, Oxford: Oxford University Press, pp. 279–304.

Rieger, E. (1995), *Bauernopfer: Das Elend der Europäischen Agrarpolitik*, Frankfurt/M.: Campus.

Rietschel, E. T. (2009), 'Evaluation of the Sixth Framework Programmes for Research and Technological Development 2003–2006. Report of the Expert Group', February.

Risse, T. (2009), 'Social Constructivism and European Integration', in A. Wiener and T. Diez (eds), *European Integration Theory*, 2nd edition, Oxford: Oxford University Press, pp. 144–160.

Risse-Kappen, T. (1996), 'Exploring the Nature of the Beast: International Relations Theory and Comparative Policy Analysis Meet the European Union', *Journal of Common Market Studies*, 34: 1, 53–80.

Roederer-Rynning, C. (2010), 'The Common Agricultural Policy: The Fortress Challenged', in H. Wallace, M. A. Pollack and A. A. Young (eds), *Policy-Making in the European Union*, 6th edition, Oxford: Oxford University Press, pp. 181–206.

Rosamond, B. (2000), *Theories of European Integration*, Basingstoke, London: Macmillan.

Rose, H. (1999), 'A Fair Share of the Research Pie or Re-Engendering Scientific and Technological Europe?', *The European Journal of Women's Studies*, 6: 1, 31–47.
Rossilli, M. (ed.) (2000), *Gender Policies in the European Union*, New York: Peter Lang.
Roth, S. (2008), 'Introduction: Gender Politics in the Expanding European Union: Mobilization, Inclusion, Exclusion', in S. Roth (ed.), *Gender Politics in the Expanding European Union*, Oxford, New York: Berghahn Books, pp. 1–16.
Rubery, J. (2005), 'Reflections on Gender Mainstreaming: An Example of Feminist Economics in Action?', *Feminist Economics*, 11: 3, 1–26.
Rubery J., M. Smith and C. Fagan (1999), *Women's Employment in Europe, Trends and Prospects*, London: Routledge.
Ruminska-Zimny, E. (2002), 'Gender Aspects of Changes in the Labour Markets in Transition Economies', UNECE Issue Paper.
Sainsbury, D. (ed.) (1994), *Gendering Welfare States*, London: Sage.
Sainsbury, D. (1996), *Gender, Equality and the Welfare State*, Cambridge: Cambridge University Press.
Sandholtz, W. and A. Stone Sweet (eds) (1998), *European Integration and Supranational Governance*, New York: Oxford University Press.
Sauer, B. (2001), 'Vom Nationalstaat zum Europäischen Reich? Staat und Geschlecht in der Europäischen Union', *Feministische Studien*, 21: 1, 8–20.
Schäfer, S. (2005), 'Das transformative Potenzial von Gender Mainstreaming in der europäischen Forschungspolitik', *Zeitschrift für Frauen- und Geschlechterstudien*, 23: 3, 36–49.
Schierup, C.-U., P. Hansen and S. Castles (2006), *Migration, Citizenship, and the European Welfare State. A European Dilemma*, Oxford, New York: Oxford University Press.
Schimmelfennig, F. (2004), 'Liberal Intergovernmentalism', in A. Wiener and T. Diez (eds), *European Integration Theory*, Oxford: Oxford University Press, pp. 75–94.
Schmidt, V. (2005), *Gender Mainstreaming – An Innovation in Europe*, Opladen: Barbara Budrich.
Schmitt, M. (1997), *Landwirtinnen: Chancen und Risiken von Frauen in einem traditionellen Männerberuf*, Opladen: Leske + Budrich.
Schmitter, P. C. (1996), 'Imagining the Future of the Euro-Polity with the Help of New Concepts', in G. Marks, F. W. Scharpf, P. Schmitter and W. Streeck (eds), *Governance in the European Union*, London: Sage, pp. 121–150.
Schmitter, P. C. (2004), 'Neofunctionalism', in A. Wiener and T. Diez (eds), *European Integration Theory*, Oxford: Oxford University Press, pp.75–94.
Schunter-Kleemann, S. (1992a), *Herrenhaus Europa: Geschlechterverhältnisse im Wohlfahrtsstaat*, Berlin: Edition Sigma.
Schunter-Kleemann, S. (1992b), 'Wohlfahrtsstaat und Patriarchat – Ein Vergleich europäischer Länder', in S. Schunter-Kleemann (ed.), *Herrenhaus Europa – Geschlechterverhältnisse im Wohlfahrtsstaat*, Berlin: Edition Sigma, pp. 141–327.
Sedelmeier, U. (2009), 'Post-Accession Compliance with EU Gender Equality Legislation in Post-Communist New Member States', *European Integration Online Papers*, Special Issue 2: 13, Online: http://eiop.or.at/eiop/index.php/eiop/article/view/2009_023a/140.
Shaw, J. (2000), 'Importing Gender: The Challenge of Feminism and the Analysis of the EU Legal Order', *Journal of European Public Policy*, 7: 3, 406–431.
Shaw, J. (2002), 'The European Union and Gender Mainstreaming: Constitutionally Embedded or Comprehensively Marginalized?', *Feminist Legal Studies*, 10, 213–226.

Sifft, S. (2003), 'Pushing for Europeanisation: How British Feminists Link with the EU to Promote Parental Rights', in U. Liebert (ed.), *Gendering Europeanisation*, Brussels: Peter Lang, pp. 149–186.

Siim, B. (1993), 'The Gendered Scandinavian Welfare States: The Interplay between Women's Roles as Mothers, Workers and Citizens in Denmark', in J. Lewis (ed.), *Women and Social Policy in Europe: Work, Family and the State*, Cheltenham: Edward Elgar, pp. 25–48.

Siim, B. (2000), *Gender and Citizenship. Politics and Agency in France, Britain and Denmark*, Cambridge: Cambridge University Press.

Silvera, R. (1998), 'Les femmes et la diversification du temps de travail: Nouveaux enjeux, Nouveaux risques', *Revue Française des Affaires Sociales*, 52: 3, 71–89.

Smith, M. and P. Villa (2010), 'The Ever-Declining Role of Gender Equality in the European Employment Strategy', *Industrial Relations Journal*, 41: 6, 526–543.

Snyder, F. (1993), 'Soft Law and Institutional Practice in the European Community', in S. Martin (ed.), *The Construction of Europe – Essays in Honour of Emile Noel*, Dordrecht: Kluwer Academic Publishers, pp. 197–225.

Sousi-Roubi, B. and I. von Prondzynski (1983), 'Women in Agriculture', Supplement No. 13 to Women of Europe', Brussels: Commission of the European Communities, Directorate-General Information, X/338/83-EN.

Spanish Presidency (2002), 'Spanish Presidency's Information Note to the Employment and Social Policy Council on Gender Mainstreaming in European Union Policies', 29 May, Brussels, 8872/02. SOC 247.

Špidla, V. (2009), 'Social Aspects of the Lisbon Treaty', Speech to Conference of European Churches 'Shaping European Economic and Social Policies in Times of Uncertainty', European Parliament, 29 April, Brussels.

Springer, B. (1992), *The Social Dimension of 1992: Europe Faces a New European Community*, New York: Praeger.

Squires, J. (2007), *The New Politics of Gender Equality*, Houndsmill, Basingstoke: Palgrave Macmillan.

Stacey, J. (2010), *Integrating Europe. Informal Politics and Institutional Change*, Oxford: Oxford University Press.

Stanko, E. (2000), 'Rethinking Violence, Rethinking Social Policy?', in G. Lewis, S. Gewirtz and J. Clarke (eds), *Rethinking Social Policy*, London: Sage, pp. 245–258.

Stone Sweet, A. and W. Sandholtz (1997), 'European Integration and Supranational Governance', *Journal of European Public Policy*, 4: 3, 297–317.

Stone Sweet, A., W. Sandholtz and N. Fligstein (eds) (2001), *The Institutionalization of Europe*, Oxford: Oxford University Press.

Stratigaki, M. (2004), 'The Cooptation of Gender Concepts in EU Policies: The Case of "Reconciliation of Work and Family"', *Social Politics*, 11: 1, 30–56.

Stratigaki, M. (2005), 'Gender Mainstreaming vs. Positive Action: An Ongoing Conflict in EU Gender Equality Policy', *The European Journal of Women's Studies*, 12: 2, 165–186.

Stratigaki, M. (2008), 'La politique du recul. De l'intégration de l'égalité 'des sexes' à l'intégration de l'égalité "pour tous"', *Cahiers du genre*, 44, 49–72.

Strid, S. (2010), *Gendered Interests in the European Union: The European Women's Lobby and the Organization and Representation of Women's Interests*, Örebro Studies in Gender Research 1, Örebro: Örebro University.

Subhan, A. and A. Angelidis (1993/1994), *Situation, Status, Role and Prospects of Women in Agriculture*, Luxembourg: European Parliament, Directorate General for Research.

Sullerot, E. (1968), *La condition feminine dans les Etats membres de la Communauté Economique Européenne*, Brussels: Etude pour la Commission européenne.

Szczepaniková, A., M. Čaněk and J. Grill (eds) (2006), *Migration Processes in Central and Eastern Europe: Unpacking the* Diversity, Multicultural Center Prague, Online: http://www.migration-boell.de/downloads/integration/Migration_Processes_in_CEE_MKC.pdf (accessed 31 March 2011).

Tanasescu, I. (2009), *The European Commission and Interest Groups*, Brussels: VUB Brussels University Press.

Theiler, T. (2005), *Political Symbolism and European Integration*, Manchester: Manchester University Press.

Threlfall, M. (1997), 'Spain in Social Europe: A Laggard or Compliant Member State?', *South European Society and Politics*, 2: 2, 1–33.

Threlfall, M. (2003), 'European Social Integration: Harmonization, Convergence and Single Social Areas', *Journal of European Social Policy*, 13: 2, 121–139.

Tickner, A. (1992), *Gender in International Relations*, New York: Columbia University Press.

Titkow, A. (1998), 'Polish Women in Politics: An Introduction to the Status of Women in Poland', in M. Rueschemeyer (ed.), *Women in the Politics of Postcommunist Eastern Europe*, New York: M. E. Sharpe, pp. 24–32.

Toemmel, I. (2009), 'The Treaty of Lisbon – A Step toward Enhancing Leadership in the EU', Paper delivered at the EUSA-Conference in Los Angeles, CA, 23–25 April.

Traser, J., M. Byrska and B. Napieralski (2005), 'Report on the Free Movement of Workers in EU-25. Who's Afraid of EU Enlargement?', Brussels: European Citizen Action Service, September.

True, J. (2003), 'Mainstreaming Gender in Global Public Policy', *International Feminist Journal of Politics*, 5: 3, 368–396.

UNIFEM (2006), *Strengthening Economic Governance: Applied Gender Analysis to Governments Budgets*, New York.

UNIFEM (2008), *Who Answers to Women? Gender and Accountability*, New York.

Vaiou, D. (2003), 'In the Interstices of the City. Albanian Women in Athens', *Espaces, Populations, Societé*, 3, 373–385.

Valiente, C. (2003), 'Pushing for Equality Reforms: The European Union and Gender Discourse in Post-Authoritarian Spain', in U. Liebert (ed.), *Gendering Europeanisation*, Brussels: Peter Lang, pp. 223–254.

Valiente, C. (2006), 'Spain at the Vanguard in European Gender Equality Policies', Paper presented at the annual meeting of the American Sociological Association in Montreal, 11 August.

Vallance, E. and E. Davies (1986), *Women of Europe: Women MEPs and Equality Policy*, Cambridge: Cambridge University Press.

van der Molen, I. and I. Novikova (2005), 'Mainstreaming Gender in the EU-Accession Process: The Case of the Baltic Republics', *Journal of European Social Policy*, 15: 2, 139–156.

van der Vleuten, A. (2004), 'Snail or Snake? Shifts in the Domain of EU Gender Equality Policies', Paper presented at the Second Pan-European Conference on EU Politics of the ECPR Standing Group on the European Union in Bologna, 24–26 June.

van der Vleuten, A. (2005), 'Pincers and Prestige: Explaining the Implementation of EU Gender Equality Legislation', *Comparative European Politics*, 3: 4, 464–488.

van der Vleuten, A. (2007), *The Price of Gender Equality. Member States and Governance in the European Union*, Aldershot: Ashgate.
van Schendelen, M. P. C. (ed.) (1998), *EU Committees as Influential Policymakers*, Aldershot: Ashgate.
Vasileva, K. (2009), 'Population and Social Conditions', *Eurostat: Statistics in Focus*, 94, 1–7.
Verloo, M. (2006), 'Multiple Inequalities, Intersectionality and the European Union', *The European Journal of Women's Studies*, 13: 3, 211–228.
Verloo, M. and A. van der Vleuten (2009), 'The Discursive Logic of Ranking and Benchmarking: Understanding Gender Equality Measures in the European Union', in E. Lombardo, P. Meier and M. Verloo (eds), *The Discursive Politics of Gender Equality. Stretching, Bending and Policymaking*, London, New York: Routledge, pp. 169–185.
Verwilghen, M. (1993), *Access to Equality between Men and Women in the European Community*, Louvain-la-Neuve: Presses Universitaires de Louvain.
Villa, P. and M. Smith (2010), 'Gender Equality, Employment Policies and the Crisis in EU Member States: Synthesis Report 2009', Expert report commissioned by and presented to the European Commission Directorate-General Employment, Social Affairs and Equal Opportunities, Unit G.1, Online: ec.europa.eu/social/BlobServlet?docId=5630&langId=en (accessed 21 March 2011).
Voet, R. (1998), *Feminism and Citizenship*, London: Sage Publications.
Vogel, S. and G. Wiesinger (2003), 'Zum Begriff des bäuerlichen Familienbetriebs im soziologischen Diskurs', *Österreichische Zeitschrift für Soziologie*, 28: 1, 55–76.
Vogel Polsky, E. (1997), 'Démocratie, femmes et citoyenneté Européenne', *Sextant*, 7, 17–40.
von Wahl, A. (2005), 'Liberal, Conservative, Social Democratic, or...European? The European Union as Equal Employment Regime', *Social Politics*, 12: 1, 67–95.
von Wahl, A. (2011), 'A "Women's Revolution from Above"? Female Leadership, Intersectionality, and Public Policy under the Merkel Government', *German Politics*, 20: 3, 392–409.
Waddington, J. and R. Hoffmann (eds) (2000), *Trade Unions in Europe: Facing Challenges and Searching for Solutions*, Brussels: ETUI.
Wajcman, J. (2000), 'Reflections on Gender and Technology Studies: In What State is the Art?', *Social Studies of Science*, 30, 447–464.
Walby, S. (1990), *Theorizing Patriarchy*, Oxford: Blackwell.
Walby, S. (1997), *Gender Transformations*, London: Routledge.
Walby, S. (2004), 'The European Union and Gender Equality: Emergent Varieties of Gender Regime', *Social Politics*, 11: 1, 4–29.
Walby, S. (2005), 'Gender Mainstreaming: Productive Tensions in Theory and Practice', *Social Politics*, 12: 3, 321–343.
Walby, S. (2009a), 'Gender and the Financial Crisis', Paper for Unesco, Online: http://www.lancs.ac.uk/fass/doc_library/sociology/Gender_and_financial_crisis_Sylvia_Walby.pdf (accessed 30 March 2011).
Walby, S. (2009b), *Globalization and Inequalities, Complexity and Contested Modernities*, London: Sage.
Wallström, M. (2005), 'Speech by Commissioner Wallström at the EP on "Women's Rights in the EU"', 8 March, Online: http://www.europa-eu-un.org/articles/en/article_4425_en.htm (accessed 1 March 2011).
Walzenbach, G. P. E. (ed.) (2006), *European Governance. Policy Making between Politicization and Control*, Aldershot: Ashgate.

Warner, H. (1984), 'EC Social Policy in Practice: Community Action on Behalf of Women and Its Impact in the Member States', *Journal of Common Market Studies*, 23: 2, 141–167.

Watson, P. (2000), 'Politics, Policy and Identity: EU Eastern Enlargement and East-West Differences', *Journal of European Public Policy*, 7: 3, 369–384.

Watson, R. and M. Shackleton (2008), 'Organized Interests and Lobbying', in E. Bomberg, J. Peterson and A. Stubb (eds), *The European Union: How Does It Work?*, 2nd edition, Oxford: Oxford University Press, pp. 92–111.

Welz, C. and C. Engel (1993), 'Traditionsbestände politikwissenschaftlicher Integrationstheorien: Die Europäische Gemeinschaft im Spannungsfeld von Integration und Kooperation', in A. von Bogdandy (ed.), *Die Europäische Option. Eine interdisziplinäre Analyse über Herkunft, Stand und Perspektiven der europäischen Integration*, Baden-Baden: Nomos, pp. 129–169.

Westphal, M. (1999), 'Familäre und berufliche Orientierungen von Aussiedlerinnen', in K. Bade and J. Oltmer (eds), *Aussiedler: deutsche Einwanderer aus Osteuropa*, Osnabrück: Universitätsverlag Rasch, pp. 127–149.

Wiener, A. and T. Diez (eds) (2009), *European Integration Theory*, 2nd edition, Oxford: Oxford University Press.

Wijers, M. (2000), 'European Union Policies on Trafficking in Women', in M. Rossilli (ed.), *Gender Policies in the European Union*, New York: Peter Lang, pp. 209–230.

Wilson, E. (1977), *Women and the Welfare State*, London: Tavistock.

Wilson, G. A. and O. Wilson (2001), *German Agriculture in Transition: Society, Policies and Environment in a Changing Europe*, Houndmills, Basingstoke: Palgrave Macmillan.

Wimer, M. (1988), *Zweierlei Leut: Patriarchalische Strukturen in landwirtschaftlichen Familien*, Witzenhausen: Ekopan Verlag.

Wobbe, T. and I. Biermann (2009), *Von Rom nach Amsterdam: Die Metamorphosen des Geschlechts in der Europäischen Union*, Wiesbaden: VS Verlag.

Woodward, A. E. (1996), 'Multi-National Masculinities and European Bureaucracy', in D. Collinson and J. Hearn (eds), *Men as Managers, Managers as Men*, London: Sage, pp. 167–185.

Woodward, A. E. (2003), 'European Gender Mainstreaming: Promises and Pitfalls of Transformative Policy', *Review of Policy Research*, 20: 1, 65–88.

Woodward, A. E. (2004), 'Velvet Triangles: Gender and Informal Governance', in T. Christiansen and S. Piattoni (eds), *Informal Governance and the European Union*, Cheltenham: Edward Elgar, pp. 76–93.

Woodward, A. E. (2007), 'Challenges of Intersectionality in the Transnational Organization of European Women's Movements: Forming Platforms and Maintaining Turf in Today's EU', in I. Lenz and C. Ullrich (eds), *Gender Orders Unbound: Towards New Reciprocity and Solidarity?*, Opladen, Framington Hills: Barbara Budrich Publishers, pp. 9–27.

Woodward, A. E. (2008), 'Too Late for Mainstreaming: The View from Brussels', *European Journal of Social Policy*, 18: 3, 289–302.

Young, B. (2000), 'Disciplinary Neoliberalism in the European Union and Gender Politics', *New Political Economy*, 5, 77–98.

Zeff, E. and E. Pirro (eds) (2006), *The European Union and the Member States*, Boulder, London: Lynne Rienner.

Zeitlin, J., P. Pocher and L. Magnussen (eds) (2005), *The Open Method of Coordination in Action: The European Employment and Social Inclusion Strategies*, Brussels: Peter Lang.

Zimmermann, K. and S. Metz-Göckel (2007), *Vision und Mission. Die Integration von Gender in den Mainstream europäischer Forschungspolitik*, Wiesbaden: VS Verlag.

Zippel, K. (2004), 'Transnational Advocacy Networks and Policy Cycles in the European Union: The Case of Sexual Harassment', *Social Politics*, 11, 57–85.

Zippel, K. (2008), 'Violence at Work? Framing Sexual Harassment in the European Union', in S. Roth (ed.), *Gender Politics in the Expanding European Union: Mobilization, Inclusion, Exclusion*, New York, Oxford: Berghahn Books, pp. 60–80.

Zulauf, M. (2001), *Migrant Women. Professionals in the European Union*, New York: Palgrave Macmillan.

Zürn, M. (2000), 'Democratic Governance beyond the Nation-State: The EU and Other International Institutions', *European Journal of International Relations*, 6: 2, 183–221.

Index

acquis communautaire, 3, 69, 104, 113
   Article 119 (EEC Treaty), 5, 18, 36–7, 63–4, 69, 73–4, 90–1, 105, 147, 155, 238
   Directive 2000/78/EC, 72, 210, 223
   Directive 2004/113/EC, 116, 170
   Directive 2010/41/EU, 123, 132, 137, 156
   Directive 86/613/EEC, 72, 123, 129, 132, 138
   Equal Treatment Directive, 70–1, 74, 146, 156, 170, 238
   gender, 15, 63–4, 69–70, 82, 111, 205
   primary law, 69–70, 72
   race Directive 2000/43/EC, 210–11, 222, 238
   recast Directive 2006/54/EU, 71, 73, 156
   secondary law, 70, 72–3, 76
   supranational norm, 26, 36
   supremacy principle, 7, 57
affirmative (positive) action, 7, 88, 94
Amsterdam Treaty, 2, 69–72, 68, 191, 211, 215
   Amsterdam Treaty (Article 13), 100, 116, 173, 181, 210, 222–3
APs (Action Programmes on Equal Opportunities), 7, 74–5, 149
Austria, 30, 104, 110–12, 116

Belgium, 78, 104–6, 111–12, 210, 214
best practice, 51, 74, 148, 194, 196, 198, 205, 211–12, 219, 221–2, 230

Charter of Fundamental Rights, 72, 100, 175, 185, 221, 224, 226, 237–8
co-decision procedure, 48, 68, 190
Commission of the EU, 7, 31, 42–7, 67–8, 75–6, 92–3, 99, 111
   DG Agriculture, 138, 141
   DG EMPL, 43, 46–7, 60–2, 67, 100, 235
   DG Research, 82, 193–4, 199, 202, 205
   Equal Opportunities Unit DG-V (European Commission), 62, 160
Committee of the Regions (CoR), 59

communism, 2, 121
compliance, 39–40, 86, 92, 104, 107–8, 112, 115–17, 235
Coreper, 50–1
Council of Europe, 62, 97–8, 103, 154
Council of the EU, 28, 38, 50–2, 68
   Employment, Social Policy, Health and Consumer Affairs Council (EPSCO), 50–1, 68
   qualified majority vote (QMV), 51–2, 61, 68, 165, 232
critical mass, 18, 191, 232, 242, 247

Delors, Jacques, 44, 149–50, 173, 233
democratic deficit, 10, 14, 59, 111, 119, 210, 231–2, 234, 246
democratization, 17–18, 97, 109, 123, 154
demographic change, 246
Denmark, 24, 29, 36, 89, 104, 106–7, 111–12, 150, 214, 238
difference feminism, 88, 96
Discrimination, 2, 9, 11, 46–7, 57, 60–1, 63–4, 67, 72–4, 88, 90, 94, 100, 108, 116, 122, 134–7, 157, 160, 162–3, 170, 173–5, 181, 199, 210, 214–16, 217, 222–3, 226, 245
   dequalification, 213
   multiple discrimination, 181, 223, 226
   positive action, 7, 9, 73, 86, 88, 93–4, 110
diversity, 15–16, 88, 99, 226, 242

employment
   Barcelona targets on childcare, 159, 168, 179
   employability, 12, 54, 159
   equal pay, 5, 36, 56, 63–4, 69–70, 90, 105–8, 146–9, 156–8, 178, 213
   European Employment Strategy (EES), 54, 151, 158, 211
   parental leave, 51, 56–7, 59, 64, 70, 72–3, 93, 101, 115, 123, 148, 156, 163, 170, 177, 240

part-time work, 32, 46–7, 59, 61, 64, 73, 93, 101, 142, 148, 156, 176, 220
retirement, 89, 92, 140, 161, 174, 178
self-employment, 70, 72, 107, 129, 132–4, 136–8, 141, 211, 236
enforcement, 6, 72, 80–1, 105, 112, 114–16, 178, 218–19
enlargement, 13, 14, 16, 23, 80, 104, 106–22, 209
  Copenhagen criteria, 113
  candidate countries, 80, 104–5, 109, 113–14, 119, 198
  Central and Eastern European Countries (CEEC), 80–1
equal opportunities, 60, 67, 73, 85, 90–2, 104–5, 107, 110, 159, 179, 219
equal rights feminism, 19, 88, 89–92
equal treatment, 7, 56, 63–4, 72–4, 88–92, 107, 155–6, 172
EU as a political system sui generis, 6, 16, 64, 65, 216
EU citizenship, 96, 210, 216, 238
Europe 2020, 158, 192, 226
European Citizens' Initiative, 234
European Coal and Steel Community (ECSC), 2, 188
European Convention, 233
European Council, 52–4
  Tampere European Council, 210–12
European Court of Justice (ECJ), 36–7, 54–7, 63, 73–4, 79, 108, 116, 148–9
  Bilka vs. Germany, 73–4
  Defrenne cases, 11, 18, 60, 63, 69–70, 73, 90, 148–9, 155, 235
  and infringement proceedings, 46, 55–6
  Kalanke case, 156
  preliminary ruling, 56–7, 60–1
  Rummler vs. Dato-Druck, 70, 73
European Economic and Social Committee (EESC), 58–9
European Institute for Gender Equality (EIGE), 43, 101
European Parliament (EP), 47–50, 68, 80, 92, 190, 234
  Committee on Women's Rights and Gender Equality (FEMM), 48–9, 60, 68, 194

female MEPs, 232
parliamentary committees, 48
EU studies
  gender/feminist EU studies, 9–15, 40, 229
  malestream in EU studies, 9–10, 228
  normative theory, 15
expert committees, 45
  Advisory Committee on Equal Opportunities for Women and Men (EU), 60, 92, 136
  Group on Women in Decision-Making, 19
  High Level Group on gender mainstreaming, 51, 212
  Women's Network of Legal Experts, 19

feminism, 5, 19, 87–9, 176
femocrats, 18, 19, 33, 60, 78, 80–1, 137, 247
Finland, 30, 102, 110–12, 224, 238
formal notice, 46, 111, 116
Framework Programme (FP), 189, 200, 222

gender (as a social construction), 9, 11–12, 24, 38–9, 89, 157
gender democracy deficit, 4, 231, 234
gender equality, 1–2, 5, 18–19, 72, 75, 77–8, 80, 85, 88–101, 152, 155–9, 170, 185–6, 236, 242–5
gender gap, 29, 32, 77, 231, 246
gender impact assessment (GIA), 185, 199–200, 203, 205, 240
gender mainstreaming, 6–7, 9, 37, 51, 66, 75–7, 81–2, 96–9, 110, 137, 140–3, 179–81, 205–6
gender regime, 1–2, 39–40, 64, 69, 82, 129
gender segregation, 152
Greece, 30, 39, 91, 108–10, 112, 116, 118, 138, 178–9, 236

hard law, 13, 93, 148, 155, 222, 224, 230, 237–9, 242
harmonization, 3, 17, 80, 105, 108–9, 121, 175, 210, 236–7
High Representative of the Union for Foreign Affairs and Security Policy, 53

278 Index

homosociality, 35
human resource approach, 202

implementation (of equality policy), 5, 12–13, 17, 33, 39–40, 46, 55, 66–9, 72–3, 75, 78–82, 98–9, 105, 111, 120, 140–2, 157, 170, 235
integration, 1, 3–4, 23
integration theory, 23–40, 64, 76–7, 228–9, 234–5, 246–7
  constructivism, 15, 26, 35, 38–9, 78, 129
  domestic politics approach, 24, 28–30
  Europeanisation, 3, 40, 82, 168
  Liberal-Intergovernmentalism, 24–7, 234
  multi-level governance, 6, 15, 17, 25, 30–1, 33–5, 86, 129, 230, 234, 240, 246
  neofunctionalism, 4, 24–5, 30–2
  new institutionalism, 12, 24, 26, 35–8, 76–7
  state-centric approaches, 27, 30
interest groups, 31–2, 57–61, 230, 234–5
  European Women's Lobby (EWL), 31, 60, 67–8, 77, 154, 177, 183
  Gay and Lesbian Rights Intergroup, 58, 60
  lobbyism, 32, 57–9
intergovernmental bargaining, 4–5, 24–30, 233
International Labour Organization (ILO), 161
Ireland, 2, 36, 89, 91, 106–10, 112, 112, 121, 142, 211

Lisbon Strategy, 13, 17, 151, 159–60, 191–2, 226, 240
Lisbon Treaty, 1–3, 9, 17, 43, 47, 50, 53, 54, 72, 83, 100, 119–20, 165–6, 175, 192, 202, 222–5, 233

Maastricht Treaty, 2–3, 74, 190
  Maastricht Treaty (Article 8), 96, 210
male-as-norm, 26, 37, 40

networks, 12, 17, 25, 33–5, 46, 58, 64–5, 67, 76–7, 83, 83, 95, 138, 157–8, 200, 207, 238–9

new social movements, 12, 77, 83, 121
NOW, 75, 158, 178

open method of coordination (OMC), 13, 54, 76, 151, 174, 180–1, 237–40

path dependence, 24, 26, 33, 35–6, 38, 77
pincer effect, 25, 33, 232, 235, 241, 245
policy cycle, 64, 66, 78–9, 82, 98
Portugal, 30, 91, 104, 108–9, 111–12, 116, 121, 145, 236
power, 15, 19, 24–7, 30, 32, 34–5, 37, 39–40, 61, 89, 215, 232, 234, 246
President of the EU, 53
PROGRESS, 46, 71, 75, 158

reasoned opinion, 46, 55, 112, 116
representation, 28, 32, 41, 50, 55, 62, 103, 154–5, 233
reproductive economy, 162

Schengen Agreement, 2, 114, 210–11, 218
Single European Act (SEA), 2, 110, 150, 165–6, 171, 189
Single European Market, 129
social policy
  social citizenship, 181–3, 185, 216, 237
  social dialogue, 32, 58, 117–18, 148, 150, 155, 174, 184, 240
  social economy, 160, 163
  social platform, 96, 183–4
  social protocol, 2, 96, 156, 163, 165–6, 170, 171
  social security, 12, 46, 56, 70, 72, 93, 107–9, 118, 132–4, 155–6, 170–2, 175–6, 178–9, 236
soft law, 32, 37, 53–4, 63–4, 69–70, 74–7, 157–8, 237
Spain, 91, 101, 108–10, 149, 236
spillover, 25, 30, 33, 216
stakeholders, 45, 58, 98, 180, 190, 201, 203, 212, 234, 243
structural funds, 45, 51, 81, 137–8, 140–1, 178, 185, 237
Sweden, 32, 39, 78, 87, 101, 110–12, 173, 197, 214, 238

transnational coalition building, 31–2, 41, 58, 60–1, 65, 95, 235, 238–9
transnational organizations, 30–2, 60
transposition, 16, 56, 86, 107–20
Treaties of Rome, 2, 23–4, 36, 105, 165–6, 170, 209

United Kingdom, 89, 91, 108, 116, 121, 149–50, 173, 224
United Nations, 85, 90–1, 132
   CEDAW, 90–1, 215
   UN Beijing Conference 1995 / UN Conferences on Women / UN Decade on Women, 6, 51, 60, 78, 84, 97, 137

velvet triangles, 13, 34, 232
violence against women, 10, 14, 64, 80, 83, 98, 119, 177
   DAPHNE, 47, 68–9, 71, 75, 83, 240
   STOP, 70–1, 75
   trafficking in women, 68, 70, 74, 77–8, 215

welfare regimes, 78, 140, 143, 236
White Paper on European Governance, 37, 234
Wollstonecroft dilemma, 88
women's movements, 31, 41, 81, 87, 89, 107
women's studies, 92, 95

CPSIA information can be obtained at www.ICGtesting.com
Printed in the USA
LVOW01*1359140114

369361LV00002B/3/P